RURAL INVESTMENT CLIMATE
IN INDONESIA

The **Institute of Southeast Asian Studies (ISEAS)** was established as an autonomous organization in 1968. It is a regional centre dedicated to the study of socio-political, security and economic trends and developments in Southeast Asia and its wider geostrategic and economic environment. The Institute's research programmes are the Regional Economic Studies (RES, including ASEAN and APEC), Regional Strategic and Political Studies (RSPS), and Regional Social and Cultural Studies (RSCS).

ISEAS Publishing, an established academic press, has issued almost 2,000 books and journals. It is the largest scholarly publisher of research about Southeast Asia from within the region. ISEAS Publishing works with many other academic and trade publishers and distributors to disseminate important research and analyses from and about Southeast Asia to the rest of the world.

RURAL INVESTMENT CLIMATE IN INDONESIA

EDITED BY

Neil McCulloch

ISEAS

INSTITUTE OF SOUTHEAST ASIAN STUDIES
Singapore

First published in Singapore in 2009 by ISEAS Publishing
Institute of Southeast Asian Studies
30 Heng Mui Keng Terrace
Pasir Panjang
Singapore 119614
E-mail: publish@iseas.edu.sg
Website: http://bookshop.iseas.edu.sg

The responsibility for facts and opinions in this publication rests exclusively with the authors and their interpretations do not necessarily reflect the views or the policy of the publisher or its supporters.

ISEAS Library Cataloguing-in-Publication Data

Rural investment climate in Indonesia / edited by Neil McCulloch.
  1. Investments—Indonesia.
  2. Indonesia—Rural conditions.
  I. McCulloch, Neil, 1964–.
HG5752 R451   2009

ISBN 978-981-230-853-5 (soft cover)
ISBN 978-981-230-854-2 (PDF)

Typeset by Superskill Graphics Pte Ltd
Printed in Singapore by Seng Lee Press Pte Ltd

Contents

List of Tables, Figures, and Boxes   vii

Abbreviations and Acronyms   xv

The Contributors   xxi

1   Introduction   1
    Neil McCulloch

2   Agricultural Demand Linkages and Growth Multipliers in
    Rural Indonesia   24
    *Asep Suryahadi, Daniel Suryadarma, Sudarno Sumarto,
    and Jack Molyneaux*

3   Trends and Constraints Associated with Labour Faced by
    Non-Farm Enterprises   50
    Armida S. Alisjahbana and Chris Manning

4   The Constraints in Accessing Credit Faced by Rural
    Non-Farm Enterprises   86
    Andi Ikhwan and Don Edwin Johnston

5   The Constraints Associated with Infrastructure Faced by
    Non-Farm Enterprises at the *Kabupaten* Level   110
    John Gibson

6   Technology/Knowledge Transfer and Diffusion in
    Indonesian Non-Farm Enterprises   140
    Tulus Tambunan and Thee Kian Wie

7   Marketing and Competition in the New Indonesia   192
     Hal Hill and Pantjar Simatupang

8   Local Tax Effects on the Business Climate   224
     Blane D. Lewis and Bambang Suharnoko Sjahrir

9   Leadership and Voice in Local Governance   246
     Christian von Luebke

10   Insecurity and Business Development in Rural Indonesia   300
     Jonathan Haughton and John M. MacDougall

Index   331

List of Tables, Figures, and Boxes

Tables

Table 1.1   Employment by Sector in Rural and Urban Areas   3
Table 1.2   Distribution of the Poor in Indonesia by
             Sector and Location, 1996–2002 (%)   7

Table 2.1   Sectoral Contributions to GDP in Indonesia,
             1990–2003 (%)   27
Table 2.2   Employment Share of Rural and Urban Areas in
             Indonesia, 1990–2003 (%)   28
Table 2.3   Sectoral Employment Share in Rural Areas in
             Indonesia, 1990–2003 (%)   28
Table 2.4   Household Income Sources in Indonesia, 1995 (%)   29
Table 2.5   Distribution of the Poor in Indonesia by Sector,
             1996–2002 (%)   30
Table 2.6   Distribution of the Poor in Indonesia by
             Rural-Urban Areas, 1996–2002 (%)   31
Table 2.7   Distribution of Agricultural Households by
             Cultivated Landholding Size (%)   31
Table 2.8   Results of Estimation of Growth Linkages Model
             (Dependent variable: Rural non-agricultural
             sector growth)   42
Table 2.A1   Contribution to GDP by Sector and Location (%),
             1984–2002   46

Table 2.A2   Results of First-Stage Regression of Growth Linkages
              Model (Dependent variable: Rural agricultural
              sector growth)   47

Table 3.1   Employment by Major Sectors, Urban and Rural Areas,
              Formal and Informal Sectors, Indonesia, 1987–2004   52
Table 3.2   Multinomial Logit Estimation: The Probability of an
              Individual Engaging in Various Categories of NFE
              Relative to Farm Employment as Main Source of Income,
              Rural Indonesia, Year 2000 ("Farm Employment" as the
              Comparison Group)   62
Table 3.3   Logit Estimation: The Probability of an Individual
              Engaging in Farm and Non-Farm Activities,
              Rural Indonesia, Year 2000   64
Table 3.4   Firms' Opinion on Labour-Related Obstacles by
              Type of Enterprise Year 2005   74

Table 4.1   Source of Credit for Non-Farm Enterprises   88
Table 4.2   Source of Credit for Non-Farm Enterprises by
              Business Sector   89
Table 4.3   Rural Non-Farm Enterprises Facing Financial
              Obstacles to Continued Operation/Growth   91
Table 4.4   Possibility to Borrow from Formal Financial Institution   92
Table 4.5   Reasons for Not Applying for Loans from Banks,
              Informal Non-Farm Enterprises Receiving Credit
              from Other Sources   95
Table 4.6   Enterprises' Willingness to Borrow from a
              Formal Financial Institution   96
Table 4.7   Business Requirements and Types of Collateral   98

Table 5.1(a) Importance of Non-Farm Activity Varies By
              Road Infrastructure   120
Table 5.1(b) Importance of Non-Farm Activity Varies By
              Road Infrastructure   121
Table 5.2   Relationship Between Electricity Supply and
              Share of Household Total Income from
              Net Revenues of Non-Farm Business   123
Table 5.3   Relationship Between Electricity Supply and
              Whether Anyone in the Household Participates in
              Non-Farm Business   124
Table 5.4   Importance of Non-Farm Activity Affected by
              Access to Telecommunications   126

Table 5.5   Importance of Non-Farm Activity and Access
             to Irrigation   127
Table 5.6   Relationship Between Changes in Village Infrastructure
             and Whether Anyone in the Household Participates in
             Non-Farm Business   129
Table 5.7   Enterprise's Perceptions of Infrastructural Obstacles to
             Operation and Growth   131
Table 5.8   Constraints Listed Most Frequently as the
             Most Important Obstacles to Enterprise Operation
             and Growth   132
Table 5.9   Effects of Infrastructure Quality on the Percentage of
             Rural Household Income Coming From Non-Farm
             Enterprises   134
Table 5.A1   Sensitivity Analysis for Table 5.9   136

Table 6.1   Differences in Labour Productivity between MNCs
             and Local Firms in Manufacturing Industry (% period
             average of value added per worker)   143
Table 6.2   Differences in Labour Productivity in Indonesian
             Manufacturing Industry by Size of Enterprise and
             Sub-Sector, 2000 (average of value added per worker;
             in thousand Rupiah)   146
Table 6.3   Productivity (P) and Output Share (Q) in
             Manufacturing by Size, 1999–2003   147
Table 6.4   Relative Position of Indonesia with Respect to
             Indicators of the Technological Capabilities of Local
             Firms in the *Global Competitiveness Report 2004–2005*   147
Table 6.5   Types of Strategic Alliances by the Surveyed Firms,
             1997   159
Table 6.6   Percentage of MIEs and SMEs in Manufacturing
             Not Participating and Participating in the Foster
             Father Scheme by Type of Assistance, 2002   163
Table 6.7   Main Problems Faced by MIEs and SEs in the
             Manufacturing Sector, 2002   166
Table 6.8   Number of Institutions and Assistance Programmes
             to Strengthen MIEs and SEs, 1997–2003   169
Table 6.9   The Proportion of Assistance Programmes to
             Strengthen MIEs and SEs Based upon the Type of
             Activities and the Implementing Institutions   170
Table 6.10   The Impact of Assistance Programmes on MIEs
             and SEs   174

Table 6.11   Banks Involved in Financing SMEs in Indonesia, 2003   176
Table 6.12   Private Companies Actively Supporting SMEs,
             1997–2003   177

Table 7.1   Contrasting Characteristics between Traditional and
             Modern Market Systems   197
Table 7.2   Cost and Profitability Indicators of Vegetable and
             Fruit Farming as a Ratio to Rice in Irrigated Land   199
Table 7.3   Procurement Area of Non-Farm Trading Enterprises
             in RICS *Kabupaten*   207
Table 7.4   Sales Area of Non-Farm Trading Enterprises in
             RICS *Kabupaten*   208
Table 7.5   Number of Trading Enterprises Who Reported That
             There are More Than Five Competitors and Buyers   212

Table 8.1   *Kabupaten/Kota* Revenue, by Type, 1994/95 to 2003   227
Table 8.2   Property Tax, by Sector, 1994/95 to 2003   230
Table 8.3   Official Tax Burden   236
Table 8.4   Problems Related to Official Taxes   237
Table 8.5   Problems Related to Compliance Costs   238
Table 8.6   Unofficial Tax Burden   241
Table 8.7   Problems Related to Unofficial Taxes   241

Table 9.1   Influence of District Policies on Business Activities
             since 2001   251
Table 9.2   Ranking of Perceived Business Problems   253
Table 9.3   District Evidence on Licence Procedures —
             Administration Time and Capture   254

Table 10.1   Crime Rates, 1998–2000   301
Table 10.2   Perceived Change in Security Situation over the
             Three Years up to 2000   304
Table 10.3   Weighted Measures of the Four Main Obstacles to
             the Enterprise's Operations and/or Growth:
             Existing Firms   308
Table 10.4   Breakdown of Government and Security Obstacles
             to Enterprise Development by Urban/Rural and
             Ownership   311
Table 10.5   Security Variables Used in KPPOD Surveys   313

Table 10.6   Scores for KPPOD Variables, 2002 and 2004   314
Table 10.7   Tax Payments and "Unofficial Payments" by Firms,
             Indonesia 2005   316
Table 10.8   Basic Regression Results   318
Table 10.A   Weighted Measures of the Four Main Obstacles to the
             Enterprise's Operations and/or Growth
             (Full Breakdown)   321
Table 10.B1 Government and Security Obstacles by *Kabupaten*   324
Table 10.B2 Government and Security Obstacles by Sector   325
Table 10.B3 Government and Security Obstacles by Location of
             Owner of Enterprise   326
Table 10.C   Estimation Results for Modes of Enterprise Sales   327

Figures

Figure 1.1   Distribution of Employment by Size of Firm in
             Six *Kabupaten*   4
Figure 1.2   Mean Share of Income by Source in 2002   5
Figure 1.3   Sectoral Distribution of Enterprises in
             RICS *Kabupaten*   10
Figure 1.4   Location of Final Consumption of Goods
             Produced by RNFEs   11
Figure 1.5   The Distribution of Firms, Employment, and
             Value-Added by Size of Firm for Manufacturing   12
Figure 1.6   Factors Affecting Demand For and Supply of
             Output from Rural Non-Farm Enterprises   14
Figure 1.7   Most Important Constraints faced by Firms
             (Urban and Rural)   15

Figure 3.1   Formal and Informal Employment in Rural and
             Urban Areas, 1996–2004   53
Figure 3.2   Formal and Informal Employment in Farm and
             Non-Farm Sectors, 1996–2004   54
Figure 3.3   The Comparison of Hiring Tax in Selected Countries
             (Hiring Tax in number of monthly wages in 1990
             and 1999)   69

Figure 4.1   Informal Micro and Small Enterprises Facing
             Credit Problems, by Sector   90

Figure 4.2   Potential for Expansion of Micro-Credit   93
Figure 4.3   Reasons Businesses Choose not to Borrow from
              Formal Financial Institutions   96

Figure 6.1   The Spillover Effects of Technology/Knowledge (T/K)
              Transfer and Diffusion   142
Figure 6.2   Distribution of Non-Farm MIEs and SEs that Received
              Supports from the Government by Region, 2003   171
Figure 6.3   Proportion of SEs and MIEs Received Assistances
              from Government by Region, 2003 (% of total SEs
              and MIEs in the Region)   172

Figure 9.1   Corruption Rankings of Indonesia and its
              Neighbouring Countries over time   248
Figure 9.2   Location of the Eight District Cases   250
Figure 9.3   Perceptions of Local Business Policies During
              Subsequent Governance Periods   252
Figure 9.4   Impressions of Local One-Stop Licensing Services   257
Figure 9.5   Satisfaction of Businesses towards their Representation
              by Local Parliaments   267
Figure 9.6   Institutional Deficiencies at National and
              District Levels   272
Figure 9.7   Counterbalancing Factors — Governmental
              Leadership and Civic Pressure   273
Figure 9.8   Overall Business Perceptions on Aspects of
              Civic Pressure   275
Figure 9.9   Governmental Leadership Indicators in Case Districts   282
Figure 9.10   Comparison of Leadership Values in Kebumen
              and Klaten   285

Figure 10.1   Incidents of Social Violence in Indonesia, 1990–2003   303

Boxes

Box 1.1   Why this Book is about Rural, Non-Farm Enterprises
           (RNFEs)   2
Box 1.2   The Structural Transformation of the Rural Economy   6
Box 1.3   The Indonesian Rural Investment Climate Survey
           (RICS)   9

Box 3.1   *Premanism* in Job Recruitment   76
Box 3.2   Unqualified Locals versus Demand for
            Employment Share   77

Box 9.1   Examples of Low District Tax Effort   261
Box 9.2   Perceptions on PNS Bribe Payments from
            Stakeholder Interviews   270
Box 9.3   Statements on Corruption in the Public Tender
            Business   278
Box 9.4   Government Reforms in Solok during the Office of
            Bupati Fauzi Gamawan   284

Abbreviations and Acronyms

ADB	Asian Development Bank
AMT	Achievement Motivation Training
APBD	*Anggaran Pendapatan dan Belanja Daerah* (Regional Budget)
ASEAN	Association of Southeast Asian Nations
BAT	British American Tobacco
BBM	*Bahan Bakar Minyak* (Fuel)
BKD	*Badan Kredit Desa* (Village Credit Institutions)
BKK	*Badan Kredit Kecamatan* (Sub District Credit Institutions)
BKPM	*Badan Koordinasi Penanaman Modal* (Investment Coordinating Board)
BPD	*Bank Pembangunan Daerah* (Regional Development Bank)
BPN	*Badan Pertanahan Nasional* (National Land Agency)
BPPT	*Badan Pengkajian dan Penerapan Teknologi* (Agency for the Assessment and Application of Technology)
BPPI	*Badan Penelitian dan Pengembangan Industry* (Industrial Research and Development Laboratory)
BPR	*Bank Perkreditan Rakyat* (People's Credit Bank)
BPS	*Badan Pusat Statistik* (Central Statistic Agency)
BRI	*Bank Rakyat Indonesia* (People's Bank of Indonesia)
BRTI	*Badan Regulasi Telekomunikasi Indonesia* (Indonesian Telecommunications Regulatory Body)
BULOG	*Badan Urusan Logistik* (the Bureau of Logistic)
BUMN	*Badan Usaha Milik Negara* (State-Owned Enterprises/SOE)
Bupati	Head of a Regency

CCP	Captive Power Plant
CEFE	Creation of Entrepreneur for Formation Enterprises
CESS	Centre for Economic and Social Study
CU	Credit Union
CUCO	Indonesian Credit Union Federation
DAI	Development Alternatives, Inc
DAK	*Dana Alokasi Khusus* (Special Allocation Fund)
DAU	*Dana Alokasi Umum* (General Allocation Fund)
DIS	Debtor Information System
DPE	*Dewan Penunjang Ekspor* (Export Support Board)
DPRD	*Dewan Perwakilan Rakyat Daerah* (Local Parliaments)
DSP	*Danamon Simpan Pinjam* (Danamon Savings and Loans)
FDI	Foreign Direct Investment
FP	Foster Parent
GDP	Gross Domestic Product
GDS	Government and Decentralization Survey
GIAT	Growth through Investment, Agriculture, and Trade
GTZ	German Development Agency
HVC	High Valued Commodities
IFAD	International Fund for Agricultural Development
IFC PENSA	Programme for Eastern Indonesian Small Medium Enterprise Assistance
IFLS	Indonesia Family Life Survey
IMB	*Izin Mendirikan Bangunan* (Building License)
INKOPDIT	*Induk Koperasi Kredit* (Credit Union Central of Indonesia)
Inpres	*Instruksi Presiden* (Presidential Instruction)
IPP	Independent Power Plants
IT	Information Technology
JBIC	Japan Bank for International Cooperation
JICA	Japan International Cooperation Agency
Kabupaten	Regency or rural district
KDP	Kecamatan (Sub-District) Development Programme
KHM	*Kebutuhan Hidup Minimum* (Minimum Basic Subsistence Needs)
KKB	*Klinik Konsultasi Bisnis* (Business Consultancy Clinic)
KOPINKRA	*Koperasi Industri Kerajinan Rakyat* (Small-Scale Handicraft Industry Cooperatives)
Kota	City or urban district
KPPOD	*Komite Pemantauan Pelaksanaan Otonomi Daerah* (Committee Monitoring the Implementation of Regional Autonomy)

KPPU	*Komisi Pengawas Persaingan Usaha* (the Supervisory Commission on Business Competition)
KSP	*Koperasi Simpan Pinjam* (Savings and Loans Cooperatives)
KUD	*Koperasi Unit Desa* (Village Cooperatives)
KUK	*Kredit Usaha Kecil* (Small Scale Credit)
KUPEDES	*Kredit Umum Pedesaan* (General Rural Credit)
kWh	Kilo Watt-hours
LDKP	*Lembaga Dana Kredit Pedesaan* (Rural Fund and Credit Institutions)
LE	Large Enterprise
LIK	*Lingkungan Industri Kecil* (Estates for Small-Scale Industry)
LIPI	*Lembaga Ilmu Pengetahuan Indonesia* (Indonesian Institute of Science)
LKD	*Lembaga Keuangan Desa* (Village Finance Institutions)
LKM	*Lembaga Kredit Micro* (Micro Credit Institutions)
LKURK	*Lembaga Kredit Usaha Rakyat Kecil* (People's Small Business Credit Institutions)
LKP	*Lumbung Kredit Pedesaan* (Rural Credit Storehouse)
LP3E FE	*Laboratorium Penelitian, Pengabdian pada Masyarakat dan* Unpad *Pengkajian Ekonomi Fakultas Ekonomi Universitas Padjajaran*
LPEM-FEUI	*Lembaga Penelitian Ekonomi dan Masyarakat – Fakultas Ekonomi Universitas Indonesia* (University of Indonesia's Institute for Economic and Social Research)
ME	Medium Enterprise
MEMR	Ministry of Energy and Mineral Resources
MNC	Multinational Cooperation
MNE	Multinational Enterprise
Mobnas	*Mobil Nasional* (National Car)
MoI	Ministry of Industry
NFE	Non-Farm Enterprise
NFRE	Non-Farm Rural Enterprise
NGO	Non Government Organization
NIE	Newly Industrialized Economies
NPWP	*Nomor Pokok Wajib Pajak* (Taxpayer Registration Number)
NRI	Natural Resource Institute
OBA	Output-Based Aid
OECD	Organization for Economic Cooperation and Development

OSR	Own-Source Revenue
OSS	One-Stop Service
P4K	*Pembinaan Peningkatan Pendapatan Petani-Nelayan Kecil* (Assistance in Income Generation for Marginal Farmers and Fishermen)
PAD	*Pendapatan Asli Daerah* (Locally Raised Revenue)
Perda	*Peraturan Daerah* (Regional Regulations)
PDRB	*Produk Domestik Regional Bruto* (Gross Regional Domestic Product)
PKWT	*Perjanjian Kerja Waktu Tertentu* (Temporary Working Agreement)
PKPS BBM	*Program Kompensasi Pengurangan Subsidi Bahan Bakar Minyak* (Compensation Reduction Programme Implementation of Refined Fuel Oil Subsidy)
PKK	*Pendidikan Kesejahteraan Keluarga* (Women Welfare Activities)
PLN	*Perusahaan Listrik Negara* (State-Owned Electricity Company)
PNM	*Permodalan Nasional Madani* (National Fund for Social Investment)
PNS	*Pegawai Negeri Sipil* (Civil Servant)
PODES	*Potensi Desa* (Village Potential Statistics)
PT	*Perseroan Terbatas* (Limited Company)
R & D	Research and Development
REDI	Rural Economic Development Initiative
RGDP	Regional Gross Domestic Product
RICA	Rural Investment Climate Assessment
RICS	Rural Investment Climate Survey
RNFE	Rural Non-Farm Enterprise
SA	Strategic Alliances
Sakernas	*Survei Tenaga Kerja Nasional* (Labour Force Survey)
SE	Small Enterprise
SIUP	*Surat Ijin Usaha Perdagangan* (Trade Business Permit)
SOE	State-Owned Enterprise
Susenas	*Survei Sosial Ekonomi Nasional* (National Socio-Economic Survey)
SUSI	*Survei Usaha Terintegrasi* (Integrated Business Survey)
SME	Small Medium Enterprise
TAF	The Asia Foundation
TDP	*Tanda Daftar Perusahaan* (Business Registration Certificate)

TFP	Total Factor Productivity
TI	Transparency International
UED-SP	*Unit Ekonomi Desa – Simpan Pinjam* (Village Economic Units – Savings and Credit)
UKM	*Usaha Kecil Menengah* (Small Medium Enterprise/SME)
UPKD	*Unit Pengelola Keuangan Desa* (Village Financial Management Units)
UPT	*Unit Pelayanan Teknis* (Technical Service Unit)
USAID	United States Agency for International Development
USO	Universal Service Obligation
USP	*Unit Simpan Pinjam* (Saving and Credit Units)
WARSI	*Warung Informasi Konservasi* (Conservation Information Kiosk)
Wartel	*Warung Telekomunikasi* (Telecommunication Kiosk)

The Contributors

Neil McCulloch is a Fellow of the Institute of Development Studies at the University of Sussex, UK. He was formerly the Director for Economic Programs of The Asia Foundation in Indonesia and a Senior Economist at the World Bank office in Jakarta. His current research interests focus on the impact of the investment climate on firm performance, economic growth and poverty reduction. Whilst at the World Bank office in Jakarta, Dr McCulloch led a major research project on the Rural Investment Climate in Indonesia — the current book pulls together all of the original background research for that project. Dr McCulloch has published papers in a wide variety of refereed journals and books and has also co-authored a book *Trade Liberalisation and Poverty: A Handbook* (CEPR) which provides a comprehensive analysis of the evidence linking trade liberalization and poverty.

Asep Suryahadi is a Senior Researcher at the SMERU Research Institute in Jakarta. His research interests are in the areas of economic development, poverty, social protection, labour, and social policy. His research papers have been published in the *Bulletin of Indonesian Economic Studies, ASEAN Economic Bulletin, Asian Economic Journal, Review of Income and Wealth, Applied Economics, Journal of International Development, World Development, Development and Change, Developing Economies, Social Indicators Research, European Journal of Development Research, Education Economics,* and *Labour.* His current research topics include economic growth and poverty reduction, economic growth and employment creation, household composition and chronic poverty, and targeting the poor in developing countries.

Daniel Suryadarma has been with the SMERU Research Institute since 2003. He is currently doing his Ph.D. in Economics at the Australian National University. His broad research interests pertain to education economics, labour economics, and applied microeconomics. His latest publications are on the issues of student achievement, teacher absence, measurement of unemployment and how to reduce unemployment, poverty and economic growth, and the effect of private sector growth on poverty. His current research is on ascertaining the effect of cognitive ability on labour market outcomes and the effect of Catholic schools on substance use.

Sudarno Sumarto is one of the founders and currently holds the position of Director at the SMERU Research Institute, Jakarta. He is an economist and his research focuses on poverty analysis, social protection, wage and employment, and other socio-economic related issues. He has written several articles published in a number of international refereed journals including *Asian Economic Journal, Journal of International Development, Bulletin of Indonesian Economic Studies, Labour, World Development,* and *Review of Income and Wealth.*

Jack Molyneaux is a Senior Economist at the World Bank. Dr Molyneaux has conducted research, policy analysis, and consultancy in a wide variety of areas, most notably on nutrition, demographics, and the analysis of household poverty. He was the lead consultant responsible for the implementation of the Rural Investment Climate Survey in Indonesia and is an expert on survey design, implementation, and analysis. When at the RAND Corporation, Dr Molyneaux was involved in the design, implementation, and analysis of the Indonesian Family Life Survey.

Armida S. Alisjahbana is Professor of Economics at the Faculty of Economics, Padjadjaran University, Bandung, Indonesia. Her main research interests are in the area of public finance, economics of education, and labour market. She received her Ph.D. in Economics from the University of Washington in Seattle in 1994. She has been involved in various research projects, among others under the United Nations University, the World Bank, Bank Indonesia, AusAID, the European Commission, JBIC, and ADB. Aside from her extensive writing in national and international economic journals, Professor Armida serves on the International Advisory Board of the *Bulletin of Indonesian Economic Studies* (BIES), the Australian National University, and is a member of the Council of Fellows, the East Asian Economic Association.

Chris Manning is Head of the Indonesia Project and a Senior Fellow, in the Division of Economics, Research School of Pacific and Asian Studies, at the Australian National University (ANU), Canberra. He has extensive research and policy experience in Indonesia since first going there as a volunteer in 1967. He has authored and edited several books and many papers on Indonesian labour and related issues, as well as on general social and economic developments, and also co-authored a book and published papers on international labour migration in East Asia. He specializes in labour economics, labour policy, and international migration related to economic growth and poverty in Southeast Asia, and particularly Indonesia.

Andi Ikhwan is a Senior Consultant specializing in the Indonesian micro and SME finance sector. Mr Ikhwan has extensive experience in the design, implementation, and analysis of financial sector surveys. He has conducted several studies on the Indonesian financial sector including assignments for a large number of donors such as Asian Development Bank (ADB), International Finance Corporation (IFC), Japan International Cooperation Agency (JICA), Kreditanstalt für Wiederaufbau (KfW), Swisscontact, United States Agency for International Development (USAID), and the World Bank.

Don Edwin Johnston, Jr is a microfinance and banking expert. He is currently the Indonesia Programme Manager for the Maximizing Financial Access and Innovation at Scale for Mercy Corps. He has extensive experience in the management and implementation of access to finance and SME/microfinance programmes, including spending nine years as the Chief of Party for Harvard's highly successful technical assistance to Bank Rakyat Indonesia, the world's largest and most financially successful commercial microfinance institution. Mr Johnston has written numerous reports and studies on microfinance and teaches on Harvard University's Executive Programme, Financial Institutions for Private Enterprise Development.

John Gibson is Professor of Economics at the University of Waikato Management School. His teaching and research interests are in microeconomics and in the microeconometric aspects of development, labour, and the international economy. His other research interests include poverty measurement, the design and analysis of household survey data, and economic development, especially in China and other Asian and Pacific economies.

Tulus Tambunan is a Lecturer at the Faculty of Economics at the University of Trisakti, Jakarta. Dr Tambunan has a broad range of research interests including: economic development, poverty, growth, income distribution, rural development, small and medium enterprises, the international economy, and industrial development. He has written extensively on the topic of small and medium enterprise development in the Asia-Pacific region and on the role of small-scale industries in rural economic development. He also acts as an advisor to the Indonesian Chamber of Commerce on industrial development.

Thee Kian Wie is Senior Economist at the Economic Research Centre, Indonesian Institute of Sciences (P2E-LIPI), Jakarta. He received his first degree in Economics from the University of Indonesia, Jakarta, and his Ph.D. in Economics from the University of Wisconsin, Madison, USA. Dr Thee's major research interests are the modern economic history of the East Asian countries, with a focus on industrialization, the role of foreign direct investment and technological development in these countries. His most recent publications in English include several papers in refereed journals and two books, namely, *The Emergence of a National Economy: An Economic History of Indonesia, 1800–2000* (co-authored with Howard Dick, Vincent Houben, and Thomas Lindblad) and an edited book, *Recollections: The Indonesian Economy, 1950s–1990s*.

Hal Hill is the H.W. Arndt Professor of Southeast Asian Economies in the Research School of Pacific and Asian Studies, Australian National University. From 1986 to 1998 he headed the University's Indonesia Project and for much of this time also edited the *Bulletin of Indonesian Economic Studies*. His general research interests are the economies of ASEAN, especially Indonesia and the Philippines; industrialization and foreign investment in East Asia; and Australia's economic relations with the Asia-Pacific region. He is the author or editor of 14 books and has written about 120 academic papers and book chapters. Titles include *The Indonesian Economy since 1966, Indonesia's Industrial Transformation*, and *The Philippine Economy* (co-edited with Arsenio Balisacan). Current and recent book projects include a textbook on the ASEAN economies, a collection of papers on the ASEAN economies, edited volumes on regional development dynamics in the Philippines, the economy of East Timor, and foreign investment in the Asia Pacific. Recent paper topics include the Indonesian economy a decade after the crisis, regional development in East Asia, Indonesian industrialization, and the political economy of reform in Southeast Asia.

Pantjar Simatupang received his master's degree in Agricultural Economics from Bogor Agricultural University in 1980 and his Ph.D. degree in Economics from Iowa State University in 1986. He is currently a Research Professor (and former Director) of the Indonesian Center for Agro Socio-Economic Studies (ICASEPS), Ministry of Agriculture, Republic of Indonesia. He is also Senior Economic Advisor at the USAID funded DAI/AMARTA project to help develop the value chains of some high-value agricultural commodities in Indonesia. His research interests focus on agricultural policy, the linkages between agriculture and rural development, food security, and the macroeconomics of agriculture.

Blane D. Lewis is an expert on the Indonesian system of intergovernmental fiscal relations. He has published many articles on the local tax system, including the effect of transfers on local revenue generation, the creation and impact of new local revenue instruments since decentralization, the cost inefficiency of local tax administration, and the performance of central government administration of the property tax, among others. Other work has focused more specifically on the Indonesian transfers system and local government borrowing and loan repayment. Currently, Dr Lewis is conducting research on local education and health service delivery in Indonesia.

Bambang Suharnoko Sjahrir is a Ph.D. student at the University of Freiburg, Germany. Prior to this, Mr Suharnoko was an Economist in the World Bank office in Jakarta. In that capacity, he conducted several pieces of research and policy analysis focused on decentralization and the analysis of public expenditure. He has also co-authored papers on the determinants of regional growth. His current research interests are in the linkages between decentralization, growth, poverty, and inequality.

Christian von Luebke is a political economist with particular interest in governance and economic development in Southeast Asia. He is a post-doctoral Fellow at the Institute for Global Political Economy (GLOPE) at Waseda University in Tokyo, Japan. Between 2001 and 2008 he has worked extensively in rural Indonesia on issues of local economic development, investment climates, and good governance — both for the World Bank and the German development agency (GTZ). In 2007/2008, he was part of an international research team at the Institute of Development Studies (IDS) analysing the effects of public-private action on investment and growth.

Dr von Luebke completed his Ph.D. in policy and governance in 2007 at the Crawford School of Economics and Government, the Australian National University.

Jonathan Haughton is Professor, Economics Department, Suffolk University, Boston, Massachusetts, USA. His research focuses on economic development, and taxation. Current projects include an examination of the Thailand Village Fund, a study of tax incidence in Vietnam, the completion of a Manual on Poverty Analysis for the World Bank Institute, and a book on analytical techniques for the study of living standards survey data.

John MacDougall has been studying and conducting research in Indonesia for the past fifteen years. During the New Order, John focused primarily on religion and the sectarian tensions experienced by Buddhists, Hindus, and Muslim Indonesians. After the fall of President Soeharto in 1998, his focus shifted as sectarian tensions quickly turned inter-generational and inter-communal as local youth groups redefined the meanings of security, tradition, and political identity. Dr MacDougall received his doctorate in Social Anthropology from Princeton University in 2005. He currently resides in Jakarta where he works as a consultant.

1
Introduction

Neil McCulloch

1. Why Do We Care about the Rural Investment Climate?

This book focuses on the investment climate faced by Rural Non-Farm Enterprises (RNFEs). By this we refer to enterprises which are not in the major metropolitan centres, but we include non-farm enterprises in both rural and smaller urban and peri-urban environments (see Box 1.1). We also include all sizes of enterprises, including medium and large, although our emphasis is on micro- and small enterprises; and both registered and non-registered enterprises.

The majority of employment in Indonesia is in non-farm enterprises. Non-farm enterprises employ 53 million people in Indonesia — 57 per cent of the working population. Of these, around 20 million are employed in rural areas. Non-farm employment, including manufacturing, trade and services, constitutes well over a third of all employment in rural areas and 88 per cent in urban areas (see Table 1.1).

Most of this non-farm employment is in micro- and small enterprises.[1] Evidence from the recently completed Indonesia Rural Investment Climate Survey (RICS — see Box 1.3) shows that 63 per cent of non-farm workers in the six *kabupaten* surveyed[2] worked in micro-enterprises, with a further 23 per cent working in small enterprises. Only 13 per cent of employment was in medium and large enterprises (see Figure 1.1). The RICS *kabupaten* are predominantly rural (with the exception of Badung) — but a similar picture is apparent at the national level. For example around 60 per cent of manufacturing employment nationally is in cottage or small businesses.

Box 1.1
Why this Book is about Rural Non-Farm Enterprises (RNFEs)

This book is about the investment climate facing Rural Non-Farm Enterprises (RNFEs). This box defines what we mean by RNFEs and why we chose to focus on this category of firms.

Rural versus Urban
The Indonesian Central Statistical Agency (*Badan Pusat Statistik* or BPS) defines villages as "urban" based on a set of characteristics that include the share of income from agriculture; population density; and the availability of a list of amenities and services that are associated with urban living. "Rural" villages are simply villages that are sufficiently agricultural, sparse, or lacking in amenities that they fail to be classified as "urban".

For the purposes of this book, there is an important problem with the BPS definition. Because the definition of "urban" is functional, some areas classified as "rural" at one period in the analysis become "urban" in a later period. These reclassifications generally take place after each decadal census, with as many as 10–15 per cent of villages being reclassified at this point. However, it is precisely the dynamic rural economies that are so successful in growing that they are reclassified as urban that we seek to understand. Therefore, although we use the term "rural" to emphasize that we are interested primarily in non-metropolitan areas, much of our analysis applies to enterprises in peri-urban and smaller urban centres too.

Farm versus Non-Farm
We focus on the investment climate facing the "non-farm" economy because the technological and policy environments facing crop and livestock production — the farm economy — have their own distinctive characteristics that have been much studied. Relatively little is known about the constraints facing non-farm enterprises. The activities of such enterprises may be associated with the farm economy — indeed, may be carried out on a farm by the same households — but are distinct from farming *per se*. "Non-farm" also includes typical manufacturing and services activities not associated with farming at all.

Household versus Enterprise
Our study focuses on enterprises. The large majority of RNFEs are household enterprises, often operated from the household premises. However, we also include in our definition stand-alone enterprises (both formal and informal), including medium and large enterprises.

National versus Local
Most of the RNFEs to which we refer are based in *kabupaten*. The statistical data gathered for this project are from six *kabupaten*, and most of the chapters report on constraints facing firms operating at this local level. However, there are many *kota* that have enterprises which we would call RNFEs, whilst some *kabupaten* have large urban enterprises that we would not include. Therefore, we prefer the term "rural" to indicate the typical location of the firm. Also, to use the term *kabupaten* might imply that it is only *kabupaten* level policies that we are interested in. Certainly the study provides

useful advice for *kabupaten* leaders (*bupati*) on how to improve the investment climate in their regions — but it also emphasizes the importance of national-level policies to improve the investment climate at the local level.

In the face of all these complexities, we choose "Rural Non-Farm Enterprises" (RNFEs) as the shorthand name for the enterprises at the heart of our analysis. Why? Because it is widely used in the development literature and is not likely to be confused with alternatives also in use, such as SMEs (small and medium enterprises) or "informal" enterprises. SMEs fails to capture the rural emphasis we want, and although many of the enterprises we will be studying are indeed informal, much of the analysis is devoted to understanding the constraints on their transition to formal status. Thus, RNFE is the term of choice. Where required, exceptions will be noted.

Table 1.1
Employment by Sector in Rural and Urban Areas

Sector	Total (000)	Share
NATIONAL		
Agriculture, Forestry, and Fishery	40,608	43.3%
Manufacturing Industry	11,070	11.8%
Wholesale/Retail Trade, Restaurants, Hotels	19,119	20.4%
Public Services	10,512	11.2%
Others	12,413	13.2%
ALL NON-FARM	53,114	56.7%
TOTAL	93,722	100.0%
RURAL		
Agriculture, Forestry, and Fishery	36,088	63.9%
Manufacturing Industry	4,549	8.1%
Wholesale/Retail Trade, Restaurants, Hotels	7,345	13.0%
Public Services	3,159	5.6%
Others	5,322	9.4%
ALL NON-FARM	20,375	36.1%
TOTAL	56,464	100.0%
URBAN		
Agriculture, Forestry, and Fishery	4,520	12.1%
Manufacturing Industry	6,521	17.5%
Wholesale/Retail Trade, Restaurants, Hotels	11,774	31.6%
Public Services	7,353	19.7%
Others	7,091	19.0%
ALL NON-FARM	32,739	87.9%
TOTAL	37,259	100.0%

Source: Sakernas (2004).

Figure 1.1
Distribution of Employment by Size of Firm in Six *Kabupaten*

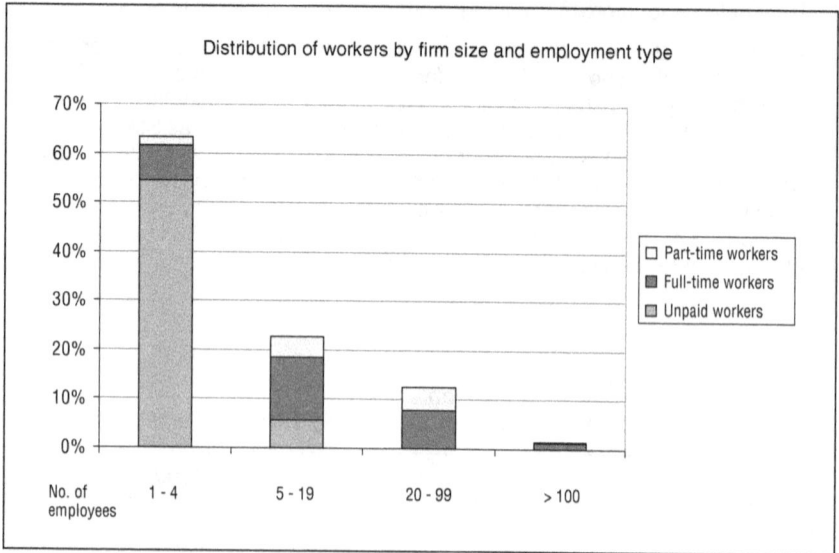

Distribution of workers by firm size and employment type

Source: RICS (2006).

The vast majority of enterprises are micro- or small firms. The RICS data show that more than 90 per cent of enterprises were micro-enterprises in all the surveyed *kabupaten* except Badung. Even in Badung, which lies near the major urban centre of Denpassar, 80 per cent of enterprises were micro-enterprises. Given the small size of most enterprises, it is not surprising that the overwhelming majority of enterprises are household enterprises[3] (as opposed to stand-alone enterprises). On average 94 per cent of rural enterprises in the RICS sample were household enterprises; even in urban villages 82 per cent were household enterprises.

A quarter of rural households and almost a third of urban households run household enterprises in the RICS *kabupaten*. Given that the RICS *kabupaten* were quite rural this suggests that running a household enterprise is quite common. Furthermore, households that run non-farm enterprises tend to have much higher incomes (almost 19 million per year) than those that do not (on average Rp 11 million).

Most non-farm enterprises in the RICS *kabupaten* are in rural villages. In the six *kabupaten* chosen, 60 per cent of the non-farm enterprises are in rural areas. To some extent this reflects the predominantly rural *kabupaten* chosen (with the exception of Badung) and there is some variability between the *kabupaten*. Nonetheless it is important to recognize that it is *not* the case that most non-farm enterprises are in urban areas, even though at a national level most non-farm employment is in urban areas.

Nationally, non-farm income constitutes half of all income (or 70 per cent if one includes income from transfers, investments, ownership, and other receipts) — see Figure 1.2. As incomes have grown over time, the relative importance of agricultural income has fallen, whilst that of non-farm income has risen. This reflects the longer-term structural transformation of the economy (see Box 1.2).

But perhaps the most important reason why we care about the investment climate faced by RNFEs is because the growth of this sector has the potential to be an important route out of poverty which we explore further in the next section.

Figure 1.2
Mean Share of Income by Source in 2002

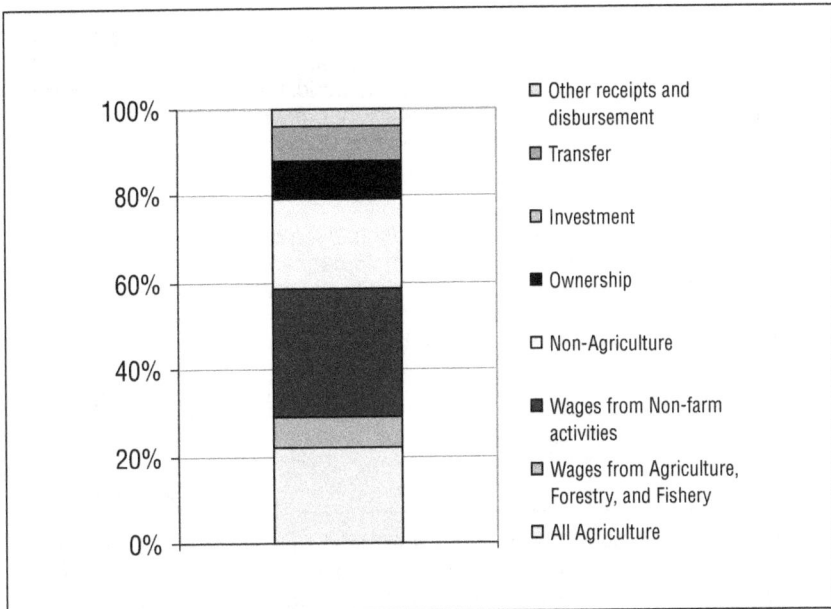

Source: Calculated from Susenas (2002).

Neil McCulloch

Box 1.2
The Structural Transformation of the Rural Economy

The Indonesian rural economy has undergone a structural transformation over the last twenty years. Since 1990, the contribution of the agricultural sector to Gross Domestic Product (GDP) has declined from 20 per cent in 1990 to just 16 per cent by 2003.

	1990	1995	2000	2003
Share of GDP (%)				
Agriculture	20	16	17	16
Industry	38	42	44	43
Services	42	42	40	41
Share of Rural Employment (%)				
Agriculture	70	60	66	68
Industry	11	15	13	12
Services	19	25	21	20

From agriculture to non-farm activities… Agriculture still represents more than two-thirds of rural employment. This average masks large differences between Java and off-Java. In 2002, 36 per cent of workers in Java (both rural and urban) were employed in agriculture, compared to 57 per cent of workers off-Java. Employment in agriculture declined rapidly prior to the crisis so that by 1995, the proportion of the rural workforce in this sector fell to 60 per cent.

…and back again. However, the economic crisis in 1997–98 pushed many of those who lost their livelihoods in urban areas back into rural agricultural activities reversing the secular decline in agricultural employment. Slow growth in the early years of the recovery has maintained a high level of agricultural employment while the proportion of the rural workforce working in the industrial and services sectors has declined during the post-crisis period.

From rural to urban… Indonesia has also seen a dramatic reduction in the share of employment in rural areas, from 75 per cent in 1990 to only 60 per cent in 2003. Some of this is as a result of rural-urban migration. Data from the inter-censal survey suggests that 1.85 per cent of the rural population physically moved from a rural to an urban area between 1990 and 1995.

	1990	1995	2000	2003
Share of Employment (%)				
Rural	75	67	62	60
Urban	25	33	38	40

…but without moving. Most of the "shift" from rural to urban is as a result of the reclassification of rural areas as urban. Thus declining non-farm employment in rural areas shown by official figures is actually an indication of the success rather than the failure of the sector. As rural areas have shifted into more non-farm activities and developed better facilities they have become reclassified as urban areas.

2. Agriculture, Rnfes, and Poverty Reduction

Most of the poor still live in rural areas. Table 1.2 shows the distribution of the poor population in Indonesia by sector and location. In 2002, 61 per cent of the poor earned their livelihood in the agricultural sector while 63 per cent of Indonesia's poor resided in rural areas.

Table 1.2
Distribution of the Poor in Indonesia by
Sector and Location, 1996–2002 (%)

Sector (%)	1996	1999	2002
Agriculture	63.2	59.3	61.1
Industry	15.5	15.8	16.1
Services	21.3	25	22.8
Rural	72	67	63
Urban	28	33	37

Source: Calculated from Susenas.

What has been the most effective way of reducing rural poverty? In the past, much poverty reduction has come from the growth of agriculture (Timmer 1988).

Agricultural growth has been very pro-poor in Indonesia because of the strong linkages between agriculture and non-farm activities. Precisely because they are rural, much of the market for RNFEs is based on demand from rural households, with growth of the agricultural sector inducing growth in the non-agricultural sector (White 1991).

Empirically, the strength of this linkage has been declining over time, but it is still extremely important. On average, 1 per cent growth in the agricultural sector induces 1.2 per cent growth in the non-agricultural sector in rural areas (see Chapter 2 of this book). A comprehensive study by Timmer (2005) has shown that the strength of these linkages was one of the reasons that the introduction of new "green revolution" agricultural techniques in the 1970s and 1980s had such a dramatic pro-poor effect.

The growth of agriculture is still an important route out of poverty. Recent evidence shows that most of those who exited poverty between 1993 and 2000 and who were working in rural agriculture in 1993, did so whilst continue working in rural agriculture (McCulloch, Timmer, and Weisbrod 2006). Within sector productivity growth and price changes are still the most important way of escaping poverty.

But productivity growth in the agricultural sector has been stagnant since the early 1990s, dropping from 2.5 per cent per year from 1968 to 1992, to –0.1 per cent per year from 1993 to 2000 (Fuglie 2004). There are several reasons for this. Investments in irrigation stalled after the crisis, with the result that much of the current irrigation infrastructure is in poor condition. In addition, agricultural extension services have suffered serious decline, particularly since decentralization, with the result that fewer farmers are actually able to receive such services. Finally, the technical options for improving agriculture are currently limited, and have been since the early 1990s, especially for rice. There are few immediately applicable new technologies likely to provide a significant boost to yields, although GM technologies hold hope for the future.

However, a more integrated domestic and international economy is now creating opportunities both in agriculture and other sectors. In the past, the strength of local linkages between the farm and the non-farm economy helped to transmit income gains in agriculture to the whole rural economy (Mellor 1976 and 2000). However, the local nature of many of these linkages is now a constraint rather than a vehicle for growth. Both in agriculture and in the rural non-farm economy, the opportunities for growth are likely to lie through greater linkages with the domestic urban economy and international markets. For example, the dramatic expansion of supermarket chains in Indonesia in recent years has created opportunities for growing high-value fruits and vegetables (see Reardon et al. 2005; World Bank 2006). Similarly, urban growth is creating strong demand for non-farm goods and services creating opportunities for firms in peri-urban and rural areas.

3. What Do We Know about RNFEs?

The Rural Investment Climate Survey (RICS) conducted in early 2006 gives a large amount of useful information about the characteristics and constraints faced by RNFEs in the six *kabupaten* surveyed (see Box 1.3). The key characteristics that emerge from this survey are outlined below.

As noted above, most RNFEs are very small. The median number of employees in firms in the RICS was 2 — even the mean, which is raised by a small number of large firms, is only 2.6. Total sales is also small: the median sales of micro- enterprises in the RICS was only Rp 11.7 million per year compared to Rp 60 million for small enterprises and Rp 867 billion for medium-sized enterprises.

Most RNFEs are focused in trade and services. Figure 1.3 shows the share of enterprises in production, trade and services in the six RICS *kabupaten*.

Box 1.3
The Indonesian Rural Investment Climate Survey (RICS)

Overview
The Indonesian Rural Investment Climate Survey (RICS) is an in-depth, quantitative survey of 2,549 non-farm enterprises, 2,782 households, and 149 communities in 6 rural *kabupaten*. Conducted in January–February 2006, the data from this survey is a valuable resource for researchers, students, and academics interested in understanding how the investment climate affects the rural economy.

Who was surveyed?
The RICS is a linked survey of non-farm enterprises and households. It excludes enterprises undertaking agriculture, forestry, and fishery activities, although the processing and trading of these commodities is included. The sample consists of:
- 1,755 Enterprise Households (i.e. with non-farm enterprises)
- 1,027 Non-Enterprise Households (without non-farm enterprises)
- 619 Stand-Alone Enterprises
- 144 Directory Enterprises
- 149 Communities
The survey includes both formal and informal businesses and examines both rural and urban areas of *kabupaten* to generate comparative data.

Where was the RIC Survey done?
The RIC Survey was conducted in six geographically distinct districts:
- Labuhan Batu, North Sumatra — a plantation area
- Kutai, East Kalimantan — an area rich in mineral resources
- Barru, South Sulawesi — a forest fringe area
- Malang, East Java — a rich agricultural area
- Badung, Bali — a peri-urban agglomeration area
- Sumbawa, NTB — a dryland area
The survey was deliberately "narrow but deep", i.e. although it was only done in six *kabupaten*, the sample size in each *kabupaten* is large enough to ensure statistical representation at the *kabupaten* level.

What was asked?
Three questionnaire modules were used:
- Household Questionnaire: which includes questions about household demographic and economic characteristics
- Enterprise Questionnaire: which asks detailed information about revenues, costs, and constraints faced by non-farm enterprises
- Community Questionnaire: which details characteristics of local infrastructure and governance

Data Access and User Support
To access the public access data set, go to <www.worldbank.org/id/rica> and click on the Survey link. Copies of all questionnaires in English and Indonesian, interviewer manuals, and annotated questionnaires are available at the site. Data are in STATA and SPSS formats.

Figure 1.3
Sectoral Distribution of Enterprises in RICS *Kabupaten*

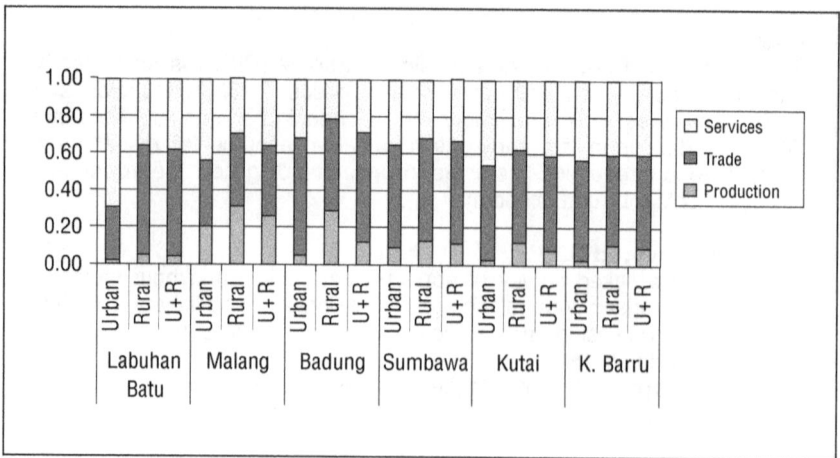

Source: Calculated from RICS (2006).

Around 45 per cent of RNFEs are trading enterprises, a further 35 per cent provide services, whilst only 20 per cent are involved in production of goods.

Most RNFEs are quite young. The median age of a RNFE is six years, with almost a third of firms three years old or less. But the age distribution is quite wide with 15 per cent of firms between 15 and 49 years old. Furthermore there appears to be a great deal of turnover. Looking just at household enterprises, perhaps 12 per cent of households started up a non-farm household enterprise in the last three years, whilst as many as a third of those households running an enterprise three years ago may have closed it down.[4]

Very few RNFEs are registered. Only 2.1 per cent of the RICS enterprises have a Business Registration Certificate (TDP); 4.4 per cent have a trading licence (SIUP); and 3.4 per cent have a building licence (IMB). Taking all of these licences together (plus application for electricity connection and worker safety permit), a mere 8.6 per cent of businesses in these six *kabupaten* had any of these licences.

RNFEs serve very local markets. Figure 1.4 shows the point of final consumption of the goods and services produced by the enterprises in the RICS. More than half of all trade and almost half of all services are supplied in the same village, and close to 80 per cent are supplied in the same *kecamatan*. Even for enterprises involved in production, more than a third of

Figure 1.4
Location of Final Consumption of Goods Produced by Rnfes

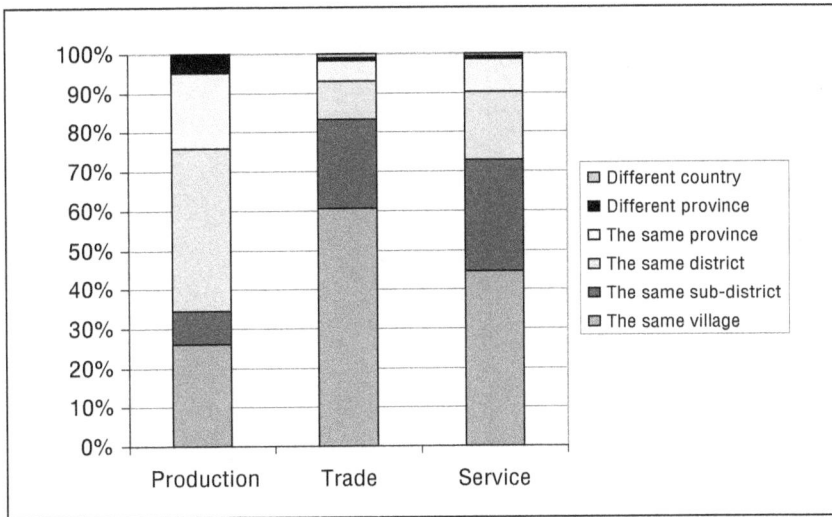

Source: Calculated from RICS (2006).

goods are consumed in the same *kecamatan* and 75 per cent are consumed in the same *kabupaten*.

Labour productivity is very low, particularly in micro-enterprises. There is a dramatic difference in the labour productivity of micro-, small and medium/large enterprises. Figure 1.5 shows the proportion of manufacturing enterprises at the national level in each size category, as well as the share of employment and the share of value-added in each category. The results are dramatic. Although more than 90 per cent of these enterprises are micro-/ cottage enterprises, and around 60 per cent of manufacturing employment is in micro- or small enterprises, more than 90 per cent of manufacturing value-added is generated by medium/large enterprises. This implies very large differences in labour productivity between micro-, small and medium/ large enterprises.

3.1. Why Bother with RNFEs?

Figure 1.5 poses a challenge. If almost all value-added is being created by medium and large firms, why should policy be concerned with RNFEs that are predominantly micro- and small firms?

Neil McCulloch

Figure 1.5
The Distribution of Firms, Employment, and Value-Added by
Size of Firm for Manufacturing

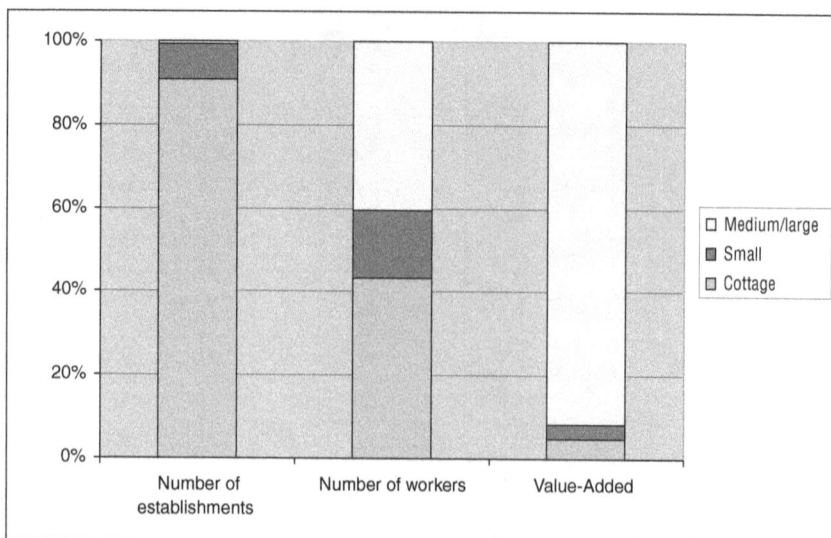

Source: SUSI (2002)/Statistik Industri (2002).

One answer is because policy is designed to promote broad-based growth. Medium and large firms are heavily concentrated in the major cities and their immediate surroundings. Growth among medium and large enterprises can have a strong positive impact, but the impact tends to be localized to the areas in which these firms are located or is spread nationally only by raising the level of real wages. By contrast RNFEs are spread throughout the country. If policy can improve the performance of such firms then the gains will be much more widely spread.

Secondly, many RNFEs are small and unproductive because they are constrained by high costs — in getting credit, in accessing markets and technology, in obtaining infrastructure services, and in dealing with government bureaucracy. Many of these costs are directly amenable to public policy — through broadening access to the banking system, building better roads, extending electricity provision, and reducing the time and cost of licensing procedures, amongst others. Of course such actions entail costs on the part of the government. The real question therefore is what sort of actions to improve the rural investment climate are likely to have benefits in terms of growth and job creation which outweigh the costs of implementation. To be able to answer this it is necessary to have an understanding of the constraints facing RNFEs.

4. What Constrains RNFEs in Indonesia?

4.1. A Framework for Understanding the Constraints on RNFEs

Figure 1.6 summarizes the framework used in this book for the analysis of constraints on *kabupaten*-level enterprises. The core of the framework is the equilibrium between supply and demand for the goods and services produced by the rural non-farm enterprise sector. It is critical to consider both sides of this equation.

(i) *Demand side:* The top section of Figure 1.6 shows the various factors influencing the demand for the output of rural non-farm enterprises. Profits from agricultural production; incomes earned in these non-farm enterprises; and demand generated outside the rural economy, either domestic or foreign, can all contribute to effective demand for the goods and services produced by RNFEs. Which of these sources of demand is the most important depends on the locale and the degree of development in the environment in which the RNFEs operate.

(ii) *Supply side:* The bottom section of Figure 1.6 shows the various sources of supply of goods and services from RNFEs. A wide variety of factors determines the ability of RNFEs to produce these goods and services and the costs which they incur in doing so. These include: issues associated with rights of access to natural resources including land; the ability to access capital and the cost of doing so; the cost and quality of labour; the quality of the local regulatory environment; the state of local infrastructure; the extent of competition; knowledge of market opportunities; and the stability and security of the area.

Typically, RNFEs are micro- or small enterprises that use rather old and highly labour-intensive technologies to deliver goods and services on a very small scale. As a result, unit costs can be high and productivity low. In these circumstances, it is only profitable for RNFEs to serve a local clientele, since high transportation costs or other constraints create a degree of natural local protection.

Figure 1.6
Factors Affecting Demand For and Supply of Output
from Rural Non-Farm Enterprises

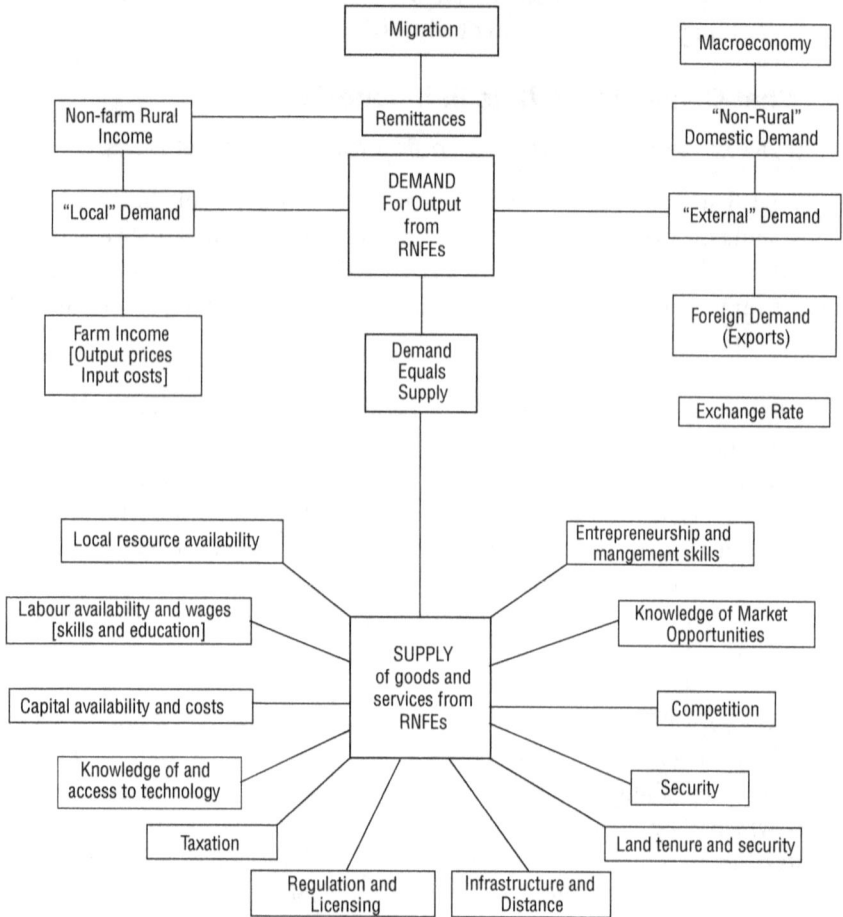

```
                        ┌──────────────┐                    ┌──────────────┐
                        │  Migration   │                    │ Macroeconomy │
                        └──────────────┘                    └──────────────┘

┌──────────────┐        ┌──────────────┐                    ┌──────────────┐
│ Non-farm Rural│───────│ Remittances  │                    │  "Non-Rural" │
│    Income     │        └──────────────┘                    │Domestic Demand│
└──────────────┘        ┌──────────────┐                    └──────────────┘
                        │   DEMAND     │
┌──────────────┐        │  For Output  │                    ┌──────────────┐
│ "Local" Demand│───────│    from      │────────────────────│"External" Demand│
└──────────────┘        │    RNFEs     │                    └──────────────┘
                        └──────────────┘
                                                            ┌──────────────┐
┌──────────────┐        ┌──────────────┐                    │Foreign Demand│
│ Farm Income  │        │   Demand     │                    │  (Exports)   │
│[Output prices│        │   Equals     │                    └──────────────┘
│ Input costs] │        │   Supply     │                    ┌──────────────┐
└──────────────┘        └──────────────┘                    │Exchange Rate │
                                                            └──────────────┘
```

Local resource availability   Entrepreneurship and mangement skills

Labour availability and wages [skills and education]   Knowledge of Market Opportunities

Capital availability and costs   **SUPPLY of goods and services from RNFEs**   Competition

Knowledge of and access to technology   Security

Taxation   Land tenure and security

Regulation and Licensing   Infrastructure and Distance

4.2. The Critical Importance of Demand Factors: Local or External Demand?

The wide variety of factors determining the investment climate suggests that lowering costs holds the potential for profitably expanding non-farm enterprises. However, this depends critically on the extent to which demand for the output of the non-farm sector is local or external.

If demand is very localized, additional output resulting from lower production costs will merely lower prices locally, undermining the profitability of the expansion.[5] In such a situation, measures to improve the local investment climate may have a very limited impact upon output and incomes. On the other hand, if demand is completely external to the local area, local firms can expand production without any impact on local prices (so long as their costs are below their competitors). Thus, the "domain of trade", or the extent to which goods are traded locally or more widely, is a key determinant of the success of measures to improve the local economy. But, of course, some interventions change the domain of trade. In particular, improvements in infrastructure — roads, electricity, communications, market facilities, etc. — tend to broaden the domain of trade and increase the size of the market, thus helping to alleviate constraints on both the demand and supply side.

4.3. What are the Most Important Constraints Faced by Indonesian RNFEs?

The RICS asked firms about the principal constraints that they faced. Figure 1.7 shows the ranking of the most important constraints mentioned by the RICS enterprises.

Figure 1.7
Most Important Constraints faced by Firms (Urban and Rural)

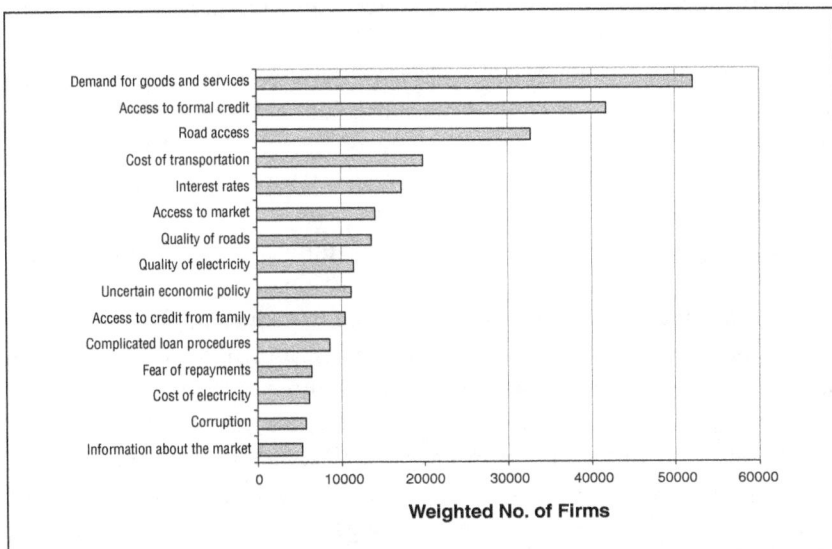

Source: Calculated from RICS (2006).

Demand, access to formal credit, and the costs associated with road transportation are the principal concerns of RNFEs. The dominant position of "demand" in the list of constraints confirms the importance given to demand constraints in the framework of Figure 1.7. But the result must also be interpreted with some caution. Most firms prefer more orders to fewer. A lack of demand may indicate that firms face very localized markets, as shown in Figure 1.4. The policy response to this is to broaden the reach of their markets by reducing the costs (both physical and information related) needed to reach markets. But it can also be an indication that the quality of the goods and services produced is low and that these firms are therefore losing customers to more modern firms producing higher quality products. Indeed the gradual reduction over time of the "natural protection" provided to rural firms by high costs of transportation may be the reason why firms are complaining about problems of lack of demand. But this is not a reason for slowing down the process of connecting the rural economy; quite the reverse, the competition provided by more productive enterprises has been shown internationally to be one of the main factors driving productivity growth (World Bank 2005).

Access to formal credit is the second most cited constraint for RNFEs. The key here is that it is formal credit that is constrained, rather than informal sources of credit. Although Indonesia is justifiably proud of its international reputation for rural banking, there is still some way to go, with a substantial minority of viable micro- and small firms still unable to access the formal banking system. Chapter 3 on Credit addresses this issue in more detail.

Thirdly, access to roads and the cost of transportation weigh heavily on RNFEs. Road access, the costs of transportation and road quality all appear among the seven most common concerns of RNFEs. This reflects the poor quality particularly of *kabupaten*-level roads. Chapter 4 on Infrastructure addresses this issue in more detail.

The top concerns of RNFEs are quite different from those of larger urban-based enterprises. Although direct comparisons are difficult, the investment climate assessments of larger urban firms tend to highlight problems of macroeconomic instability, policy uncertainty, corruption, the legal system and taxation issues (World Bank 2004). Whilst some of these feature amongst the concerns of RNFEs, it is clear that they are not the principal concerns.

In one sense this is a problem since it indicates that most RNFEs simply do not participate in the formal economy. Policies applied to formal firms are not applied to them, most have few dealings with the bureaucracy and are therefore less concerned with corruption, the legal system or taxation. As the productivity of such enterprises increases it is likely that the advantages of participating in the formal economy will increase and so such issues will rise in the rankings of importance. But, at least for now, it is clear that the actions needed to stimulate growth among RNFEs are likely to be rather different than those needed to improve the performance of larger urban enterprises.

5. The Chapters of this Book

The ranking in Figure 1.7 identifies the priorities of RNFEs. But clearly actions are needed in many different areas to improve the rural investment climate. This book explores different aspects or themes of the rural investment climate: labour; credit; infrastructure; the diffusion of technical knowledge; competition and marketing; the political economy of licensing reform; taxation; and security. Each chapter asks the same four questions:

1. What is the size and nature of the constraint that RNFEs face?
2. What is the impact of the constraint on RNFE performance?
3. What is the policy and institutional environment and how does it give rise to the constraint?
4. What policy reforms at both the national and local level can lead to a better investment climate?

However, because of the close linkage between the farm and the non-farm sector in rural areas, we start with a key chapter on Agricultural Demand Linkages. Chapter 2, therefore, explores the question of whether growth in agriculture drives non-agricultural growth in rural areas, or whether, in fact, non-agricultural growth is driven by non-agricultural growth in nearby urban areas. Combining a panel of GDP and household survey data, Suryahadi, Suryadarma, Sumarto, and Molyneaux find that the growth of the agricultural sector strongly induces the growth of non-agricultural sector in rural areas. They estimate that on average 1 per cent growth of the agricultural sector induces 1.2 per cent growth of the non-agricultural sector in rural areas, vindicating the view that rising incomes in the agricultural sector stimulate demand for locally-produced goods and services in rural areas. Given the synergistic relationship between the farm and non-farm sectors, their results suggest that efforts to improve the investment climate for non-farm enterprises in rural areas should be designed to benefit all enterprises, or at least should not discourage the growth of agriculture since it represents an important source of demand for the output of the non-farm sector.

Chapter 3 analyses the impact of labour market regulations and informal labour market practices on the performance of RNFEs. Alisjahbana and Manning examine the trend in both formal and informal non-farm employment. They show that employment in the formal sector, both agricultural and non-agricultural, has been stagnant or declining, whilst informal employment has been growing in both sectors. They review the extensive literature on the factors that determine participation in non-farm economic activities and then empirically assess the relevance of these factors in Indonesia using the Indonesia Family Life Survey data from 2000. In addition to the commonly-found influence of individual characteristics they reveal interesting new evidence about the importance of social networks and community facilities for participation in the non-farm sector.

The chapter then turns its attention to the impact of labour policies on the growth of non-farm enterprises since the crisis. They review the recent evidence on the impact of minimum wages, severance pay, and outsourcing regulations on employment growth in Indonesia. In addition, the Indonesian Rural Investment Climate Survey (RICS) data is used to identify the key labour problems faced by non-farm enterprises and further understanding of the impact of local labour regulations is obtained from recent case study data. The chapter reviews the current state of the other major labour issue in Indonesia — domestic and international migration — and the impact of such migration on the creation and growth of non-farm enterprises. The chapter concludes with some implications for policy arising from the analysis.

Chapter 4 looks at financial services and the constraints that small businesses face in obtaining credit. Difficulty in accessing finance represents one of the most important constraints facing RNFEs in Indonesia. Lack of access to formal credit is the second most often cited constraint by firms in the Rural Investment Climate Survey (RICS) and more than half of the enterprises surveyed mentioned finance-related obstacles as a problem, with almost a quarter saying that finance was the most important problem that they faced. After reviewing the financial services available to RNFEs in Indonesia, Ikhwan and Johnston use the RICS and other recent data to assess the extent to which financing is a problem for such enterprises. They find that the majority of RNFEs do not use credit from either formal or informal sources. Moreover, perhaps a quarter of existing enterprises would like to borrow; meet lenders' criteria; are prepared to pay the costs; but are still failing to gain access to financing.

Having obtained an indication of the magnitude of the constraint, they then proceed to explore the reasons given by household businesses and small enterprises for not applying for loans from banks or other formal sector institutions. These include some motives not easily affected by policy, such as the desire to avoid indebtedness and the fear of not being able to repay. However, interest rates, collateral concerns, and the perceived complexity and cost of application procedures, including the high costs of formal registration of a business required by formal lending institutions, are also considered important by a large proportion of firms. The authors also examine the constraints to lending from the supply side. Banks are constrained from making loans to small enterprises because of the difficulty and cost of identifying micro- and small enterprises that could potentially become successful borrowers. The chapter concludes with a range of policy recommendations to reduce the credit constraints faced by small and micro-enterprises through supporting pro-competition policies and reinforcing competitive behaviour at the micro-level.

Chapter 5 examines infrastructure, including roads, electric power, and telecommunications. Gibson underlines the critical role of infrastructure investments in generating economic growth and structural change. However, in reviewing the literature on the linkages between infrastructure and the development of non-farm enterprises, he highlights the methodological difficulty of drawing causal inferences about the role of infrastructure from the available evidence.

The two main sections of the chapter report new evidence on the effect that infrastructure has on the importance of non-farm enterprises in rural Indonesia. This evidence comes from two surveys: the Indonesia Family Life Survey (IFLS) and the RICS. Gibson exploits the panel nature of the IFLS data to explore how changes in infrastructure can affect households' participation in non-farm enterprises in the rural economy. The RICS data is then used to identify the extent to which infrastructure represents an important constraint for RNFEs and how this constraint has changed over time, as well as an indication of which types of infrastructure have the largest impact on the extent to which household income comes from the non-farm sector.

Chapter 6 discusses the diffusion of technical knowledge to small enterprises (both rural and urban). Tambunan and Thee point to the very low levels of technological capacity in many micro- and small enterprises. This suggests that improving the diffusion of technical knowledge to such enterprises may be an important part of boosting their growth and development. After reviewing the literature on the current technological capabilities of Indonesian firms, the authors lay out the channels through which international technical knowledge is typically obtained by Indonesian enterprises. These include: foreign direct investment; technical licensing agreements; imports of intermediate and capital goods; and participation in world trade. In addition they review the mechanisms through which the domestic diffusion of knowledge typically occurs, notably subcontracting, strategic alliances, and clustering.

Tambunan and Thee then turn to the constraints typically faced by rural non-farm enterprises, and discuss how constraints in the access to technology have affected the growth of non-farm enterprises. The authors review the role of supporting agencies and SME promotion programmes, pointing to the large number of such programmes and the limited evidence for their success. They conclude with a set of recommendations for policy.

Chapter 7 on marketing and competition, breaks with the non-farm focus of most of the other chapters by exploring the marketing of both agricultural and non-agricultural goods. The reason for this is that so many non-farm goods are derived from agricultural goods that it makes little sense to consider their marketing channels in isolation. Hill and Simatupang point to the dramatic changes in marketing in Indonesia over the last decade, contrasting the characteristics of traditional marketing channels with the rapidly growing modern retail-driven value chains. In the case of agriculture, they draw on case study work in East Java to point to the importance of the "supermarket revolution" in modernizing agricultural marketing and their growing role in extending the market for rural agricultural goods.

For non-farm marketing channels, the authors review the surprisingly limited recent literature on the evolution of marketing in Indonesia and draw out the factors which appear to have been associated with success. In particular it appears to be the case that the most successful examples of marketing have arisen from within the private sector, rather than through government intervention, but that national and local governments do have an important role to play in facilitating market linkages and ensuring the availability of appropriate market infrastructure. They also draw on the RICS data to highlight the extremely limited geographical range of procurement and sales from most non-farm enterprises. The limited scope of existing markets helps to explain why lack of demand is the most important constraint cited by RNFEs in the RICS.

Finally, Hill and Simatupang briefly review the related literature on competition. They exploit the RICS data to show that the markets in which most micro- and small businesses operate are very competitive, with large numbers of competitors and buyers, even at the local level. From a policy perspective, they review the role of the competition commission (KPPU) and more generally the influence of Indonesia's broader political transition in creating a more competitive commercial environment. The chapter concludes with some key lessons and recommendations for policy.

In Chapter 8, Lewis and Sjahrir review the state of our knowledge about local taxation in Indonesia and analyse the effects of local taxation on the business climate. They examine local government own-source revenue and (central) property tax revenue, pre- and post-decentralization, and review certain issues related to newly created local taxes and charges during the post-decentralization period. The authors then outline their cost-benefit analytical framework. Costs include the revenue burdens and compliance costs associated with local taxation that are borne by private businesses. Benefits comprise the public services delivered to businesses that are funded from local tax payments. The authors look at the available evidence regarding the costs and benefits of local taxation and the impact of administrative ineffectiveness and inefficiency and corruption on such costs and benefits. In their concluding section, they summarize the main points of the chapter and draw some conclusions that may be important for the future development of sub-national tax policy.

Chapter 9 broadens out the discussion from specific constraints faced by non-farm enterprises to examine the political economy of investment climate reforms at the local level. Drawing on a set of eight case studies at the district level undertaken by the author, von Luebke assesses how business conditions have changed in the five years since decentralization. A majority of districts have seen rising administrative capture practices, unsatisfactory one-stop licensing services, and a local revenues management that follows vague "target systems" rather than sound accounting standards. The author presents evidence that this outcome is related to institutional deficiencies, both at the national and district level: at the national level ambiguity of national tax laws and restricted supervision creates room for misconduct of local governments; at the district level inverted incentive structures and adverse bureaucratic conventions negatively affect administrative practices.

Yet, despite institutional impediments, some districts appear to be more conducive for local business than others. Von Luebke's cross-district analysis shows that better regulatory policies and more conducive tax and licensing practices are more closely related to the quality of district leadership than pressure from local businesses. This suggests that the options for "voice" and "exit" often cited in the fiscal federalism and anti-corruption literature as mechanisms in which the private sector can improve the business climate that they face, appear to be less prominent in Indonesia's current setting.

Finally, Chapter 10 examines the critical issue of how insecurity (in the sense of crime, violence, and coercive behaviour), affects non-farm enterprises at the district level. Haughton and MacDougall attempt to move beyond the abundant anecdotal evidence to assess how widespread insecurity is in Indonesia, and specifically in rural Indonesia, which has traditionally been viewed as more peaceful and safer than the urban areas. They find that insecurity in Indonesia, as measured by murder rates, is comparable to that of the United States, and far higher than portrayed in standard international statistical comparisons. Furthermore, this insecurity is found throughout the country, and not just in large urban centres.

The authors then attempt to assess the extent to which violence, or the threat of violence, limits business development using data from the RICS. They find that concerns about safety — whether criminality, theft and lawlessness, or conflict and social friction — rank near the bottom of the list of perceived challenges faced by business people. This by no means implies that security issues are irrelevant, but of the micro- and small rural enterprises surveyed, there are other more pressing concerns. However, the authors point out that uncertainty induced by government policies, whether because of corruption, uncertainty in economic policies, or restrictive laws and regulations, are a significant concern. This appears to be particularly important in the mining sector and in transportation — indeed transportation is the main sector where "criminality, theft and lawlessness" are reported to be serious, as trucks and buses are especially vulnerable to extortion.

NOTES

1. We define micro-enterprises as 0–4 employees; small as 5–19 employees; medium as 20–99 employees; and large as 100+ employees.
2. Indonesia has more than 480 districts — these include cities known as *kota*, and regencies known as *kabupaten*. The Rural Investment Climate Survey covered six *kabupaten*: Labuhan Batu, Malang, Badung, Manggarai, Barru, Sumbawa.
3. Household enterprises are defined as those which take place in the household residence or which are mobile and operated by household members.
4. The figure for firm exit ranges from only 10 per cent to 32 per cent depending on one's assumption about the population of firms three years ago.
5. More precisely, we are referring to the price elasticity of demand for the output of RNFEs. If it is low, as is the case with very localized economies, prices will fall substantially when output expands; if it is high, as is typical of more widely integrated economies, prices only fall slightly if at all. In the extreme, exports to the world market are usually at a constant "border price". In such cases, the cost structure of supplying firms determines the scale of output and demand is not a constraint.

REFERENCES

Fuglie, Keith O. "Productivity Growth in Indonesian Agriculture: 1961–2000". *Bulletin of Indonesian Economic Studies* 40, no. 2 (2004): 209–25.

McCulloch, Neil, Julian Weisbrod, and C. Peter Timmer. "The Pathways out of Rural Poverty in Indonesia". Paper for the Indonesian Poverty Assessment, World Bank, Jakarta processed, 2006.

Mellor, John W. *The New Economics of Growth: A Strategy for India and the Developing World*. Ithaca, NY: Cornell University Press, 1976.

———. "Agricultural Growth, Rural Employment, and Poverty Reduction: Non-Tradables, Public Expenditure, and Balanced Growth". Prepared for the World Bank Rural Week, 2000.

Reardon, Thomas et al. "Farmer Organization to Access Markets for High Value Products: Challenges and Innovations". Presentation at World Bank, Washington D.C., 15 December 2005.

Suryahadi, Asep, Daniel Suryadarma, Surdarno Sumarto, and Jack Molyneaux. "Agricultural Demand Linkages and Growth Multiplier in Rural Indonesia". In *Rural Investment Climate in Indonesia*, edited by Neil McCulloch. Singapore: Institute of Southeast Asian Studies, 2009.

Timmer, C. Peter. "The Agricultural Transformation". In *The Handbook of Development Economics*, Vol. I, edited by Hollis B. Chenery and T.N. Srinivasan. Amsterdam: North-Holland, 1988.

———. "Operationalizing Pro-Poor Growth: A Country Case Study of Indonesia". Washington D.C.: PREM/World Bank, July 2005.

White, Benjamin. "Economic Diversification and Agrarian Change in Rural Java, 1900–1990". In *In the Shadow of Agriculture: Non-farm Activities in the Javanese Economy, Past and Present*, edited by Paul Alexander, P. Boomgaard, and Benjamin White. Amsterdam: Royal Tropical Institute, 1991.

World Bank. "Making Indonesia Competitive: Promoting Exports, Managing Trade". PREM East Asia and Pacific, November 2004.

———. "A Better Investment Climate for Everyone". World Development Report 2005.

———. "The Supply of High Value Crops to Supermarkets in Malang District — Trends and Implications for Small Farmers". Rural Investment Climate Assessment Case Study 1, Jakarta, 2006.

2

Agricultural Demand Linkages and Growth Multipliers in Rural Indonesia

Asep Suryahadi, Daniel Suryadarma, Sudarno Sumarto, and Jack Molyneaux

1. Background

Although declining, rural areas still make up an important part of the Indonesian economy. The majority of Indonesians still live in rural areas. According to data from the Population Census 2000, around 58 per cent of Indonesians are rural residents. Aside from providing food supplies for the whole economy, the rural areas also contribute importantly to foreign exchange earnings from export of commodities. However, rural areas apparently lag behind compared to urban areas, both in terms of physical infrastructure as well as the socio-economic welfare of the populace. As a consequence, around 80 per cent of all the poor in the country are found in rural areas.

This obviously calls for more focused attention and more rigorous efforts on rural development. This, however, requires a clear and effective strategy to jump-start and sustain economic growth in rural areas. Since rural areas are closely identified with the agricultural sector, a more specific question is whether investments should be directed to improve productivity in the agricultural sector or whether it is more effective to invest to develop the rural non-agricultural sector directly. Ultimately, the answer to this question, and hence the rural development strategy adopted, should depend on its potential to push growth for the whole rural economy.

The agricultural and non-agricultural sectors in rural areas are closely linked. Hence, growth in one sector will induce growth in the other. However, despite the fact that there is a relatively long history of studies focusing on the subject of rural sectoral linkages, there remains debate on whether the most effective route for rural development is through firstly developing the agricultural sector or through directly developing the non-agricultural sector.

Among one strand of the literature, there is a consensus that agriculture has strong linkages and has a large growth multiplier to other sectors in the rural economy and, because of that, it is essential to develop the agriculture sector first in order to develop the whole rural area. Not all rural development thinkers and practitioners agree to the agriculture-first strategy, however. Some have argued for the opposite, that it is the non-agriculture sectors that have strong potential to push economic growth in the rural areas and pull the poor, who mostly live in the agriculture sector, out of poverty. Others, meanwhile, have argued that both agricultural and non-agricultural sectors have strong potential to become the engine of growth in rural areas and, hence, call for a more balanced growth strategy.

In the context of Indonesia, unfortunately, there is no known or published study on sectoral demand and growth linkages in rural areas. This is unfortunate considering the importance of rural areas for the Indonesian economy, in particular as the location where the majority of workers find employment. Furthermore, the vast majority of the poor in Indonesia live in rural areas and work in the agricultural sector.

This study tries to fill in the gap by examining the empirical evidence on the strength of agricultural demand linkages and estimating the agricultural growth multipliers in rural Indonesia. It is hoped that the results of this analysis will provide the foundation for formulating the most effective strategy for stimulating economic growth in rural Indonesia, which is crucial for improving the welfare of its residents as well as effectively resolving a large part of the poverty problem in Indonesia.

2. Sectoral Linkages in Rural Areas

There are several types of sectoral linkages in rural areas. The most well-known linkages are production and distribution linkages. A production linkage occurs when a sector produces an output which is then used as an intermediate input by another sector. An example of this is the linkage between a farm producing food commodities and a food-processing industry. From the point of view of a certain sector, there are two types of production linkages: backward and forward linkages. For example, from a farm's point of view, the linkages to fertilizer and seed producers are backward linkages. On the other hand, the linkages from the farm to food-processing industries are forward linkages.

Meanwhile, distribution linkages act as an intermediary between two sectors. A farm may supply its output directly to a food-processing industry, but it may also sell its output to a trader who then re-sells it to the food-processing industry. In this case, the trader plays the role of a distribution linkage. In general, a distribution linkage provides two types of services. First, it provides location value added by transporting a good from one place to meet its demand in another place. Second, it provides time value added by storing a good to meet its demand in the future.

Another type of linkage which is less well known, but whose strength and impact is no less important, is consumption linkage. This linkage refers to the consumption demand from households for the output of a sector. The importance of this linkage is mainly due to the second round effect of growth in the economy as a whole, induced by increasing demand from households due to increasing income driven by growth in a particular sector. Hence, the consumption patterns of households play a crucial role in determining the importance of this linkage.

The following is an example of how consumption linkage boosts the growth of an economy from an increase in output of the agricultural sector. Suppose an exogenous technological improvement is introduced to the agricultural sector, which then resulted in an increase in farm productivity. As a result, households supplying factors of production to this sector experience increases in real incomes. Due to the increase in income, the households' demand for various goods and services increases. In particular, the increase in demand for the outputs of the non-tradable sector will stimulate the local economy, hence increasing the total income of the local economy further.

The extent to which an increase in income in a particular sector induces an increase in income of the whole economy is referred to as the sectoral growth multiplier. Hence, the agricultural growth multiplier quantifies the impact of a certain increase in income in the agricultural sector on the growth of income in other sectors. Early on, it was thought that this multiplier is small because agriculture is considered a low-linkage sector. This conclusion is later proved wrong because it only looked at production linkages. Once consumption linkages are taken into account, the multiplier turned out to be quite large (Haggblade, Hazel, and Brown 1989).

Aside from production and consumption linkages, there are other linkages across sectors in a rural economy. One such linkage is the investment linkage. For example, part of increased income in the agricultural sector may be saved. These savings may constitute an important source of funds for investments in the non-agricultural sector. On the other hand, capital flows from other sectors also provide important sources of fund for investments in the agricultural sector.

Other than capital, there are also labour flows across sectors in the rural economy. In particular the labour flows between the agricultural sector and non-agricultural sector can be quite intensive. Because the nature of agricultural production is in general seasonal, consequently the pattern of labour use in agriculture is also seasonal. Partly as an effort to smooth income stream, during the low season agricultural labour will temporarily move to work in other sectors. On the other hand, during the peak season non-agricultural labour can also join the agricultural sector.

Another possible cross-sectoral linkage in a rural economy is the transfer linkage. This type of linkage occurs whenever a household transfers part of its income to another household for purposes other than production, consumption, or investment. This may take place in the form of charity to help relatives or friends in need, which constitutes an important part of informal social safety nets in rural areas.

3. The Indonesian Rural Economy

In developing countries, rural areas and the agricultural sector usually make up an important part of the economy, either in terms of output, employment, or both. In the case of Indonesia, Table 2.1 shows that since 1990, the contribution of the agricultural sector to Gross Domestic Product (GDP) has

Table 2.1
Sectoral Contributions to GDP in Indonesia, 1990–2003 (%)

Sector	1990	1995	2000	2003
Agriculture	22	17	16	15
Industry	39	42	40	39
Services	39	41	45	46

Source: BPS, Statistik Indonesia, various years.

already been low compared to industry and services. Furthermore, the share has been continuously declining over time, falling from around 22 per cent in 1990 to just 15 per cent in 2003.

On the other hand, the contribution of the service sector has continued to increase during the period, from 39 per cent in 1990 to 46 per cent in 2003. For the industrial sector, meanwhile, which expanded before the occurrence of the economic crisis in 1997–98, its contribution to GDP has declined again during the post-crisis period. After reaching 42 per cent in 1995, the contribution of the industrial sector to GDP declined to 39 per cent in 2003, similar to its level in 1990. This provides evidence that Indonesia has experienced a deindustrialization during the post-crisis period.

At a glance, the declining contribution of agriculture to GDP gives an indication that the role of agriculture in the national economy has become less important. However, the existence of forward and backward production linkages means that the importance of the agricultural sector cannot be simply implied just from the value of its direct output. In 2003, for example, the food, beverages and tobacco sub-sectors alone contributed 28 per cent to the total output of manufacturing industry. Similarly, a significant part of the output of the service sector is also strongly related to agriculture.

Table 2.2
**Employment Share of Rural and Urban Areas
in Indonesia, 1990–2003 (%)**

Area	1990	1995	2000	2003
Rural	75	67	62	60
Urban	25	33	38	40

Source: Calculated from Sakernas data.

Table 2.3
**Sectoral Employment Share in Rural Areas
in Indonesia, 1990–2003 (%)**

Sector	1990	1995	2000	2003
Agriculture	70	60	66	68
Industry	9	11	10	9
Services	22	29	24	24

Source: Calculated from Sakernas data.

Furthermore, until now rural areas and the agricultural sector still provide important sources of livelihoods for a large proportion of the Indonesian population. Table 2.2 shows the shares of rural and urban areas in providing employment opportunities for the working population. Meanwhile, Table 2.3 disaggregates employment in rural areas by sector. These tables indicate that the importance of rural areas and agricultural sector in terms of employment is higher than implied by output data.

Table 2.2 shows that, although continuously declining, the majority of workers in Indonesia still find employment in rural areas. In 1990, fully three-quarters of Indonesian workforce worked in rural areas. By 2003, although the proportion of rural workforce had declined substantially, around 60 per cent of the working population still worked in rural areas. Interestingly, the table shows that there is no evidence that the economic crisis has reversed the trend of urbanization in the country.

Within the rural areas, as shown in Table 2.3, the majority of rural workers stated that their main occupation was in the agricultural sector. In 1990, around 70 per cent of the rural workforce worked mainly in the agricultural sector. This proportion declined substantially during the pre-crisis era, so that by 1995 the proportion of agricultural workforce had fallen to 60 per cent. After the onset of the economic crisis in 1997–98, however, the role of the agricultural sector in providing employment opportunities in rural areas regained its importance. As a result, in 2003 the proportion of the rural workforce who worked in the agricultural sector had increased again to 68 per cent. On the other hand, after increasing during the pre-crisis period, the proportion of the rural workforce who worked in the industrial and services sectors declined during the post-crisis period.

Consistent with the employment data, a large proportion of Indonesian households, particularly in rural areas, derive their income from agriculture, either as a sole income source or in combination with other sources. Table 2.4

Table 2.4
Household Income Sources in Indonesia, 1995 (%)

Income Source	Rural	Urban	Total
Agriculture	46.3	6.0	24.9
Non-agriculture	27.4	84.0	52.5
Mixed:	26.3	10.0	22.6
– Mainly agriculture	13.2	2.6	9.9
– Mainly non-agriculture	13.1	7.4	12.7

Source: Booth (2002).

shows the household income sources in Indonesia in 1995 based on the Intercensal Population Survey (Supas) data. Nationally, slightly less than a half of all households derived their incomes wholly or partly from the agricultural sector. In rural areas, 72.6 per cent of households derived at least part of their incomes from the agricultural sector. This shows the strong potential of the agricultural sector to stimulate growth of the whole rural economy. Growth of the agricultural sector, which is translated as increases in income of more than 70 per cent of the rural population, will provide a strong stimulus for a second round of growth in other sectors by increasing local demand.

However, there are some constraints that may affect the potential of the agricultural sector as the driving factor of growth in the rural economy. Table 2.1 indicates that the Indonesian economy has undergone massive structural transformation from an economy where the agricultural sector plays a dominant role in the country's output production to an economy where agriculture's contribution becomes much less important. This is more evident over a long-term horizon, where the contribution of agriculture to GDP has declined from around 45 per cent in 1971 to just 15 per cent in 2003. Meanwhile, the pace of structural transformation in the labour market has been much slower. Over the same period, the proportion of the agricultural workforce has declined from around 67 per cent in 1971 to 46 per cent in 2003.

Since agriculture's share of output fell faster than its share of employment, output per agricultural worker fell in relative terms compared to output per worker in other sectors. This implies that over time agricultural workers become relatively poorer than non-agricultural workers. Unsurprisingly, therefore, the agriculture sector has the highest poverty incidence compared to other sectors and contributes the largest proportion of the poor in the country. Table 2.5 shows the distribution of the poor population in Indonesia across sector. In 2002, more than two-thirds of the poor had livelihood in the

Table 2.5
Distribution of the Poor in Indonesia by
Sector, 1996–2002 (%)

Sector	1996	1999	2002
Agriculture	68.5	58.4	67.4
Industry	6.7	8.7	10.3
Services	24.7	32.9	22.4

Source: Calculated from Susenas data.

agricultural sectors. This is similar to the level reached in 1996. Meanwhile, due to the economic crisis, which hit the modern sectors harder, in 1999 the proportion of the poor who had a living in the agricultural sector fell to below 60 per cent.

Because most of the poor have a livelihood in the agricultural sector, this implies that most of the poor live in rural areas. In fact, Table 2.6 shows that in 2002 almost 80 per cent of Indonesia's poor population resided in rural areas. This proportion has declined from the 1996 level which reached 85 per cent. Again due to the economic crisis, this proportion reached its lowest level in 1999 with 76 per cent.

There are at least three interrelated reasons why people who have a living in agriculture tend to be poorer than those who are not in agriculture. First, the quality of human resources in agriculture is very low compared to those in non-agriculture. Second, in general they have low access to capital. Third, their landholding size is small. Table 2.7 shows the distribution of agricultural households by size of cultivated landholding. The table shows that in 2003 around 75 per cent of Indonesian farmers cultivated land with sizes less than one hectare. This proportion has increased from around 70 per cent in 1984 and 1993. More worrying is the proportion of farmers who cultivate land

Table 2.6
Distribution of the Poor in Indonesia by
Rural-Urban Areas, 1996–2002 (%)

Area	1996	1999	2002
Rural	85.0	76.2	79.7
Urban	15.0	23.8	20.3

Source: Calculated from Susenas data.

Table 2.7
Distribution of Agricultural Households by
Cultivated Landholding Size (%)

Size of Cultivated Land-holding (ha)	1984	1993	2003
< 0.1	8.5	7.0	17.2
0.1 – 0.49	37.7	40.7	39.2
0.50 – 0.99	24.1	22.4	18.4
≥ 1.0	29.7	29.9	25.2

Source: Calculated from Agricultural Census data.

with sizes less than 0.1 hectare, which has increased substantially from 7 per cent in 1993 to 17 per cent in 2003.

In terms of demand linkages and growth multipliers to the non-agricultural sector in the rural economy, the fact that the majority of farmers are poor and small constitutes a constraint for two reasons. First, it means that farm households have relatively low purchasing power to boost the rural economy through consumption demand for locally produced goods and services. Second, there is evidence from other countries that poor and small farm households spend a smaller proportion of their expenditure on locally made goods and local services than large farm households (Hazell and Röell 1983).

4. Methods for Estimating Linkages: Literature Review

The literature on sectoral linkages in rural areas has largely focused on attempts to estimate agricultural growth multiplier in rural economy. Most of the studies have been inspired by Mellor's tradition to prove that agriculture has a potent power to boost rural economic growth (Mellor 1976). These empirical studies are mostly confined to African countries and parts of Asia, where the majority of workers are still employed in the agriculture or agriculture-related sectors. In analysing the linkages, these studies have invariably focused on production and consumption linkages.

In terms of the methods used to estimate the sectoral growth multiplier, these studies can be broadly grouped into three types: (i) studies which use a micro-econometric approach, (ii) studies which employ a macro-econometric approach, and (iii) studies which utilize input-output table (IOT), social accounting matrix (SAM), or computable general equilibrium (CGE) modelling. Each of these approaches has its advantages and disadvantages. Each approach requires different type of data and data availability often determines the approach used in a particular study.

4.1. Studies Using Micro-Econometric Approach

Studies that can be included in this approach include among others: Foster and Rosenzweig (2004 and 2005), Haggblade and Hazell (1989), Haggblade, Hazell, and Brown (1989), Hazell and Röell (1983), and Simphiwe (2001). Studies of this type are usually based on household survey data that records detailed household expenditures. The method examines household consumption patterns so as to know the proportion of household budget spent on locally produced goods and services, i.e. the non-tradable, and that spent on goods imported from outside regions.[1] Based on the results of estimation of an Engel function or a Working-Leser model,[2] evaluated at the mean value, the marginal budget share, i.e. the change in household budget share from an increase in income, can be calculated for each commodity. These marginal budget shares are then used to calculate the agricultural growth multiplier. Higher marginal budget shares for non-tradable goods and services will lead to a higher multiplier.

One of the classics of this type of study is Hazell and Röell (1983). This study utilized data from two areas where World Bank agriculture development projects were implemented. The first area is Muda in northwest Malaysia, where an irrigation project was implemented. The other area is Gussau in northern Nigeria, where an agriculture development project was put in place. Through these projects, household data was collected weekly for about a year. The household expenditures were annualized to overcome the problems of seasonality and unevenness of expenditure patterns.

They find that the linkages from the agricultural sector to local non-farm economy are much stronger in Muda. In this region, households on average spent 18 per cent of their total budget on locally produced non-food goods and services. Furthermore, they allocated 37 per cent to these items of any incremental increase in their total expenditures. In Gussau, meanwhile, the average and marginal budget shares on the same items of locally produced goods and services were only 8 and 11 per cent respectively.

Furthermore, based on the analysis of budget shares across income levels and farm sizes, they found that richer and larger farms in both regions had the most desired expenditure patterns for stimulating secondary growth in the local economy than smaller farms. Hence, they concluded that larger farm households are the suitable targets for technology or public investments to increase agricultural output in order to stimulate growth of the whole rural economy.

Two studies by Foster and Rosenzweig in 2004 and 2005 utilized the same data source from India. This is a continuing survey of rural households residing in approximately 250 villages located in the 17 major states of India that began in 1968. The survey has been carried out by the National Council of Applied Economic Research (NCAER). The two studies, however, analysed the survey data of two different interval periods.

Foster and Rosenzweig (2004) used a panel data of the villages for the period 1971–99 to review the impact of the Green Revolution, which has increased agricultural productivity, on non-farm sector in rural areas. They found that the growth of the non-farm sector is not determined by the increase in agricultural productivity. In fact, areas that have the highest non-farm sector growth are areas that have benefited relatively less from agricultural productivity growth. They concluded that focus and resources should be shared to equally promote non-farm and farm growth in India, because non-farm growth can also play a direct and important role in rural growth.

Meanwhile, Foster and Rosenzweig (2005) used the village and household panel data for the period of 1982–99 to assess empirically the contributions of agricultural productivity improvements and rural factory expansion to rural income growth, poverty reduction, and rural income inequality. In this study, they developed and tested a simple general equilibrium model of farm and non-farm sectors in a rural economy. The key prediction of their model is that while both agricultural development and capital mobility and openness increase rural incomes, the growth of a rural export-oriented manufacturing sector reduces both local and spatial income inequality relative to agriculture-led growth.

Empirically they found that the non-tradable, non-farm sector is driven by local demand conditions and, hence, is positively influenced by growth in agricultural productivity. On the other hand, the tradable non-farm sector, which consists of relatively small-scale factories, enters areas with relatively low wages and hence is negatively influenced by growth in agricultural productivity. Both agricultural technical change and factory employment growth increase rural incomes and wages, and hence reduces poverty. Consistent with the model's prediction, they found that factory investment in a locality reduced both spatial wage inequality and local household income inequality, while agricultural technology improvements increased inequality.

Similarly, Eapen (2003) argued that an excessive concentration on agricultural linkages has resulted in an underestimation of rural non-farm linkages. She states that since agriculture linkages to the non-agricultural sector in a rural economy mostly stem from consumption linkages, there is still much benefit that could be realized by expanding non-agricultural sectors, especially since those sectors provide considerable scope to stimulate growth in the rural economy through production linkages.

However, Kimenyi (2002) argued that many studies in developing countries have found that agricultural growth contributed the most to poverty reduction, especially in countries whose labour force is largely engaged in agriculture.[3] There are two channels where agricultural growth can spur large poverty reduction. The first is the direct linkage between agriculture and its input and output industry, which includes urban industries, where growth in the agricultural sector would create, among other things, more jobs and higher income both within the sector itself and in other sectors. The second channel is through the increase in non-agricultural sector growth in rural areas that resulted from the increase in income of agriculture households.

This positive effect on poverty reduction constitutes an advantage of an agriculture-led growth in rural areas.

4.2. Studies Using Macro-Econometric Approach

Studies that can be included in this approach include among others: Block (1999), Ravallion and Datt (1996), Datt and Ravallion (1998), Fan, Hazell, and Thorat (1999), and Rock (2002). The main difference between this type of macro-econometric study and micro-econometric studies is the data used. Rather than using household survey data, these studies analysed aggregate data at the national, state, provincial, or regional level. Hence, this type of study requires the availability of relatively long-spanning time series or panel data for the analysis to be statistically meaningful. The data is used to analyse a macro-economic model, which could be either a structural model or a reduced-form model.

Block (1999) developed a four-sector numerical simulation model of economic growth in Ethiopia. He defined the four sectors as agriculture, services, traditional industry, and modern industry. In order to calculate the macroeconomic growth multipliers resulting from exogenous income shocks in each sector, the model specifies a set of intersectoral linkages through which the output of one sector can contribute, either through forward and backward linkages or indirectly through effects on prices and investment, to output in other sectors.

The sectoral growth multipliers which resulted from the simulated income shocks are 1.80 for the service sector, 1.54 for agriculture, 1.34 for modern industry, and 1.22 for traditional industry. These results suggest that intersectoral linkages in the economy operate unevenly. Linkages operate robustly between agriculture and services, and to some extent from agriculture to traditional industry. Services provide important stimulus to modern industry. However, the industrial sectors have limited impact on services and agriculture. Even though the service sector has the highest multiplier, he argued that since most of the poor are confined in the agriculture sector, focusing on developing that sector would yield the most benefit in efforts to reduce poverty in the country.

The natural extension of the literature on agriculture growth multiplier is to relate it to poverty reduction. This is quite straightforward since economic growth has been proven in many studies to be one of the most effective ways to reduce poverty. One of the pioneering studies in this area is Ravallion and Datt (1996), which analysed data from India. They estimated the impact of urban and rural growth on urban, rural, and national poverty using the Indian national time-series data spanning from 1951 to 1991. They concluded that rural growth benefits both urban and rural poor, while urban growth has adverse distributional impact on urban poor, which undermines the gains the urban poor receive, and no impact on rural poor.

Furthermore, when investigating the probable reasons why some Indian states managed to reduce rural poverty better than others, Datt and Ravallion (1998) analysed panel state-level data from 1957 to 1991. They found that agriculture technology growth, measured by output per acre, and initial agriculture infrastructure and human resource conditions, measured by initial irrigation rate, female literacy rate, and infant mortality rate, are the main determinants of success in reducing rural poverty.

Meanwhile, Rock (2002) investigated the impact of agriculture growth and government intervention on the agricultural sector, such as rice stabilization policies, in Indonesia, Malaysia, and Thailand. He argued that studies such as these are important because most industrial analysts believe that developing country economies are bifurcated between the traditional agriculture sector and the modern sector and the two sectors have little connection. He stated that growth in agriculture, particularly agricultural exports, can facilitate the growth of manufacturers by providing foreign exchange to import capital goods, semi-processed goods, and spare parts to the manufacturing sector. He used panel data of the three countries and found agricultural growth and rice stabilization policies to have significant and positive impact on growth in the manufacturing sector.

In contrast to putting the agriculture sector in the spotlight and measuring its multiplier on other sectors, there are also studies that focus on other sectors and measure their multipliers on agricultural growth. An example of such studies is Fan, Hazell, and Thorat (1999). They estimated a simultaneous equation model to trace the effects of government expenditure items on productivity growth and poverty alleviation, including their trade-offs and complementarities. They found that investments in rural roads, rural infrastructure, and agricultural research and development have the greatest impact on reducing rural poverty and agricultural productivity growth, while expenditure on direct poverty reduction programmes such as employment programmes only have modest effects.

In addition, they also estimated the marginal returns to agricultural productivity growth and poverty reduction from additional government expenditure and found that investments on roads have the highest marginal return in both areas, while other types of spending benefit one more than the other. The important contribution of this study is the finding that government spending on rural infrastructure and agricultural research and development have a higher impact on reducing poverty, both directly and indirectly, through increased agricultural productivity. This implies the government would be wise to direct its spending on these aspects rather than concentrating on direct poverty reduction programmes.

4.3. Studies Using IOT, SAM, and CGE Modelling

Studies that can be included in this type, among others, are Byerlee (1973), Byerlee et al. (1977), Rangarajan (1984), Adelman (1984), and Bautista and Thomas (1998). The advantage of using a general equilibrium modelling approach is that it can measure the full direct impact of rural agricultural growth in the national economy. The precision of the measured impact, however, depends on the fit of the model and the accuracy of the database in representing the economy in reality.

Byerlee (1973), who applied a general equilibrium model for Nigeria, and Byerlee et al. (1977), who applied a similar model for Sierra Leone, are the pioneering studies in this subject which utilize general equilibrium modelling. Studies using the general equilibrium modelling approach in the context of Asia came later, pioneered among others by Rangarajaran (1982) for India and Adelman (1984) for South Korea. Confirming findings from studies using other methods, the results of these general equilibrium modelling studies also suggest that linkage effects from agricultural growth to non-agricultural growth are stronger in Asia than in Africa.

More recently, Bautista and Thomas (1998) calculated national-level agricultural growth multiplier using a macro-modelling based on SAM in Zambia. In their model, they divide the agriculture sector into five sub-sectors: (i) agriculture, which consists of all crop and livestock commodities; (ii) smallholder agriculture, which includes all smallholder activity; (iii) food crops, consisting of maize and other grain commodities; (iv) traditional export crops, which includes tobacco and cotton; and (v) non-traditional export crops that consist of horticulture commodities.

They found that agriculture growth linkages are high with smallholder agriculture having the largest GDP multiplier of 1.92. Based on these results, and since a large portion of the poor are in rural areas and engaged in the agriculture sector, they concluded that investment in this sector would yield the optimum advantage to overall growth and poverty reduction. Hence, they advocate countries to switch their focus from solely concentrating on the industrial sector and mainly urban investments to also include investments in the agriculture and rural sector.

5. The Model

As described in the introduction section, the aim of this study is to examine empirically the strength of agricultural demand linkages and estimate the agricultural growth multiplier in rural Indonesia. In particular, the research question that will be addressed in this study is how growth in the agricultural sector in rural areas affects the growth of the non-agricultural sector in rural areas. Following the macro-econometric approach discussed in the literature review, the analysis will be based on a simplified model of the inter-relationships of growth across sectors in the whole economy.

Let us split the whole economy into three sectors: (i) the rural agricultural sector, (ii) rural non-agricultural sector, and (iii) urban sector. Therefore, the economy's total Gross Domestic Product (GDP) can be defined as the sum of GDP of the three sectors:

$$Y = Y_R^A + Y_R^N + Y_U \tag{1}$$

where Y is the real GDP, the subscripts R and U refer to rural and urban areas, and the superscripts A and N refer to the agricultural and non-agricultural sectors respectively. Differentiating equation (1) and then dividing by Y result in:

$$\frac{dY}{Y} = \frac{dY_R^A + dY_R^N + dY_U}{Y} \tag{2}$$

$$\dot{y} = \frac{Y_R^A}{Y}\frac{dY_R^A}{Y_R^A} + \frac{Y_R^N}{Y}\frac{dY_R^N}{Y_R^N} + \frac{Y_U}{Y}\frac{dY_U}{Y_U} = H_R^A\,\dot{y}_R^A + H_R^N\,\dot{y}_R^N + H_U\,\dot{y}_U \tag{3}$$

where $\dot{y} = \frac{dY}{Y}$ refers to real GDP growth. Equation (3) says that the total GDP growth is the sum of its sectoral GDP growth components weighted by each sector's share (H) in the total GDP.

Now let us assume that the total economic growth is a function of a vector of exogenous variables X:

$$\dot{y} = \dot{y}(X) \tag{4}$$

Since the total GDP growth is a function of X, then implicitly all of its components are also a function of X. This means that:

$$\dot{y}(X) = H_R^A \, \dot{y}_R^A(X) + H_R^A \, \dot{y}_R^N(X) + H_U \, \dot{y}_U(X) \tag{5}$$

Rearranging equation (5):

$$H_R^N \, \dot{y}_R^N(X) = \dot{y}(X) - H_R^A \, \dot{y}_R^A(X) - H_U \, \dot{y}_U(X) \tag{6}$$

$$\dot{y}_R^N(X) = \frac{1}{H_R^N} \, \dot{y}(X) - \frac{H_R^A}{H_R^N} \, \dot{y}_R^A(X) - \frac{H_U}{H_R^N} \, \dot{y}_U(X) \tag{7}$$

Equation (7) is an identity, defining the GDP growth of the rural non-agricultural sector. Behaviourally, it implies that the GDP growth of the rural non-agricultural sector can be defined as a function of the GDP growth of the other two sectors in the economy, each weighted by the ratio of its GDP share to the GDP share of the rural non-agricultural sector, conditional on X:

$$\dot{y}_R^N = f\left(\dot{y}_R^{A*}, \dot{y}_U^* ; X\right) \tag{8}$$

where $\dot{y}_R^{A*} = \dfrac{H_R^A}{H_R^N} \, \dot{y}_R^A$ and $\dot{y}_U^* = \dfrac{H_U}{H_R^N} \, \dot{y}_U$.

Imposing a linear functional form, the estimable model of rural non-agricultural sector growth is:

$$\dot{y}_R^N = \alpha + \beta_1 \, \dot{y}_R^{A*} + \beta_2 \, \dot{y}_U^* + \gamma X + \varepsilon \tag{9}$$

If rural non-agricultural sector growth does not affect rural agricultural sector growth and urban sector growth, then equation (9) can be estimated using the Ordinary Least Squares (OLS) procedure. This is quite likely to be true for the case of urban sector growth. However, it is more likely that this condition is not true for the case of rural agricultural sector growth. In this case the estimates obtained from OLS will be inconsistent, so the model has to be estimated using the Instrumental Variable (IV) procedure.

The coefficient of interest in this study is β_1. This coefficient shows the percentage growth of the rural non-agricultural sector due to growth in the rural agricultural sector by one per cent times the inverse of the ratio of rural agricultural sector GDP share to rural non-agricultural sector GDP share. For example, if the ratio of rural agricultural sector GDP share to rural non-agricultural sector GDP share is 50 per cent, then β_1 is the per cent growth of the rural non-agricultural sector due to 2 per cent growth in the rural agricultural sector. Note that 50 per cent times 2 per cent is 1 per cent.

6. Empirical Estimation

6.1. The Data

The database that is used to estimate the model is a panel data of sectoral GDP growth with province as the unit of observation. The source of the data is the province-level Regional Gross Domestic Product (RGDP) publication from BPS. The RGDP data for each province is already disaggregated by sector, but is not yet divided into rural and urban areas. Therefore, to split the sectoral RGDP data by rural-urban areas in each province, the proportions of aggregated sectoral rural and urban household expenditures in each province calculated from the Susenas Consumption Module data are applied to the RGDP data. The time period covered in the panel data is from 1984 to 2002 with a three-year interval in accordance with the Susenas Consumption Module survey.

The resulting sectoral and rural-urban disaggregation of GDP at the national level is presented in Table 2.A1 in the Appendix. The disaggregation results make sense and confirm what is commonly known about the rural and urban economies in Indonesia. First, the order of sectoral importance in urban areas is services, industry, and agriculture in the last position. Second, the order of sectoral importance in rural areas is agriculture, services, and industry. Third, the agriculture sector makes up only a very small part of the urban economy. Fourth, in the long run the importance of the urban economy has been increasing, while the importance of the rural economy has been decreasing. This shows that the method used to disaggregate the sectoral GDP by rural-urban areas is justified and, hence, provides confidence for using the data in the estimations.

However, Table 2.A1 also shows a peculiarity in the rural-urban GDP disaggregation method that needs to be taken into account when using the resulting data. This has to do with the fact that the Susenas sampling frame is always updated following a population census, which is conducted every ten years. This update in the sampling frame takes into account the changes in population, administrative boundaries, as well as the urban-rural status of villages across regions. The data used in this study consists of three different sampling frames. The 1984, 1987, and 1990 surveys used a sampling frame based on the results of the 1980 Population Census. The 1993, 1996, and 1999 surveys used a sampling frame based on the results of the 1990 Population Census. Meanwhile, the 2002 survey used a sampling frame based on the results of the 2000 Population Census.

The consequence of the changes in sampling frames is reflected in the urban-rural share of GDP shown in Table 2.A1 in the Appendix. For example, between 1984 and 1990 the urban share of GDP tended to decline. However, as a result of reclassification of successfully developed rural areas to become urban areas, the urban share of GDP in 1993 jumped significantly. Likewise, between 1993 and 1999 the urban share of GDP tended to decline, but it increased again significantly in 2002. This means that the original rural areas tend to grow faster that the original urban areas, but since successfully developed rural areas are reclassified as urban areas, over the long run the GDP share of urban areas increases while that of rural areas decreases.[4]

6.2. Estimation Results

Within a region, growth of various sectors may or may not be highly correlated with one another. It depends on whether the sectors in question are integrated or not. In a dualistic economy, for example, the modern sector could be booming with little effect on the traditional sector since they are practically insulated from each other. In an integrated economy, on the other hand, each sector is strongly interrelated with the other sectors in the economy, making growth in one sector affect growth in the other sectors significantly.

Table 2.8 shows the results of estimating equation (9) using both Ordinary Least Squares (OLS) and Instrumental Variable (IV) procedures. In both estimations, the dependent variable is rural non-agricultural sector growth and the independent variables are rural agricultural sector growth and urban sector growth.[5] The control variables are rural population growth, initial rural poverty rate, initial rural Gini ratio as a measure of inequality in income distribution, initial proportion of rural population with junior secondary education and above as a measure of human resources quality, and log of total real expenditures of village governments within a province. In addition, to take into account the effects of changes in Susenas sampling frame following a population census, two dummy variables on 1990 and 2000 sampling frames are also included as control variables.

Table 2.8
Results of Estimation of Growth Linkages Model
(Dependent variable: Rural non-agricultural sector growth)

Independent Variable	OLS	IV
Rural agricultural sector growth	0.5805**	1.8504*
	(3.33)	(2.44)
Urban sector growth	−0.2539**	−0.3113**
	(−7.40)	(−5.91)
Rural population growth	−0.0247	−0.0189
	(−0.95)	(−0.61)
Initial rural poverty rate	0.1871	−0.0042
	(1.21)	(−0.02)
Initial rural Gini ratio	−0.6237	−0.1636
	(−0.74)	(−0.16)
Initial proportion of rural population with junior secondary education and above	0.3468	0.5586
	(0.92)	(1.19)
Log of total real expenditures of village governments	0.0058	0.0705
	(0.19)	(1.35)
1990 Susenas sampling frame	−0.2677**	−0.2056*
	(−3.84)	(−2.26)
2000 Susenas sampling frame	−0.1738	−0.0333
	(1.91)	(0.25)
Constant	0.4351	−0.2607
	(1.53)	(−0.50)
Number of observations	132	132
F-value (9, 122)	11.26**	7.65**
R-squared	0.4538	0.2166

Notes: − Numbers in parentheses are t-values
  − ** is significant at 1 per cent level
  − * is significant at 5 per cent level
  − Rural agricultural sector growth is treated as an endogenous variable and instrumented by rainfall and number of trucks

In the IV estimation, rural agricultural sector growth is treated as an endogenous variable and instrumented by rainfall and number of trucks. The reason for using rainfall as an instrument for rural agricultural sector growth is obvious. Meanwhile, the number of trucks is also used as another instrument for rural agricultural sector growth because both agricultural inputs and outputs are bulky, so that the number of trucks available in a province provides a good indication of the intensity of economic activities in the agricultural sector in that province. On the other hand, urban sector growth is treated as an exogenous variable as there is no strong reason to believe that there is a significant feedback effect from rural non-agricultural sector growth to urban sector growth. The results of the first stage regression of the IV estimation are presented in Table 2.A2 in the Appendix.

In both OLS and IV estimation results, the coefficients of both rural agricultural sector growth and urban sector growth are statistically significant. However, the magnitudes of the coefficients obtained from the IV estimation are larger than those obtained from the OLS estimation. Except for change in Susenas sampling frame, none of the control variables in both estimations have statistically significant coefficients, although the signs of the coefficients are in general as expected. Since it is more likely that the endogeneity problem does exist in the data, the following discussion on the estimation results is based on the IV estimation results.

The coefficient of rural agricultural sector growth is positive. This indicates that the growth of the agricultural sector does indeed positively induce growth of the non-agricultural sector in rural areas. This vindicates the view that rising incomes in the agricultural sector in rural areas stimulate demand for local goods and services, in particular those produced by the non-tradable sector. This positive effect combines both the production and consumption linkages, so it is not possible to tell which one is more dominant.

On the other hand, the coefficient of urban sector growth is negative. This indicates that urban development is not complementary directly to the development of the non-agricultural sector in rural areas. Rather, urban sector growth suppresses rural non-agricultural sector growth, perhaps because both sectors produce similar goods and services which compete with each other. Indirectly, however, Table 2.A2 in the Appendix shows that urban sector growth has a positive and statistically significant effect on rural agricultural sector growth. Since rural agricultural sector growth positively affects rural non-agricultural sector growth, this means that the net effect of urban growth on rural non-agricultural growth depends on the balance of these two opposing effects.

In interpreting the magnitude of the coefficient of the rural agricultural sector growth variable as the agricultural growth multiplier to non-agricultural sector growth in rural areas, it is important to keep in mind that in the estimation this variable is weighted by the ratio of rural agricultural sector GDP share to rural non-agricultural sector GDP share in total GDP. Hence, as discussed in the previous section, the coefficient represents the percentage growth of the rural non-agricultural sector due to the growth in the rural agricultural sector by one per cent times the inverse of the ratio of rural agricultural sector GDP share to rural non-agricultural sector GDP share.

Therefore, to obtain the multiplier of one per cent growth of the agricultural sector to non-agricultural sector growth, the coefficient needs to be multiplied by the ratio of rural agricultural sector GDP share to rural non-agricultural sector GDP share. Based on the sectoral and locational share of GDP in Table 2.A1 in the Appendix, this ratio has declined during the pre-crisis period from 0.75 in 1984 to 0.55 in 1996, reflecting the declining role of the agricultural sector in the total output produced, even in rural areas. After the crisis, however, the ratio has tended to increase again, reaching 0.73 in 2002. The mean of the ratio over time is 0.6.

Based on the coefficient obtained from the IV estimation of 1.8504, this implies that in 1984 one per cent growth of the agricultural sector was able to induce 1.4 per cent growth of the non-agricultural sector in rural areas. During the high economic growth pre-crisis period, this multiplier declined to just 1.0 by 1996. After the crisis, however, the multiplier increased again, reaching 1.3 by 2002. The mean of the multiplier over time is 1.2.

By any standard, this estimated agricultural growth multiplier is considered large. Measured in a different way, Haggblade, Hazell, and Brown (1989) estimated that the agricultural growth multiplier in Asia is around 1.8, which in their study means that a certain increase in the income of the agricultural sector will stimulate an increase in the income of the non-agricultural sectors by 80 per cent. At the same time, they estimated that the agricultural growth multiplier in Africa is around 1.5.

This finding implies that, although declining, the agricultural sector still has a large potential to become the driving force in the Indonesian rural economy. Formulated appropriately, a rural development strategy through developing the agricultural sector could provide an impetus for achieving a fast-growing and vibrant rural sector in Indonesia.

7. Conclusion

In a fast-urbanizing Indonesia, the rural sector still plays an important role in the country's economy. The majority of the population, and hence the workforce, still live and find employment in rural areas. Rural areas also provide crucial services to the whole economy, in particular by providing food supplies for all of the population. In addition, rural areas also contribute importantly to foreign exchange earnings from export of commodities.

On the other hand, rural areas lag behind compared to urban areas, both in terms of physical infrastructure as well as the socio-economic welfare of its inhabitants. Strong evidence of this is that around 80 per cent of all the poor in the country are found in rural areas. Although in the long run Indonesia will be more urbanized and the rural areas can be expected to diminish in the future, there is still a need for more focused attention and more rigorous efforts on rural development.

This requires a clear and effective strategy to jump-start and sustain economic growth in rural areas. Specifically, since rural areas are closely identified with the agricultural sector, the question is that in order to push growth for the whole rural economy is it more effective to improve productivity in the agricultural sector first or is it better to invest in the rural non-agricultural sector directly?

This study examines the empirical evidence on the strength of agricultural linkages and estimating the agricultural growth multiplier in rural Indonesia. It finds that the growth of the agricultural sector does indeed strongly induce growth of the non-agricultural sector in rural areas. Although it has been fluctuating over time, it is estimated that on average, one per cent growth of the agricultural sector will induce a 1.2 per cent growth of the non-agricultural sector in rural areas. This finding vindicates the view that rising incomes in the agricultural sector stimulate demand for locally produced goods and services in rural areas, in particular those produced by the non-tradable sector. Formulated appropriately, a rural development strategy through developing the agricultural sector could provide a major impetus for achieving a fast-growing and vibrant rural sector in Indonesia.

On the other hand, this study also finds that urban development is not complementary directly to the development of the rural non-agricultural sector. Rather, urban sector growth suppresses the growth of the rural non-agricultural sector, perhaps because both sectors produce goods and services which compete with each other. Indirectly, however, urban sector growth has a positive effect on rural agricultural sector growth. Since rural agricultural sector growth positively affects rural non-agricultural sector growth, this means that the net effect of urban growth on rural non-agricultural growth depends on the balance of these two opposing effects.

APPENDIX

Table 2.A1
Contribution to GDP by Sector and Location (%), 1984–2002

Year	Urban				Rural			
	Agriculture	Industry	Services	Total	Agriculture	Industry	Services	Total
1984	1.53	17.94	35.57	55.04	18.56	10.50	14.22	43.28
1987	1.32	17.90	33.75	52.70	18.30	11.36	16.24	45.90
1990	1.29	18.55	30.36	50.20	17.37	11.56	20.19	49.12
1993	2.08	21.52	37.97	61.57	15.26	9.51	13.67	38.44
1996	1.79	21.87	37.39	61.05	13.77	10.30	14.89	38.96
1999	2.12	21.40	35.76	59.28	15.02	11.06	14.65	40.73
2002	2.75	25.53	40.08	68.36	13.34	6.91	11.38	31.63
Mean	1.95	21.32	36.35	59.62	15.40	9.93	14.71	40.04

Table 2.A2
Results of First-Stage Regression of Growth Linkages Model
(Dependent variable: Rural agricultural sector growth)

Independent Variable	IV
Urban sector growth	0.0480**
	(2.84)
Rural population growth	–0.0039
	(-0.30)
Initial rural poverty rate	0.2163**
	(2.73)
Initial rural Gini ratio	–0.6104
	(–1.42)
Initial proportion of rural population with junior secondary	–0.1893
education and above	(–1.00)
Log of total real expenditures of village governments	–0.0097
	(–0.49)
Rainfall	–0.0000
	(–0.66)
Number of trucks	–0.0000**
	(–3.10)
1990 Susenas sampling frame	–0.0594
	(–1.68)
2000 Susenas sampling frame	–0.0959*
	(–2.14)
Constant	0.3432*
	(2.28)
Number of observations	132
F-value (7, 124)	3.61**
R-squared	0.2298

Notes: – Numbers in parentheses are t-values
– ** is significant at 1 per cent level
– * is significant at 5 per cent level

NOTES

1. Information on the origin of goods consumed by households is usually not available in a regular household survey. Therefore, this type of study usually requires special data collection effort.
2. An Engel function maps the relationship between household expenditure on food with total household expenditure. A Working-Leser model is a version of Engel function defined in terms of expenditure share.
3. Mellor (1999) has compiled a thorough review of the relationship between agriculture growth and poverty reduction.
4. For discussion on rural-urban reclassification of villages, see Firman (1992).
5. An attempt to estimate the model in levels instead of growth was dropped due to multicollinearity problem. Sectoral GDP levels are highly correlated with each other.

REFERENCES

Adelman, Irma. "Beyond Export-led Growth". *World Development* 12, no. 9 (1984): 937–49.

Bautista, Romeo M. and Marcelle Thomas. "Agricultural Growth Linkages in Zimbabwe: Income and Equity Effects". TMD Discussion Paper no. 31. Washington D.C.: International Food Policy Research Institute, 1998.

Block, Steven A. "Agriculture and Economic Growth in Ethiopia: Growth Multipliers from a Four-Sector Simulation Model". *Agricultural Economics* 20 (1999): 241–52.

Booth, Anne. "The Changing Role of Non-Farm Activities in Agricultural Households in Indonesia: Some Insights from the Agricultural Censuses". *Bulletin of Indonesian Economic Studies* 38, no. 2 (2002): 179–200.

Byerlee, Derek. "Indirect Employment and Income Distribution Effects of Agricultural Development Strategies: A Simulation Approach Applied to Nigeria". African Rural Employment Paper no. 9. East Lansing, MI: Department of Agricultural Economics, Michigan State University, 1973.

Byerlee, Derek, Carl K. Eicher, Carl Liedholm, and Dunsian S.C. Spencer. "Rural Employment in Tropical Africa: Summary of Findings". African Rural Economy Working Paper no. 20. East Lansing, MI: Michigan State University, 1977.

Datt, Gaurav and Martin Ravallion. "Why Have Some Indian States Done Better than Others at Reducing Rural Poverty?". *Economica* 65 (1998): 17–38.

Eapen, Mridul. "Rural Industrialization in Kerala: Re-examining the Issue of Rural Growth Linkages". Working Paper no. 348. Kerala: Center for Development Studies, 2003.

Fan, Shenggen, Peter Hazel, and Sukhadeo Thorat. "Linkages between Government Spending, Growth, and Poverty in Rural India". Research Report 110. Washington D.C.: International Food Policy Research Institute, 1999.

Firman, Tommy. "The Spatial Pattern of Urban Population Growth in Java, 1980–1990". *Bulletin of Indonesian Economic Studies* 28, no. 2 (1992): 95–109.

Foster, Andrew D. and Mark R. Rosenzweig. "Agricultural Productivity Growth, Rural Economic Diversity, and Economic Reforms: India, 1970–2000". *Economic Development and Cultural Change* (2004): 509–42.

————. "Agricultural Development, Industrialization and Rural Inequality". Mimeographed. Brown University and Harvard University, 2005.

Haggblade, Steven and Peter Hazell . "Agriculture Technology and Farm/Non-Farm Growth Linkages". *Agriculture Economics* 3 (1989): 345–64.

Haggblade, Steven, Peter Hazell, and James Brown. "Farm-Nonfarm Linkages in Rural Sub-Saharan Africa". *World Development* 17, no. 8 (1989): 1173–201.

Hazell, Peter B.R. and Ailsa Röell. "Rural Growth Linkages: Household Expenditure Patterns in Malaysia and Nigeria". Research Report 41. Washington D.C.: International Food Policy Research Institute, 1983.

Kimenyi, Mwangi S. "Agriculture, Economic Growth and Poverty Reduction". KIPPRA Occasional Paper no. 3. Nairobi: Kenya Institute for Public Policy Research and Analysis, 2002.

Mellor, John W. *The New Economics of Growth: A Strategy for India and the Developing World*. Ithaca, NY: Cornell University Press, 1976.

————. "Faster, More Equitable Growth — The Relation between Growth in Agriculture and Poverty Reduction". Agricultural Policy Development Project Research Report no. 4. Cambridge, MA: Abt Associates Inc., 1999.

Rangarajan, C. "Agricultural Growth and Industrial Performance in India". Research Report no. 33. Washington D.C.: International Food Policy Research Institute, 1982.

Ravallion, Martin and Gaurav Datt. "How Important to India's Poor is the Sectoral Composition of Economic Growth?". *World Bank Economic Review* 10, no. 1 (1996): 1–25.

Rock, Michael T. "Exploring the Impact of Selective Interventions in Agriculture on the Growth of Manufactures in Indonesia, Malaysia, and Thailand". *Journal of International Development* 14, no. 4 (2002): 1–26.

Simphiwe, N. "Prospects for Rural Growth? Measuring Growth Linkages in a South African Smallholder Farming Area". Working Paper no. 2001–11. Pretoria: Department of Agricultural Economics, Extension and Rural Development, University of Pretoria, 2001.

3

Trends and Constraints Associated with Labour Faced by Non-Farm Enterprises

Armida S. Alisjahbana and Chris Manning

1. Introduction

This chapter examines trends in non-farm employment and associated labour market constraints that have hindered the growth of non-farm employment (NFE) since the economic crisis in 1997–98. Declining rural NFE is of particular concern as it is related to stagnant or even declining investment and output growth. This chapter also examines the human capital dimension of labour markets, key labour regulations and migration that are thought to hinder, or encourage, NFE creation.

The chapter is organized as follows: the second part of the chapter looks at NFE trends in urban and rural areas, by sector, according to formal and informal work status, and by type of employment. In the third part, a brief literature survey deals with labour market-related aspects of NFE. Evidence for Indonesia on labour market aspects of NFE is presented in part four, by estimating a model of NFE probabilities. This is followed by an examination of labour regulations and their effects on NFE creation. A discussion of migration as it relates to NFE follows. The last part concludes with a brief look at policy implications.

2. Trends in Non-Agricultural and Non-Farm Employment[1]

Rapid economic growth before the crisis created opportunities for households from a range of classes to become involved in a range of service and sales activities stimulated by the new prosperity, particularly in rural Java (Effendi and Manning 1994, pp. 233–36).

However, during the crisis and recovery in Indonesia in 1997–2000, the rural non-farm sector experienced a major downturn. The Indonesian Family Life Surveys conducted in the pre-crisis period (1997) and in the post-crisis period (2000) show how people responded to the crisis: labour force participation rates rose; more women became involved in NFE; and in many areas both women and men diversified their earnings activities (Strauss et al. 2004). More women worked in self-employment and family workers rather than in formal employment. The following section describes several important trends in employment growth since the crisis.

The first trend is the apparent negative correlation between employment growth in agriculture and NFE (see Table 3.1). As the agriculture sector declined in importance, employment growth in the sector was negative for the ten years prior to the crisis. However, during the crisis and in its aftermath the agriculture sector absorbed large numbers of workers displaced from non-farm jobs. Employment in this sector grew by 4.2 per cent between 1997 and 2000. However this growth proved to be short-lived. Since 2000, the employment in the agricultural sector has again declined.

By contrast, non-agricultural employment grew strongly prior to the crisis, particularly in urban areas and in manufacturing. During the crisis and its aftermath, employment in this sector declined dramatically, with annual declines of 1.4 per cent from 1997 to 2000. Employment in trade and services was particularly hard hit, as apparently was *rural* NFE. However, from 2000 non-agricultural employment recovered in both rural and urban areas, growing at almost 2 per cent a year. This was driven by growth in the trade and service sectors, while employment in manufacturing continued to decline.

The second trend relates to the rate of urban employment growth, which was more than double the rate in rural areas. Moreover, the data suggest that rural NFE suffered a severe decline of almost 8 per cent per year during and immediately after the crisis, whilst non-agricultural employment continued to grow in urban areas. Since 2000, the contrast between the rate of employment in the rural and urban areas appears to have been less marked, although at much lower overall rates of growth.

However, the picture from official figures of urban dynamism and rural decline should be treated with some caution. The distinction between "rural"

Table 3.1
Employment by Major Sectors, Urban and Rural Areas, Formal and Informal Sectors, Indonesia, 1987–2004

	Distribution				Growth Rates		
	1987	1997	2000	2004	1987–97	1997–2000	2000–04
All Sectors							
Agriculture	55	41	45	43	−0.77%	4.21%	−0.04%
Manufacturing	8	13	13	12	6.56%	1.25%	−1.26%
Other	37	46	42	45	4.36%	−2.13%	2.85%
Total	100	100	100	100	2.12%	1.05%	1.06%
Non-Agriculture							
Urban	43	53	62	62	6.84%	3.53%	1.96%
Rural: Non-Farm	57	47	38	38	2.90%	−7.95%	1.89%
Total	100	100	100	100	4.80%	−1.36%	1.94%
Wage	46	50	48	44	5.63%	−2.72%	−0.24%
Non-Wage	54	50	52	56	4.03%	−0.05%	3.79%
Total	100	100	100	100	4.80%	−1.36%	1.94%
Total Employment (000)	70,402	87,050	89,838	93,722			

Source: World Bank's calculation based on Sakernas (1987, 1997, 2000, 2004).

and "urban" is not a clear cut binary distinction, nor is it fixed and immutable. The manner in which areas are classified — and reclassified — as either urban or rural has a dramatic impact on the conclusions drawn. The villages in which the labour force survey (Sakernas) is undertaken are classified by BPS as either rural or urban based upon a range of criteria including: the share of agricultural households; the presence of various urban facilities; and the population density. Thus, precisely when a rural area experiences economic growth, it becomes more likely that it will be classified as urban. Consequently, the apparently much more impressive rate of NFE growth in urban areas may arise precisely because dynamic growth in the rural non-farm sector has meant that rural areas have been reclassified as urban ones. A large number of areas were reclassified in 1990 and in 2000, after the population censuses. Recent work by McCulloch, Weisbrod and Timmer (2006) suggests that these affects on apparent employment growth trends may be very significant.

The third trend has been the slow growth of formal sector employment — in both rural and urban areas and in farm and non-farm sectors. Figure 3.1 shows that formal sector employment in urban areas was stagnant from 2001–04, whilst that in rural areas experienced a steady decline from 1999. The reclassification of rural villages may exaggerate the rural decline, but the overall picture of formal sector stagnation is clear.

Figure 3.1
Formal and Informal Employment in Rural and Urban Areas, 1996–2004

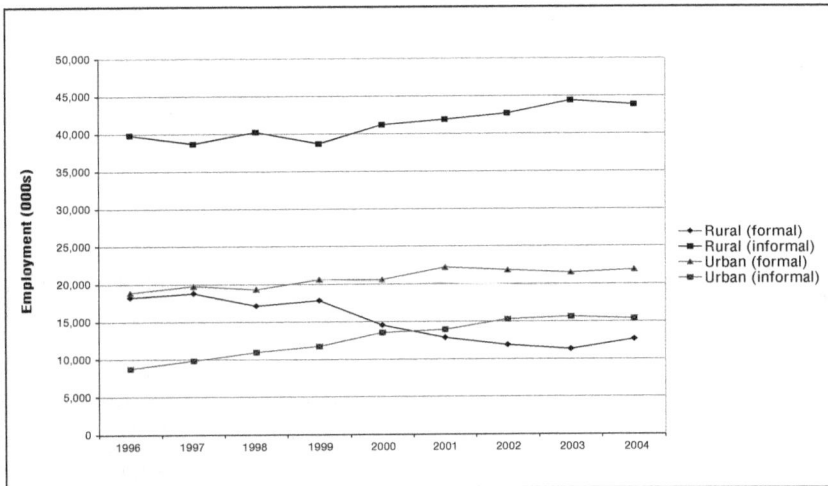

Source: World Bank's calculation based on Sakernas (1996–2003).

As employment growth in the formal sector has slowed, the informal sector has expanded to absorb the large numbers of new entrants into the labour force. The rates of informal employment in both urban and rural areas have been growing steadily at least since the crisis. This is a potentially worrying trend, since many (although certainly not all) informal sector jobs are likely to be low-wage and low-productivity jobs with few prospects for long-term income growth. Figure 3.2 shows the formal and informal employment broken down by sector. Again, the stagnation of the formal non-farm sector from 2000 is apparent, with formal employment in agriculture actually declining. By contrast, informal employment rose steadily in both agriculture and non-farm jobs.

Trends in NFE with regard to some human capital dimensions show the following patterns. Along gender lines, more than 60 per cent NFE in rural areas is male. Female employment in non-farm activities had experienced a declining trend during the period of 1996–2003, in contrast to that in urban areas where there was a slight tendency for employment to rise. In terms of age structure of the workers, NFE in rural areas is dominated by those aged 25–54 (over 65 per cent), followed by youth aged 15–24 (about 16–20 per cent). The trend in NFE was downward for all age groups from 1996.

Figure 3.2
Formal and Informal Employment in Farm and
Non-Farm Sectors, 1996–2004

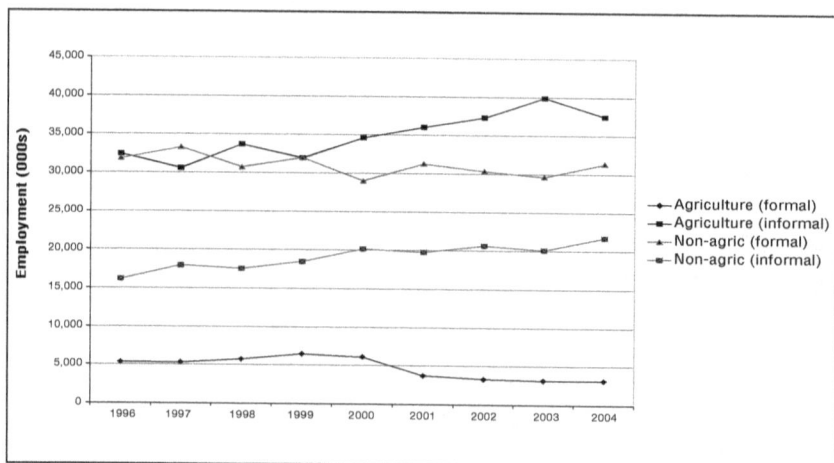

Source: World Bank's calculation based on Sakernas (1996–2003).

The quality of the workforce is another important aspect of NFE, and here the trends were more positive. Sakernas (1996–2003) shows that both farm and NFE is dominated by workers with primary education. Although the share of secondary and tertiary educated workers in rural areas was still low, it increased during 1996–2003 from 32 to 40 per cent and from 3 to 5 per cent respectively.

3. Literature Review

The participation of individuals or households in non-farm economic activities in the rural economy can be viewed as determined by two major factors: motivation and ability to participate. Motivation relates to incentives, while ability is the capacity of individuals or households to engage in a preferred sector.

The motivation to participate in the preferred sector can be classified into two types, *demand-pull motivation* and *distress-push motivation* (Davis 2003). *Demand-pull motivation* is motivation to diversify employment, related to wage and risk differentials associated with each type of employment. When returns to non-farm economic activities are higher and less risky than farming, "pull" factor are at work. Ellis (2000) noted that a rise in rural non-farm wages or greater opportunities to undertake remunerative NFE is likely to increase the tendency to diversify. On the contrary, an increase in the returns to farm activities would tend to reduce the motivation to diversify. *Distress-push motivation* is the motivation related to inadequate income and the lack of opportunities for consumption smoothing, such as through credit and crop insurance.

The ability to participate in non-farm economic activities is associated with the access of individuals or households to those activities, and therefore is not uniform, and more likely to vary compared with the motivation to engage in non-farm economic activities. Some individuals or households may face barriers to entry to engage in non-farm economic activities related to their human capital endowment. Janowski and Bleahu (2001) observed that poor households, without either material or human capital engage in non-farm economic activities because of distress-push factors, while better-off, higher status households were involved because of demand-pull considerations.

3.1. Human Capital

Numerous studies on rural non-farm economic activities emphasize the importance of human capital aspects that affect a household's ability to engage in non-farm economic activities (Gordon and Craig 2001; Lanjouw and Shariff 2002; and Davis 2003). A household's human capital comprises education and training, skills and health status. Age and sex can also be closely related to human capital attributes.

(i) *Education*
Education or formal schooling is important because it enables households to access higher income employment. For example, Lanjouw (1995) found that the probability of employment in regular-wage work in the non-agricultural sector increases as the education level increases, but the opposite is often observed for employment in the casual non-agricultural sector. Using data from Bangladesh, Islam (1997) shows that households with higher levels of education are more likely to be engaged in rural industry (compared with the rural population as a whole). Furthermore, Islam (1997) reports that education, particularly primary and secondary education, contributed to the growth of the non-farm sector in village and small rural towns. Primary education enhances work force productivity, while secondary education may contribute to entrepreneurial capacity. Better-educated members of the rural population have better access to any NFE, and are also more likely to establish their own non-farm business. Other studies by Lanjouw and Sharif (2002) observed that those with no education are more likely to be employed as agricultural wage employees.

Gordon and Craig (2001) noted several processes that reinforce the influence of education on household access to income-generating activities:

• Education increases skill levels, which are required for some non-farm economic activities, contributes to increased productivity, or may be an employment rationing device;
• Education can set in training processes that increase confidence, establish useful networks or contribute to productive investment (through exposure outside the home village, migration, using increased earnings to educate other family members to invest in rural enterprises);
• Education tends to be closely correlated with other variables that also improve access to higher income employment (pre-existing wealth, useful social networks, and confidence);
• Non-educated family members may benefit from advice given by more educated relatives.

(ii) *Training and skills*
Skills can be obtained by vocational training or outside the schooling system. In addition to formal education, skills are important. The skills required to

engage in many rural non-farm economic activities are either very simple or acquired outside the formal school system, through relatives and friends and on-the-job training (Cannon and Smith 2002; Som et al. 2002; Coppard 2001; Zwick 2001). For example, the positive impact of training and extension services on women's non-farm economic activities is documented for Tanzanian women (Gordon and Craig 2001). Women exposed to extension services may be more dynamic and entrepreneurial individuals. During the training, women also made contacts that contributed to the success of their business. Wandschneider (2003) observes that group strategies illustrate the potential of social capital to address credit and market access constraints, improve access to service provision, and overcome barriers to entry into income-generation activities.

(iii) *Health*
Health plays a significant role in income-generating activities through its effect on workers' productivity. Islam (1997) discusses the importance of investment in health more broadly, which results in morbidity reduction and improved nutrition, and thereby increases labour productivity, in both farm and non-farm sectors.

(iv) *Age*
Age is a dimension of human capital and it is important to understand how it affects an individual's participation in non-farm economic activity. Smith (2000) notes that younger household members generally migrate in search of NFE opportunities. Mature women, on the other hand, are more likely to take up a business at home. Women in their twenties and at older ages are more active in the non-farm economic activities that involve periods away from their home.

3.2. Social Capital

(i) *Gender dynamics*
Many studies report that women have less access to rural non-farm economic activities compared to men (Coppard 2001 in Davis). For example in India, women are rarely involved in enterprise management and in higher-level positions in the public sector. Women have also been constrained in the activities in which they are permitted or able to participate, by tradition, religion, or other social constraints. Greater involvement of women in the informal sector relative to the formal sector occurred because of childcare responsibilities, lower levels of education, and social expectations.

(ii) *Social networks*

Fafchamps and Minten (1998) describe social network as similar to social capital, with special emphasis on benefits that agents realize from knowing others with whom they form networks. Supplier and customer networks influence the returns to social capital, including the number of traders that the respondent knows of and the number of suppliers and clients that the respondent knows personally (Gordon and Craig 2001). Smith (2000) found that individuals and households with better social networks have greater opportunities to be engaged in the non-farm sector.

(iii) *Family size and structure*

Lanjouw and Sharif (2002) estimate that household size is positively and significantly related to own-enterprise and regular NFE, but not to casual NFE. Further, Lanjouw and Sharif indicate that individuals from large households are particularly likely to be engaged in own-enterprise and regular NFE, relative to agricultural labour.

4. Understanding Factors Affecting Households Rural Non-Farm Employment: Evidence for Indonesia

This section discusses evidence for Indonesia on factors that determine whether households engage in non-farm economic activities, by paying particular attention to labour-related factors such as the household's physical and human capital, and social networks. In addition to the household's own labour endowment, labour regulations may affect the non-farm business environment in which households have to operate. Labour regulations affect employment in the formal sector, but may also have indirect effects on informal sector employment creation. The last factor that is thought to hinder the development of non-farm enterprises especially in rural areas is migration (both domestic and international).

With regard to physical capital, studies of rural Java in particular have found that access to land is a major factor determining household's capacity to invest in non-farm work (White and Wiradi 1989; Breman and Wiradi 2002). Land-owning households have tended to invest much more in non-farm enterprises, whereas those without land are engaged in agricultural labouring on a casual basis and in the informal sector, often with very low returns to labour. Both poor and middle class rural households found jobs through circular migration to urban areas, especially involving factory work in the 1990s before the crisis (see below).

At the same time, rapid economic growth rates before the crisis provided an opportunity for households from a range of classes to become involved in new service activities in rural Java, such as selling snacks and gasoline, as minibus and truck drivers and *kenek* (assistants), and TV/radio and motorcycle repair activities (Effendi and Manning 1994, pp. 233–36). It is noteworthy, moreover, with regard to human capital, that this latter study found those involved in the "new" service activities tended to be better educated than those engaged in traditional areas of non-farm work, such as traditional healers and masseurs (*tukang pijit* and *dukun*), tailors and trishaw drivers.

During the crisis and recovery in Indonesia 1997–2000, both "push" and "pull" factors were at work in affecting non-farm work. The IFLS conducted just before the crisis and then again in the year 2000 suggested that labour force participation rates rose. More women in particular became involved in NFE, and in many areas both women and men diversified their earnings activities (Strauss et al. 2004). The main transition was from wage employment to self-employed and family work, especially among females.

Nevertheless, demand factors have also played a major role not only in the loss of jobs but also the emergence of new employment activities after the crisis. Although many households sought refuge in agricultural jobs, and NFE continued to grow very slowly at a national level, NFE expanded significantly in some rural areas. Export prices had risen as a result of the large devaluation in 1998 and provided opportunities for non-farm work in activities like rattan and furniture, with flow-on effects for informal sector activities (SMERU 2004).

As the later discussion of labour regulation in Indonesia shows, restrictive labour regulations will have an adverse impact on formal sector employment with the consequent increase in informal sector employment absorption. An example to be discussed below is the case of restrictive severance regulations. In addition to labour regulations at the national level, the non-farm business environment will be affected by other restrictive labour regulations comprising "nuisance" retributions or user fees, and restrictions on employing workers who originate from outside the region.

To corroborate the effects of restrictive labour regulations on NFE creation, a survey was conducted during September 2005 in the District or *Kabupaten* of Serang in the Banten region west of Jakarta. The survey conducted twenty-nine semi-structured interviews involving representatives from local government, business associations, trade unions, owners of small and medium enterprises, and representatives of large firms. Relevant findings which are referred to in this chapter relate to the impact of minimum wage, severance pay, contract worker, outsourcing, and informal labour regulations on businesses in Serang District.[2]

4.1. Non-Farm Employment Probabilities

Let us now turn to an examination of individual, household, social network and community facility characteristics associated with NFE probabilities using a multinomial logit regression model. The data employed for this purpose is the Indonesian Family Life Survey 2000 (IFLS-3). The survey contains extensive information on household characteristics, health, education, economic activities such as expenditure, production activities as well as asset holdings. Selected household members were asked about their current and retrospective wages and employment patterns, and migration. For the analysis of non-farm economic activity, we use the household modules of IFLS-3.

A multinomial logit regression model, or Model (1) is employed to explore the association between individual and household characteristics, social networks, and community facilities, and the probability of NFE in rural Indonesia. We consider four broad categories of occupations in this case: farm employment, non-farm self-employment, non-farm formal worker, non-farm family worker. In this model, we concentrate the analysis on the reported principal occupation of each individual. The subsequent logit regression model, or Model (2) analyses the issues associated with combining farm with non-farm activities, focusing on farm households engaging in non-farm economic activities as a secondary source of income. A set of explanatory variables comprises individual and household characteristics, social networks, and community facilities.

At the individual level, we consider the gender, marital status, age, and educational attainment of the household head. At the household level, we have information on household size, the household's per capita landholding, and the percentage of household members engaging in cultivation activities (cultivating households). The variables are chosen to capture some of the possible interaction between agriculture and non-farm economic activities at the household level (Lanjouw and Shariff 2002). It may be the case that the size of landholdings indicate a household's ability to engage in farm activities, or alternatively it may act as a proxy for household wealth, enabling the better off to take advantage of non-farm economic activities. Similar reasoning may be applied to household cultivation, as a proxy for the degree of a household's specialization in agriculture. Alternatively small areas cultivated may indicate a household's need to diversify out of agriculture.

To capture household interaction within a social network, we included three proxy variables, namely whether any household members are active in any rotating saving scheme (*arisan*); whether they participate in women's welfare activities (PKK), or whether any household members participate as member of a cooperative. Household participation in any one of these social network activities is expected to yield positive externalities in terms of contacts and knowledge diffusion. We have also included three community facility variables which may influence the probability of households engaging in non-farm activities, i.e. whether the village has a bank or financial institution, a local market, or a transport terminal (bus or microlet). In a vast country such as Indonesia, geographic variations may become additional variables that capture NFE patterns. The set of location variables comprises whether households reside in one of the major island groupings (Java, Sumatra, and the "Other" islands).

Table 3.2 provides parameter estimates of the multinomial logit estimation for the probability of households engaging in NFE activities, or Model (1). Table 3.3 reports results for the logit estimation of farm households who were also engaged in non-farm activities, or Model (2). The multinomial logit model requires that a particular occupational category be designated as numeraire against which all results should be compared. We have chosen farm employment as the designated comparison group. Results of the multinomial logit model will be interpreted as whether the set of non-farm occupational categories are systematically different from the farm employment category. The parameter estimates show the strength of association of a particular explanatory variable with the respective occupational category relative to the same explanatory variable with the comparison group, i.e. farm-employment.

Table 3.2 shows parameter estimates of the multinomial logit model where men are strongly and significantly more likely to be involved in any category of NFE than in the farm category. The parameter estimate on age indicates that the older an individual is, the more likely he/she is to be engaged in non-farm self-employment relative to farm employment as the main occupation. Relative to farm employment, the probability of employment in non-farm formal jobs or as a family worker increases among married individuals.

Education is strongly associated with employment outside farm activities. Higher levels of education would increase a household's probability in engaging in any employment outside the farm sector. This is indicated by the significant and positive coefficient for all education levels relative to the

Table 3.2
Multinomial Logit Estimation: The Probability of an Individual Engaging in Various Categories of NFE Relative to Farm Employment as Main Source of Income, Rural Indonesia, Year 2000 ("Farm Employment" as the Comparison Group)

Independent variable	Coefficient	Standard error	z		ME
Non-farm self-employment					
Individual characteristics:					
Male	0.474	0.067	7.090	***	0.067
Age	0.052	0.011	4.590	***	0.008
Age squared	−0.001	0.000	−4.720	***	−0.00008
Married	0.007	0.083	0.090		0.010
Primary education	0.288	0.095	3.030	***	0.032
Secondary education	0.725	0.117	6.180	***	0.079
Tertiary education	1.263	0.254	4.980	***	0.104
Household characteristics:					
Household size	−0.012	0.017	−0.700		−0.005
Per capita land owned	0.000	0.003	−0.010		0.000
Per capita land owned squared	0.000	0.000	−1.320		0.000
Cultivating household	0.000	0.000	0.500		0.000
Social networks:					
Whether participate in PKK[#]	0.216	0.144	1.500		0.042
Whether participate in *koperasi*	0.332	0.079	4.220	***	0.059
Whether participate in *arisan*[##]	0.426	0.072	5.950	***	0.057
Community facilities:					
Whether have bank or financial institution in the village	0.251	0.124	2.030	**	0.022
Whether have local market in the village	0.095	0.072	1.320		0.021
Whether have terminal in the village	0.390	0.070	5.550	***	0.050
Location:					
Whether live in Sumatra	−0.536	0.083	−6.430	***	−0.051
Whether live in other islands	−0.103	0.079	−1.290		0.003
Constant	−2.957	0.292	−10.110	***	
Non-farm formal worker					
Individual characteristics:					
Male	0.139	0.070	1.970	**	−0.002
Age	0.017	0.013	1.320		0.001
Age squared	0.000	0.000	−2.700	***	0.000
Married	0.215	0.089	2.420	**	0.028
Primary education	0.354	0.117	3.020	***	0.038
Secondary education	0.954	0.133	7.150	***	0.110
Tertiary education	2.686	0.221	12.130	***	0.463
Household characteristics:					
Household size	0.094	0.017	5.530	***	0.013
Per capita land owned	−0.008	0.003	−2.680	***	−0.001
Per capita land owned squared	0.000	0.000	1.290		0.000
Cultivating household	0.000	0.000	−0.320		0.000

Social network:

Whether participate in PKK#	−0.215	0.169	−1.270	−0.036
Whether participate in *koperasi*	−0.329	0.075	−4.380 ***	−0.066
Whether participate in *arisan*##	0.291	0.077	3.790 ***	0.024

Community facilities:

Whether have bank or financial institution in the village	0.524	0.134	3.900 ***	0.072
Whether have local market in the village	−0.199	0.081	−2.460 **	−0.032
Whether have terminal in the village	0.304	0.075	4.040 ***	0.027

Location:

Whether live in Sumatra	−0.923	0.090	−10.200 ***	−0.746
Whether live in other islands	−0.530	0.086	−6.150 ***	−0.361
Constant	−1.771	0.316	−5.600 ***	−1.151

Non-farm family worker

Individual characteristics:

Male	0.868	0.137	6.330 ***	0.023
Age	−0.004	0.022	−0.200	−0.001
Age squared	0.000	0.000	−0.330	0.000
Married	0.522	0.152	3.440 ***	0.016
Primary education	0.426	0.215	1.980 **	0.009
Secondary education	0.999	0.248	4.030 ***	0.022
Tertiary education	1.261	0.528	2.390 **	−0.002

Household characteristics:

Household size	0.042	0.032	1.340	0.001
Per capita land owned	−0.012	0.010	−1.270	−0.0003
Per capita land owned squared	0.000	0.000	−0.130	0.000
Cultivating household	0.000	0.001	0.610	0.000

Social network:

Whether participate in PKK#	0.050	0.287	0.170	0.001
Whether participate in *koperasi*	1.066	0.214	4.970 ***	0.026
Whether participate in *arisan*##	0.361	0.142	2.540 **	0.007

Community facilities:

Whether have bank or financial institution in the village	0.076	0.245	0.310	−0.003
Whether have local market in the village	0.460	0.137	3.360 ***	0.010
Whether have terminal in the village	0.216	0.141	1.530	0.007

Location:

Whether live in Sumatra	−0.667	0.167	−3.980 ***	−0.011
Whether live in other islands	−0.229	0.158	−1.450	−0.004
Constant	−4.721	0.594	−7.940 ***	

LR Chi2	1,088.87 ***	
Pseudo R2	0.0683	
Observations	7,365	

Note: *** Significant at a 1 per cent level
  ** Significant at a 5 per cent level
  # PKK= Women' Welfare Organisation
  ## Arisan = Rotation Savings Scheme
Source: Estimation using the IFLS 2000 (IFLS-3).

Table 3.3
Logit Estimation: The Probability of an Individual Engaging in Farm and
Non-Farm Activities, Rural Indonesia, Year 2000

Independent variable	Coefficient	Standard error	z		ME
Individual characteristics:					
Male	0.575	0.092	6.220	***	0.080
Age	−0.039	0.015	−2.620	***	−0.006
Age squared	0.001	0.000	3.230	***	0.000
Married	0.260	0.120	2.180	**	0.035
Primary education	0.167	0.115	1.460		0.024
Secondary education	0.588	0.156	3.760	***	0.075
Household characteristics:					
Household size	0.052	0.022	2.390	**	0.007
Social network:					
Whether participate in PKK	−0.126	0.240	−0.530		−0.019
Whether participate in *koperasi*	0.146	0.095	1.540		0.021
Whether participate in *arisan*	−0.051	0.104	−0.490		−0.007
Community facilities:					
Whether have bank or financial institution in the village	−0.049	0.185	−0.270		−0.007
Whether have local market in the village	−0.185	0.093	−1.980	**	−0.027
Whether have terminal in the village	0.255	0.105	2.440	**	0.035
Location:					
Whether live in Sumatra	−0.367	0.101	−3.640	***	−0.055
Whether live in other islands	−0.313	0.103	−3.040	***	−0.047
Constant	1.436	0.383	3.750	***	
LR Chi2	130.060	***			
Pseudo R2	0.0327				
Observations	4,177				

Note: *** Significant at a 1 per cent level
    ** Significant at a 5 per cent level
Source: Estimation using IFLS 2000 (IFLS-3).

no-schooling option as the omitted category. Note that the coefficient for secondary education is larger than for primary education. It is clear that this indicates a household is more likely to be engaged in any non-farm activities as main source of income than farm employment the higher the education level of its head.

Turning to household size, this was positively and significantly related to non-farm formal sector employment, indicating that individuals from large households are more likely to be engaged in non-farm formal activities relative to farm employment. To the extent that non-farm formal economic activities are more productive activities, these findings lend support to the notion that larger households may not be necessarily poorer households. It is interesting to note that per capita landholdings had significant and negative effect only on the probability of non-farm, "formal" sector employment. This suggests that household heads without much land were "pushed" to seek wage employment in the formal sector, but were not necessarily overrepresented in self-employed jobs in the non-farm sector.[3] The results also indicate a negative effect of the size of landholdings on the probability of NFE among formal workers. As landholdings per capita increase, this may lead to greater specialization on the part of households to engage in farm activities.

When we consider social network variables, the results in Table 3.2 show that they have the expected positive effect on all categories of NFE particularly for those households active in *arisan*. Arisan is a social gathering which functions as a rotating saving scheme, but more importantly, it is a medium for individuals to expand social and business networks, contacts and information. However, positive effects for membership of a *koperasi* are only evident for those households engaging in self-employment and as family workers in non-farm activities; the effect is negative for those households engaged as formal workers in the non-farm sector, relative to the farm sector.

Interesting results are evident from the effect of a set of community facilities, in which availability of a transport terminal and bank/financial institution appears to facilitate a household being engaged in either self-employment or in the formal worker category of non-farm activities, relative to farm employment. In contrast, the availability of a local market in a village is associated with higher probability of a household being employed as family workers in non-farm activities, relative to the farm sector. A set of locational variables indicate the expected negative effect of residence outside Java, especially Sumatra, relative to Java. These regions are generally more dependent on agriculture, and are less developed than many regions on Java.

Model (2) is a logit model where the dependent variable is 1 if the individual is engaged in both farm as principal occupation and non-farm economic activities as secondary source of income, and 0 otherwise. The explanatory variables consist of individual characteristics, household characteristics, social networks, community facilities, and location. Results in Table 3.3 should be interpreted differently from those of Table 3.2. The logit estimation in Table 3.3 is estimated to derive the probability of an individual engaging in farm and non-farm business activities simultaneously. It may be possible for a farm household to derive supplementary source of income from such activities.

In general, the results of Table 3.3 were quite similar to Table 3.2. Thus households headed by men are more likely to derive incomes from both farm and non-farm activities than women. Again, secondary education attainment or higher of the household head is the most significant factor (positively) influencing the probability of a farm household being engaged in non-farm activities as a supplementary source of income. The ability of a farm household to take advantage of additional income from non-farm activities is more likely for households having an individual member that is well educated. However, the parameter estimate on age indicates that the young are relatively more likely to be engaged in both farm and non-farm activities. And, household size parameter estimates show a positive and significant effect (it was negative in the case of self-employed work in Table 3.2), perhaps indicating the need of larger farm households to derive supplementary incomes from non-farm activities.

As with Table 3.2, the availability of a bus terminal in a village appears to facilitate a farm household being active in non-farm activities, most probably enabling greater market access for their non-farm products.

Turning finally to location characteristics, we find that individuals in Java are again more likely to be engaged in farm and non-farm activities relative to regions outside Java. Java appears to have a sizable number of farm households deriving supplementary income from non-farm sectors relative to their outer islands neighbours.

In sum, the results from the logit analysis were broadly as we expected: non-farm employment tended to be dominated by males, and by more educated household heads. It was associated with greater participation in social networks, and also with some infrastructure variables, included in the equation as proxies for greater economic diversity and better transport networks to the communities where the households resided.

4.2. Labour Regulations and Non-Farm Employment Creation

(i) *More restrictive national labour regulations*

Minimum wage regulations
Indonesian labour market has experienced a significant change since the early 1990s with the establishment of several independent labour unions and the implementation of regional minimum wage regulations (UMR), which from this period have been updated annually. Although, minimum wages were first introduced in the early 1970s, attention to their impact began in the late 1980s, as minimum wages became an important plank of government labour market policy.

Annual increases in minimum wages have occurred from 1990. The SMERU Research Institute (2001) reports that the government tripled the minimum wage in the first half of the 1990s and the nominal wage continued to increase during the second half of the 1990s. The real value of minimum wage increases began to taper off after 1996, and fell significantly in 1998. In 2000, when the economy began to recover, the government vigorously pursued a minimum wage policy and the real minimum wage increased significantly in 2000–02.

In 1995, the government changed the basis for calculating the UMR to include a broader basket of goods, as part of minimum subsistence needs or KHM (*Kebutuhan Hidup Minimum*). Since the implementation of decentralization in 2001, the other important development was the transfer of the power to determine minimum wages to the heads of regional governments, i.e. governors, mayors, and regents (*Bupati*). The framework for setting minimum wages was established by the national government and is implemented by provinces and districts. A province's minimum wage is set to cover the lowest minimum wage across all districts in the province. Minimum wages are increased every year in line with estimated increases in the KHM.

Minimum wage policy has been widely, although not uniformly, adopted by businesses in the modern formal sector which is confirmed by our field study of large foreign-owned firms in Kabupaten Serang. Large foreign-owned businesses usually do not see minimum wage as an important cost burden, and it was not among the most important factors for potential investors in choosing a location for their investment. It is a problem, however, for those labour-intensive industries facing stiff competition from similar producers elsewhere in the region, notably Vietnam and China. In Kabupaten Serang, large and foreign owned firms claim that they pay their workers at or above the minimum wage, but many small, medium-sized or larger Indonesian firms still pay their workers below the minimum wage. An enterprise can propose to postpone wage increases to comply with minimum wage to the District Manpower Office for economic reasons. The District Manpower Office in theory may impose sanctions on non-compliant firms, but in practice they have never done so.

Severance pay

In addition to minimum wage law, severance pay regulations may restrict mobility in the formal sector labour market. Dismissal regulations that include severance pay have been part of Indonesia's labour policies and have been subjected to significant changes since 1996, both in terms of rates and coverage to various groups of workers. The regulation distinguishes the rights, rates of severance pay, and long-service payment depending on the cause of separation. Three broad categories of reasons for separation include: voluntary quits, dismissal for economic reasons (i.e. downsizing and bankruptcy), and violations (minor and major violations or offences).

The introduction of Ministerial Decree No. 3, 1996 increased rates of severance and long-service payment for dismissals and minor offences significantly, over 50 per cent compared to the Ministerial Decree No. 4, 1986. In the year 2000, Ministerial Decision No. 150, 2000 (*Kepmen 150*) replaced Ministerial Decree No. 3, 1996 and the new Decree included a further rise in severance rates for workers with ten or more years of service, and granted long-service pay to all workers who quitted their jobs voluntarily. A 15 per cent gratuity for all severance and long-service leave was also granted to all workers, including those that were dismissed for minor offences. The implementation of the Basic Manpower Act No. 13, 2003 further increased rates of severance pay for workers with longer years of service compared with those given under *Kepmen 150*, 2000. Based on this Act, in the case of workers dismissed for economic reasons, the overall rate of severance has increased almost three-fold compared with the 1986 regulation.

Figure 3.3 compares the so-called "hiring tax" in terms of the number of months for which severance pay has to be paid to the worker in the event that the worker quits or is dismissed for a minor violation or for economic cause. The Indonesian tax is then compared with hiring tax estimated in studies for other developing and industrial countries. The trend for Indonesia's hiring tax is clear. While several countries are reforming their severance pay systems, Indonesia is going in the opposite direction and making dismissal costs more expensive.

Results from our field survey in Kabupaten Serang, however, confirm that this regulations is rarely practised or enforced by small and medium businesses as well as large labour-intensive firms. Severance payments were not considered as an important issue for medium-sized firms surveyed, they simply ignored or were unaware of the stipulations. The practice was to pay severance payment of about one to two months of salary. In the event of economic downsizing, many entrepreneurs claimed that they could not afford to pay according to the law, and opted for a compromise settlement through tripartite bargaining. There were cases of management fabricating the cause of retrenchment by accusing workers of committing a "major offence", as a way of avoiding the high severance payment for dismissal based on economic cause. Workers in these cases of dismissal are not protected because of the ineffective legal system that has hindered a fair process of dismissal.

Figure 3.3
The Comparison of Hiring Tax in Selected Countries
(Hiring Tax in number of monthly wages in 1990 and 1999)

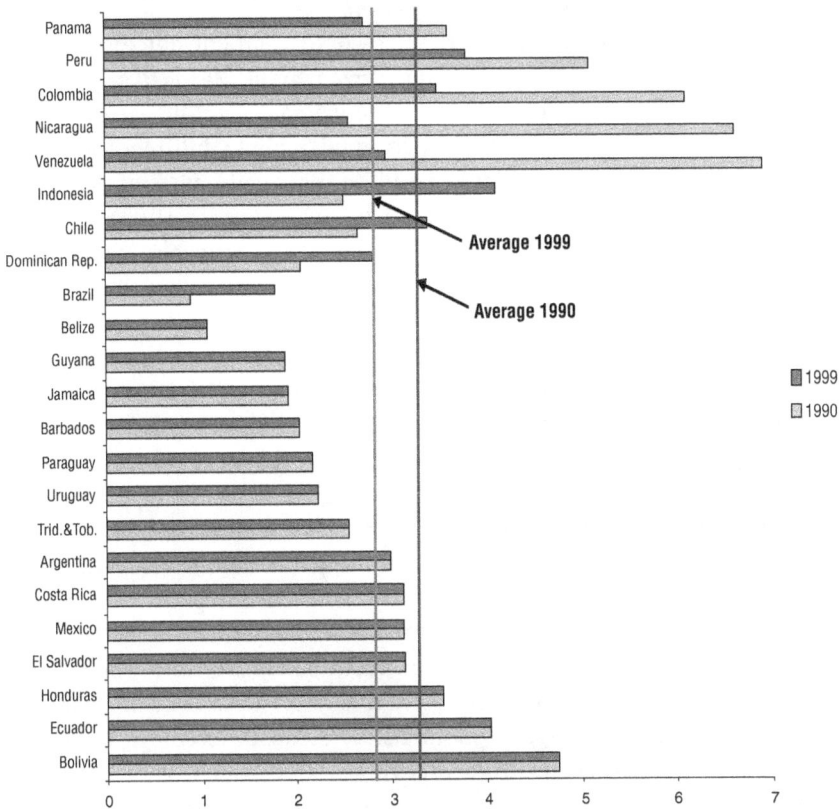

Source: Alejandra Cox Edwards (2002), "The lost decade and road to reform", cited from *LP3E UNPAD-GIAT* (2004).

Despite pragmatism and compromises in severance payment settlements, the law still worries business. Firms worry about staying competitive in the face of slow business growth and fierce competition. There is a tendency for firms to increase the use of short-term contract workers and outsource their orders, especially among firms with fluctuating sales and orders. The shift in worker management practices is in anticipation of firms having to make large severance payments in the event of downsizing or closure. The growth in the number of contract workers and outsourcing activities has occurred despite strict limitations on the use of both these modes of employment (see below).

Short-term contract workers and outsourcing

Regulation of the employment of contract workers and outsourcing through the 2004 Decree on Temporary Working Agreement or *Pekerjaan kerja Waktu Tertentu* (PKWT) has become more restrictive compared with the Decree issued in 2003. The previous decree permitted a single, full renewal of the contract. Also, there are the requirements to report all names of daily and fixed-term contract workers to the local manpower office (LP3E Unpad-GIAT 2004). Under the new decree, employers can only hire workers on limited term contracts of no more than two years, with a one-year extension permitted only for specific reasons.[4] Employers can hire workers on contract for seasonal work or on daily contracts for no longer than three months; beyond this period the appointees must be promoted as permanent workers. In addition, the new law also limits labour outsourcing of production and services to "non-core" activities, such as cleaning, security, and catering.

As noted, the survey in Kabupaten Serang confirms the trend towards the use of contract workers and outsourcing, due to slow business growth. Firms' hiring practices have shifted to limiting the number of permanent workers hired or not hiring permanent workers altogether. It is not uncommon to find firms with fluctuating orders to have 20 to 30 per cent of their workers employed on daily contracts. There are cases where firms employs up to 70 per cent of their workers as short-term contract workers, paid on a daily basis. The survey found little evidence of contract workers being hired on a permanent basis after their 2–3 year contract period had expired. Firms often re-contract the workers for yet another short-term term, and without heeding the required maximum contract period of 2–3 years or the 30-day grace period required between completion of one short-term contract and the start of the next.

Despite the recognition of a firm's right to outsource their non-core business activities according to Manpower Act 13/2003, the field survey in Kabupaten Serang found that there was lack of agreement as to what constitutes "non-core" activities. Firms argued against limiting non-core activities to include only cleaning, catering services, and security. They argue that different industries have their own definition of core and non-core activities. The trend since 2003 in Kabupaten Serang has been for firms to rely more on outsourcing as a response to economic pressures, and to benefit from this lack of clarity in the definition of "non-core" activities. Like the employment of contract workers on a short-term basis, outsourcing has benefited private companies by providing a more flexible labour force, which can be adjusted to deal with fluctuations in sales. The discrepancy between what the Law states with the actual practice reflects a condition of labour market surplus. Many job-seekers are willing to accept temporary employment without meeting basic legal requirements with regard to minimum wages and other mandated benefits.

The impact of restrictive national labour regulations on formal sector employment

How do minimum wage, severance pay, and contract workers regulations affect employment creation in the formal sector? The imposition of minimum wage affects both supply and demand in the labour market. Several studies, most notably by SMERU (2001) suggested a negative relationship between minimum wages and employment in the modern formal sector after the crisis. The results of this study showed that increases in the minimum wages have a negative effect on urban formal sector employment, except for white-collar workers. This negative effect was greatest for those groups that are most vulnerable to change in labour market conditions, such as females, young workers, and less educated workers.

Studies undertaken before the crisis when employment was growing strongly and compliance rates relatively low suggest that the minimum wage impact on employment was much smaller. This may have been because larger firms, in particular, had developed strategies to circumvent the legislation in an environment where labour unions were tightly controlled by the government. Alatas and Cameron (2003) found different results from a study of the impact of minimum wages under more favourable labour market conditions prior to the crisis. Their study looked at the impact of minimum wages on employment in the clothing, textiles, footwear, and leather industries.[5] The results of the study suggest that the increase in minimum wages had no significant employment effect for large firms, both domestic as well as foreign. In contrast, the increase of minimum wages had a significant negative impact on employment in small domestic firms. An earlier study by Rama (1996) also found similar results, in that employment in smaller firms was adversely affected by the minimum wage increases, while employment in large firms was unaffected. Very different results found in studies undertaken after the crisis suggest that higher rates of compliance can affect employment negatively (and also may bring only limited benefits in terms of consumption) under less favourable labour market conditions.

The impact of severance regulations is similar to a "tax" on employment, or hiring new workers. An increase in severance rates could be expected to reduce the demand for workers in the modern sector. A LP3E Unpad-GIAT study concluded that the high-cost severance system has three major effects on the Indonesian labour market:

- The system is discouraging employers from hiring workers on a permanent basis.
- The system hurts employment of younger workers and low educated workers. For example, firms will tend to keep older workers even if they are less productive than younger ones because it is more expensive to lay off older workers. In this way the current structure of severance payments is biased against employing young people.
- The system enhances problems of dualism and social exclusion in the labour market. High costs of severance disadvantages workers who fail to gain access to these sorts of "protected" jobs.

Aside from increases in rates and coverage of severance pay with subsequent regulations culminating in the Manpower Act of 2003, several other developments have contributed to employers' increasing concern over the severance pay regulation (LP3E Unpad-GIAT 2004). First, severance regulation has been more binding especially since the *reformasi* era after the fall of the Soeharto government. Labour unions have become more active in enforcing regulations and consequently compliance with severance pay regulations have increased. Labour disputes over severance pay have become more common especially in sectors that face economic difficulties (due to weak domestic demand or a tougher export market), and are forced to lay off workers. Examples can be found in the textile and textile products, and footwear industries.

Another aspect of severance pay regulations that has raised concerns among employers relates to the large recent increases in minimum wages. As overall severance pay is calculated as a multiple of monthly wages, large increases in minimum wages would entail significant increases in the overall severance pay to dismissed workers, especially those laid off due to economic reasons. The combination of much higher severance rates, and large increases in minimum wages have resulted in the new severance regulation being relatively among the most costly in the developing world.

Restrictions on the choice employment arrangements, combined with large increases in minimum wages, and the high severance cost of permanent workers has discouraged firms from hiring new permanent workers in the formal sector. This is especially the case for non-agricultural employment in the modern sector, in both urban and rural areas. But it is unlikely to apply to NFE in informal sectors where the regulations are not binding, as is supported by evidence from the Indonesian Rural Investment Climate Survey (RICS) 2006 conducted in six *kabupaten*, as part of the Rural Investment Climate Assessment in Indonesia (see Table 3.4). Labour-related regulations in the form of inflexible hiring and firing, which increased costs mostly affect large enterprises, but are not considered to be a problem for smaller and informal sector enterprises.

Interestingly, the majority of large firms in the RICS have been affected by the difficulties of finding skilled labour, and of hiring workers from outside the region. This is part of the local labour regulations that are prevalent in some *kabupaten*, as will be discussed in the following section. Further tabulation of the RICS data reveals a quarter of workers in household enterprises are illiterate and another quarter do not finish primary school. Larger enterprises have better educated workers with more than three-quarters of their workers having finished primary schooling or higher. About 40 per cent of workers completed senior secondary schooling or higher in the RICS sample of large firms. Skill acquisition through training also seems to be much higher for medium and and large enterprises (30 per cent and 40 per cent of their workers respectively). On the other hand, household enterprises in the RICS do not seem to pay enough attention to workers' need for training, since hardly any of their workers received any training, either prior or during employment.

(ii) *A plethora of local labour regulations and informal labour practices*
At the regional and local level, labour regulations are mostly concerned with issues such as the employment of local workers, labour protection, and regional minimum wages. The first two relate to licensing in the form of payments for certain permits/licences for which the company has to pay the local labour office. Since decentralization, this form of local regulation has mushroomed in the interest of local government's raising more of their own revenues (PAD). Many labour regulations are administered by district governments through retributions or user charges concerning various permits, such as permission for overtime work, compliance with workers' safety regulations, etc. In many cases, there are no clear services or licences provided in return for the fees, and most of the administration can be categorized rather as "nuisance" taxes.

Another disturbing area of local labour regulation trend has been restrictions imposed in certain regions on the employment of workers from outside the region. The local practice of restricting employment of workers from outside the region usually takes the form of a letter issued by the district head (*Surat Edaran Bupati*) requiring firms to employ a certain

Table 3.4
Firms' Opinion on Labour-Related Obstacles by Type of Enterprise Year 2005
(percentage of firms surveyed)

Type of obstacle	Degree of problem	Household Enterprise	Medium-Scale Enterprise	Large Enterprise	All firms
Inflexible hiring and firing regulations	Not a problem	85.28	86.3	67.77	85.41
	Minor problem	5.16	7.37	13.27	5.63
	Moderate problem	6.62	3.55	15.17	6.05
	Big problem	2.94	2.78	3.79	2.92
High labour cost due to government regulations	Not a problem	85.04	83.19	55.77	84.55
	Minor problem	5.33	5.86	19.23	5.49
	Moderate problem	6.68	8.44	18.27	7.08
	Big problem	2.96	2.51	6.73	2.88
Obtaining work permits for foreigners	Not a problem	85.3	89.82	67.48	86.12
	Minor problem	5.3	3.56	16.5	5.01
	Moderate problem	6.1	3.52	12.62	5.62
	Big problem	3.3	3.1	3.4	3.26
Lack of skilled labour	Not a problem	82.73	81.57	3.17	82.18
	Minor problem	6.77	4.82	8.47	6.39
	Moderate problem	6.82	8.93	84.66	7.55
	Big problem	3.68	4.68	3.7	3.88
Difficulties hiring labour from outside region	Not a problem	84.51	86.17	3.23	84.51
	Minor problem	5.65	7.63	8.06	6.05
	Moderate problem	6.94	3.92	76.34	6.62
	Big problem	2.91	2.28	12.37	2.82

Source: Indonesian Rural Investment Climate Survey (2006).

percentage of the workforce from the local population. For example, in Kabupaten Bekasi, a letter issued by the district head (*Surat Edaran Bupati No. 560/334*) required any firms located in the district of Bekasi to employ 50 per cent of its workforce from among local citizens. Also located in Kabupaten Bekasi, the Sukadana village sets a worker quota based on the worker's place of origin, i.e. 50 per cent to be recruited from among village inhabitants, 29 per cent from the district of Bekasi, 20 per cent Indonesian citizens, and 1 per cent expatriates.

Another example is the case of of the city of Pekanbaru (Central Sumatra). Regional Regulation (*Perda*) No. 4/2000 on Local Worker Placement aims to overcome potential social problems caused by the domination of employment by workers from outside the region. The regulation requires: (1) firms or employers to give local workers priority; (2) the firm must appoint local workers for the human resources development manager position; (3) a worker must pay Rp 10,000 for a membership card annually; and (4) a worker's agent pays Rp 500,000 per hired worker for the purpose of a skill improvement programme, in cases where the worker comes from outside Pekanbaru.

Many other regions have regulations that restrict employment from outside the region including Kabupaten Musi Banyu Asin in South Sumatra that sets an employment charge of Rp 1,000,000 for each worker from outside the region. Kabupaten Maluku Tenggara sets more specific charges based on job qualifications. For example, every worker from outside the region at manager and researcher level is charged Rp 250,000 per month; sailors, teachers, and other similar types of worker are charged Rp 200,000 per month; actors/actresses are charged Rp 5,000,000 per month; and general workers are charged Rp 150,000 per month.

Aside from local labour regulations mentioned above, our field survey in Kabupaten Serang uncovered informal labour practices in the form of informal employment recruitment. Two forms of the most common informal recruitment practices are pressure from local communities to employ locals and payments to third parties to secure employment. The practice of *premanism* (boss boys) in employment recruitment is widespread in Kabupaten Serang, and although *preman* do not usually interfere in firms' recruitment procedures, they consitute a financial burden to firms as well as creating an insecure business environment (see Box 3.1). On the other side of the coin, there is a widespread practice of paying a third party to secure a job. This practice affects all workers, locals and migrants seeking work in foreign and domestic owned firms.

The Serang case study highlights another aspect of informal labour practices in the sense of entitlements to jobs among local residents, although

---

Box 3.1
Premanism in Job Recruitment

Preman or *jawara* (local term) are small-time gangsters who make their living extorting money from businesses in a number of ways, including direct demands for money and threats of either violence to persons or damage to property, including demands that an enterprise use certain service providers for activities such as waste disposal. A respondent from a large foreign-owned manufacturing firm stated that he received demands for payment when the firm hired additional workers. *Premans* hang around outside firms and note any new employees arriving for work and then "charge" the firm for hiring new workers. The firm has hired military personnel as well as civilian security guards to secure the premises, as such harassment adds to operational costs. However, several respondents noted that from April 2005 the district police launched an operation to combat *premanism* by rounding up suspects, which seems to have reduced the problem, at least temporarily.

Source: Field survey in Kabupaten Serang.

---

their educational level generally does not meet with formal requirements. Kabupaten Serang's large number of unemployed and low skilled workers has exerted considerable pressure on firms to provide employment opportunities for locals. The pressure is felt especially by large firms requiring skilled workers. Most of these firms have expressed their preference to employ workers who meet certain minimum skill and educational requirements, although this generally means hiring workers from outside the region. To cope with this problem, many large firms have opted to develop a mechanism to ensure that certain lower level jobs are given to members of the local community. These attempts do not appear to have always been successful, as was the experience of PT JRD (see Box 3.2).

The informal practices of *premanism* and demands of locals for employment are prevalent across Kabupaten Serang, and nearly all employers interviewed reported this as a burden to their enterprise. It interferes with recruitment, forces enterprises to employ unqualified workers and unnecessarily adds to the number of employees. This kind of practice adds unnecessary extra financial costs to the firm's budget, in addition to the nuisance caused.

4.3. Domestic and International Migration

Based on Indonesia's current pattern of population mobility, its population mobility has entered the "late transitional society" stage (Tjiptoherijanto

---

Box 3.2
Unqualified Locals versus Demand for Employment Share

When PT JRD first opened it needed many workers who had graduated at the senior high school level. The firm is located in a community where most people are primary school graduates. The local community demanded a share of the job openings, however PT JRD only recruited those that met the requirement. The crowd from the local community protested; and it turned violent. Some of the recruited workers were barred from going to work at PT JRD, the personnel manager even got punched. This is an example where the local community does not understand that their educational background does not meet the level required. What they understand is that they are entitled to a share of the employment opportunities since their land has been converted to an industrial area.

Source: Field survey in Kabupaten Serang.

2005). Indonesia's population mobility at this stage is characterized by: (1) large long-term rural urban movements with the target cities as the primary targets, intermediate centres being bypassed, and the emergence of "megacities"; (2) increasing urban to urban movement among circular or non-permanent migrants; (3) increasing international migration; (4) decreasing rural-based circulation associated with decline in the rural population in many regions.

Migration may have positive and negative impacts on the region of origin. The negative impact from the perspective of labour for non-farm economic activities will especially be felt if the best human resources migrate outside an area. This is especially true since migration is often closely related to levels of education. Those who are more educated often record higher rates of out-migration, compared to less educated people. More young men also tend to migrate from rural areas compared with women. However, in the case of Indonesia, increasing numbers of young women tend to migrate not only into urban areas, but abroad as overseas contract workers. In a study of Sub-Saharan Africa, Gordon et al. (2000) report that the ability to migrate and the choice of destination for migration is also influenced by social networks, in addition to education and gender.

In the case of Indonesia, many households withdrew from factory and informal sector work in the cities during the economic crisis, as wage jobs were lost, and more villagers became more heavily involved in agricultural work or NFE in their home villages than in earlier periods (Suryahadi et al. 2000; Strauss et al. 2004). However, as the national-level data on employment suggest (see above), many of these informal sector workers from rural areas returned to cities to find jobs in the post-crisis period (Manning 2000). However, in some locations many did not, and their return to the village placed additional pressure on the village economy, manifested in greater competition for scarce rural jobs, mostly outside agriculture (Breman and Wiradi 2002).

In the pre-crisis period, circular migration was a major feature of rural urban migration, with household heads leaving their families for periods of several weeks to several months, depending on their occupation and village of origin (Silvey 2004). However remittances were a major feature of support for rural households in many places (Hetler 1989). A high proportion of these circular migrants were employed in the informal sector, although wage employment especially among young, single females in manufacturing was a feature of migration flows during the deregulation period in the 1990s. The decline in employment in labour-intensive manufacturing industries such as garments and footwear after the crisis meant, however, that one avenue for employment outside the village was closed to many potential rural urban migrants (Tjandraningsih 1999).

In addition, after the crisis relatively high costs of transport to rural locations far from the villages, meant that support from urban residents for rural households back home declined substantially. This was in contrast to support for home villages that were closer to places where urban migrants worked.[6]

Inter-provincial migration, mostly from poorer rural environments to urban areas has been an important feature of the labour market in Indonesia. In the period 1995–2000, inter-provincial migration was still substantial in many Outer Island regions, especially the resource-rich provinces of Riau, Central and East Kalimantan. In these regions, the percentage of recent migrants (movements over the five-year period prior to the census in 2000), ranged from 7–13 per cent of the total population aged five years and above (Sugiyarto et al. 2005, p. 19). Notably, the proportion of in-migrants increased in all these provinces compared with five years earlier, especially in Riau province where the proportion of recent migrants more than tripled compared with five years earlier. Jakarta and Banten, centres of manufacturing and services, were the main provinces of high net in-migration on Java. As might be expected, regions with low rates of internal migration (mostly net out-migration provinces) consisted of the relatively poorer regions of Central and East Java, and West and East Nusa Tenggara, and Maluku.

Nevertheless, as noted above, additional barriers to (and costs of) inter-regional migration would appear to have increased since decentralization, although these pressures have probably been much greater in many of the Outer Island districts than in Java. District and provincial governments now responsible for their own budgets had become more wary of employing outsiders, especially in government jobs, and in extreme cases such as in Papua and parts of Kalimantan, there was an exodus of outsiders, often after social conflict, partly as a result of competition for jobs.

In addition to domestic migration, international migration became more common for Indonesians in the 1990s. Difficulties in coping with the household economy led many Indonesians to work overseas as *Tenaga Kerja Indonesia* (TKI) or Overseas Contract Workers (OCW). The main destination of OCW was Malaysia, both East and West, followed by the Middle East. Malaysia alone provided employment for around 1.5 million Indonesians at the outset of the crisis, and the Middle East (mainly Saudi Arabia) hosted another half a million. From the mid-1990s, smaller numbers of mainly female household helpers found jobs in Singapore and Hong Kong, and construction workers in Taiwan.

The movement of OCW processed by the Ministry of Manpower increased rapidly during the 1990s, especially following the onset of the economic crisis in 1997 (Hugo 2004). Almost universally, the migrants were unskilled workers from rural villages, both from Java and especially from the poorer regions of Eastern Indonesia, who found jobs in domestic service, construction, and plantation agriculture (the latter mainly in Malaysia). Although many migrants suffered poor working conditions while abroad (and among married females often did so at considerable personal cost to their families), village studies have found that they mostly found work abroad preferable to staying at home. This is despite the fact that remittances were often only sufficient for limited consumption benefits — purchase of some consumer durables and improvement in housing conditions (Breman and Wiradi 2002, pp. 116–28). The impact on rural non-farm work was therefore relatively small for many poorer families.

However, in some locations, international labour migration has also had an important impact on regional development, and hence the creation of non-farm economic activities. A study cited by Hugo (2004) in Kabupaten Flores, East Nusa Tenggara (NTT) Province reported that overseas contract workers from Flores and NTT were agricultural workers before leaving. The majority of OCW worked in Sabah, Malaysia and they remitted significant amounts of money to their families in their hometown and village, periodically. The largest use of remittance was for daily expenses (34 per cent), while housing improvements and debt repayment accounted for 24 per cent and 15 per cent respectively. One interesting point was that there were substantial investments of remittance in schooling (20 per cent). This resulted in a tendency for the children and siblings of migrant workers, who benefited from this investment of remittances, to settle elsewhere in Indonesia. Thus remittances indirectly contributed to brain drain, as the more educated children of migrants sought work where there were more opportunities for people with skills and with higher levels of education. Further, there is some evidence of remittances being invested in productive activities such as transport and small shops. This improvement in local transport and hence local economy contributed to the creation of NFE. The other positive impact is the ease of underemployment problems and pressures on land resources in areas of origin.

5. Policy Implications

What are the policy implications from our findings on rural NFE, and the impact of national and regional policies, both formal and informal, on the job prospects and welfare of rural households? Given a history of repressive policies towards organized labour and worker rights in Indonesia under Soeharto, it is not surprising that a plethora of new regulations have emerged in recent years that seek to protect wage workers, both at the national and district levels. With the reaffirmation of rights to organize, to form trade unions and bargain collectively, organized labour now has a significant role in determining labour outcomes in Indonesia for the first time in thirty years, in the post-Soeharto era.

In the current much more democratic polity, there is a perception that the government was anti-labour under Soeharto: neglecting all labour rights in its efforts to accommodate the interests of employers. This has meant that both central and local government parliaments are now wary of any moves which might be seen to be against the interests of workers. The bureaucracy (most obviously Ministry of Manpower officials in Jakarta and in the regions) has moved quickly to distance itself from the alleged "anti-labour" stance of the previous regime.[7] It was the Ministry of Manpower, for example, rather than trade unions, which took the running on the revised Manpower Protection Act No. 13/2003.[8] Further, the centralized nature of government decision-making in the past (and absence of any significant independent local representation in national and regional politics), has added to pressures on local politicians and officials to be seen to be developing policies which protect the jobs of local residents.[9]

While endorsing major achievements in the area of labour rights since the fall of Soeharto, we have argued implicitly that the emphasis appears to have moved too far in the direction of narrowly defined "pro-labour" policies. The upshot has been an emphasis on labour protection for those already with more stable and higher paying jobs, frequently at the expense of those without jobs. Labour policy *"kebablasan"* (gone too far) would seem to accurately describe what has happened through legislative processes in recent years. Improved worker welfare, and also a greater voice for workers in general, depend on the creation of more jobs and "better" jobs. We have suggested that on this score the previous regime performed better than successive governments in the post-Soeharto era.

The crux of the issue is slower economic growth and deterioration in the investment climate which have negatively affected employment (as various chapters in this volume suggest, especially with regard to infrastructure and local incentives for economic activity). Nevertheless, labour policies have also been important. We have drawn attention to both national and local (some informal) regulations that have tended to discourage job creation. These interact with the economic environment and policies. Thus we saw, for example, that minimum wages have begun to bite partly because economic conditions are unfavourable to enterprise and investment, in addition to greater pressures for compliance with new legislation, especially in larger scale firms. While the impacts have no doubt been greatest in urban areas, they have also flowed through to regional and rural environments, both indirectly (as rural people find it harder to gain modern sector jobs in towns and cities), and directly through the hiring and firing policies of firms operating in regional centres and their environs.

Redressing the balance in favour of those without jobs requires action at both national and regional levels. In recent years, the Directorate of Manpower at the National Planning Agency (Bappenas) has sought to engage stakeholders within and outside the government on policies to restore some balance in labour polices. The emphasis has been on policies to support job creation. At the national level, it would appear necessary for the Ministry of Manpower to work more closely with Bappenas (in cooperation with other key technical ministries, most importantly Industry and Agriculture) in providing better information on labour policy options to stakeholders, politicians, and the general public. Stress would be on the potential conflicts between a narrow pro-labour policy which only, or mainly, benefits the employed (and especially those in more secure jobs), at the expense of those seeking jobs for the first time, or seeking to shift out of agriculture and low-paying informal jobs.

Efforts were made in early 2006 to revise key articles in Law 13/2003 through tripartite negotiations.[10] However, to be successful these efforts will need to be accompanied by serious endeavours to "socialize" the main ideas in collabouration with unions, through media and advocacy campaigns, if they are to be accepted by key political actors, both at the national and provincial and district level. Social support policies for the working poor (such as the cash compensation programme for those most affected by the rise in oil prices) and public works schemes for the poor, can be an important complement to assist those affected by changes in the regulatory environment for labour.

More effort could also be directed towards limiting local government discrimination in employment against outsiders. Anti-discrimination legislation is frequently interpreted as pertaining mainly to equal rights for females or ethnic minorities, rather than inter-regional migrants. At the Central Government level, it seems important to reassert the rights of all Indonesians to work, regardless of their place of residence and birth, and to provide a mechanism whereby discrimination against outsiders can be reviewed on a regular basis (in much the same way as the Government reviews restrictions to trade or new taxes and charges levied at the district and provincial level). The new labour courts, once established, might become an important forum for dealing with complaints from outsiders regarding discrimination in employment. At the same time, special attention could also be given to possible discrimination against locals by firms in their hiring procedures, to ensure a level playing field for all people seeking new jobs.

NOTES

1. This section draws heavily from results of the Rural Investment Climate Assessment for labour as reported in "Revitalizing the Rural Economy: An Assessment of the Rural Investment Climate in Indonesia", World Bank, 2006.

2. The complete report of the field survey is available as a separate report. Peter Rosner, Novi Anggriani, and Gregorious Kelik, "The Impact of Formal and Informal Labor Regulations on Business in Serang District", field survey report, RICA World Bank, Jakarta, 11 December 2005.

3. Of course another probability is that of reverse causation: wage employees in the formal sector dispensed with their landholdings once they had obtained more secure wage employment.

4. These include a one-off activity or temporary job, a specified job to be completed in a maximum of three years, or a job related to the introduction of new products on trial.

5. The estimates of the employment effect due to increases in minimum wage were obtained by comparing the average change in the number of workers employed within firms in Jakarta with the average change within similar firms in Botabek areas (Bogor, Tangerang, and Bekasi).

6. For example, Silvey (2004, pp. 139–43) documents the greater capacity for West Java (Priangan) urban migrants to support their families in nearby villages during and after the crisis, compared with urban workers in Bekasi, whose families resided far away in Central Java.

7. See especially papers on local voice and its political manifestations in Edward Aspinall and Greg Fealy (2003), for a fascinating discussion of local versus national interests in political processes in Indonesia after the crisis.

8. This needs to be viewed in a historical context in which the Ministry of Manpower was increasingly discredited during the period of the second last Soeharto cabinet (1993–98). Pressures for industrial relations reform mounted as the broader opposition to non-democratic institutions gained momentum. The Ministry of Manpower was especially discredited when it was revealed that workers' social insurance funds were used by the Ministry to pay for a hotel in Jakarta to draft a new (now discarded) labour law, on the eve of the crisis.

9. These pressures are not entirely new. Large-scale firms were frequently pressed to give priority to employment of locals in earlier times. In contrast to the Soeharto era, however, employers can no longer override local aspirations willy-nilly by appealing to the security forces or politically powerful forces in Jakarta.

10. Discussions had begun on several key articles, especially the criteria for setting minimum wages (too much oriented towards welfare rather than broader employment considerations), the harsh severance pay regulations (by international standards), and restrictions on the employment of contract workers and over outsourcing and subcontracting activities.

REFERENCES

Alatas, Vivi and Lisa Cameron. "The Impact of Minimum Wages on Employment in a Low Income Country: An Evaluation Using the Difference-In-Difference Approach". World Bank Policy Research Working Paper no. 2985, March 2003.

Alisjahbana, Armida S. and Chris Manning. "Employment, Labour Standards and Flexibility: Getting the Balance Right". Forthcoming.

Aspinall, E. and G. Fealy, eds. *Local Power and Politics: Decentralisation and Democratisation*. Singapore: Institute of Southeast Asian Studies, 2003.

Breman, Jan and Gunawan Wiradi. *Good Times and Bad Times in Rural Java*. Singapore: Institute of Southeast Asian Studies, 2002.

Davis, Junior R. "The Rural Non-Farm Economy, Livelihoods and Their Diversification: Issues and Options". NRI Report no. 2753, 2003.

Effendi, Tadjuddin and Chris Manning. "Rural Development and Non-Farm Employment in Java". In *Development or Deterioration: Work in Rural Asia*, edited by Bruce Koppel, John Hawkins, and William James. Boulder: Lynne Reinner, 1994.

Ellis, F. "The Determinant of Rural Livelihood Diversification in Developing Countries". *Journal of Agricultural Economics* 51, no. 2 (2000*a*): 289–302.

Fafchamps and Minten. "Return to Social Capital Amongst Traders". Markets and Structural Studies Division Discussion Paper no. 23. Washington D.C.: International Food Policy Research Institute, 1998.

Gordon, Ann and Catherine Craig. "Rural Non-Farm Activities and Poverty Alleviation in Sub-Saharan Africa". Policy Series 14. UK: University of Greenwich, Natural Resources Institute, 2001.

Haggblade, Steven. "The Rural Non-Farm Economy: Pathway Out of Poverty or Pathway In?". Paper prepared for the research workshop "The future of small farms". Withersdane Conference Centre, Wye, Kent: UK IFPRI, ODI, Imperial College, 2005.

Hetler, Carol. "The Impact of Circular Migration on a Village Economy". *Bulletin of Indonesian Economic Studies* 25, no. 1 (1989): 53–75.

Hugo, Graeme. "International Labor Migration and Rural Dynamics: A Study of Flores, East Nusa Tenggara". In *The Indonesian Rural Economy: Mobility, Work and Enterprise*, edited by Thomas Leinbach. Singapore: Institute of Southeast Asian Studies, 2004.

Islam, N. "The Non-Farm Sector and Rural Development". Food, Agriculture and Environment Discussion Paper no. 22. Washington D.C.: International Food Policy Research Institute, 1997.

Lanjouw, Jean O. and Peter Lanjouw. "Rural Non-Farm Employment: A Survey". Washington D.C.: The World Bank Office of the Vice President Development Economics, 1995.

Lanjouw, Peter and Abusaleh Shariff. "Rural Non-Farm Employment in India: Access, Income and Poverty Impact". Working Paper Series no. 81. New Delhi: National Council of Applied Economic Research, 2002.

Leinbach, Thomas R., ed. "The Indonesian Rural Economy". In *The Indonesian Rural Economy: Mobility, Work and Enterprise*. Singapore: Institute of Southeast Asian Studies, 2004.

LP3E FE Unpad and GIAT. "Indonesia's Employment Protection Legislation: Swimming Against the Tide?". LP3E FE Unpad and GIAT, 2004.

Malik, Sohail J. *Pakistan Rural Investment Climate Survey: Background and Sample Frame Design*. Project funded by the UK Department for International Development (DFID) for the benefit of developing countries, 2001.

Manning, Chris. "Labour Market Adjustment to Indonesia's Economic Crisis: Context, Trends and Implications". *Bulletin of Indonesian Economic Studies* 36, no. 1 (2000): 105–36.

McCulloch, Neil, Julian Weisbrod, and C. Peter Timmer. "The Pathways out of Rural Poverty in Indonesia". Paper for the Indonesian Poverty Assessment. Jakarta: World Bank, 2006.

Rama, M. "Consequences of Doubling the Minimum Wage: The Case of Indonesia". Policy Research Working Paper 1643. Washington D.C.: World Bank, 1996.

Silvey, Rachel. "Gender, Socio-Spatial Networks, and Rural Non-Farm Work Among Migrants in West Java". In *The Indonesian Rural Economy: Mobility, Work and Enterprise*, edited by Thomas Leinbach. Singapore: Institute of Southeast Asian Studies, 2004.

Smith, D. "The Spatial Dimension of Access to the Rural Non-Farm Economy". Draft Paper. Chatham, UK: Natural Resource Institute, 2000.

Strauss, John et al. *Indonesian Living Standards: Before and After the Financial Crisis.* Singapore: Institute of Southeast Asian Studies, 2004.

Sugiyarto, Guntur, Mayling Oey-Gardiner, and Ninasapti Triaswati. "Improving the Labor Market Condition in Indonesia". Manila: Asian Development Bank, 2005.

Sumarto, Sudarnon, Asep Suryahadi, Yusuf Suharso, and Lant Pritchett. "The Evolution of Poverty During the Crisis in Indonesia, 1996–1999". World Bank Staff Working Paper no. 2435. Washington D.C., 2000.

Tjandraningsih, Indrasari. "Krisis dan Buruh Pabrik: Dampak dan Masalah Jender" (The Crisis and Factory Workers: Some Gender Issues). Jakarta: SMERU, 1999.

The SMERU Research Institute. *Wage and Employment Effect of Minimum Wage Policy in the Indonesian Urban Labor Market.* Jakarta, 2001.

————. "Transitions to Non-Farm Employment and the Growth of Rattan Industry: The Example of Desa Buyut, Cirebon". In *The Indonesian Rural Economy: Mobility, Work and Enterprise*, edited by Thomas Leinbach. Singapore: Institute of Southeast Asian Studies, 2004.

Tjiptoherijanto, Prijono. "Pola mobilitas penduduk Indonesia". Paper presented at Seminar on "West Java Migration", organized by Center for Population and Human Resources Development, Padjadjaran University in cooperation with the West Java Planning Agency in Bandung, Indonesia, 2005.

Wandschneider, Tiago. "Determinants of Access to Rural Non-Farm Employment: Evidence from Africa, South Asia and Transition Economies". NRI Report no. 2758, 2003.

4
The Constraints in Accessing Credit Faced by Rural Non-Farm Enterprises

Andi Ikhwan and Don Edwin Johnston

1. Introduction: The Importance of Credit

International evidence suggests that access to credit is important for firm performance and growth. For example, Vogelgesang's (2001) study on the impact of micro-credit on productivity and growth of borrowers in Bolivia showed that those borrowers with larger numbers of loans and greater average values of loans than in their previous loans had a higher rate of growth than did other borrowers. An analysis of cross-section data on sales revenues showed that borrowers who had previously taken loans experienced greater increases in sales revenues than did others with a given level of assets.

Similar results have been found in Indonesia. For example BRI and the Center for Business and Government, JFK School of Government, Harvard University (2001) showed that the businesses of customers of BRI Units' Rural General Credit (Kredit Umum Pedesaan, KUPEDES) showed better performance over the previous five years than did non-KUPEDES-customer respondents.[1] In all such studies, strict causality — i.e., does credit cause enterprise success, or do successful firms get credit? — is difficult to establish, but it is also somewhat beside the point. There can be no doubt that credit can and does help increase the growth rate of the substantial proportion of firms that are *ready to grow* and also plays a useful role in improving the investment and consumption patterns of households with stable businesses but more limited enterprise growth prospects.

This chapter presents an analysis of the constraints to credit access facing rural non-farm enterprises (RNFEs) in Indonesia and of the extent to which these constraints inhibit enterprise growth. The map for this chapter is as follows:

(i) An Overview of Financial Services Available to RNFEs. This section provides a brief snapshot of the institutions and financial services available to RNFEs in Indonesia.
(ii) Is Financing a Problem? This section discusses the extent of credit constraints for households and small businesses.
(iii) The Nature of Credit Constraints. This section contains a discussion of the factors that constrain non-farm enterprises' access to credit, from the perspective of both borrowers and lenders.
(iv) Policy Recommendations. This section presents recommendations for action, prioritizing interventions that are likely to have the greatest impact on enterprise growth.

2. An Overview of Financial Services Available to RNFEs

2.1. Formal and Informal Sources of Credit

A number of types of financial institutions provide credit to non-farm enterprises in Indonesia. Several studies have shown that both rural and urban micro, small, and medium-scale enterprises use credit from both formal and informal financial institutions (see for example results of the DAI and REDI study of small enterprises in East Java, October 2004, and the SUSI 2003 survey of informal enterprises). These sources of credit for non-farm enterprises are shown in Table 4.1.

2.2. Composition and Relative Importance of Sources of Capital and Credit

BPS data reveals much about the composition and relative importance of the various sources of financing for non-farm enterprises.[2] This data shows that of non-farm enterprises that sought and obtained financing, the four most frequently cited sources for loans (respondents were allowed to indicate more than one source) were:

Table 4.1
Sources of Credit for Non-Farm Enterprises

Informal Loans/Capital:	Friends or family Money lenders Pawn shops
Business-Linked Credit:	Suppliers Buyers
Non-Bank Microfinance:	Cooperatives Microfinance institutions Government & donor programmes
Microfinance-Oriented Banks:	Microfinance arms of commercial banks (conventional and syariah) BPRs – Bank Perkreditan Rakyat or People's Credit Bank (conventional and syariah)
SME Finance:	Commercial Banks (nearly all compete for SME business), provincial venture capital companies (conventional and on syariah principles) Formal non-bank financial institutions (vehicle/ equipment finance, leasing and factoring) true venture capital

- Individuals other than family members (33 per cent);
- Banks (24 per cent);
- Family (20 per cent); and
- Other sources (28 per cent).

As Table 4.2 demonstrates, the relative importance of these different sources of credit varies significantly across different business sectors. Overall, informal sources of finance are more frequently used by informal enterprises than formal sources, but banks remain by far the most common formal source of finance. Furthermore, banks are the most significant single source of finance in the wholesale, retail, restaurant, and accommodation services sector, and the financial institutions, real estate, leasing business, and services sector.

The large amount of financing for business activities deriving from informal sources such as individuals and family suggests that many RNFEs in Indonesia still face substantial constraints in their access to credit. The next section explores the evidence that access to credit really is a constraint for RNFEs.

Table 4.2
Source of Credit for Non-Farm Enterprises, by Business Sector

Economic Sector	Bank	Cooperative	NBFI	Venture Capital	Individual	Family	Others
Smallholder Mining and Quarrying, Non-PLN Electricity, and Construction	18	0	2	1	28	31	30
Manufacturing Industries	17	5	4	0	44	15	32
Wholesale Trade, Retail Trade, Restaurants, and Accommodation Services	34	9	8	1	29	24	20
Transportation and Communication	6	1	2	1	36	12	45
Financial institutions, Real Estate, Leasing, and Services	32	6	5	2	20	30	24
Total	24	6	6	1	33	20	28

Source: SUSI (2003), BPS.

3. How Many Firms are Credit Constrained?

The only nationally representative source of data on micro and small non-farm enterprises is the Integrated Business Survey (*Survei Usaha Terintegrasi*, or "SUSI"), conducted by the Central Statistical Agency (BPS). SUSI (2003) surveyed micro and small non-farm informal enterprises regarding their perceptions of the main problems that they faced. Of the 15.8 million micro and small enterprises in the country, the survey results suggest that more than half currently face business problems of some sort, with a larger proportion of *kabupaten* (town and rural) enterprises (54.6 per cent) than *kota* (located in municipalities) enterprises (41.7 per cent) making this claim.

Of those that said they were facing problems, the most commonly identified major problems were Marketing (with 39 per cent of respondents mentioning this) and Financing (37 per cent). The proportion of respondents claiming to face credit constraints was higher amongst businesses involved in trading, financial services, and manufacturing, than in mining, and transportation (see Figure 4.1). A quarter of informal small enterprises (informal firms with 5–19 employees) cited Finance as their main business problem, a higher percentage than for micro-enterprises (19 per cent). When one includes firms that did not register any problems, almost one-fifth of informal micro and small enterprises mentioned credit as a problem.

More recent data from the RICS suggests that, in the six *kabupaten* surveyed, access to finance was a very significant problem. More than half of

Figure 4.1
Informal Micro and Small Enterprises Facing Credit Problems, by Sector

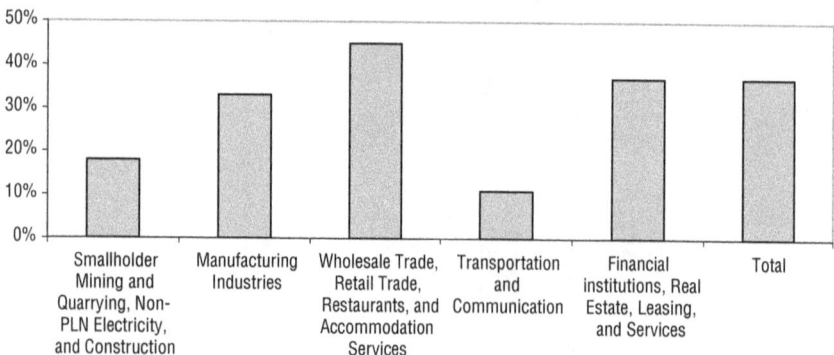

Source: Calculated from SUSI (2003).

the enterprises sampled reported that they faced financial obstacles in continuing to operate their firm or in expanding it (see Table 4.3). Nearly a quarter of the firms listed financial obstacles as the main impediment.

Table 4.3 demonstrates that while more than half of informal firms faced credit problems of some sort, these firms did not all face the *same* financial obstacles. The single most important financial obstacle, the possibility to borrow from a formal financial institution, accounts for just less than half of firms citing financial obstacles as their main business problems. Interest rates and other obstacles together accounted for the remainder.

Second, Table 4.4 shows that micro (12 per cent) and small enterprises (8 per cent) were much more likely than medium and large enterprises (2 per cent) to report obstacles in borrowing from formal financial institutions as their main constraint.

The evidence cited above only show respondents' perceptions of credit problems. However, some borrowers may perceive themselves to be "credit constrained" because a lender will not lend to them whereas in fact the refusal to lend is based on a realistic analysis of its business prospects. Conversely, some businesses will not perceive themselves as being credit constrained simply because they do not wish to borrow, even though they might find it difficult to borrow if they wanted to. Others may be genuinely not credit

Table 4.3
Rural Non-Farm Enterprises Facing Financial Obstacles to
Continued Operation/Growth

Potential Finance-Related Obstacles	Is a Problem (Per cent Firms)	Is the Main Problem (Per cent Firms)	Median Expected Increase in Income if Obstacle Removed (Per cent)*
Possibility to Borrow from Family, Friends or Others	33	3	40
Possibility to Borrow from Formal Financial Institution	46	11	45
Interest Rate	47	5	40
Complicated Bank Loan Procedures	45	2	50
Fear of Not Being Able to Pay Instalments	45	2	40
All Financial Obstacles	52	23	

Note: *Applies to Main Problem.
Source: Calculated from RICS (2006).

Table 4.4
Possibility to Borrow from Formal Financial Institution

Firm Size (Size of Sample)	Firms Viewing Lack of Ability to borrow from FFI as:	
	An Obstacle to Growth	The Main Obstacle to Growth
Micro (2090)	46%	12%
Small (226)	44%	8%
Medium/Large (50)	36%	2%
All Firms (2366)	46%	11%

Source: Calculated from RICS (2006).

constrained because they can borrow from informal sources (such as friends and family) even though they might not be able to obtain funding from formal financial institutions.

Theoretically, defining a credit constraint is straightforward: a credit constraint exists if a firm is not able to access credit on terms reflecting the cost and risk of providing these funds for purposes which will generate sufficient revenues to successfully repay the loan. Unfortunately, in practice, it is extremely difficult to tell whether or not a loan would have been repaid had it been offered. However, one survey which comes closer to the ideal approach is the MASS survey conducted in 2002.

3.1. The MASS Survey: Moving Beyond Perceptions

The 2002 MASS survey makes it possible to go beyond perception-based measures of credit constraints. This survey, in addition to asking about credit constraints, also included an assessment by independent BRI credit officers of whether the interviewee was a viable borrower or not (i.e. whether or not the credit officer would have approved a loan if one had been sought). The survey concluded that approximately two-thirds of households would qualify for credit from a commercial microfinance institution (an institution with requirements similar to those of BRI units), though a large proportion of non-borrowing households were unaware that they met the requirements for a micro-scale loan. Just over a fifth of qualified households (21.6 per cent of total households) were actually borrowing. Moreover, 41 per cent of qualifying non-borrowers (19 per cent of total households) indicated that they would like to borrow, while 53 per cent of non-qualifying households (17 per cent of total households) would like to do so (see Figure 4.2).

Figure 4.2
Potential for Expansion of Micro-Credit

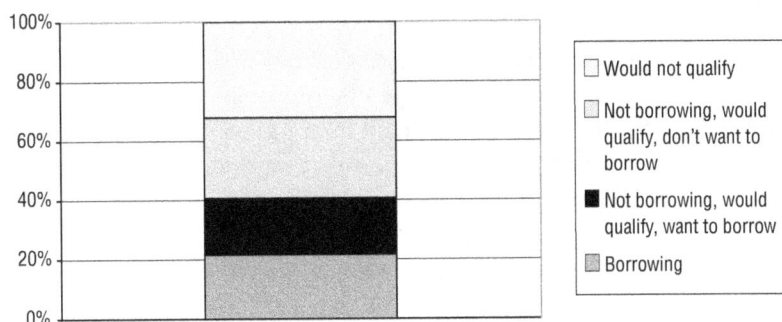

Source: MASS (2002).

This study suggests that: (i) the potential exists to almost double microfinance lending if ways can be found to address the constraints faced by households and firms that would qualify for loans and wish to borrow, but do not currently do so; (ii) the remaining majority of qualifying non-borrowing households are not interested in borrowing given the terms and products currently available — lower rates, increased competition and product innovation are the best options for inducing more of these households to borrow; and (iii) there continues to be a need for outreach-oriented microfinance institutions willing to lend to firms which would not qualify for commercial micro-credit but which are either creditworthy or could be made creditworthy with modest business development inputs. In the MASS survey sample, 54 per cent of non-qualified households would like to borrow if they had the opportunity. Finally, of the qualified non-borrowers, more than one-third appeared to lack information on whether and from where they could successfully obtain a loan.

For SMEs, rather than micro-enterprises, there is less information available. Judging the effective level of access to SME credit is much more difficult given the greater complexity of the application process. The available data suggest a more nuanced picture: the large majority of SMEs have access to and knowledge regarding credit sources for micro-level loans.[3] However, constraints often relate to the size of available loans, rather than access to a loan of any size.

4. The Nature of Credit Constraints

4.1. The Reasons for Not-Borrowing from Formal Financial Institutions

The evidence presented above suggests that systemic barriers to lending remain for many enterprises. For large enterprises and conglomerates, the main systemic hindrances to lending tend to be related to failures in the legal system. For small and medium enterprises that want to borrow much of the systemic problem is caused by more tractable policy issues.

The SUSI survey asks household and small informal enterprises that obtained credit but who did not apply for a loan from a bank, why they did not apply for a loan from a bank. The results in 1999 and 2003 by business sector, are shown in Table 4.5.

Leaving aside the third of respondents who were simply not interested in applying for a loan, Table 4.5 suggests that the principal reasons for not applying for a bank loan were: perceived lack of collateral (31 per cent); ignorance of the procedures for application (16.7 per cent); and the complexity of loan procedures (10.8 per cent). Interestingly, interest rates in 2003 did not represent a major reason for not applying for a bank loan.

More recent evidence from the RICS (2006) also shows that many micro and small firms who say that they need finance do not wish to approach a formal financial institution. Table 4.6 shows that 58 per cent of surveyed firms reported that they needed additional funding, but only 25 per cent of enterprises needing funding were planning to apply to a formal financial institution.

The reasons varied widely (see Figure 4.3), the most common being concerns over ability to repay and associated concerns over high interest rates and fear of debt. This undoubtedly reflects the large increase in interest rates during 2005 resulting in part from the rising oil prices and the reductions in the fuel subsidy which occurred in the months prior to the survey.

However, perceptions of insufficient collateral and complicated procedures again feature strongly among the reasons for not borrowing from a formal financial institution. Interestingly, in the six *kabupaten* surveyed lack of knowledge of the procedures did not appear to be as important a constraint on borrowing, though it was more prominent among micro-scale than small or medium/large firms.

Overall it is clear that there is no single dominant reason why firms do not borrow from formal financial institutions. Risk aversion, interest rates, collateral, complex procedures, and lack of information all matter to greater or lesser degrees depending on the particular enterprise. We therefore explore

Table 4.5
Reasons for Not Applying for Loans from Banks, Informal Non-Farm Enterprises
Receiving Credit from Other Sources

Type of Business	Don't Know Procedure		Complex Procedure		No Collateral		High Interest Rates		Not Interested		Proposal Rejected	
	1999	2003	1999	2003	1999	2003	1999	2003	1999	2003	1999	2003
Smallholder Mining and Quarrying, Non-PLN Electricity, and Construction	20.30	18.00	14.60	16.90	20.70	20.10	8.60	13.00	35.20	31.80	0.60	0.30
Manufacturing Industries	15.30	16.10	11.30	10.00	25.80	29.20	8.50	9.40	38.60	35.00	0.60	0.30
Wholesale Trading, Retail Trading, Restaurants, and Accommodation Services	17.60	16.90	12.50	13.30	27.30	29.10	11.50	10.90	30.30	29.00	0.80	0.80
Transportation & Communication	15.40	17.50	7.70	6.60	32.20	36.90	6.90	4.60	37.40	33.00	0.40	1.50
Financial institutions, Real Estate, Leasing, and other Services	10.50	13.50	10.60	14.90	22.60	27.30	12.50	10.30	43.00	32.50	0.70	1.60
Total	16.40	16.70	11.10	10.80	27.90	31.10	9.90	8.80	34.00	31.60	0.60	0.90

Source: SUSI (1999) and (2003), BPS.

Table 4.6
Enterprises' Willingness to Borrow from a Formal Financial Institution

Firm Size with Size of Sample	Percentage of Firms Needing Additional Funding	Of Firms Needing Additional Funding, Percentage Planning to Apply for a Loan from a FFI	Median Amount Willing Firms would Borrow (Rp)
Micro (1954)	58	24	10,000,000
Small (220)	53	37	50,000,000
Medium/Large (49)	45	42	500,000,000
All Enterprises (2,223)	58	25	10,000,000

Source: Calculated from RICS (2006).

Figure 4.3
Reasons Businesses Choose not to Borrow from Formal Financial Institutions

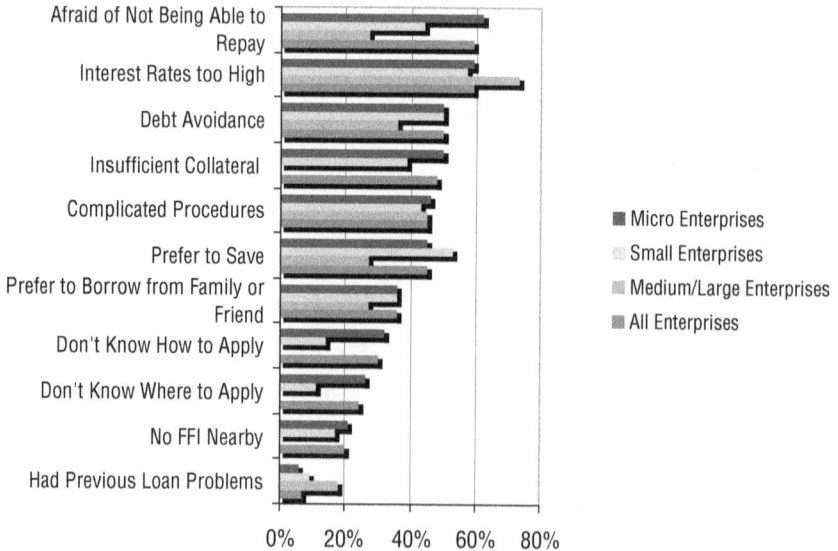

Source: Calculated from RICS (2006).

the constraints facing borrowers, including issues of collateral, business registration, and transaction costs (cost of information, complexity of procedures, and the cost of finance) in more detail below.

5. Constraints Facing Borrowers

5.1. The Issue of Collateral

The surveys conducted by DAI and REDI in East Java (2004); ADB TA 3417-INO in the cities of Medan and Semarang (2001); and ADB TA 3829-INO in four districts/cities in the provinces of Central Java and South Sulawesi (2003), confirm that collateral issues are still an important constraint for non-farm enterprises in obtaining credit from commercial banks. Furthermore, the RICS (2006) shows that, of those enterprises listing collateral as a problem, about half reported inadequate assets for the size of loan desired. For the rural non-farm enterprises surveyed, up to 21 per cent may have problems of inadequate collateral.

There are at least three issues related to collateral in the allocation of credit from commercial banks to non-farm enterprises:

- Non-farm enterprises do not have the types of assets required to apply for loans from commercial banks;
- Non-farm enterprises do have the types of assets required by commercial banks, but to use these assets as collateral entails additional effort and therefore additional costs; and
- Non-farm enterprises have to put up collateral with a value significantly higher than that of the loan that is received.

The results of the CESS and IFC PENSA study (2005), showing the business requirements and the types of collateral required to obtain credit from the micro-banking units of commercial banks and BPRs, are shown in Table 4.7.

The requirement of commercial banks that collateral be provided in the form of fixed assets, such as land and building certificates, was until recently mandated by Bank Indonesia Regulations. Until the end of 2004,[4] commercial banks could not accept movable assets as deductions in determining loan loss reserve when allocating credit to micro, small, and medium-scale enterprises. Consequently, many micro, small, and medium-scale enterprises could not apply for credit from commercial banks (as opposed to the more lenient BPRs) because they could not provide the types of collateral required.

Table 4.7
Business Requirements and Types of Collateral

Item	Mandiri Micro-Banking	Danamon Savings and Loan	BRI Unit
Business Requirement	Have own business for at least two years (proven with SIUP or TDP)	Have own business	Have own business for one year
Type of Collateral	Collateral in form of land certificate, house, car or motorcycle, or time deposit for loan of over Rp 10 million (US$1,053)	Collateral in form of land and building certificate, motorcycle, or car, for loan of over Rp 10 million (US$1,053)	Collateral in form of house and land ownership certificate, provisional ownership deed (girik) or sale deed, certificate that collateral is not in dispute, most recent PBB (property tax) receipt

5.2. Business Registration Issues

According to Bank Indonesia Regulations, applying for credit from commercial banks requires that the prospective loan recipient have legal business status, whether in the form of a Company Registration Certificate or of a special permit, such as a Trading Business Permit or Industry Registration Certificate. To obtain a loan of Rp 50 million or more, the prospective borrower must also have a Taxpayer Number (NPWP).

The ADB TA study 3829-INO, conducted in the cities of Pare-Pare and Sragen, showed that 12.5 per cent and 27 per cent, respectively, of the sample of household, small and medium-scale industries did not apply for loans from commercial banks even though they needed credit because of the issue of legal business status. These data confirm that although this problem is not as serious as the issue of collateral, household, small, and medium-scale industries mentioned legal status as one of the three main problems that usually prevent them from obtaining credit from commercial banks.

The DAI and REDI study (2004) showed that 70 per cent of small business respondents have one or more permits for their businesses' operations. Around 61 per cent of respondents stated that they have a trading business permit (SIUP), and around 58 per cent stated they have a taxpayer number (NPWP). Of the small businesses that have both

SIUP and NPWP, around 66 per cent said that by having SIUP and NPWP, they were free to do business and did not fear intervention by government officials. Only around 21 per cent stated that they would also obtain a further benefit in the form of access to credit from commercial banks. On the other hand, this study also found that by having SIUP and NPWP, their businesses were often subject to inspections by government officials. Around 20 per cent of these businesses stated that they gave bribes to the government officials who conducted these inspections.

Thus, when non-farm enterprises have SIUP and NPWP, they meet the requirements to apply for loans from commercial banks, but they also bear additional costs because they are subject to taxation — and become the object of inspections by government officials. Thus, even though the DAI and REDI study (2004) found that a majority of small (not micro) enterprise respondents said they would like to acquire SIUP and NPWP to ensure the legal status of their businesses, the majority of micro-enterprises prefer not to obtain formal business status.[5]

5.3. Transaction Costs

There are three major types of transaction costs faced by firms in applying for a loan:

- The cost of obtaining the necessary information;
- The complexity and cost of the procedures; and
- The direct cost (fees, etc.) of obtaining the finance.

Evidence from a number of studies suggests that the first two are significant disincentives for firms to apply for credit. For example, the two main reasons why small and medium-scale enterprises in the cities of Medan and Semarang that need credit do not apply for credit from commercial banks are: (i) fear that the company will not meet the requirements set by the banks; and (ii) lack of knowledge regarding the procedures (Ikhwan and Hiemann 2001). Similar reasons were expressed by small businesses in East Java (DAI and REDI 2004).

Non-farm enterprises' relative lack of knowledge about the requirements, procedures and effective strategies for applying for loans from formal financial institutions (especially commercial banks) has several significant effects: (i) lack of knowledge is costly in itself, increasing the time and effort needed to complete the application process; (ii) lack of knowledge contributes to entrepreneurs' feelings that the procedures are too difficult; and (iii) lack of knowledge contributes to firm owners' fears about being unable to meet the requirements set by banks, discouraging applications.

These reasons continue to resonate: as noted above, the RICS 2006 data for six *kabupaten* show that lack of knowledge and/or concerns about the complexity of the process contribute to the decision not to apply for credit from formal financial institutions in more than one-third of cases of firms needing funds but which do not apply to formal institutions (see Figure 4.3). Still, concerns about taking on debt, ability to repay, or high interest rates dominate these procedural problems.

Because it is far more effective to gather information by meeting directly with a financial institution's credit officer, non-farm enterprises located in rural areas must spend much more to obtain information about requirements and procedures, even though it is not certain that their credit applications will be approved. Consequently, the shortage of information about requirements and procedures for applying for loans is closely related to the transaction costs faced by non-farm enterprises (especially those located in rural areas) to obtain such information.

6. Constraints Facing Commercial Banks

6.1. Lack of Information

The various studies examined in the previous section show that only a small number of micro and small enterprises have obtained credit from commercial banks. Although they need credit, micro and small enterprises do not apply for credit from commercial banks. On the other hand, the commercial banks would like to grant loans to micro and small enterprises,[6] but the necessary information is not available. The limited network of branch offices and the limited number of credit officers mean that most commercial banks experience serious constraints in identifying micro and small enterprises that could potentially become borrowers. The lack of adequate information for commercial banks means that they tend to provide credit only to the same sectors or commodities that have obtained financing in the past.

In general, the branch offices of commercial banks are located in urban areas. Thus, they have difficulty in granting loans to micro and small enterprises, which are located mostly in rural areas. The greater the distance between the commercial banks' branch offices and the location of the micro and small enterprises, the higher the transaction costs that the banks must bear. These high transaction costs result not only from the high transportation costs entailed in evaluating the credit requests of micro and small enterprises, but also the costs of monitoring.

The lack of quick and accurate information for commercial banks in channelling credit to micro and small enterprises, especially those located in rural areas, creates a perception of high risk in allocating credit to micro and small enterprises. In allocating credit to micro and small enterprises, the results of several studies show that the character of the business owner is a key factor. In addition, prior experience in obtaining loans from financial institutions greatly helps commercial banks in assessing character as a part of the overall risk assessment of micro and small business operators who take loans from commercial banks.

Bank Indonesia now has a Debtor Information System (DIS) that can provide information to commercial banks about micro, small, and medium-scale enterprises that have obtained loans from commercial banks. Formerly this information only related to borrowers that obtained loans greater than Rp 50 million. In theory, it now covers all sizes of loans.[7] However, in practice the loan records of many micro-enterprises that have obtained loans from commercial banks are not yet included in the current database of DIS, let alone those micro-enterprises and small enterprises that have no experience in obtaining loans from commercial banks. Moreover, the DIS only has information on outstanding loans from commercial banks and, beginning soon, BPRs and finance companies. It therefore lacks broader payment information from utility companies and other sources which could shed light on the potential creditworthiness of non-borrowers. Perhaps most importantly, the DIS currently provides only the status of outstanding loans — it does not yet have information about the repayment record of borrowers

6.2. Land Certification Issues

Theory suggests that greater security of land ownership will increase the collateral value of land which will in turn increase the land owner's access to credit. In Indonesia, an initiative was undertaken in 2003 to improve access for micro and small business operators to credit from commercial banks through a land certification programme, through a memorandum of understanding between the State Ministry of Cooperatives and SMEs and the National Land Agency (BPN) and a joint agreement among the State Ministry of Cooperatives and SMEs, the BPN, and PT Bank BRI. Under the terms of this agreement, it was explicitly stated that only micro and small business operators who are applying for credit or who have already taken loans from BRI units or BRI branches but do not yet have certificates for the land that is to be used, or has been used, as collateral are entitled to take part in the programme. Every micro or small entrepreneur taking part in the programme is granted funds for the certification fee from the State Budget of around Rp 175,000 or US$17.50 (around 10 per cent of the average cost set by BPN),[8] with the remainder of the necessary costs borne by the micro and small entrepreneurs.

Interviews with Bank BRI staff show that although the cooperation agreement states that micro and small business operators who are applying for loans from BRI units or BRI branches can join the land certification programme, in practice the programme has focused only on micro and small business operators who have already taken loans from BRI units and do not have collateral in the form of land certificates. In 2003, out of 3 million borrowers from BRI Units, there were around 900,000 with credit ceilings below Rp 10 million (most of the loans had ceilings of Rp 3 million) who did not have collateral in the form of land certificates. Under BRI's loan provisions, debtors of BRI units with loans of up to Rp 10 million do not need to provide land certificates as collateral. On the other hand, even if their businesses are viable but they cannot provide a land certificate as collateral, micro and small business operators are not eligible to take out loans of over Rp 10 million.

From the start of the programme in 2003 to 2004, 43,200 land certificates were issued to micro and small business operators who were borrowers from BRI units in all provinces in Indonesia, except in regions facing security problems and traditional land right (*ulayat*) issues. For 2005, it was planned that 40,000 micro and small business operators would receive assistance of Rp 250,000, or roughly US$25, for each micro and small business operator who takes part in the land certification programme. Thus, it is predicted that by the end of 2005, around 10 per cent of the debtors of BRI units with credit ceilings of Rp 10 million will have obtained land certificates.

This land certification programme does not automatically mean that BRI units will increase the supply of credit to micro and small business operators whose land has undergone the certification programme. In principle, the value of the credit that is approved is determined mainly by the nature of the borrower's business and its prospects, and not by the certified land that is to be put up as collateral. However, the land certification programme will indirectly have the positive impact of enabling micro and small business operators whose businesses are viable but who previously had only land without certificates to serve as collateral to obtain loans of over Rp 10 million from BRI units.

Ultimately, the approaches described above are at best reactive; they are only capable of assisting borrowers and committed credit applicants. By design, such programmes are unlikely to assist owners of untitled land in making a decision to borrow in the first place; few prospective borrowers would be in a position to learn about the programme prior to applying for a loan.

A far better approach, and one with many non-credit benefits (e.g. increased land value, increased liquidity of land parcels), would be to embark on a programme of automatic, universal land titling. While having formal title to land is not an absolute requirement for borrowing at the micro-level, it certainly helps to facilitate borrowing and ensure greater borrower choice among financial institutions. In most cases (excluding equipment and vehicle loans), formal land title is a requirement for borrowing at the small enterprise level. Ensuring that all landowners have formal title increases the value of their land assets, supports legal ownership rights, and greatly facilitates the use of the land as collateral.

6.3. Difficulties Resolving Credit Problems through the Courts

According to commercial banks, the currently existing judicial system provides a strong disincentive for banks to resolve credit problems through the courts. The length of time, uncertainty, high costs, and lack of transparency are the main problems perceived by commercial banks (Ikhwan and Hiemann July 2001). Although weaknesses in the judicial system is not the main reason for banks' unwillingness to provide credit to micro and small businesses, banks often impose a number of requirements that were not previously required as a protective measure in case of defaults that cannot be remedied through the judicial system. This situation occurs because even though some debtors with problems with commercial banks have been taken to court, there is a serious lack of transparent information about these defaulting borrowers. As a consequence, it often happens that debtors who have been taken to court are still able to obtain loans from other banks.

6.4. Institutional Problems from Internal Policies

Micro and small enterprises that intend to apply for credit from commercial banks lack information on the requirements and procedures for obtaining credit. On the other hand, formal credit sources would like to provide credit but lack information on the prospective borrowers' wishes and their ability to repay. The unavailability of the information needed by credit providers creates the perception that granting credit to micro and small enterprises entails high risk.

Most cases of problems of access, especially among formal financial institutions, are caused in part by institutional problems, and especially the formal financial institutions' internal policies on allocating credit. This situation is indicated in the form of the provisions on minimum value of loans, complicated loan application procedures, and provisions limiting the use of credit to certain purposes. In addition, loan terms, repayment schedules, specified types of collateral, and provision of additional services are often not aligned with the needs of the target groups, and so micro and small businesses that could potentially be borrowers do not apply for loans.

The study by DAI and REDI (2004) in East Java confirmed that there is an information gap between banks and small businesses that are their potential borrowers. Small business operators that do not borrow suffer from a shortage of knowledge and information about the borrowing requirements, the process for loan approvals, and strategies for success in obtaining loans.

7. Conclusion

Many micro and small enterprises need credit for their business operations but do not apply for credit from formal financial institutions, especially commercial banks, either because they lack one of the basic requirements for a loan or because they think they would not qualify. In addition, some micro and small enterprises have experienced credit problems in the past or have applied for credit but have been rejected. This situation occurs because of a number of constraints, both on the side of the micro and small enterprises and on the side of the formal financial institutions, especially commercial banks.

Rather than attempt to resolve all of these constraints directly, it is useful to keep in mind that several could simply be swept away or at least be relieved by competitive pressure. This is particularly true of information problems: a firm credit offer from a competitive micro-lender is by far the best information potential borrowers can receive.

With this in mind, the following recommendations are made for financial-sector reforms:

7.1. Support Pro-Competition Policies and Reinforce Competitive Behaviour at the Micro-Level

Key components of this recommendation include:

(i) **Improved financial institution access to full credit and payment histories for micro and small enterprises:** The key to achieving this lies in the development of an access-promoting credit bureau (full credit and payment histories for a broad set of micro and small enterprises) and standard requirements for the sharing of credit information among financial institutions (usually as part of an application to another institution). Ultimately, BI should implement a transition towards greater private sector involvement in the provision of credit bureau services, with BI acting as a "data wholesaler".

(ii) **Common on-line savings initiative involving BPRs:** Although BPRs have done a good job in microfinance outreach (as a whole, trailing only BRI in terms of outreach to micro-enterprises), these lower-tier banks are at present uncompetitive in mobilizing funds, placing them at a serious disadvantage relative to the microfinance-oriented commercial banks with whom they compete directly for funds. Essentially, a shared approach to IT development and network participation is needed to ensure that BPRs can offer competitive savings products at an affordable cost to themselves.

(iii) **Ending of BPD quasi-monopolies on lending to civil servants:** At present, virtually all BPDs retain a privileged, protected position, serving the basic credit needs of civil servants, typically based on their role as the region's paymaster for civil servants. Unfortunately, this has had several anti-competitive effects beyond the maintenance of high margins with little product innovation in lending to civil servants. With only a few exceptions, most BPDs have been very slow to move out of their sheltered markets into the more competitive but still profitable micro and SME lending segments in their respective provinces, and new micro-banking entrants have been unable to tap this market segment as part of an overall rural service strategy. As banks with mandates to serve their respective provinces, BPDs typically have the second-best rural branch networks in their working areas after BRI.

7.2. Make Commercial Banks (and BPRs) more Transparent

This initiative would require some technical expertise and a willingness to push financial institutions to be more transparent in the way they report micro and SME lending. For example, BRI has established itself as perhaps the world's best micro-enterprise finance institution, currently lending to more than three million micro-borrowers nationwide. However, the current approach to reporting by BRI, most BPDs and other banks that claim to focus on micro/SME lending, makes it difficult to determine how much lending has actually gone to micro/small enterprises versus consumer lending to individuals.

For example, banks are often reluctant to show micro-enterprise lending separate from micro-scale lending to civil servants and employees, and they tend to emphasize cumulative disbursement rather than outstanding loan amounts and number of borrowers. The point here is not to embarrass banks or to add an additional reporting burden. Rather it is to require them to provide a more accurate picture of their current microfinance activities.

In practice, the actual additional information required from banks is fairly modest:

(i)   Greater emphasis on orang (account) figures for reporting micro and SME loans, not just Rupiah values;
(ii) Improved practice in loan reporting, accurately distinguishing between enterprise and consumption lending; and
(iii) Measures aimed at encouraging state-owned banks (including BPDs) to uphold their special commitments to providing financial access by:
   •   requiring that the profit and loss of the banks be disaggregated according to business line — at the very least, this should discourage consistent loss-making in "non-core" activities.
   •   Requiring that these banks formulate strategies for increasing micro and SME lending. Beyond this, it may be worthwhile to work with certain SME lenders to ensure that profitability both drives decision-making and leads to incentive payouts to staff.

7.3. Support for One or More Outreach Initiatives Aimed At Connecting New Micro-Borrowers to the Financial System

The basic job of ensuring basic financial coverage for all Indonesian households is far from complete, and well-designed, large-scale outreach initiatives — efficient, modestly subsidized credit programmes — have the potential to be part of a solution. Despite an overwhelming number of failed credit programmes, Indonesia can also point to some successes in this area. For example, many aspects of the ADB-financed P4K credit programme, implemented over several phases in twelve Indonesian provinces, would be worthy of replication in such an effort — the programme produced good repayment rates among borrowers on a wide scale while scaling down (that is, efficiently reaching even small clusters of borrowers) in rural areas better than virtually any other programme tried in Indonesia.

In order to be a long-term success, though, a new initiative would need to have as its objective the bringing of borrowers into the financial system — an area of conspicuous failure for the P4K despite considerable effort. In the past, credit programmes attempted to accomplish this by institutionalizing the programme — an approach that worked in the case of the BRI units but which has failed in most other instances. A better approach at this point is to provide incentives for commercial micro-lenders to begin lending to borrowers before the programme ends (rather than attempt end-of-project handovers which often do not work). The key here appears to be early involvement of genuinely interested commercial microfinance institutions.

NOTES

1. Performance of KUPEDES borrowers was far superior to non-KUPEDES borrowers who had businesses which were deemed not to be viable by BRI credit officers. The performance of businesses of KUPEDES customers was also slightly better than those of non-KUPEDES customers with viable businesses, although the difference was not statistically significant.

2. The questions posed by BPS in SUSI 2003 cause significant under-reporting of debt from owner-operated enterprises. Nonetheless, the data are still revealing about the composition and relative importance of the various sources of enterprise finance.

3. The definition of this sum depends on the institution. For example, BRI defines "micro-credit" in terms of loans under the value of Rp 25 million. According to Bank Indonesia's definition, the ceiling is up to Rp 50 million.

4. With the issuance of Bank Indonesia Regulation No. 7/2005 concerning the Evaluation of Quality of Assets of Commercial Banks, which has only been in force since January 2005, the types of collateral that can be used as deductions in loan loss reserve now include not only fixed assets, time deposits, savings, and government bonds, but also movable assets and inventory.

5. The reasons for not obtaining formal business status are not only the costs that must be borne after the business becomes formal, but also the complexity and uncertainty of the formalization process.

6. In Indonesia, for example, the experience of the economic crisis meant that commercial banks changed their lending strategy, which had been oriented towards large businesses, shifting to a focus on micro and small enterprises. One indication of the banks' granting of credit to small enterprises is that the banks experienced an increase in their outstanding loans during 2003, and in 2004 this figure exceeded the situation before the economic crisis.

7. With the issuance of Bank Indonesia Regulation No. 7/8/PBI 2005 on the Borrower Information System, the coverage of information that must be reported by commercial banks is the entire loan portfolio.

8. The average fee for the certification process set by BPN is Rp 1,750,000, and the process takes around six months. Procedurally, BPN does not make any exceptions for micro and small business operators who take part in the programme, but it

does provide greater certainty regarding the time required to complete the certificates.

REFERENCES

ADB SME Development TA. "Improving the Regulatory Framework for SMEs: Streamlining Business Formalization Procedures and Facilitating One-Stop-Services". Policy Paper No. 7, 2001–02.

Bankakademie International. "Report on Rural Microfinance". ADB PPTA, 2003.

Badan Pusat Statistik. "Profil Usaha Kecil dan Menengah Tidak Berbadan Hukum Indonesia Tahun 1999". Jakarta, Indonesia: Survei Usaha Terintegrasi, 1999.

―――. "Profil Usaha Kecil dan Menengah Tidak Berbadan Hukum Indonesia Tahun 2003". Jakarta, Indonesia: Survei Usaha Terintegrasi, 2003.

Bank Indonesia Regulation No. 7/2/PBI/2005, on Evaluation of Quality of Assets of Commercial Banks.

Bank Indonesia Regulation No. 7/8/PBI/2005, on Debtor Information System.

Bank Rakyat Indonesia and Center for Business and Government John F. Kennedy School of Government Harvard University. "BRI Micro Banking Services: Development Impact and Future Growth Potential", 2001.

Beck, Thorsten, Ash Demirg̃,Á-Kunt, and Vojislav Maksimovic. "Financing Patterns around the World: Are Small Firms Different?", August 2004.

Center For Economic and Social Studies (CESS) and IFC PENSA. "Commercial Bank Financing and Other Credit Issues for BPRs", July 2005.

Development Alternatives, Inc and Regional Economic Development Institute. "Finance for Small and Medium Enterprise in Indonesia". Final Report prepared for Japan Bank for International Cooperation (JBIC), August 2004.

Field, E. and M. Torero. "Do Property Titles Increase Credit Access Among the Urban Poor?". Evidence from a Nationwide Titling Program, January 2004.

Hans Dieter Seibel. "The Microbanking Division of Bank Rakyat Indonesia: A Flagship of Rural Microfinance in Asia". In *Small Customers, Big Market: Commercial Banks in Microfinance*. ITDG Publishing, 2005.

Hiemann, Wolfram. "Enhancing The Role of Factoring as a Tool for Financing Small and Medium Enterprises in Indonesia". Background Report ADB SME Development TA 3417-INO, November 2001.

Ikhwan, Andi. "Strengthening Venture Capital Company as Source of Mid-Term Finance for SME in Indonesia". (In Indonesian) Background Report ADB SME Development TA 3417-INO, November 2001.

―――. "Penggunaan Movable Asset Sebagai Agunan dalam Penyaluran Kredit Bank Umum Kepada UKM: Pengalaman International". Background Report ADB Strengthening BDS TA 3829-INO, 2003.

Ikhwan, Andi and Wolfram Hiemann. "Strategi Meningkatkan Penyaluran Kredit Kepada Usaha Kecil dan Menengah dengan Prinsip Pasar" (Strategies for

Increasing Allocation of Credit to SMEs through Market Principles). Background Report — ADB SME Development TA 3417-INO, July 2001.

————. "Enhancing The Role of Leasing as a Tool for Financing Small and Medium Enterprises in Indonesia". (In Indonesian) Background Report ADB SME Development TA 3417-INO, November 2001.

Kementerian Koperasi dan UKM, R.I. "Petunjuk Teknis Program Pemberdayaan Pengusaha Mikro dan Kecil Melalui Kegiatan Sertipikasi Hak Atas Tanah", 2004.

Masuko, Louis and Desmond Marufu. "The Determinants of Transactions Cost and Access to Credit by SMEs and the Poor in Zimbabwe". IFLIP Research Paper 03-9, ILO, May 2003.

Vogelgesang, Ulrike. "The Impact of Microfinance Loans and the Clients' Enterprises: Evidence from Caja Los Andes, Bolivia". Mannheim, Germany: University of Mannheim, CDSEM, 68131, 2001.

5

The Constraints Associated with Infrastructure Faced by Non-Farm Enterprises at the Kabupaten Level

John Gibson

1. Introduction

Infrastructural investment is fundamental to economic growth and to the development and structural change of low-income economies. Yet when considering the role that infrastructure can play and the size of investments by developing countries in infrastructure, there are surprisingly few studies of the way in which inadequate infrastructure can constrain enterprises and affect household living standards (Gibson and Rozelle 2003). In part, this lack of evidence reflects the difficulty of drawing causal inferences about the role of infrastructure from the available evidence. Therefore the methodological issues that arise when studying infrastructural constraints are discussed in the next section of this chapter.

Another constraint to understanding the role of infrastructure is a general lack of detailed information on the quality of infrastructure. Many surveys simply provide evidence on access to infrastructure but evidence is accumulating that the poor quality of rural infrastructure may be the more binding constraint on the activities of households and enterprises. Therefore the two main sections of this chapter report new evidence on the effect that infrastructure has on the importance of non-farm enterprises in rural Indonesia. This evidence comes from two surveys: the Indonesia Family Life Survey (IFLS) and the Rural Investment Climate Survey (RICS) carried out as part of the World Bank analysis of the rural investment climate in Indonesia. While most of the evidence comes from cross-sectional snapshots that are subject to certain interpretational difficulties, the two surveys are from different periods (2000 and 2005) so they can help to show whether infrastructural constraints are changing for the better or worse. Moreover, there is a limited analysis of the evidence about how changes in infrastructure can affect the importance of non-farm enterprises in the rural economy.

Although the chapter reports on a number of new analyses of Indonesian data, it does not suggest any new policy solutions for overcoming infrastructural constraints. However the results can at least guide the search for policy solutions because they show that the poor quality of infrastructure is a more major problem than a lack of infrastructure, especially for electricity and roads. Hence any policy solutions have to consider quality issues rather than just the more widely discussed access issues.

2. Literature Review

There is a large international literature on the role of infrastructure in economic growth and development. However, certain characteristics of both infrastructure and the nature of the evidence pose interpretation difficulties when we want to apply that literature to the question of how infrastructural constraints might affect non-farm rural enterprises at the *kabupaten* level. This section discusses the international evidence and the methodological problems that exist in assessing the impact of infrastructure.

Key features of infrastructure are that it has (i) scale economies in production; (ii) consumption externalities (which may be negative in the case of congestion, and positive in the case of networks); and (iii) non-exclusivity (Jimenez 1995). These characteristics make it harder to evaluate the overall contribution of infrastructure to economic growth than would be the case for other productive inputs. For example, network effects introduce a time-dependent element to any evaluation because the productive value of a given stock of infrastructure may grow over time, as more users join the network (or fall, with congestion). The consumption externalities also make it harder to value the aggregate benefit by simply adding up benefits at an individual or firm level, because some of the external benefits and costs are unlikely to be captured.

2.1. Sources of Evidence on the Effects of Infrastructure

Despite these conceptual problems there have been many studies on either the value of infrastructure or the constraints posed by (lack of) infrastructure. However some of these studies of infrastructural investment in rural areas, and especially rural roads, have only considered producer benefits in agriculture rather than for non-farm employment (de Walle 2002). Amongst the more limited set of applicable studies, there are three main sources of information used:

(i) Qualitative enterprise surveys. These surveys typically ask a sample of firms to rank the major impediments to either their current business or to new investment. For example, electricity outages were listed as one of the top four constraints to expansion of small firms in Ghana (Steel and Webster 1991). Although these qualitative surveys are straightforward to field, it can be difficult to translate the evidence into a framework for evaluating infrastructural investments, particularly in the presence of multiple impediments because something that is listed as a priority may in fact have only a marginal impact on productivity.

(ii) Quantitative enterprise surveys. Firm-level censuses and surveys typically have reasonable measures of outputs and also purchased inputs, from which enterprise productivity (and profitability, if more assumptions are made about capital costs) can be calculated. But firm surveys rarely contain adequate infrastructure measures to relate back to the firm's productivity or profitability, especially when the problem is more about the quality of the infrastructure (e.g. interrupted electricity supply) rather than either the payments for it, or its availability.

  Occasionally it is possible to look at evidence of duplication because unreliable public utilities may cause firms to produce their own infrastructure services. For example, in Nigeria, 92 per cent of surveyed firms owned their own electricity generators (Lee and Anas 1992). This sort of duplication can be very costly; in the Nigerian example the cost of the electricity input into the firm's production was very high because each firm had to invest large fixed costs for small volumes of electricity output, and there was no way to move down their marginal cost curve by selling electricity back to the state generator.

(iii) Quantitative household surveys. These surveys typically have information on household access to infrastructure (travelling times to roads and other transport facilities, connections to electricity, water and telecommunications) and household economic activities. Thus, it is possible to relate the choice of farm versus non-farm activities, and sometimes the productivity of the non-farm activities, to the availability of infrastructure.

The evidence from these household surveys in rural areas of various developing countries shows a large effect of infrastructure access on the pattern of rural economic activity. For example, in rural Cambodia, profits from non-farm businesses make up twice the share of income for households in villages with an all-weather road, compared with those with no road access (Gibson 2004).[1] Similar evidence comes from rural El Salvador, where living in a household with an electricity connection raises the predicted probability of someone working in high-productivity, non-farm jobs by over a quarter, compared with the mean probability (Lanjouw 2001).

These household surveys are often clustered by first selecting a community and then selecting households within the community. This makes it possible to consider the relationship between infrastructure and economic activity at the neighbourhood (survey cluster) level as well. For example, in rural Honduras, in neighbourhoods where all households have electricity, the share of income from non-farm sources is 22 percentage points higher than in neighbourhoods where none have access to electricity (Isgut 2004). Within neighbourhoods, those households with electricity are more likely to have members engaged in non-farm self-employment and the income of these self-employed workers is almost 50 per cent higher than for workers in other households.

Although this evidence from household surveys is useful, it is only partial. In addition to the methodological problems discussed below, the other problem with household survey evidence is that the sampling frame rules out enterprises that are not owned at a household level. Thus, the constraints from infrastructure to a considerable part of the non-farm rural economy may be missed and even if a household survey covers the employees in these enterprises it is unlikely to collect information on the infrastructural problems faced by these enterprises.

2.2. Methodological Problems in Assessing the Impact of Infrastructure

Even if appropriate information on infrastructure and rural non-farm enterprises can be obtained, there are at least four methodological problems that plague attempts to infer what the effects of new infrastructural investment will be from the observed correlations between existing infrastructure and economic outcomes:

- Reverse causality from growth to infrastructure rather than from infrastructure to growth;
- Omission of unobserved, productive factors that are correlated with infrastructure;
- Heterogeneity in terms of the varying quality of infrastructure and the varying quality of the non-farm employment that infrastructure may promote; and
- Multiple objectives for infrastructural investments.

Because these factors make it difficult to measure the impact of infrastructure they also make it difficult to see what constraint is posed by either the absence or the insufficiency of infrastructure. For example, if the effect of infrastructure on growth is overstated because of reverse causation then the absence of infrastructure may not be as binding on firms as expected. Similarly, whether limited infrastructure is a constraint may depend on what the objective for the infrastructural investment is — if there are distributional rather than solely efficiency objectives, evidence of attenuated output due to poor infrastructure may not be relevant to the assessment.

2.3. Reverse Causation

Empirical correlations between higher infrastructure spending and higher output do not necessarily reflect the causal effect of infrastructure, and hence they may not reflect the binding effect of a lack of infrastructure. Instead, reverse causation (or simultaneity bias) may be occurring. In a time-series context, reverse causation occurs when income growth increases the demand for infrastructure, rather than infrastructure causing the growth in output. In a cross-sectional context, this reverse causality is reflected in the endogenous placement of infrastructure such as roads in richer areas. Specifically, if richer areas attract investment while poorer areas do not, the correlation between access to infrastructure and income is unlikely to reflect the true causal effects of infrastructure.

Two methods of dealing with the reverse causation problem are to either use panel data, or to use instrumental variables methods (or equivalently simultaneous equations methods). There are very few examples of either approach for developing countries. One panel data study that allows the before and after impacts of infrastructure to be observed is Latif (2002). A baseline household survey was carried out in Bangladesh in 1995–96 just before implementation of a major infrastructure project. A follow-up survey was carried out five years afterwards, to capture the post-investment impact (Latif 2002). The results suggested significant positive impacts of the development of transport networks on income, consumption, and poverty. Ideally, such studies should also have control groups who did not get the project, in case the observed change just reflects general development and macroeconomic conditions (these control groups allow a difference-in-differences estimator to be used).

An instrumental variables approach to studying the effect of road access on household consumption and poverty is used by Gibson and Rozelle (2003). They use the year in which Papua New Guinea's national highway system penetrated into each district as an instrumental variable explaining current rural road density but not consumption (except through its impact on roads).[2] The two key assumptions behind the use of this variable are that (i) districts that have had a national highway for a longer time are likely to have a larger network of feeder roads and shorter travel times for households, and (ii) the year of joining the network is not necessarily correlated with a district's wealth or productivity (independent of its effect on the building of feeder roads). This second assumption is made because the national highway started at the coast and proceeded inland, often needing to go through low productivity areas before it reached higher productivity areas. It is not clear that a similar instrument can be created in other countries where highway development proceeded less linearly.

2.4. Omission of Unobserved Productive Factors

If improvements in infrastructure are systematically located in places where firms were already more likely to succeed (because of some unobserved sources of productivity) the estimated effects of infrastructure will be biased upwards because they will measure the combined effects of the infrastructure and the valuable unobserved factors. Specifically, as Jacoby (2000) notes, rural roads may be more abundant in relatively more productive regions, and so may be correlated with unobserved (to the econometrician) regional productivity. One solution to this problem is to use panel data so that time-invariant unobserved productivity can be controlled for by differencing (e.g. by estimating the relationship between the change in infrastructure and the change in non-farm productivity). Another solution is to include good controls for unobserved productivity by using richer data (e.g. by building a database with area characteristics using Geographic Information Systems).

Another form of bias due to unobservables could come from the adaptation of enterprises to a lack of infrastructure. For example, when discussing the effect of infrastructure on agricultural productivity, Jacoby (2000, p. 714) notes that the problem with studies that regress agricultural productivity or profits on distance from market is that these studies assume a fixed technology (which is not observed) and do not account for potential adaptation of producers to their remoteness from markets. For example, this substitution might include switching from modern to traditional inputs or away from transport intensive crops, both of which would change productivity but not because of infrastructure per se.

A similar problem could affect studies of non-agricultural enterprises. For example, Deichmann, Fay, Koo, and Lall (2000) construct market access indicators to explain the variation in productivity across manufacturing firms in Mexico. Market access was calculated from the size of the potential markets that can be reached from a particular point, given the density and quality of the transportation network. Results suggest that a 10 per cent improvement in market access raises labour productivity by 6 per cent. However, this may not be a causal relationship because producers with poorer market access may find it optimal to use a different technology, which delivers lower productivity but perhaps is more profitable. Unless the technology can be observed and controlled for it is difficult to make the claim that the greater market access causes the higher productivity.

The solution that Jacoby (2000) uses to calculate the productive benefit of rural roads is to look at land prices rather than production and profits. The argument is that land prices should capture the expected value of future profits that result from lower transport costs, without this being conditional on unobserved technology choices. However, applying this method to non-farm rural enterprises would be harder because there is no single asset like land which reflects the capitalized value of future profits. A more diverse set of assets are used by non-farm enterprises.

2.5. Varying Quality of Infrastructure and Non-Farm Rural Employment

Infrastructure can vary widely in quality. This is most apparent for roads, which range from dirt roads to super highways. Consequently, simply measuring the quantity of infrastructure, such as the length of roads or the average travelling time of households to the nearest road, may not be sufficient. In particular, the relationship between infrastructure quantity and economic output may be biased if variation in quality is not taken account of. For example, China expanded the length of its expressway system by 44 per cent per annum since 1988 (from 147 km to 25,130 km) while the length of low quality, mostly rural roads expanded by only 3 per cent per annum over the same period. Yet, while a one yuan investment in low-quality roads raises non-farm rural GDP by five yuan, expressways have no significant effect. There is a similar divergence between the effects of the two types of roads on overall GDP (Fan and Chan-Kang 2005). Thus, there is a need for disaggregation, because the returns to infrastructure investment (and hence the constraint from lack of investment) can vary substantially with the quality of the infrastructure.

In addition, the type of non-farm rural employment that is promoted by infrastructure spending can vary widely. Lanjouw (2001) distinguishes between *safety net* non-farm activities and *mobility* activities. The safety net activities are "last resort" activities with low labour productivity. These are typically chosen by people unable to obtain agricultural work and are tied closely to agricultural fluctuations. In contrast, the mobility activities are more productive and are less exposed to climate and other risks than are agriculturally-related activities. Moreover, at least in El Salvador, where Lanjouw (2001) draws these distinctions, the mobility enterprises have sub-contractor relationships with the larger formal sector.

The distinction between the two types of non-farm activities matters because infrastructural constraints may bind differently on each type of activity. For example, in Honduras, living in a household with an electricity connection has a stronger effect on the probability of participation in mobility activities than in safety net activities (Lanjouw 2001). This distinction also goes to the issue of how "pro-poor" is infrastructure spending. One line of thought is that because the poor typically have lesser access to infrastructure they will benefit the most when new infrastructure reaches them (Gibson and Rozelle 2003). The opposite argument is that the poor are constrained by other factors so that even when infrastructure becomes accessible they are much less well placed to benefit from it. For example, Hughes (2005) reports on a study of rural roads in Indonesia, the Philippines, and Sri Lanka which finds that increased mobility benefits the better off rather than the poor in helping them to seek employment outside their rural community. The very low levels of road travel by the poor in the Indonesian case study (less than 6 trips per month compared with more than 30 trips per month for the well off) was not primarily a function of poor road conditions but rather due to a lack of economic resources to pay for transport services. Thus, rather than being a highly effective means of reducing income inequality, investments like rural road construction may be more like a tide that lifts all boats (Jacoby 2000).

2.6. Multiple Objectives for Infrastructure

Investments in infrastructure may have both growth and poverty reduction objectives. Although these can often go hand-in-hand, there are examples where they do not. In China, investments in roads provide the highest economic returns in the eastern and central regions. However, there is more poverty reduction from a given amount of road investment if it is concentrated in western China (Fan and Chan-Kang 2005). A somewhat similar example comes from the Lao PDR, where an investment in roads between 1997–98 and 2002–03 helped to bring dry weather roads up to a wet weather standard. This improved road access contributed to the poverty reduction that occurred over the period (Warr 2005). However, it is arguable that a greater poverty reduction might have occurred by instead allocating road investment so that those areas with no road access (containing 32 per cent of rural households) got to at least a dry weather standard. This possible trade-off suggests that a clear sense of the objectives is needed when evaluating whether, and how, infrastructure acts as a constraint.

Another example of the multiple objectives for infrastructure concerns the impact on income variability rather than income growth. Specifically, because roads and other transport infrastructure give rural households better access to markets, they are likely to enable them to engage in a wider range of economic activities. This diversification can help not only to raise, but also to stabilize cash incomes. Evidence from Papua New Guinea shows a significant decline in the number of income-earning activities that household members participate in for every one-hour increase in travelling time to the nearest road (Gibson and Rozelle 2003). This evidence persists even with fixed effects for the region, so it is unlikely to reflect unobserved regional productivity and the endogenous placement of roads.

3. Evidence from the Indonesian Family Life Survey

In this section we use data from the Indonesia Family Life Survey (IFLS) to study the associations between various types of infrastructure and the non-farm business activity of rural households. We note at the outset that there are several methodological reasons why this evidence is not ideal for understanding the ways in which infrastructural constraints affect the non-farm rural economy:

(i) the sampling frame of a household survey rules out enterprises that are not owned by households. Although some wage work reported by household members may be in non-household rural enterprises, those workers are not asked (and probably could not answer) questions on the infrastructural problems faced by these non-household enterprises,

(ii) most of the evidence presented is cross-sectional, from the IFLS3 which took place in mid-2000. In addition to being a snapshot that may be prior to some more recent disruptions, such as heavy rains affecting roads, there are two other problems of interpretation which mean that the reported statistical associations cannot necessarily be treated as the causal effects of infrastructure on the pattern of rural economic activity:

- reverse causation, whereby infrastructure is endogenously placed in areas with richer and more diversified rural enterprises, so the causality is from a strong non-farm rural economy to infrastructure, rather than the reverse, and

- omitted factors (e.g. environmental quality, proximity to some productive inputs) that influence both infrastructure and the economic health of rural households and the non-farm rural economy so that the statistical associations between infrastructure and the non-farm rural economy reflect the causal impact of the unobserved factor, rather than of infrastructure.

Despite these interpretation problems it is still worthwhile to have a basic understanding of the cross-sectional associations between infrastructure access and quality, and the pattern of rural non-farm enterprise (NFE). Moreover, at the end of this section a limited analysis is made using the panel element of the IFLS, based on the effect that changes in infrastructure between 1993 and 2000 had on household involvement in NFE activities. This analysis is necessarily limited because even in that time span, only limited changes in infrastructure are recorded in the data (e.g. 36 out of the 311 communities in the survey report that the predominant road type in the village changed to asphalt or cement from something of lower quality). Moreover, the areas that gained improved infrastructure may already have been more economically dynamic. In the absence of some exogenous factors affecting the geographical pattern of infrastructure spending it is still difficult to place a strong causal interpretation upon the statistical evidence even when focusing on changes rather than levels.

There are three measures from the IFLS that are used to indicate the importance of NFE: the share of household total income that comes from the net revenue of non-farm businesses, whether any household member worked in a non-farm business within the previous twelve months, and the total number of non-farm businesses operated by all household members during the previous twelve months. For rural households in the IFLS, the share of total income from NFE is 3.8 per cent (9 per cent amongst those households who participate in NFE), with 41 per cent of households having at least one member involved in the NFE sector and a mean of 0.5 NFE activities per household.[3]

3.1. Relationship Between Road Access and Quality and the Importance of NFE

All three of these measures show significant relationships with indicators for the quality of road infrastructure, even after controlling for overall remoteness of their village (see Table 5.1(a)). Unsurprisingly, the further a village is from the provincial capital, the lower is the share of household income from NFE, and the less likely is anyone in the household to be working in an NFE. But after controlling for this effect of remoteness, two indicators of the quality of road infrastructure are still associated with variations in the household reliance on the NFE. The first indicator is the (log) average speed of travel between the village and the provincial capital (which averages 52 km/hour).[4] The better the quality of roads (relative to the traffic load), the faster the average speed of travel, and according to the regression results the greater the

Table 5.1(a)
Importance of Non-Farm Activity Varies By Road Infrastructure

	Share of household income from non-farm business net revenue	Does any household member work in a non-farm business?	Number of non-farm activities participated in by household members
Log distance to provincial capital	−0.014	−0.020	−0.018
	(4.72)**	(1.74)+	(1.11)
Log (average speed)	0.011	0.053	0.062
	(2.74)**	(3.08)**	(2.69)**
Dirt road (=1, otherwise 0)	−0.016	−0.072	−0.135
	(3.72)**	(4.02)**	(5.71)**
Constant	0.072		0.414
	(5.44)**		(5.47)**
Observations	3,844	3,989	3,989
R-squared	0.01		0.01

Note: Robust t-statistics in parentheses. * significant at 5%; ** significant at 1%; + significant at 10 per cent.
Column (2) is from a probit model, with marginal effects reported.
Source: Author's calculations from IFLS3 data, for rural households.

importance of NFE for households. The final indicator of road quality concerns the predominant type of road within the village: when this is something other than asphalt or cement (denoted "dirt road" in the table) there is a significantly lower likelihood of household members being involved in NFE, and a significantly lower share of total income coming from NFE.

The magnitude of the coefficients on the infrastructure quality variables in Table 5.1(a) is quite large. All else the same, if the predominant road in the village is a dirt road, the share of household income from NFE is 40 per cent below the mean share, and the number of NFE activities goes down by about one-quarter of the mean number.

One problem with interpreting the results in Table 5.1(a) is that the distance and speed measures are based on the provincial capital but this may not be where the NFE markets its output or sources its inputs. Unfortunately IFLS data do not inform us about either the market linkages or the supply chain of the household-level NFE activities. However, to build a more complete picture Table 5.1(b) considers distance from the village of residence to the nearest transport point (which averages three km). This can be considered a more micro-measure of inaccessibility than the distance from the provincial capital.

Table 5.1(b)
Importance of Non-Farm Activity Varies By Road Infrastructure

	Share of household income from non-farm business net revenue	Does any household member work in a non-farm business?	Number of non-farm activities participated in by household members
Distance to nearest transport[a]	−0.001	−0.003	−0.004
	(4.74)**	(3.15)**	(3.27)**
Dirt road (=1, otherwise 0)	−0.017	−0.074	−0.134
	(3.99)**	(4.23)**	(5.83)**
Constant	0.049		0.568
	(14.67)**		(33.28)**
Observations	3,932	4,081	4,081
R-squared	0.01		0.01

Note: Robust t-statistics in parentheses. * significant at 5 per cent; ** significant at 1 per cent; + significant at 10 per cent.
Column (2) is from a probit model, with marginal effects reported.
[a] Nearest bus stop, terminal (for vehicle with four wheels) or pier.
Source: Author's calculations from IFLS3 data, for rural households.

The results in Table 5.1(b) are consistent with those in Table 5.1(a) — the less locally accessible transport facilities are, the lower the share of rural household income from NFE, the lower the likelihood of household members participating in the NFE sector and the fewer NFE activities per household. Moreover, conditional on local accessibility, local road quality also matters: having a predominantly dirt road in the village lowers the share of household income from NFE by about 40 per cent below the mean share. Because a large share of the rural population (37 per cent) live in villages where the predominant type of road in the village is neither sealed nor asphalt, there is considerable scope for an upgrading of local road quality. The patterns shown by the regressions in Table 5.1(a) suggest that this upgrading could do much to boost participation in, and income returns from, NFE activity.

3.2. Relationship Between Rural Electrification and the Importance of NFE

Access to electricity may affect the importance of NFE for rural households through at least two pathways. First, on the supply-side, if a household has electricity it opens up a wider range of activities (e.g. minor construction or assembly tasks requiring electrical equipment, food stalls where refrigeration is required). Second, on the demand side, if other households in the community have electricity it may change the range of activities that a household can become involved in as an input supplier (or sub-contractor). To look at both of these effects, the share of rural household income from NFE is regressed on indicators for household-level and village-level electrification. The regression also controls for the (log) distance from the provincial capital because otherwise the electrification variables may simply be acting as a proxy for overall remoteness.

According to the results in Table 5.2, the demand-side pathway appears to be a more significant way in which electrification affects the share of rural household income coming from NFE. The regression in column (1) uses dummy variables for whether the household utilizes electricity and for whether electricity is available in the village. The village-level dummy variable is not statistically significant, but this may be because only 3 out of the 311 communities in the data do not have electricity available (so there is not much variation in this variable). When another village-level measure, the percentage of households in the village who use electricity, is added to the regression, the household level variable becomes statistically insignificant while village-level electrification is a highly significant influence on the NFE share of income at household level. Specifically, a 10 percentage point increase

Table 5.2
Relationship Between Electricity Supply and Share of Household Total
Income from Net Revenues of Non-Farm Business

	(1)	(2)	(3)	(4)
Log distance to provincial	–0.010	–0.008	–0.008	–0.009
capital	(4.30)**	(3.39)**	(3.34)**	(3.81)**
Household has electricity	0.016	–0.002		
(=1, else 0)	(2.77)**	(0.28)		
Village has electricity	–0.004			
(=1, else 0)	(0.28)			
% of household in village		0.049	0.060	0.040
with electricity		(5.94)**	(7.50)**	(5.44)**
Main source in village			–0.024	
is PLN			(3.05)**	
PLN blackout at least				–0.031
weekly				(4.27)**
PLN blackout less than				–0.016
weekly				(2.31)*
Constant	0.078	0.043	0.055	0.067
	(4.39)**	(3.10)**	(3.69)**	(4.78)**
Observations	3,844	3,844	3,844	3,844
R-squared	0.01	0.01	0.02	0.02

Note: Robust t-statistics in parentheses. * significant at 5 per cent; ** significant at 1 per cent; + significant at 10 per cent.
The omitted category in column (4) is villages where the electricity is never blacked out. Note that questions on the quality of supply are available for other sources, but because of the dominant position of PLN as a supplier, details were just used for this source of supply.
Source: Author's calculations from IFLS3 data, for rural households.

in households in the village using electricity (the mean is 74 per cent) would raise the average income share of NFE by 0.6 percentage points, equivalent to about one-sixth of its mean value.

In addition to information on access to electricity, the IFLS asks about the quality of the electricity supply. Even though PLN was the dominant supplier (listed as the main source in 98 per cent of the villages), it seems to have a constraining effect on the importance of NFE to rural household income. The share of rural income from NFE is 2.4 percentage points lower (about two-thirds of the mean value) if PLN is the main source of electricity supply in the village.

Interruptions to supply also matter. The IFLS asks (at community level) how often there was an electricity blackout in the previous year. Based on this, two dummy variables were created, the first indicates whether there were blackouts either every day or at least once a week (15 per cent of rural households live in villages where this occurs). The second indicates whether there were less frequent blackouts (which affect villages containing 70 per cent of rural households). Relative to the excluded group, who live in villages that never suffer blackouts, the income share from NFE is 3.1 percentage points lower (equivalent to four-fifths of the mean) if there are at least weekly blackouts, and 1.6 percentage points lower (equivalent to four-tenths of the mean) if there are less frequent blackouts.

Table 5.3 reports on a parallel set of analyses to those in Table 5.2, except this time the results are from a probit model of whether anyone in the household is involved in NFE activities. The results are largely the same as for the income shares, with one exception. Even after controlling for the percentage of households in the village who use electricity and the quality of supply, a dummy variable for whether the particular household uses electricity remains statistically significant. According to the coefficient on this dummy variable, the participation rate in NFE goes up by about 11 percentage points (slightly over one-quarter of its mean value) when the household utilizes electricity.

Table 5.3
Relationship Between Electricity Supply and Whether Anyone in the Household Participates in Non-Farm Business

	(1)	(2)	(3)	(4)
Log distance to provincial capital	−0.000 (0.02)	0.007 (0.73)	0.008 (0.79)	0.005 (0.49)
HH has electricity (=1, else 0)	0.162 (6.90)**	0.113 (4.53)**	0.126 (4.93)**	0.109 (4.34)**
Village has electricity (=1, else 0)	0.032 (0.58)			
% of HH in village with electricity		0.177 (4.77)**	0.233 (5.49)**	0.155 (4.09)**
Main source in village is PLN			−0.132 (2.94)**	
PLN blackout at least weekly				−0.078 (2.64)**
PLN blackout less than weekly				−0.025 (1.08)
Observations	3,989	3,989	3,989	3,989

Note: Robust z-statistics in parentheses. * significant at 5 per cent; ** significant at 1 per cent; + significant at 10 per cent.
The estimates are from a probit model for whether anyone in the household participated in non-farm business in the previous 12 months. The coefficients reported are marginal effects. The omitted category in column (4) is villages where the electricity is never blacked out. Note that questions on the quality of supply are available for other sources, but because of the dominant position of PLN as a supplier, details were just used for this source of supply.
Source: Author's calculations from IFLS3 data, for rural households.

Contrasting the results of Tables 5.2 and 5.3, it seems that when a household connects to the electricity network it expands the range of activities that household members can participate in even if this does not show up in higher NFE income shares. But having more of the surrounding households electrified appears to raise the income share coming from NFE, allowing diversification and higher overall income levels. For both participation and income, the quality of supply matters even after controlling for access to electricity.

3.3. Relationship Between Rural Telecommunications and the Importance of NFE

The IFLS data record whether there is a public telephone in the village where the household resides, and the distance and travelling time to this public phone. To see whether this particular type of access to telecommunications matters for the importance of NFE, the regressions reported in Table 5.1(a) were repeated, but adding a dummy variable for villages where there was no public telephone (which is the situation for two-thirds of rural households).

The results in Table 5.4 show that even conditioning on road access and quality, those households living in villages with no public telephone have a lower reliance on NFE. Specifically, the NFE income share is 1.3 percentage points lower (equivalent to one-third of its mean value) and the participation rate in NFE activities is 4.5 percentage points lower (one-tenth of its mean value). The results are qualitatively the same if either the distance or travelling time to the nearest public telephone are used instead of the simple dummy variable reported in Table 5.4. Hence, lack of access to at least one form of telecommunications appears to be associated with a somewhat attenuated NFE sector in rural areas.

3.4. Relationship Between Irrigation and the Importance of NFE

The constraints to NFE activity posed by poor access to and poor quality of rural roads, electricity, and telecommunications are fairly intuitive. But there may also be pathways from other rural infrastructure, such as irrigation, although the pathways are not as obvious. On the one hand, by potentially improving the productivity of agriculture irrigation might be expected to reduce the importance of NFE activities. But richer rural areas that are supported by irrigation investments may also generate a more diversified pattern of economic activity, which could provide scope for an enlarged NFE sector. To see if either of these pathways describe the data the regressions reported in the first two columns of Table 5.4 were repeated, but adding two,

Table 5.4
Importance of Non-Farm Activity Affected by
Access to Telecommunications

	Share of household income from non-farm business net revenue	Does any household member work in a non-farm business?	Number of non-farm activities participated in by household members
Log distance to provincial capital	-0.014	-0.018	-0.013
	(4.55)**	(1.53)	(0.82)
Log (average speed)	0.011	0.051	0.058
	(2.64)**	(3.02)**	(2.56)*
Dirt road (=1, otherwise 0)	-0.015	-0.067	-0.126
	(3.50)**	(3.75)**	(5.37)**
No public phone in village	-0.013	-0.045	-0.088
	(2.55)*	(2.45)*	(3.38)**
Constant	0.078		0.459
	(5.75)**		(5.91)**
Observations	3,844	3,989	3,989
R-squared	0.01		0.01

Note: Robust t-statistics in parentheses. * significant at 5 per cent; ** significant at 1 per cent; + significant at 10 per cent.
Column (2) is from a probit model, with marginal effects reported.
Source: Author's calculations from IFLS3 data, for rural households.

alternate, dummy variables for the presence of irrigation. The first dummy variable is simply the response to the (community-level) question: are there any irrigated rice fields in this village? The second dummy variable indicates whether there is "technical irrigation" in the village, with "semi-technical", "simple", and non-irrigated as the excluded categories. One third of households in the rural IFLS are in villages with technical irrigation, while two-thirds are in villages with some form of irrigation.

The simple dummy variable for whether there are any irrigated rice fields in the village does not appear to be related to either the NFE income share or the participation rate of household members in NFE. In contrast, the presence of a "technical" irrigation system appears to have statistically significant offsetting effects, in lowering the share of rural household income from the NFE sector but raising the participation rate of household members in NFE. Thus, there may be some effects of irrigation investments on the importance of rural NFE but they are less clear-cut than for the other infrastructure investments considered above.

Table 5.5
Importance of Non-Farm Activity and Access to Irrigation

	Share of household income from non-farm business net revenue	Does any household member work in a non-farm business?	Share of household income from non-farm business net revenue	Does any household member work in a non-farm business?
Log distance to Prov capital	-0.013 (4.50)**	-0.018 (1.52)	-0.014 (4.66)**	-0.015 (1.27)
Log (average speed)	0.011 (2.70)**	0.051 (3.03)**	0.012 (2.79)**	0.045 (2.71)**
Dirt road (=1, otherwise 0)	-0.014 (3.51)**	-0.067 (3.74)**	-0.015 (3.53)**	-0.066 (3.66)**
No public phone in village	-0.014 (2.93)**	-0.047 (2.44)*	-0.016 (3.00)**	-0.024 (1.24)
Is there any irrigation?	-0.006 (1.31)	-0.006 (0.35)		
Is there technical irrigation?			-0.012 (2.36)*	0.090 (4.59)**
Constant	0.082 (5.94)**		0.084 (6.04)**	
Observations	3,844	3,989	3,844	3,989
R-squared	0.01		0.02	

Note: Robust t-statistics in parentheses. * significant at 5 per cent; ** significant at 1 per cent; + significant at 10 per cent.
Column (2) is from a probit model, with marginal effects reported.
Source: Author's calculations from IFLS3 data, for rural households.

3.5. Do Improvements in Infrastructure Affect Participation in NFE?

The cross-sectional relationships reported above are subject to various interpretation problems which weaken the inferences that can be drawn from the results for the infrastructure variables. In particular, it may just be that more productive areas (due to environmental and other factors) have both more infrastructure and more NFE activity. Alternatively, NFE activity may drive demand for infrastructure, rather than the reverse.

Because IFLS is a panel survey it is possible to at least partially deal with this problem. If we assume that infrastructure is endogenously placed then the communities with the most favourable attributes should receive infrastructural investment before less well-endowed communities. Hence, information on access to infrastructure for the same community in a previous period can help to control for some of this unmeasured productivity attributes (also known as omitted heterogeneity). Similarly, there are characteristics of households (such as education, attitudes to risk, and entrepreneurship, etc.) which are likely to affect their current participation in NFE activities, irrespective of the infrastructural constraints that they face. So if we regress current NFE participation on previous participation in NFE activities this effectively controls for the other household-level characteristics affecting their choice of economic activities.

Therefore the strategy in this section of the chapter is to run probit analyses of whether any household member worked in a non-farm business within the previous twelve months (that is, for the year 1999, given that the data were collected in mid-2000), conditioning upon the participation of the same household in non-farm businesses in 1993. We also condition on variables measuring infrastructure access for their village in 1993. Note again that the sample is restricted to rural households who stayed in the original IFLS villages, so it cannot tell us about outcomes for households who moved, whether in search of better infrastructure or for other reasons.[5] The key explanatory variables are the *change* in infrastructure availability at the village level between 1993 and 2000. Once we have conditioned on previous household behaviour (did they participate in NFE or not?) and previous infrastructure access, the coefficients on the change in infrastructure should have a stronger causal interpretation for the effects of infrastructure on the importance of NFE than was possible in the cross-sectional analysis. Note also that it would be possible to do this analysis in another way, by relating changes between 1993 and 2000 in the household's NFE participation to changes in village-level infrastructure. But because households can drop out of NFE activities as well as starting them up, the dependent variable would take three values (-1, 0, and 1) and a more complicated analysis would be required (using an ordered logit or ordered probit).[6]

The results in column (1) of Table 5.6 suggest that improvements in village infrastructure, in the form of upgrading from dirt roads to asphalt or cement and connecting to an electricity network, raise the likelihood of households participating in NFE activities, even after conditioning on previous infrastructure and previous household participation. Improvements in village access to electricity and in the predominant type of local road are positively correlated ($p < 0.001$) so the results in columns (2) and (3) separate out the effects of roads and electricity in case multi-collinearity is affecting the coefficients. In both cases the results are largely the same.

Conditional on previous infrastructure and previous household participation in NFE activities, upgrading the local road increases the likelihood of a household being engaged in an NFE by just over 4 percentage points (equivalent to one-tenth of the mean participation rate). Connecting the village to the electricity network raises the likelihood of NFE participation by 13 percentage points, which is an increase equivalent to about one-third of

Table 5.6
Relationship Between Changes in Village Infrastructure and Whether Anyone in the Household Participates in Non-Farm Business

	(1)	*(2)*	*(3)*	*(4)*
Household participated in NFE in 1993?	0.376 (20.28)**	0.380 (20.61)**	0.378 (20.42)**	0.376 (20.07)**
Village had dirt road in 1993	-0.022 (0.98)	-0.039 (1.85)+		
Village road improved since 1993	0.042 (2.04)*	0.046 (2.41)*		
Village had electricity in 1993	0.154 (2.95)**		0.163 (3.23)**	
Village gained electricity since 1993	0.134 (2.47)*		0.130 (2.41)*	
% of household with electricity in 1993				0.190 (5.59)**
Change in % of household with electricity				0.087 (2.17)*
Observations	4,244	4,274	4,244	4,162

Note: Robust z-statistics in parentheses. * significant at 5 per cent; ** significant at 1 per cent; + significant at 10 per cent.
The estimates are from a probit model for whether anyone in the household participated in non-farm business in the previous twelve months. The coefficients reported are marginal effects.
Source: Author's calculations from IFLS3 and IFLS1 data, for rural households.

the mean. The final column in Table 5.6 uses an alternative measure of improvements in electrification — the change in the share of households within the village who use electricity. Once again, the results suggest that improvements in infrastructure are associated with higher participation rates in NFE, even after controlling for previous infrastructure availability.

3.6. Summary

This section of the chapter has used IFLS household survey data to show that lack of access to infrastructure and poor quality of infrastructure both constrain the non-farm economic activities of rural households in Indonesia. Households are less likely to participate in non-farm activities and have a lower income share from them if they are more remote, have lower quality roads, lack access to electricity and telecommunications, and live in areas that suffer from frequent electricity blackouts. Moreover, it appears that improvements in village-level infrastructure between 1993 and 2000 are associated with higher participation rates in non-farm activities.

4. Evidence from the Rural Investment Climate Survey (RICS)

The analysis of IFLS data suggests that both lack of access to infrastructure and poor quality of infrastructure constrain the non-farm enterprises of rural households. In this section, more direct evidence is reported which supports these conclusions. This evidence comes from the Survey of the Rural Investment Climate (RICS) carried out in late 2005 in six selected *kabupaten*. In this survey households who had desired to start a non-farm enterprise were asked about the obstacles that had blocked them, and existing enterprises (which could be household businesses or stand-alone businesses) were asked about the obstacles to the operation and/or growth of their enterprise.

Amongst those households who had once been interested in starting an enterprise, electricity and transportation were obstacles that were seen as a "major problem" by 14 and 21 per cent of respondents respectively.[7] The other three types of infrastructure considered (telecommunications, water, and postal services) were viewed as major problems by no more than 4 per cent of respondents.

The importance of electricity and transportation as obstacles to growth is mirrored in the responses from existing enterprise operators. The cost of transport, road quality and access, and the cost and quality of electricity are the infrastructural obstacles that are listed by the highest percentage of these respondents as major problems for either their enterprise's operation or growth (see Table 5.7). It is notable that with the exception of

Table 5.7
Enterprise's Perceptions of Infrastructural Obstacles
to Operation and Growth

Obstacles to enterprise operation and/or growth	Listed as a "major problem"	Change since 2002		
		Improved	Worsened	Net Change
Electricity	%	%	%	%
Access	6.3	10.3	6.0	4.3
Quality	11.2	6.0	10.9	−5.0
Cost	13.5	3.4	16.4	−13.0
Telecommunications				
Fixed line access	2.9	10.5	1.1	9.3
Fixed line quality	2.2	9.5	0.7	8.8
Fixed line cost	3.1	8.0	1.8	6.2
Cellular access	2.1	12.2	0.8	11.4
Cellular quality	1.9	11.9	0.8	11.1
Cellular cost	4.7	8.5	3.0	5.5
Water				
Access	6.2	6.0	2.7	3.4
Quality	7.2	4.6	4.1	0.5
Cost	5.3	4.4	3.0	1.4
Postal services				
Access	1.2	8.9	0.1	8.8
Quality	1.3	8.9	0.7	8.2
Cost	1.7	8.2	1.6	6.6
Transportation				
Road access	13.9	15.0	6.7	8.3
Road quality	17.6	14.7	10.7	4.0
Cost	19.1	5.5	19.0	−13.4
Traffic	11.7	7.7	7.0	0.7
Facilities to transport goods	11.2	8.3	6.7	1.6

Note: Estimates of the percentage listing the potential obstacle as a major problem come from samples of between 2,140 and 2,206 enterprises, depending on the obstacle, and for the change since 2002 come from samples of between 1,853 and 1,906 enterprises. The estimates are weighted by sampling weights that reflect the inverse probability of selection.
Source: Author's calculations from RICS data.

telecommunications, the quality of the infrastructure is seen as more of a major problem than is access to that particular kind of infrastructure.

Enterprise operators were also asked their opinion about whether there had been an improvement since 2002 in each of the obstacles to operation and growth (that is, a reduction in the importance of the obstacle). More than 10 per cent of respondents felt that the cost and quality of roads and the cost and quality of electricity had become worse obstacles to growth since 2002 (see Table 5.7, column 4). While some enterprises experienced reductions in these obstacles (column 3), these were insufficient to offset those experiencing a worsening situation in terms of the cost and quality of electricity and the cost of transport. For the other types of infrastructure, and especially cellular telecommunications, there has been a net improvement since 2002. Thus according to this evidence both roads and electricity are seen by enterprise operators as major obstacles to their enterprise's operation and growth, and if anything, these problems have got worse rather than better since 2002.

The information on the infrastructural obstacles to the operation and growth of enterprises comes from a section of the RICS questionnaire where there are eleven other groups of obstacles. It is possible that respondents see all of these obstacles as "major problems" which could undermine the interpretation placed on the evidence in Table 5.7. Respondents were therefore asked to prioritize by choosing the *most* important obstacle to their enterprise's operation and growth, from amongst the list of fifty-seven potential obstacles that they had previously been asked about.

Table 5.8 reports the ten obstacles that were listed most frequently as the *most* important obstacle to operation and growth. It also reports the ten that were listed as the *second* most important. Five of the ten most frequently cited obstacles relate to electricity and road infrastructure and in total these five are listed by one-quarter of respondents.[8] For both electricity and roads, quality of the infrastructure is listed more frequently as the major problem than either the cost or the access to that particular type of infrastructure. Road

Table 5.8
Constraints Listed Most Frequently as the Most Important Obstacles to Enterprise Operation and Growth

	Most important obstacle	%	Second most important obstacle	%
1	Market demand	15.7	Interest rates	10.5
2	Accessing formal sector loans	15.4	Accessing formal sector loans	10.0
3	Electricity quality	7.0	Complicated bank procedures	7.0
4	Interest rates	5.9	Transport cost	6.3
5	Access to market (distance/cost)	4.9	Market demand	6.3
6	Electricity cost	4.9	Road quality	6.1
7	Uncertain economic policy	4.5	Electricity quality	5.1
8	Road quality	4.1	Market information	5.0
9	Transport cost	4.0	Access to market (distance/cost)	4.5
10	Road access	4.0	Fear of loan default	4.2

Note: Estimates for the most important obstacle come from the reports by 2,179 enterprises, and for the second most important from 1,878 enterprises. Respondents could choose from 57 different obstacles.
Source: Author's calculations from RICS data.

quality and electricity quality are also amongst the top ten items listed as the second most important constraint to enterprise's operation and/or growth.

In addition to the qualitative data on obstacles to their enterprise's operation and/or growth, respondents in the RICS also supplied quantitative information that enables some similar analyses to those reported above with the IFLS data. Specifically, a series of regressions were carried out to explain the variation in the percentage of rural household income that comes from non-farm enterprises. On average, enterprise income contributes 23 per cent of rural household cash income in the *kabupaten* surveyed by RICS, but with a considerable variation (the standard deviation is 34 per cent). The aim of the regression models is to see whether variations in infrastructure quality can explain some of this variation in the importance of enterprise income to these rural households.

To parallel the analyses reported above with IFLS data, the regressions control for the overall remoteness of the villages that rural households are located in, proxied by the (log) distance to the sub-district centre.[9] Road quality is indicated by two dummy variables, for whether roads within the village are predominantly dirt roads (10 per cent of rural households live in such villages) and whether inter-village road surfaces are predominantly dirt (affecting 3 per cent of rural households). The quality of electricity supply is measured by the proportion of time in the last month that electricity was blacked out, which averaged 2 per cent but in some villages was up to 50 per cent of the time.[10]

The regression results suggest that the share of rural household income coming from non-farm enterprises is approximately 12 percentage points lower when there are mostly dirt roads leading out of the village (see Table 5.9, column 2).[11] In addition, the results show that the greater the proportion of time in the last month that the electricity was blacked out, the lower the share of enterprise income in total rural household income. Specifically, an increase by one standard deviation in the total amount of time that the village was blacked out would reduce the share of enterprise income by two percentage points.

There are a large number of households with no income from non-farm enterprises, and the presence of these zeros in dependent variables is sometimes dealt with by using the Tobit model. The results of this estimator (see Table 5.9, column 3) largely mirror those for the OLS model, once it is noted that infrastructural constraints can have two effects: they may prevent households from participating in non-farm activities and for those households who do participate, they may reduce the intensity of their activity. In the current context, the interest is in the unconditional expected value of the dependent

Table 5.9
Effects of Infrastructure Quality on the Percentage of Rural Household Income Coming From Non-Farm Enterprises

	OLS	Tobit	Range with other covariates	
Log distance to sub-district centre	−0.030	−0.022	−0.030 to	−0.124
	(0.53)	(0.24)	(0.52)	(2.18)*
Mostly dirt roads in the village	−4.560	−4.654	−0.893 to	−4.913
	(1.20)	(0.81)	(0.23)	(1.29)
Mostly dirt roads between villages	−12.495	−17.627	−12.849 to	−15.194
	(2.33)*	(1.95)+	(2.38)*	(2.84)**
Blackout periods (proportion of last month)	−20.809	−32.102	−18.705 to	−20.346
	(1.92)+	(1.69)+	(1.74)+	(1.92)+
Constant	44.611	33.996		
	(40.45)**	(20.72)**		
R-squared	0.012	0.006		

Note: Robust t-statistics in parentheses. * significant at 5 per cent; ** significant at 1 per cent; + significant at 10 per cent.
Full results with other covariates included are reported in Table 5.A1 in the Appendix.
Tobit coefficients need to be multiplied by the proportion of non-limit observations (0.6) to give the unconditional effect of changes in the explanatory variables on the income share from NFE, which is comparable to what the OLS coefficients measure.
Source: Author's calculations from RICS data, for 1,795 rural households.

variable, which takes into account the probability of being above the limit and the expected value conditional upon being above the limit. In this case, the Tobit coefficients should be multiplied by the fraction of non-limit observations (McDonald and Moffitt 1980) and a close approximation to this product is given by the OLS coefficients estimated on the full sample of limit and non-limit observations.[12]

Further confirmation of the robustness of these results is given in the last column of Table 5.9, which summarises the range of coefficient values when other covariates are added to the regression models. The full results with the other covariates are reported in Table 5.A1 in the Appendix. A summary of the results for the additional covariates is as follows: the share of household income coming from non-farm enterprises is greater when households are larger and richer,[13] for households who do not own land, for households where the head is a migrant from outside of the district, and for households where the household head is literate.

The extent of the losses due to electricity blackouts can also be established from the RICS enterprise questionnaire (which covers household and stand alone enterprises). On average, the revenue losses from blackouts amongst all electricity using businesses are equivalent to 1.1 per cent of the annual enterprise sales in 2005. Amongst those businesses that experience a revenue loss, the average loss is equivalent to 3.4 per cent of annual enterprise sales in 2005. In addition, there is the loss from enterprises investing in their own generators which would not be needed if the electricity supply was more reliable.

Another form of obstacle that enterprises face is the amount of time that it takes to get a new electricity connection. According to the RICS data, amongst those businesses that applied to PLN for a new connection in 2005, one-third faced a delay of more than four weeks. This delay is likely to impose substantial costs on the enterprises, although these costs are not captured in the RICS data.

There also appears to be some evidence that the problems caused by blackouts are getting worse, corroborating the perceptual evidence on infrastructural obstacles reported in Table 5.7. Amongst those enterprises that could make comparisons with 2002, 19 per cent reported that the revenue losses due to blackouts were higher in 2005 than in 2002, compared with only 14 per cent reporting them to be lower (and 67 per cent unchanged).

5. Conclusion

In this chapter we have used several indicators of rural infrastructure quality, including the predominant type of roads inside of, and connecting, villages, the average speeds the roads allow, and the frequency and length of electricity blackouts. Results using both IFLS data for the year 2000 and RICS data from 2005 suggest that the lower the quality of infrastructure, the less likely are rural households to be involved in non-farm enterprises and the less important is non-farm enterprise income as a share of rural household income.

These findings are largely mirrored when opinions are obtained from enterprise operators about the obstacles to the operation and growth of their enterprise. Both electricity and road transport appear to be significant obstacles to the operation and growth of enterprises at the *kabupaten* level in Indonesia. Other infrastructure such as telecommunications, water, and postal services are much more minor obstacles. Moreover, many of the problems relate to the quality of the infrastructure rather than the access that households and enterprises have to infrastructure. Hence, any policy solutions should give quality problems at least as much attention as the more widely discussed access issues.

APPENDIX
Table 5.A1
Sensitivity Analysis for Table 5.9

	(1)	(2)	(3)	(4)	(5)	(6)
Log distance to sub-district centre	-0.030 (0.52)	-0.109 (1.97)*	-0.092 (1.50)	-0.099 (1.77)+	-0.117 (2.05)*	-0.124 (2.18)*
Mostly dirt roads in the village	-4.913 (1.29)	-2.352 (0.63)	-2.943 (0.77)	-1.346 (0.35)	-0.893 (0.23)	-1.035 (0.27)
Mostly dirt roads between villages	-12.849 (2.38)*	-13.497 (2.58)*	-14.525 (2.81)**	-15.194 (2.84)**	-14.916 (2.77)**	-15.215 (2.81)**
Blackout periods (proportion of last month)	-19.095 (1.75)+	-19.138 (1.83)+	-18.956 (1.80)+	-20.346 (1.92)+	-18.705 (1.74)+	-18.893 (1.78)+
Household size	1.367 (2.82)**	2.257 (4.73)**	2.103 (3.77)**	2.483 (5.14)**	2.320 (4.74)**	2.508 (5.15)**
Log per capita income				8.137 (7.96)**	7.483 (7.14)**	7.935 (7.15)**
Household owns land		8.087 (7.91)**	6.246 (2.26)*	-8.093 (3.78)**	-6.818 (3.17)**	-6.570 (3.07)**
Area of paddy land owned (hectares)				-0.336 (1.55)	-0.311 (1.41)	-0.325 (1.49)
Age of household year					-0.062 (0.83)	-0.125 (1.58)
Household head is migrant (out of district)					5.418 (2.55)*	5.643 (2.66)**
Household head is illiterate					-6.405 (1.82)+	
Dummy variables for highest education level of household head	No	No	No	No	No	Yes
Constant	38.637 (15.99)**	-30.100 (3.34)**	-14.660 (0.62)	-25.464 (2.79)**	-18.571 (1.88)+	-19.878 (1.97)*
R-squared	0.02	0.07	0.07	0.08	0.08	0.09

Notes: Column (3) is from an instrumental variables estimator, with log per capita consumption as the instrument for log per capita income. The dummy variables for highest education distinguish between nine schooling levels.

Source: Author's calculations from PICS data for 1,705 rural households.

NOTES

1. Across all villages, non-farm profits are 14 per cent of average rural household income, but they are only 9 per cent for those without roads, and 17 per cent for those with all-weather roads.

2. Implicitly, this approach has an equation for infrastructure as a dependent variable as well as an equation with infrastructure as an explanatory variable. A different simultaneous equation set-up is used by Fan, Jitsuchon, and Methakunnavut (2004) who account for the simultaneous effects of infrastructure investment in factor and product markets in rural Thailand. They find that non-agricultural rural employment is strongly correlated with rural roads and electrification but not with rural telephony.

3. The analysis is restricted to those households in the original 311 villages surveyed by the IFLS in 1993. While data are available on households who moved out of those villages, the detailed community-level questions on infrastructure are not available for the non-IFLS villages.

4. This is derived from two questions on the distance to the capital city and the time taken for a one-way trip.

5. This is because the detailed infrastructure variables are only collected in the original IFLS villages and not in the new villages that people may have moved to.

6. It would also be possible to look at changes in the income shares accounted for by NFE but it is an onerous task to construct the total income estimates in the IFLS data, particularly because there were changes in the questionnaire structure between 1993 and 2000.

7. These are weighted proportions. The unweighted estimates are 12 and 18 per cent. In addition to "major problem" respondents were allowed to categorize a potential obstacle as "not a problem", "a minor problem" or "somewhat of a problem".

8. Access to markets (distance and cost) is grouped with Market obstacles in the questionnaire rather than infrastructural ones, but can be considered as a reflection on infrastructural constraints as well.

9. The RICS did not include information on distance to the provincial capital, unlike the IFLS.

10. Calculated from the product of the number of blackouts and the average length of each blackout, relative to the total number of minutes in the month.

11. The regression coefficients come from unweighted regressions which are used for two reasons. First, future versions of these models will consider spatial lags and spatial errors (Anselin 1988) and these methods require a spatial weight to be defined, which cannot be combined with sampling weights. Second, there is considerable debate about the appropriateness of using sampling weights with regressions, unlike the situation for descriptive statistics where weights are almost always appropriate (see Deaton 1997, pp. 67–71 for a summary of the issues).

12. Greene (1981) shows that approximate Tobit coefficients can be obtained by dividing OLS coefficients by the sample proportion of non-limit observations.
13. The effect of household per capita income on the composition of income is likely to be affected by endogeneity, so an instrumental variables estimate was also used (using log per capita consumption as the IV) and results were largely the same.

REFERENCES

Anselin, L. *Spatial Econometrics: Methods and Models*. Dordrecht: Kluwer, 1988.

Deaton, A. *The Analysis of Household Surveys*. Baltimore: Johns Hopkins University Press, 1997.

Deichmann, U., M. Fay, J. Koo, and S. Lall. "Economic Structure, Productivity, and Infrastructure Quality in Southern Mexico". Policy Research Working Paper Series no. 2900. Washington D.C.: World Bank, 2000.

Fan, S. and C. Chan-Kang. "Road Development, Economic Growth, and Poverty Reduction in China". Research Report no. 138. Washington D.C.: International Food Policy Research Institute, 2005.

Fan, S., P. Hazell, and S. Thorat. "Linkages between Government Spending, Growth, and Poverty in Rural India". Research Report no. 110. Washington D.C.: International Food Policy Research Institute, 1999.

Fan, S., S. Jitsuchon, and N. Methakunnavut. "The Importance of Public Investment for Reducing Rural Poverty in Middle-Income Countries: The Case of Thailand". DSGD Discussion Paper no. 7. Washington D.C.: International Food Policy Research Institute, 2004.

Gibson, J. "A Quantitative Analysis of Rural Livelihoods in Cambodia Based on Evidence from the 1999 Cambodia Socio-Economic Survey". Prepared for the Rural Sector Strategy Note. Phnom Penh: World Bank, 2004.

Gibson, J. and S. Rozelle. "Poverty and Access to Roads in Papua New Guinea". *Economic Development and Cultural Change* 52, no. 1 (2003): 159–85.

Greene, W. "On the Asymptotic Bias of the Ordinary Least Squares Estimator of the Tobit Model". *Econometrica* 49, no. 2 (1981): 505–13.

Hughes, P. "The Difficult Problem of Measuring the Village-Level Socio-Economic Benefits of Road Rehabilitation Projects in Rural Asia and Papua New Guinea". Resource Management in Asia-Pacific Working Paper no. 62. Canberra, ACT: Australian National University, 2005.

Isgut, A. "Non-Farm Income and Employment in Rural Honduras: Assessing the Tole of Locational Factors". *Journal of Development Studies* 40, no. 3 (2004): 59–86.

Jacoby, H. "Access to Markets and the Benefits of Rural Roads". *The Economic Journal* 110 (July 2000): 713–37.

Jimenez, E. "Human and Physical Infrastructure: Public Investment and Pricing Policies in Developing Countries". In *Handbook Of Development Economics 3*, edited by J. Behrman and T.N. Srinivasan. Amsterdam: Elseiver, 1995.

Lanjouw, P. "Nonfarm Employment and Poverty in Rural El Salvador". *World Development* 29, no. 3 (2001): 529–47.

Latif, M. "Income, Consumption and Poverty Impact of Infrastructure Development". *Bangladesh Development Studies* 28, no. 3 (2002): 1–35.

Lee, K. and A. Anas. "Impacts of Infrastructure Deficiencies on Nigerian Manufacturing". Infrastructure Department Discussion Paper no. INU 98. Washington D.C.: World Bank, 1992.

McDonald, J. and R. Moffitt. "The Uses of Tobit Analysis". *Review of Economics and Statistics* 62, no. 3 (1980): 318–21.

Steel, W. and L. Webster. "How Small Enterprises in Ghana have Responded to Adjustment". *World Bank Economic Review* 6, no. 3 (1992): 423–38.

van de Walle, D. "Choosing Rural Road Investments to Help Reduce Poverty". *World Development* 30, no. 4 (2002): 575–89.

Warr, P. "Road Development and Poverty Reduction: The Case of Lao PDR". Research Paper no. 64. Manila: Asian Development Bank Institute, 2005.

⑥
Technology/knowledge Transfer and Diffusion in Indonesian Non-Farm Enterprises

Tulus Tambunan and Thee Kian Wie

1. Introduction

Non-farm firms must develop their capacity to enhance their efficiency and competitiveness to ensure their viability and sustained growth. A key element of capacity building is knowledge or technology development, that is the development of a firm's technological and associated managerial and marketing capabilities.[1] This technology development can take place internally (inside the firm) or can be fostered through access to outside sources, including domestic firms, multinational companies (MNCs), technical licensing agreements, imported capital goods and the associated technical advice from the foreign equipment suppliers, technical information and advice from the firm's foreign buyers, universities, and government or private research institutes. Knowledge from outside sources can take various forms. For instance, in the form of technology embodied in imported capital goods or transferred through MNCs, or through the external economies from "knowledge or technical spillovers" from MNCs or modern local firms. Through these spillovers, non-farm firms, including firms in rural areas, can benefit from the "demonstration effects" of the use of modern technologies and management methods used by these MNCs. Since Indonesia, like other developing countries, is a net technology importer, knowledge/technology transfer from the advanced countries, plays a crucial role in developing the country's technological capabilities. Whether technology transfer will have a positive effect on the recipient firms or countries largely depends on the absorptive capacity of the firms/host countries, that is their ability to understand, assimilate, and make effective use of the transferred technology.

The purpose of this chapter is to study the international or cross-border technology transfer to Indonesia and the domestic diffusion of these transferred technologies among Indonesian firms. Based on a review of the international and Indonesian literature, the major channels of international technology transfer from foreign firms to local firms will be analysed and assessed as well as the subsequent domestic diffusion of these imported technologies among domestic non-farm firms. This domestic diffusion of imported technologies is at least as important as the international technology transfer, as the effective and widespread diffusion of the transferred technologies determines whether the technological capabilities (TCs) and associated managerial capabilities of Indonesia's non-farm firms will be enhanced. This is by no means a foregone conclusion because the domestic diffusion of transferred or imported technologies may be hampered by the restrictive conditions imposed by the foreign technology suppliers (licensors) on the Indonesian technology buyer (licensee) on the sale of their technologies or by erroneous policies of the government.

This study deals primarily with three related issues: (i) the international transfer of technology from the advanced countries to Indonesia; (ii) the domestic diffusion of imported technology from one firm to other domestic firms,[2] and (iii) the spillover effects, that is the total effects of technology transfer from multinational companies (MNC)/foreign direct investment (FDI) on a local firm or group of local firms (see Figure 6.1).

2. Current Technological Capabilities of Indonesian Non-Farm Firms

Productivity, either total factor productivity (TFP), or partial productivity (e.g. labour productivity), is often used as a proxy for the technological development of a firm, an industry or a country.[3] One way to measure the current technological capabilities of Indonesian non-farm firms is by comparing their labour productivity with that of foreign firms or MNCs. A study by Takii and Ramstetter (2005) on differentials in average labour productivity

Figure 6.1
**The Spillover Effects of Technology/Knowledge (T/K) Transfer
and Diffusion**

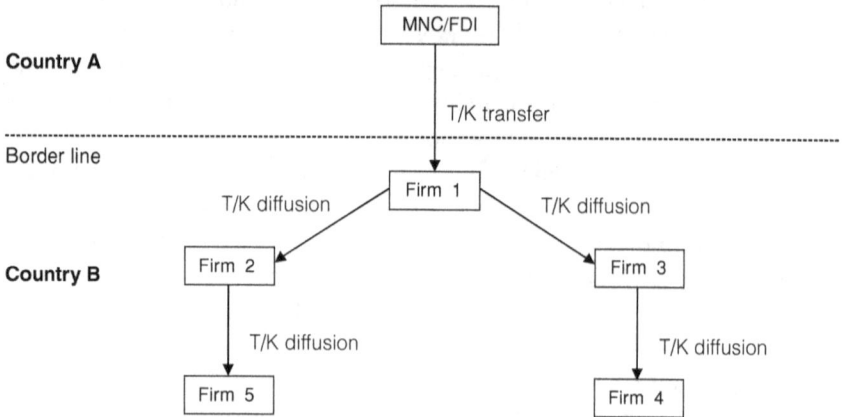

(value added-labour ratio) between MNCs and domestic medium- and large-scale industries in Indonesia found that MNCs were generally more productive than the local firms. The reason for these differentials is that the MNCs have relatively large endowments of firm-specific, generally intangible assets, including technology.

MNCs are thought to restrict or control the access of minority-owned foreign affiliates to these firm-specific assets in order to avoid losing control of them. This in turn implies that minority-owned foreign firms may be less productive than the majority-owned or fully-owned subsidiaries of MNCs. The data in Table 6.1 show that labour productivity differentials are very large in Indonesian manufacturing, not only over time but also across industries. If all manufacturing industries are combined, average labour productivity was 388 per cent to 745 per cent higher in minority-owned MNCs than in local firms (those with no foreign ownership shares); 436 per cent to 594 per cent higher in majority-owned foreign MNCs; and 164 per cent to 542 per cent higher in MNCs with foreign equity shares of 90 per cent or more. Negative differentials, suggesting higher labour productivity in local firms than in MNCs, were extremely rare, if not non-existent.

Although this study has an important shortcoming in that it cannot distinguish between differences in labour productivity resulting from the presence of foreign ownership and those resulting from variation in other factors such as factor intensity and firm size, the labour productivity of firms

Table 6.1
Differences in Labour Productivity between MNCs and Local Firms in Manufacturing Industry
(% period average of value added per worker)

Ownership group	1975–85	1986–91	1992–94	1995–97	1998–99	2000–01
Manufacturing (all industries)						
foreign dominated	542	351	164	375	401	281
foreign majority	594	533	487	501	562	436
foreign minority	388	499	650	745	707	468
Food						
foreign dominated	505	508	322	448	677	347
foreign majority	608	394	445	441	398	382
foreign minority	183	437	226	283	394	289
Textiles						
foreign dominated	230	156	78	108	247	124
foreign majority	442	474	313	366	412	218
foreign minority	168	139	281	266	175	113
Apparel						
foreign dominated	–78	–10	83	108	158	662
foreign majority	–36	58	102	163	368	132
foreign minority	–36	–20	107	134	167	78
Footwear						
foreign dominated	202	80	83	67	138	95
foreign majority	288	245	14	80	172	183
foreign minority	—	26	–2	4	38	50
Chemicals						
foreign dominated	190	270	214	325	381	168
foreign majority	295	271	465	379	524	246
foreign minority	375	392	334	345	555	147

continued on next page

Table 6.1 — *cont'd*

Ownership group	1975–85	1986–91	1992–94	1995–97	1998–99	2000–01
Rubber						
foreign dominated	134	181	106	152	104	178
foreign majority	161	104	80	198	193	193
foreign minority	42	303	99	24	18	−6
Plastics						
foreign dominated	24	1	125	2,076	418	232
foreign majority	1,431	387	185	221	310	234
foreign minority	650	680	145	322	195	167
Metal products						
foreign dominated	1,534	344	148	149	264	121
foreign majority	394	402	728	553	1,166	816
foreign minority	182	280	513	238	487	242
Electric & precision machinery						
foreign dominated	146	−32	119	90	229	109
foreign majority	355	271	83	146	86	41
foreign minority	324	277	135	77	56	44
Transport machinery						
foreign dominated	—	—	−54	450	161	225
foreign majority	228	288	257	281	214	121
foreign minority	139	527	283	360	509	832
Other manufacturing						
foreign dominated	938	410	200	265	454	246
foreign majority	743	786	561	591	487	395
foreign minority	334	410	1,406	1,705	1,294	664

Source: From Table 5 in Takii and Ramstetter (2005).

is used as a proxy for the technological capabilities of Indonesian firms as compared to that of the MNCs.

A study by Sjoholm (1999*a*, *b*) comparing the labour productivity between MNCs and domestic firms in Indonesia found that the labour productivity of the MNCs was much higher than that of the Indonesian firms. Sjoholm attributed these differences to the higher technological capabilities and better-skilled human resources of the MNCs. Both Sjoholm and Takii and Ramstetter only distinguished between the labour productivities of the MNC plants and the domestic plants in the various manufacturing industries, without differentiating between the labour productivities of the large enterprises (LEs) and the SMEs.[4]

A study by Shepherd et al. (1998) presents some industry-of-origin comparative estimates of labour productivity in Indonesian and Australian manufacturing industries. This study made binary comparisons for the benchmark year 1987, and extrapolated the 1987 benchmark backward and forward using national time series to derive comparisons for the period 1975–90. Expressed in purchasing power parities (PPPs), the study found that in 1987 Indonesian manufacturing labour productivity was on average only 16 per cent of that in Australia. However, during the period 1975 to 1990 Indonesia's average manufacturing labour productivity was catching up. Unfortunately, this study did not reveal whether the growth in Indonesian manufacturing labour productivity was a result of the transfer and diffusion of technology either through the technical spillovers from MNCs or from the technological efforts of the local firms themselves.

Data from the Department of Industry (MoI) and BPS indicate the differences in technological capability by size of firms at the national level. The data in Table 6.2 show that on average, the value added-labour ratio increases by size of enterprise, suggesting that in larger enterprises the level of technology is higher than in the smaller ones. This finding is not surprising because micro or cottage enterprises (MIEs) in Indonesia (as in most developing countries) are traditional enterprises with little, if any, mechanization. They also lack the necessary means to increase their productivity and efficiency, such as skilled workers, capital to buy new machines and modern tools, information on new machines, and know-how to improve their methods of production.[5] By contrast, large enterprises are usually highly mechanized/computerized, their production processes much better managed and organized, and they generally employ highly skilled workers. This is not only a problem in Indonesia as the labour productivity gap between small and medium enterprises (SMEs) and LEs is very large in developing countries, because LEs have more and better assets, including technology and know-how.[6]

Tulus Tambunan and Thee Kian Wie

Table 6.2
Differences in Labour Productivity in Indonesian Manufacturing Industry by Size of Enterprise and Sub-Sector, 2000
(average of value added per worker; in thousand Rupiah)

ISIC		MIEs	SEs	MEs	LEs
31	Food, beverages & tobacco	2,339	2,539	25,806	67,309
32	Textiles, garments, leather & footwear	1,746	4,855	24,271	27,237
33	Wood & wood products	2,103	6,743	12,403	30,236
34	Paper, printing & publications	3,981	5,723	18,953	103,938
35	Chemicals (including fertilizers) & rubber products	1,782	7,812	50,849	68,968
36	Cement & non-metallic mineral products	3,346	3,071	8,849	63,327
37	Basic iron & steel products	3,374	7,011	395,344	142,243
38	Transport means, machinery & its tools	5,492	5,402	45,127	130,589
39	Other manufacturing	4,973	6,097	12,701	22,946

Note: MoI defines SEs as business establishments having assets (excluding land and building) of maximum Rp 200 million and revenues per year of maximum Rp 1 billion. The Ministry does not define explicitly micro-enterprises. In this table, the Ministry adopts the definition of Biro Pusat Statistik (BPS) that is micro: 1–4 workers; SEs: 5–19 workers; MEs: 20–99 workers; and LEs: 100 or more workers.
Source: MoI (database).

BPS data on MIEs and SEs in manufacturing industry show that labour productivity increases with the size of a plant. First, the average value added-labour ratio in the MIEs and SEs combined is lower than that in the medium and large enterprises combined. The labour productivity in MIEs and SEs is so low that although the total number of their establishments and their workers are much larger than those in MLEs, their share in total output (gross value added) in manufacturing industry is much smaller than that of the MLEs (see Table 6.3). Second, the average labour productivity in MIEs is lower than that in SEs. The gap in productivity varies not only over time, but also across industries (see Table 6.2).

If labour productivity can be treated as a proxy of technological capability, then the evidence shown above suggests that in some industries, the smallest and the most traditional units of production, namely the MIEs, are able to improve their technological capability. This does not really come as a surprise, since many studies including from Sandee (1994; 1995; 1996) and Sandee et al. (1994; 2000; 2002) show that MIEs are sometimes in a better position to adopt innovations in products and in the production process.[7]

Table 6.3
Productivity (P) and Output Share (Q) in Manufacturing by Size, 1999–2003

Size of firm	1999		2000		2001		2002		2003	
	P	Q	P	Q	P	Q	P	Q	P	Q
MLEs	115.28	90.52	143.99	91.65	167.70	91.50	166.31	89.94	196.26	90.68
SEs & MIEs	8.35	9.48	9.11	8.35	10.98	8.50	12.36	10.06	13.55	9.32

Note: P in Rp million and Q in per cent.
Source: BPS (*Profil Industri Kecil dan Kerajinan Rumah Tangga*), various issues.

Table 6.4
Relative Position of Indonesia with Respect to Indicators of the Technological Capabilities of Local Firms in the Global Competitiveness Report 2004–2005

Indicator	Rank (total 104 countries)
Firm-level technology absorption	85
Capacity for innovation	28
Production process sophistication	45

Source: WEF (2004).

No data is available on the productivity of the MIEs and SMEs in the rural and urban areas. Since the majority of MIEs and SMEs are found in rural areas, while the large companies, including MNCs, are located in or near big cities like Jakarta and Surabaya, it can be assumed that the productivity of most MIEs and SEs are low. This assumption is based on the fact that in rural areas, especially in the provinces outside Java, the physical infrastructure is not yet well developed, transport facilities are bad, access to information and the capital market is limited, if not non-existent, and good facilities for education not widely available and highly skilled workers are scarce.

The annual Global Competitiveness Report of the World Economic Forum (WEF) also provides information about the technological capabilities of Indonesian firms and firms in other countries. Based on the Global Competitiveness Report 2004–05, Table 6.4 presents three indicators of the technological capabilities of Indonesia's domestic firms. The first indicator on firm-level technology absorption indicating the technology absorptive capacity of Indonesia's firms shows that Indonesia ranks very low, since in general domestic firms in Indonesia are very weak in absorbing new technologies. The second indicator is innovative capacity which indicates whether a company obtains its technology exclusively from licensing or imitating foreign companies or by conducting formal R & D and developing their own product and process technologies. On this indicator, the position of Indonesia is much lower than the advanced industrial countries, since most Indonesian companies are dependent on licensing for their technology development. The third indicator, production process sophistication, indicates the type of production processes used, that is whether labour-intensive production processes or obsolete process technologies are used rather than the world's best and most efficient process technologies. On this indicator, Indonesia is ranked in forty-fifth place, since most local firms in Indonesia adopt relatively old technologies due to their weakness in absorptive capacity.

3. Channels of Technology Transfer and Diffusion: A Review of the Literature

3.1. Channels of International Transfer of Technology to Developing Countries

There are several channels or modes of international technology transfer open to developing countries, including Indonesia (World Bank 1996, Kim 1999, and Thee 2005). They include:

(i) *Formal channels of technology transfer*

These channels involve formal arms-length transactions between the buyer and seller of a specific technology which are mediated by the market. These include: (a) foreign direct investment (FDI); (b) technical licensing agreements between a foreign firm (licensor) and a local firm (licensee); (c) imports of capital goods; (d) education and training in the advanced countries; (e) turnkey plants and project contracts; and (f) technical consultancies by foreign companies/consultancy firms.

(ii) *Informal channels of technology transfer*

Through these channels, foreign technology is transferred to local buyers without mediation by the market. In such cases the technology transfer takes place without formal agreements and payments (Kim 1999*a*, p. 126; Thee 2005). These informal channels include: (a) copying or reverse engineering; and (b) participation in world trade.

International technology transfer can also take place in the public sector through the technical assistance programmes of individual donor countries or multilateral aid agencies to state-owned enterprises or government research institutes. However, in most developing countries, including Indonesia, technology transfer in the public sector is much less important than in the private sector.

Thus far the most important channels of international technology transfer to Indonesia have been (Thee 2005): (1) foreign direct investment; (2) technical licensing agreements; (3) imports of intermediate and capital goods; and (4) participation in world trade.

(iii) *Foreign direct investment (FDI)*

Studies on the impact of foreign direct investment (FDI) on international technology transfer have usually adopted one of two main approaches, namely an econometric approach which is used by quantitative economists, and a more traditional, micro approach which is largely qualitative and based on in-depth interviews at the firm-level (Hill and Athukorala 1998, p. 42). The first approach uses a large secondary data set in which foreign and domestic firms are separately identified. These studies focus on productivity (either total factor or labour productivity) trends among the two groups of firms and across industries to find out whether the presence of foreign firms has affected the productivity levels and growth rates of the domestic firms. These studies are mainly concerned with the issue of whether or not technologies have been transferred, rather than with the transmission mechanism, that is how these technologies have been transferred. These studies are unable to estimate the relative importance of FDI among other factors accounting for the productivity growth in the domestic firms. However, they do provide presumptive evidence of causation (Hill and Athukorala 1998, p. 42).

The results of the econometric studies on technology transfer show a great variance across countries and industries, which indicate that technology spillovers do not occur automatically. Some authors hypothesize and sometimes demonstrate empirically that spillovers are positively associated with the level of competition (which pushes firms to adopt improved technologies) and negatively associated with the productivity gap between foreign and domestic firms (assuming that a very large gap makes it difficult for the local firms to absorb the advanced technologies from the foreign-invested enterprises (Hill and Athukorala 1998, p. 42).

An econometric study by Fredrik Sjoholm on technology transfer and spillovers from foreign-invested establishments on domestic establishments in a number of Indonesia's manufacturing industries found that the foreign-controlled establishments in these industries had higher total factor productivities (TFPs) than the establishments of domestic firms. This empirical evidence indicated that the transnational corporations (TNCs) were able to transfer more advanced technologies to their Indonesian affiliates. The study also found that the structure of ownership, whether fully-owned subsidiary, joint venture with foreign majority ownership or joint venture with foreign minority ownership, had no effect on their TFP levels (Sjoholm 1999, p. 611). In these latter joint ventures, high productivities could be maintained because most foreign companies were generally able to retain management control over these joint ventures, even if they had divested their shares to minority ownership.

The technologies used by the foreign-controlled establishments also appeared to have benefited domestic establishments through favourable technological spillovers, as domestic establishments in industries with relatively high levels of FDI were found to have comparable high levels of factor productivity. To the extent that strong presence of foreign-invested establishments in some manufacturing industries is associated with higher factor productivities of the domestic establishments in these industries, Sjoholm's findings indicate that FDI is beneficial for Indonesia's manufacturing sector because of the favourable technological spillovers from these foreign-controlled establishments (Sjoholm 1998, p. 611). These favourable technological spillovers indicate that the domestic diffusion of the transferred technologies took place in these industries by, amongst others, labour turnover from the foreign-controlled to domestic establishments and the technical assistance by a foreign assembly firm to local supplier firms (Sjoholm 1999, p. 589).

An econometric study by Sadayuki Takii on productivity spillovers from foreign-controlled establishments in Indonesia's manufacturing industries came up with slightly different conclusions than Sjoholm's study. Takii found that positive spillovers were smaller in industry-year combinations in which the foreign equity share in foreign-controlled plants was relatively high. This result could be caused by the fact that foreign-controlled plants in which the foreign partner held majority equity ownership were able to control or limit the diffusion of their firm-specific assets better than other foreign-controlled plants and that, as a result, the magnitude of spillovers from these plants was smaller (Takii 2001, p. 19).

Takii's study also found that spillovers tended to be relatively large in industries where the technological gaps between foreign-controlled and locally-owned firms were relatively small in the initial year. This result suggests that technological levels in locally-owned firms were not high enough in some industries to facilitate large technological spillovers from foreign-controlled firms. These results indicate that encouraging more FDI by TNCs does not necessarily lead to more favourable spillovers, especially in technologically backward industries (Takii 2001, p. 20).

The second, more qualitative approach usually involves case studies of firms in which the assessment of the impact of FDI on technology transfer in the recipient firms is based on case studies of individual firms, the information on which is obtained from questionnaire surveys and in-depth interviews with the managers of these firms. One advantage of this approach is that it can give a greater understanding and insight into the ways and mechanisms in which technologies are transferred to the local employees of foreign-controlled firms or diffused to local firms. The disadvantage of such an approach is that its findings are merely indicative rather than explanatory. Moreover, because these case studies were based on interviews with the managers of firms which were generally not randomly selected, the findings of these studies cannot be generalized.

The evidence on FDI as a channel for technology transfer is mixed. The literature on productivity spillovers from FDI has generally found a positive effect on mid-stream local firms (i.e. the supplier firms to the multinationals), and a mixed or negative effect on the productivity of other local firms in the same sector. There are several factors that determine the maximum technology transfer from FDI to local firms. The most important ones are the technology prevailing in the industry where MNCs operate and the absorptive capacity of local firms or host countries in general. These are in turn determined by learning and the R & D capabilities of local firms, the number and quality of local managers, technicians and workers, infrastructure, policies and the institutional environment, and other factors. All these factors appear to be firm-industry or host economy-specific in nature.

Based on his studies on the experiences of the East Asian countries, including Japan, South Korea and Taiwan, in technological development, Yusuf (2003) came up with the same conclusion:

> However, diffusion of technology through FDI is not automatic. An important mediating factor is the local supply of skills and R&D capability… This supply influences the volume of FDI, the sectors to which it flows, and the assimilation of technology by domestic industry. Without investment in basic skills and the constant upgrading of skills, host countries cannot hope to assimilate the technologies brought by FDI. Furthermore, both the absorption of technology and the development of new technologies in collaboration with foreign firms rest on the scale of domestic R&D and on the degree to which it moves domestic firms closer to the technology frontier (p. 153).

Hence, without adequate investment in basic skills and constant upgrading of skills and in physical infrastructure, and a conducive business environment, non-farm firms, particularly the MIEs and SMEs in the rural areas (*kabupaten*), have not much chance to assimilate and master the technologies transferred by foreign-invested enterprises. Unfortunately, in the rural areas, particularly in those areas far from big cities like Jakarta, Bandung, Semarang, Surabaya, Makassar and Medan, infrastructure is underdeveloped and good educational facilities, including technical training institutes, are lacking.

There are only a few case studies available on the development of technological capabilities and associated managerial and marketing abilities of Indonesian firms through FDI. These studies include Thee (1990*a*, 1991), Hill (1988), Thee and Pangestu (1998), and Sato (1998). Thee (1990*a*) found that while MNCs are important for Indonesia's technology development, the technological efforts of Indonesian firms that have joint ventures with MNCs are less than those of the national companies without foreign equity participation.

In their study, Thee and Pangestu (1998) attempted to assess the technological capabilities of export-oriented Indonesian textile, garment, and electronics firms. Their study found that to raise their technological capabilities, the Indonesian textile and garment firms had established strategic alliances with their foreign (Japanese) counterparts. This way has been the most important channel of technology transfer for these firms. However, the technology transfer was mainly limited to the basic production or operational capabilities, that is the capabilities to operate a plant efficiently. With respect to the domestic electronics firms, business linkages with foreign companies were very important for technology transfer, especially for the consumer electronics and electronic components firms.

In her study, Sato (1998) assessed the transfer of Japanese management technology, that is "all the knowledge to manage production and supply activities in various aspects", to the domestic firms. This involved mainly quality control (QC) and total quality control (TQC) from Japanese MNCs to the domestic firms. Based on her case study of the big Astra International business group, Sato found concrete evidence of the transfer of Japanese management technology to the Astra firms, in particular in the quality control (QC) and total quality control (TQC) methods.

(iv) *Technical licensing agreements*
A significant "unpackaged" (non-equity) channel of technology transfer from advanced country firms to Indonesian firms has been technical licensing agreements (TLAs). During the import-substitution period of the 1970s and early 1980s several foreign firms signed technical licensing agreements with Indonesian firms when they could not export their products to Indonesia because of its high import barriers (Thee 1990*a*, p. 205). In view of the concerns of the foreign firms that the terms of the licensing agreements would not be faithfully observed by the Indonesian licensees because of Indonesia's weak protection of intellectual property rights, many foreign firms preferred to choose large and bona fide local firms with a good reputation as their licensees rather than with SMEs unknown to them (Thee 1990*a*, pp. 205, 209).

Although no quantitative data is available on the number of these TLAs, circumstantial evidence indicates that these TLAs often involve the transfer of older and mature technologies that do not offer the recipient country a long-term competitive advantage in the global market (Marks 1999, p. 6). However, for a late-industrialising economy like Indonesia, acquiring and mastering these mature technologies first is an important step to develop and master the important basic industrial technological capabilities (ITCs), namely the production, investment, and adaptive capabilities (Thee 2005, p. 231).

The TLAs, however, often contain restrictive conditions for their licensees, including clauses obliging the licensee to purchase materials, components or capital equipment from the licensor, often at excessive prices, limitations of sales to the domestic market, and grant-back provisions, giving the licensor all rights to technological improvements made by the licensee (Frank 1980; Thee 1990*a*).

(v) *Imports of intermediate and capital goods*
Capital goods, specifically capital equipment and machinery, embody technological know-how. Capital goods imports are therefore embodied technology flows entering a country. They introduce into the production processes new machinery, other capital equipment and components that incorporate technologies which do not necessarily incorporate high or frontier technologies, but are nevertheless new to the recipient firm (Soesastro 1998, p. 304). In fact, imports of capital goods provide another way of acquiring the means of production without the transactional costs involved in FDI or TLAs (Dahlman, Ross-Larson, and Westphal 1987, p. 768).

In view of Indonesia's relatively backward capital goods industries, imports of intermediate and capital goods are an important channel of technology transfer to Indonesia. A study by Jacob and Meister (2005) which assessed the contribution of foreign technologies to Indonesia's manufacturing sector found that intermediate and capital goods imports had made a significant contribution to the performance of this sector. This contribution was particularly significant during the period after the significant liberalization of the trade and foreign investment regimes (1988–96).

Imported capital goods can be a cheap way to develop local technological capabilities (TCs) if they can be used as models for reverse engineering to produce the capital goods locally, like the dynamic Korean small firms did to develop their operational capabilities by producing imitative goods through reverse engineering (Dahlman et al. 1987, p. 304; Kim 1997, p. 38). Indonesian firms, however, have in general not engaged in reverse engineering on a large scale (Thee 2005, p. 221), although some firms, such as the Jarum business group used reverse engineering to make its own capital equipment and components.

Capital goods imports also contain a significant disembodied element, because the foreign suppliers of these capital goods, specifically machinery, often send technical experts to Indonesian firms to train the workers of these firms how to operate, maintain and repair the imported machinery. This training is crucial as the mere imports of capital goods do not automatically lead to an enhancement of local technological capabilities if local employees do not know how to operate, maintain or repair the imported machinery (Thee 2005).

This fact has been confirmed by a study on technological development in Indonesia's textile industry by van der Kamp et al. (1998). He found that (i) the training of newly recruited personnel and instruction in the use of new equipment and technologies were important in this industry; (ii) technological progress in the weaving industry was very rapid, largely because of the replacement of older machinery with more modern ones; (iii) technological progress in the spinning industry was less rapid because this progress was caused by improvements in existing technologies rather than the introduction of new ones; and (iv) the level of human capital was an important determinant of the speed and nature of technological progress in the Indonesian textile industry.

(vi) *Participation in world trade*
Since the mid-1970s an important informal channel of international technology transfer for Indonesian firms, including small and medium-scale enterprises (SMEs), has been their participation in world trade, specifically through exporting their products. This informal channel was utilised effectively by local firms, particularly electronics firms, in the four East Asian NIEs, including the Republic of Korea, Taiwan, Hong Kong and Singapore which, based on low wage rates, were able to build up basic operational (production) capabilities through simple assembly of mature products for exports, often developed through technical assistance provided by foreign buyers (Hobday 1994, p. 335; World Bank 1996, p. 4). This process of coupling exports with technology development was called "export-led technology development" (Hobday 1994, p. 335).

Although not as technologically advanced as the East Asian NIEs' "export-led technology development", the remarkable export performance which the garment industry and other export industries in Bali and Jepara, Central Java, Indonesia, have experienced since the mid-1970s is somewhat similar to the experience of these East Asian firms. The remarkable growth of Bali's export industries, starting with the garments industry in the mid-1970s, and followed by various handicraft industries was based on vital information flows which these Balinese firms received through strategic business alliances with foreign firms and businessmen (Cole 1998, p. 257).

Through the vital information transfer and technical and managerial assistance and advice on plant lay-out, the purchase of the most appropriate machines, quality control methods, provided by the foreign buyers who often acted as technical consultants to the mostly small firms, these firms were able to achieve high levels of efficiency and accuracy. This assistance was provided on a for-profit basis, as it was specifically tied to tangible product output results (Cole 1998, p. 275). The ongoing interaction of these two parties started a virtuous cycle of technological improvements and learning that was self-replicating and largely self-financing, which led to rapid and sustained export growth (Cole 1998, p. 275).

A similar type of vital information transfer and technical, managerial and marketing assistance by foreign buyers who also acted as technical consultants, is found in the development of the export-oriented furniture industry in the town of Jepara, Central Java. As a result, the quality of Jepara furniture has been steadily upgraded (Sandee, Andadari, and Sulandjari 2000, pp. 5–7), as has been the case with Bali's export products.

The studies by Berry and Levys (1994) and Schiller and Martin-Schiller (1997) on the export-oriented SME furniture manufacturers in Jepara also confirm the crucial role which foreign buyers have played and are playing in providing vital information and guidance to these SMEs on the furniture designs popular in the export markets and the required quality standards to penetrate these markets. An important conclusion from these studies is that local SMEs must have some basic industrial competence in their particular field of activity, so that the inflow of technology or knowledge from outside will have an optimal impact.

The above studies indicate that non-farm firms in the rural areas in Bali and in and around Jepara have benefited from the inflows of technologies (in the broad sense of the word) through their participation in foreign trade. The more open the regional economy, as is particularly the case in Bali, the greater their chances of upgrading their skills and technologies. However, the Bali and Jepara cases are exceptional cases, because in general, the capability of Indonesian non-farm firms, specifically the MIEs and SEs in the rural areas, in adopting and deploying new technologies is limited, due to the lack of the necessary assets, especially competent management having access to information, skilled workers, and capital.

3.2. Domestic Diffusion of Technology/Knowledge

The maximum spillover effect of technology transfer from an MNC to its subsidiary in a developing country depends on the domestic diffusion of these technologies to other local firms. The nature of this domestic diffusion of the transferred technology is arguably a significant determinant of spillover effects.[8]

The domestic diffusion of the transferred or imported technology or knowledge can occur in various ways. For instance, when an Indonesian manager or senior technician employed with a foreign firm leaves this firm to work with a domestic firm. The knowledge and experience he or she received while working for the foreign firm is then applied in the local firm. Another way is the technical assistance and guidance which a large assembling firm, whether foreign or domestic, provides to its local supplier firms with an opportunity to produce various parts and components according to the strict quality standards and delivery schedules set by the assembling firm. The assembling firm can also play an important role in training the workers of their local supplier firms in the required skills and in providing technical advice to the managers on quality control, plant lay-out, purchase of the best, and low cost capital equipment.

(i) *Subcontracting*

In Indonesia, the government has encouraged partnerships between SMEs and Les, especially in the form of subcontracting arrangements in the manufacturing sector. In the late 1970s the government introduced mandatory deletion programmes (local content programmes) for the engineering goods industries, including the automotive, machinery and electronic industries. Under these deletion programmes the assembling firms were required to purchase progressively more locally made parts and components from local supplier firms, preferably SMEs (Thee 1994; TAF 2000).

However, because of the shortage of competent local supplier firms, many of the local supplier firms which emerged as a result of the deletion programmes were large supplier firms. Most of these large supplier firms were joint ventures with large parts makers in the advanced countries, particularly Japan, which in the automotive industry became the first tier component makers. The SMEs which emerged as supplier firms were second tier or third tier parts makers, supplying parts and sub-components to the first tier component makers. The relatively few SMEs which became supplier firms were only able to become third or at best second tier supplier firms.

Since the deletion programmes were introduced during the import-substitution period, these programmes were generally not successful in developing SMEs to become viable and efficient supplier firms. The reason was that in the import-substitution period, the large assembler firms were not efficient because they were not able to enjoy economies of scale in the relative small, fragmented domestic market. Because the large assembling firms were not able to enjoy economies of scale, it was equally difficult for the SMEs to become efficient supplier firms. The only local supplier firms which emerged as viable and efficient firms were the export-oriented first tier component makers which were joint ventures with the large foreign, mostly Japanese, component makers (Aswicahyono, Atje, and Thee 2005). For this reason the deletion programmes were discontinued in 1993. Thus far, production linkages in terms of subcontracting between LEs and SMEs are still weak, mainly because most SMEs cannot meet the required quality standards because of their limited technological capabilities and lack of proper skills.

In a research report issued in 2000 the Asia Foundation (2000) concluded that the lack of success of the deletion programmes in fostering strong linkages between LEs, MIEs, and SMEs was due to the government's excessive interference aimed at replacing the market mechanisms. Other studies too concluded that subcontracting arrangements between SMEs and LEs are weak, mainly because SMEs cannot meet the required quality standard due to the lack of the required skills and technological abilities.[9]

Although the mandatory deletion programmes of the late 1970s and early 1980s were largely unsuccessful in developing viable domestic supplier firms, over time several SMEs were able to grow into efficient and viable supplier firms. A successful case of developing viable supplier firms is the experience of the Astra Otoparts group, part of the big Astra International business group. Through Astra Otoparts, Astra International, Indonesia's largest automotive company, was able to develop several SMEs into efficient and viable supplier firms. Thanks to the rigorous training which Astra gave to local supplier firms with potential, most of them SMEs, over time these supplier firms were able to produce a wide range of parts and components according to the strict quality standards set by Astra's automotive firms (including both cars and motorcycles) and also meet the strict delivery schedules set by Astra's automotive firms.

Although there is a much richer literature on international technology transfer than on the internal diffusion of new technologies within the country, there is a growing literature on the importance of networks in disseminating knowledge internally. These studies found that through networks an entrepreneur can learn or obtain his technology or knowledge from other entrepreneurs in the same industry.[10] The literature can be classified according to two main issues: the one on strategic alliances (SAs) and the other one on clustering. In the first group, authors such as Perry and Pyatt (1995), Rowbotham (1991), Koch (1995), and Styles (1995), suggest that a strategic alliance (SA), or partnership based on a long term and stable relationship with other enterprises, is a key factor of a firm's competitiveness. A partnership can take several forms, including subcontracting, joint ventures, and cooperation in R & D activities. A partnership is especially important for SMEs (including MIEs), which in general face several constraints in their business, including lack of capital, skilled labour, vital information flows, and technology. Through a partnership or strategic alliance with a large enterprise, whether foreign or domestic, these SMEs can obtain several benefits. The reason is that these LEs usually have better facilities and know-how than SMEs. According to Weaver and Dickson (1995), "the need to acquire resources assumed to be unobtainable internally will motivate SMEs to seek out cooperative linkages with firms possessing the requisite resources" (p. 13).

(ii) *Strategic alliances*

A study on strategic alliances by Tambunan (2005) found that out of a total of 124 respondents, most of whom were medium enterprises (MEs), more than 50 per cent had established strategic alliances (SAs) with other firms. However, the percentage of those who had established strategic alliances varied among the various industries. The industries in which firms had established the most strategic alliances with other firms included the food products and metal goods industries.

Many of the surveyed firms had established more than one strategic alliance with other firms. The data in Table 6.5 show the ranking of the importance of the various types of strategic alliances. The most important types were long-term marketing agreements (cooperation among firms in marketing their output), purchaser-supplier alliances (cooperation between input suppliers and their purchasers), joint ventures with other SMEs, and cooperation in technology.

The most important types of assistance the surveyed firms received from their strategic alliance partners were technology support, market information, and training of workers. These can be considered as other forms of benefits from a strategic alliance which can improve the production capacity, quality of products, efficiency in production process, productivity of workers, and hence the competitiveness of the firms.

Table 6.5
Types of Strategic Alliances by the Surveyed Firms, 1997

Types	Percentage Use
Long-term marketing agreements	25.3
Purchaser-supplier alliances	23.9
Joint venture with other SMEs	22.8
Technology alliances	22.0
Outside contracting/Licensing	21.2
Joint venture with LEs	20.0
Equity investments	18.9
Export management	14.8
	13.4

Source: Tambunan (2005).

A second study sponsored by The Asia Foundation (2000) on strategic alliances established by SMEs surveyed 300 enterprises in the food, garments and wood products industries in six regions, namely North Sumatra, Jakarta, West Java, Central Java, East Java, and Bali. This study found that the most prevalent strategic alliances that were established by these firms involved cooperation in marketing, rather than in technology.

(iii) *Clusters*
The literature on SMEs also indicates that in many developed countries clusters can be an effective means for SMEs to overcome their constraints, including in technology. By cooperating in a cluster, SMEs can take advantage of the presence of suppliers of raw materials, parts and components, new technologies embodied in new machinery and parts; the presence of workers with sector-specific skills; and the presence of workshops that make or service the machinery and production tools (Humphrey and Schmitz 1995). With enterprises operating in clusters, it becomes easier for the government, LEs, universities and research institutes, and other supporting agencies to provide services, such as technical development and management training, and the provision of general facilities, such as machineries for raw material drying and processing into half-finished goods. The services and facilities would be very costly for the providers if given to individual enterprises in dispersed locations (Tambunan 2000).[11]

The development of SME clusters in Indonesia has been an important subject of several studies, including by Sandee (1995), Sandee and Weijland (1989), and Sandee and ter Wingel (2002). These studies found that internal networks among firms inside clusters as well as external networks are important for the technological upgrading of firms operating in the clusters. Sandee et al. (2002) found that traders, suppliers of raw materials and other inputs, and other market agents played a leading role in introducing new technologies into the clusters. Weijland's studies (1992, 1994) indicated the importance of middlemen or traders as a source of knowledge transfer to the clusters. However, some other field studies came up with different findings. For instance, Sato (2000) saw little evidence of positive effects of clustering, as she found no inter-firm specialization of work processes and no joint actions in marketing, production, distribution or technological development among the firms inside the clusters. Supratikno's studies (1996, 2001, 2002) also found that in general inter-firm specialization and cooperation among producers inside the clusters were very limited. He found that the importance of a cluster for production development, including technology and marketing, depends on whether inside the cluster there are leading/pioneering firms, usually larger and faster growing firms that are able to manage a large and differentiated set of relationships with firms and institutions within and outside the clusters. He found that such firms had utilized cutting-edge technologies in production. This happened, for instance, in the clove cigarette cluster in Kudus, Central Java; the tea-processing cluster in Slawi; and the tourism cluster in Bali. The clove cigarette cluster in Kudus, for instance, was able to outperform products from Philip Morris and BAT. Similarly, the tea-processing cluster in Slawi, led by a big domestic company, Sosro, had developed into the market leader in the Indonesian soft drink market, leaving giant Coca Cola behind.

In general, the studies on clusters have found that some clusters are relatively more advanced in technology and innovation, while most of the others are less developed. The advanced clusters show that internal networks among firms inside clusters as well as external networks are important for the development of technology in the clusters; while the less developed clusters show lack of these networks. The creation of advanced networks should be market driven rather than supply-driven (by the government). The role of government is only to create an undistorted market mechanism.

3.3. Knowledge Diffusion from Universities and Research Institutes

There is a growing literature on knowledge diffusion from universities and research institutes to non-farm firms, particularly manufacturing firms, through publications, patents, and consulting (Agrawal 2001, p. 285). The literature discusses the relative importance of various diffusion pathways between universities and firms, such as publications, patents, and consultancies.[12] However, studies focusing on knowledge diffusion from universities or research institutes to non-farm firms in Indonesia are rare. In Indonesia the public science and technology (S & T) institutes consist of twelve national and several regional R & D centres of the Agency for Industrial Research and Development (BPPI), Department of Industry, and the research centres of the non-departmental government research institutes, particularly the Indonesian Institute of Sciences (LIPI) and the Agency for the Assessment and Application of Technology (BPPT). However, BPPI's R & D centres are mostly engaged in product certification, training and testing activities for manufacturing firms, particularly the SOEs and SMEs. Their research staff are generally not well trained, and are often not aware of the latest technological developments in their fields. Moreover, much of their laboratory equipment is obsolete because the centres are under-funded (Lall and Rao 1995, p. 84), even more so after the Asian economic crisis. Hence, in general they are not able to provide adequate technical information or technology support services to Indonesia's manufacturing firms (Thee 1998, p. 125). After the Asian economic crisis no new evidence has emerged about the establishment of linkages or cooperation between R & D institutes or universities with non-farm firms, including SMEs.

The non-departmental government institutes, particularly LIPI and BPPT, are better funded, equipped, and better staffed with highly-trained researchers, many of whom had pursued postgraduate training abroad. However, like the Department of Industries R & D institutes, the research centres of LIPI and BPPT have not played a significant role in developing the technological capabilities of Indonesia's non-farm firms, particularly the manufacturing firms. The reason for this is that they have generally not been able to establish mutually profitable linkages with national industry, particularly private industry. Because of their lack of contact with national industry, they are generally not aware of the technological needs of private industry and therefore lag behind world technological frontiers (Lall and Rao 1995, p. 84). As a result of their failure in establishing mutually profitable linkages with non-farm firms, particularly manufacturing firms, most, if not all, of their research is supply- rather than demand-driven (Thee 1998, p. 126).

(i) *Foster-Father scheme*

Another hope for source of knowledge diffusion is provided by the involvement of MIEs and SMEs in the "Foster Father" (*Bapak Angkat)* scheme, which was introduced in 1992. In this scheme large enterprises (LEs) were urged and all state-owned enterprises (SOEs) were required to assist the SMEs in providing financial assistance, training in marketing, technical assistance, and raw material procurement (see Table 6.6). For instance, in marketing the large private firms or SOEs, Foster Fathers provide promotion facilities, such as trade fairs or study tours, for the MIEs and SMEs or act as a trading house for them. The Foster Fathers also assist the SMEs in upgrading their technologies by, for instance, financing the purchase of new machinery or in providing technical training to the workers of the SMEs.

Besides Table 6.6, BPS has presented more information on the implementation of the Foster Father scheme and the participation of MIEs and SMEs in this scheme. However, these data are input data, that is they mention participation in this scheme, but they do not reveal the outcomes, that is whether or not they were successful in developing viable enterprises.

Table 6.6
Percentage of MIEs and SMEs in Manufacturing Not Participating and Participating in the Foster Father Scheme by Type of Assistance, 2002

	MIEs (%)	SMEs (5)
Not participating	93.5	85.2
Participating:	6.5	14.8
– capital assistance	–44.4	–39.4
– training and technical assistance	–11.2	–3.0
– marketing	–43.7	–57.9
– raw material procurement	–39.2	–38.3
– other assistance	–3.0	–1.4

Source: BPS.

The data in Table 6.6 show that the percentage of non-participating MIEs and SMEs is much higher than the percentage of MIEs and SMEs which were participating in the Foster Father scheme. The likely reason for this low percentage might be due to the fact that the private LEs in particular were reluctant to participate in this scheme, as it did not provide them with any tangible benefit, except perhaps some political goodwill from the authorities. After the fall of Soeharto, the large private enterprises were not pressured anymore to participate in the Foster Father scheme. Hence, they withdrew from participating in this scheme which did not confer any benefit to them. Moreover, most of these large enterprises were burdened with high debts as a result of the Asian economic crisis, and therefore had to focus all their efforts on surviving.

The relatively few large enterprises which continued participating in the Foster Father scheme were the state-owned enterprises. These SOEs could not just withdraw from participating in this scheme, even though they too had suffered as a result of the Asian economic crisis. It is likely for this reason that the MIEs and SMEs which participated in this scheme were few in number. This Foster Father scheme is now rarely, if ever, mentioned as a suitable means to develop viable MIEs and SMEs.

The above discussion on technology diffusion among non-farm firms indicates that knowledge diffusion among these firms depends to a great extent on close networks among them and between them and other institutes such as universities and R & D institutes. However, the creation of such networks should be market-driven rather than promoted through government intervention. The role of government, including the central and regional governments, is only to establish a conducive business environment.

4. Constraints Faced by Non-Farm Enterprises

4.1. Nature of the Constraints

The development of viable and efficient SMEs, particularly non-farm enterprises, is hampered by several constraints.[13] The constraints may differ from region to region or between rural and urban areas, between sectors, or between individual enterprises within a sector. However, there are a number of constraints common to all SMEs. These common constraints faced by SMEs are the lack of capital, difficulties in procuring raw materials, lack of access to relevant business information, difficulties in marketing and distribution, low technological capabilities, high transportation costs, communication problems, problems caused by cumbersome and costly bureaucratic procedures, especially in getting the required licences, and policies and regulations that generate market distortions.

Among these various constraints, three major constraints need to be discussed, namely: (1) cumbersome and onerous business regulations and restrictions; (2) lack of finance; and (3) low technological capabilities.

(i) *Cumbersome and onerous business regulations and restrictions*
Basically, the cumbersome and onerous business regulations and restrictions which hamper business activities in Indonesia reflect the poor governance in Indonesia. Some of the most egregious restrictive regulations which hampered bona fide business in Indonesia, including the non-farm enterprises, were the policy-generated barriers to domestic competition and trade. These policy-generated barriers included the barriers to inter-regional and inter-island trade and proliferation of several state and private monopolies which proliferated during the late Soeharto era (Thee 2002). The policy-generated barriers to domestic competition and trade included barriers to entry in certain economic activities, officially sanctioned cartels and monopolies, price controls, dominance of state-owned enterprises in certain sectors and preferential treatment for favoured enterprises (Iqbal 2002).

These barriers created rent-seeking opportunities which benefited well-connected businessmen, but hurt the business of the large majority of bona fide businessmen, including the numerous non-farm firms. Most of the policy-generated barriers to domestic competition and trade, both at the national and regional levels, were abolished after the Asian economic crisis as part of the structural reforms mandated by the government's agreements with the IMF. Unfortunately, after the introduction of regional autonomy in early 2001, several restrictive regulations on domestic competition and trade were re-introduced by the regional governments. These onerous restrictive regulations have worsened the business environment for business, including the many rural non-farm enterprises.

Indonesia's poor governance is reflected in the very high levels of corruption in the government bureaucracy, the legislature and judiciary, the lack of legal certainty and poor law enforcement, and the lack of adequate security and law and order. Obviously, these three aspects of poor governance hamper business and raise the costs of doing business in Indonesia. In particular, administrative corruption, that is the corruption that firms, specifically the non-farm firms, encounter in their-day-to-day dealings with mostly lower-level government officials, raises the transaction costs of these firms. It also increases the uncertainty that firms face, reduces productivity of these firms, and their incentives to invest (World Bank 2005, p. 31). Although non-farm firms, in particular the SMEs, are considered to be mostly owned and run by the "economically weak groups in society", SMEs, no less than LEs, are subjected to various illegal levies and so-called "contributions", both at the central government and the regional government levels.

(ii) Lack of finance
Both financial markets and institutions in Indonesia are relatively underdeveloped. This condition constrains the supply of capital to non-farm firms, including SMEs, particularly the fast-growing SMEs. Insufficient competition in the SME financing sector means that the available financial institutions are not vigorously scanning the entire SME market and are not motivated to create innovative financial products that would adequately serve the SME market. Moreover, "entrepreneurial finance", often involving the non-collateralised forms of lending, is inadequate which particularly constrains the supply of capital to fast-growing SMEs which could act as an important "engine of growth" for the Indonesian economy (PPTA and The Asia Foundation 2005, pp. 94–95).

Despite the well-known success of Bank Rakyat Indonesia (BRI) in providing microfinance to micro-enterprises (MIEs), SME access to finance is inadequate. Microfinance is not suitable for the SMEs as they are more complex economic organizations which require managerial skills which few MIE owners have. Hence, analysis of the risks associated with lending to SMEs is more complex and less readily suitable to the "mass market" approaches adopted by the microfinance institutions. A higher percentage of the SMEs are growth-oriented firms with the possibility of becoming nationally or even internationally competitive. Since SME finance is considered to be a separate business line by financial institutions, the Indonesian government has to recognize that the approaches to microfinance, such as "group lending", are not suitable for SMEs (PPTA and The Asia Foundation 2005, pp. 95–96).

(iii) *Low technological capabilities*
In a conducive business environment technology upgrading by Indonesia's SMEs, which focuses on higher product quality, productivity, and efficiency, is a crucial factor in determining the competitiveness of the SMEs, both in the domestic and export markets. Unfortunately, in recent years many Indonesian SME clusters have experienced declining sales and consequent reductions in employment because of the strong competition from China and Vietnam. Hence, in order to compete successfully with China and Vietnam and other emerging competitors, non-farm firms, particularly the SMEs, must increase their productivity and product quality, both of which depend on technology upgrading (PPTA and The Asia Foundation 2005, p. 77).

Interestingly, although the lack of adequate skills and technological and managerial capabilities are major constraints to SMEs, a survey by BPS on rural non-farm enterprises, including MIEs and SMEs operating in manufacturing, indicated that these enterprises did not consider the lack of skills and technological capability as a serious problem (see Table 6.7). This

Table 6.7
Main Problems Faced by MIEs and SEs in
the Manufacturing Sector, 2002

	SEs	MIEs	Total SEs and MIEs
Have no problem	46,485 (19.5)*	627,650 (25.2)	674,135 (24.7)
Have problem	192,097 (80.5)	1,862,468 (74.8)	2,054,565 (75.3)
– Raw material	20,362 (10.6)	400,915 (21.5)	421,277 (20.5)
– Marketing	77,175 (40.2)	552,231 (29.7)	629,406 (30.6)
– Capital	71,001 (40.0)	643,628 (34.6)	714,629 (34.8)
Transportation/Distribution	5,027 (2.6)	49,918 (2.7)	54,945 (2.7)
– Energy	40,605 (2.4)	50,815 (2.7)	55,420 (2.7)
– Labour cost	2,335 (1.2)	14,315 (0.8)	16,650 (0.8)
– Other	11,592 (6.0)	150,646 (8.0)	162,238 (7.9)
Total SEs & MIEs	238,582 (100.0)	2,490,118 (100.0)	2,728,700 (100.0)

Note: * = percentage
Source: BPS.

may be due to the fact that many owners of the MIEs and SEs were not aware that their productivity is low and the quality of their products inferior compared to the products of the large enterprises or imported products.

Although both the government and the private sector have undertaken various programmes to help the technology upgrading of SMEs, a survey by the ADB PPTA Project found that most SMEs are relatively unorganized. Hence, they have few channels of communication with government agencies, and are unaware of the available public business development services (BDS). Sometimes the SMEs are unaware of technology upgrading possibilities or, when aware of these services, may be unwilling or unable to pay for these services. As a result of the lack of access to relevant information on feasible technologies for SMEs, this important information on improving technologies is often not available to the SMEs. This finding is similar to the findings of the survey as presented in Table 6.9. Government agencies and private BDS providers are also not networked, so that BDS providers are often unaware of the technology needs of SMEs. For this reason these BDS providers spend much time working on technologies that are of little relevance or interest to local SMEs (PPTA and The Asia Foundation 2005, p. 80).

4.2. How Constraints in the Access to Technology have Affected the Growth of Non-Farm Enterprises

With the exception of some econometric and some case studies on the technological capabilities of large manufacturing firms, there have not been many studies on the technological development of rural non-farm enterprises in Indonesia. So far there is only one study from Sandee (1995) who specifically investigated the technological progress in a SME cluster. His study found that, first, SMEs are able to improve their technology, even without much support from the government. Secondly, technological capability is a major determinant of the performance of the SMEs he studied.[14] Sandee's finding suggests that SMEs obtain substantial benefits from improving their technological capability.

At the request of the Indonesian government in 1994–96 the Foreign Investment Advisory Service (FIAS) conducted a study on the feasibility of promoting backward linkages between export-oriented foreign-invested firms in the electronics and electrical goods industries and Indonesian supplier firms, mostly SME supplier firms. The study concluded that there was a need for backward linkages, both to strengthen domestic supporting industries and improve the investment climate for foreign investment. However, the study also identified a number of policy and procedural impediments, and weaknesses in the programmes to enhance the capabilities, including technological capabilities, of SMEs which could grow into viable and efficient supplier firms (FIAS 1996, p. i).

The FIAS study identified three major impediments to developing viable and efficient supplier firms, namely policy and procedural impediments, the lack of finance, and the weak technological capabilities of the potential supplier firms. These impediments are similar to the three constraints mentioned in Part 4.1. However, because of the weak supply-side capabilities of most supplier firms, particularly in technological capability, many potential supplier firms were not able to meet the required high standards set by the electronics and electrical goods assembling firms with regard to product quality, cost, and meeting strict delivery schedules. As a result, the MNC electronics and electrical assembling firms continued to rely mostly on imported parts and components. Not much has changed in this situation ten years later.

Indonesia's failure to develop efficient and competitive supporting industries was clearly reflected by the serious problems which the manufacturing sector experienced after the onset of the Asian economic crisis. After the collapse of Indonesia's banking sector because of the crisis, foreign banks did not want to accept the letters of credit (LCs) issued by Indonesian banks. As a result, many assembling firms were unable to import the parts and components needed to assemble the products they produced.

Non-farm firms, including SMEs, have only been able to upgrade their capacities, including technological and design capabilities, where they had access to foreign buyers who also acted as consultants, like in the case of Bali's garment and other export-oriented industries and Jepara's furniture industry. Unfortunately, these examples of the successful development of SMEs are an exception rather than the rule in Indonesia.

5. The Role of Supporting Agencies and SME Promotion Programmes

While it is impossible to itemize all government programmes, The SMERU Research Institute has been able to map most of existing important assistance programmes to strengthen MIEs and SEs provided by government and non-government institutes during the period 1997–2003. The data in Table 6.8 show there were 64 institutions whose assistance programmes to strengthen MIEs and SEs were successfully mapped and they were categorized into 6 groups. A total of 594 programmes were identified and most of them were provided by the government (65 per cent). Other programmes were conducted by NGOs (18 per cent), donor agencies (8 per cent), banking institutions

Table 6.8
Number of Institutions and Assistance Programmes to Strengthen
MIEs and SEs, 1997–2003

Institutions	Number of institutions	Number of assistance programmes		
		Total	Still continuing	
			Total	%
a) Government institutions	13	388	127	32.7
b) Banking institutions	7	31	25	80.7
c) Private companies	10	12	12	100.0
d) Donor agencies	8	46	15	32.6
e) NGOs	20	109	79	72.5
f) Others	6	8	8	100.0
Total	64	594	266	44.8

Source: SMERU (2004).

(5 per cent), private companies (2 per cent), and other institutions. The scale of each assistance programme varied greatly based on the amount of funds, time frame, and geographical scope. Hence, one programme cannot be directly compared to another.[15]

Table 6.9 shows that the type of assistance activities varied. The number of activities within each programme also varied, but generally ranged from between one and three. Hence, of the 594 assistance programmes, there were 1,044 types of activities. In total, the most common types of activities were the provision of training (22.9 per cent), capital assistance/credit (17.3 per cent), facilitation (16.1 per cent), and the dissemination/ introduction of new technology (15.2 per cent).

The data in Table 6.9 show that government agencies are the most common institutions which introduced new technology (27.9 per cent) and provided training (21.1 per cent), whereas other institutions mostly provided capital assistance. Of all the institutions, government agencies played the most prominent role (50.9 per cent), followed by NGOs (29.4 per cent) and donor agencies (10.1 per cent). Based on the type of activity, training was mostly undertaken by government institutions (46.9 per cent) and NGOs (37.2 per cent). Capital assistance was mostly provided by local and international NGOs (50.3 per cent), followed by government institutions (15.5 per cent) and banking institutions (14.9 per cent). Facilitation was mainly provided by NGOs (52.4 per cent) and government institutions (35.7 per cent).

Table 6.9
The Proportion of Assistance Programmes to Strengthen MIEs and SEs
Based upon the Type of Activities and the Implementing Institutions

	A*	B	C	D	E	F	Total
Capital assistance	5.3	52.9	25.0	21.0	29.6	28.6	17.3
Training	21.1	13.7	22.2	19.0	29.0	21.4	22.9
Facilitation	11.3	9.8	19.4	7.6	28.7	0.0	16.1
Information	1.9	7.8	2.8	3.8	1.6	21.4	2.6
Facilities	16.2	2.0	5.6	8.6	1.0	0.0	9.7
Promotion	3.0	3.9	13.9	6.7	1.0	7.1	3.3
Dissemination/introduction of new technology	27.9	0.0	0.0	6.7	1.3	0.0	15.2
Guidelines	4.3	0.0	0.0	0.0	0.7	0.0	2.4
Others	9.0	9.8	11.1	26.7	7.2	21.4	10.5
Types of activities	531	51	36	105	307	14	1,044

Note: * See Table 6.8.
Source: SMERU (2004).

5.1. The Role of Government Promotion Programmes

In Indonesia numerous government promotion programmes for non-farm firms, particularly SMEs, have over the years been implemented, including the nation-wide Small Enterprise Development or generally known as KIK/KMKP subsidized credit programme for MIEs and SMEs; the Small Enterprise Credit (KUK) scheme; the credit programme for village units (KUPEDES); the establishment of small rural development banks (BKD); human resource development training programmes, such as in production techniques, general management (MS/MUK), management quality systems (ISO-9000), quality control methods, entrepreneurship (CEFE, AMT), and extension services; the establishment of Cooperatives of Small-Scale Industries (KOPINKRA) in clusters; the establishment of small-scale industrial estates (LIK), the Foster Father scheme; the establishment of Small Business Consultancy Clinics (KKB); the establishment of the Export Support Board of Indonesia (DPE), the establishment of common service facilities (UPT) in clusters; and the introduction of an incubator system for promoting the development of new entrepreneurs.

Government departments, specifically the Directorate-General of Small-Scale Industry, Department of Industry, and the Office for the State Minister for Cooperatives and SMEs have taken the lead in the implementation of the SME development programmes. These departments, like other departments, have regional offices for the delivery of these various services in their respective regions.

The data from the Integrated Business Survey 2003 from BPS show that the government played a significant role in supporting the development of SEs and MIEs. The Survey indicated that, out of a total 481,714 units of non-farm MIEs and SEs receiving government support in 2003, 203,563 firms (or 43 per cent of the total) received support through one or more of the various government programmes. The remainder (52 per cent of the total) received support from NGOs, foreign foundations, and a number of large private companies. The distribution by region shows that the majority of those receiving support from the government are located in Java and Bali (see Figure 6.2). However, as a percentage of the total number of MIEs and SMEs receiving government support in a region, the region of Nusa Tenggara (both Barat and Timur) scored the highest, while Java and Bali ranked third (see Figure 6.3).

For the government, success is measured by the number of MIEs and SMEs participating in a programme, while the outcome of a programme has never been assessed. A more realistic measure of success of a programme

Figure 6.2
Distribution of Non-Farm MIEs and SEs that Received Supports from the Government by Region, 2003

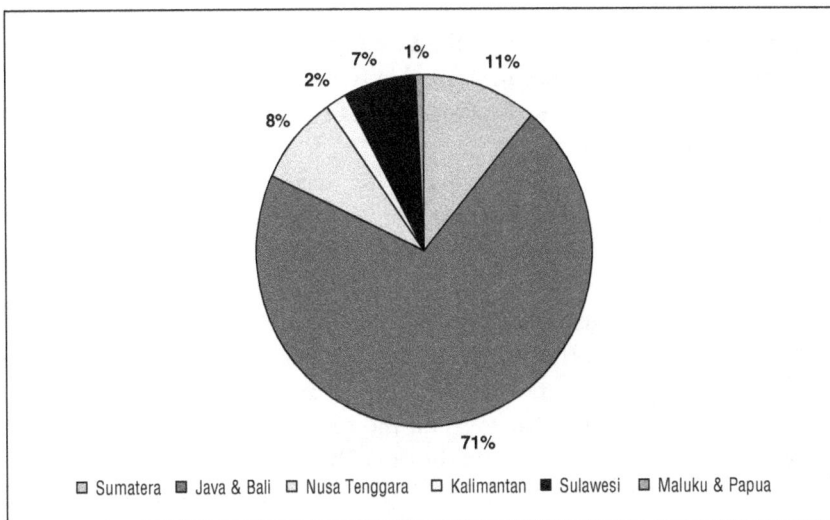

□ Sumatera ■ Java & Bali □ Nusa Tenggara □ Kalimantan ■ Sulawesi □ Maluku & Papua

Source: BPS (SUSI 2003).

Figure 6.3
Proportion of SEs and MIEs Received Assistances from Government by
Region, 2003 (% of total SEs and MIEs in the Region)

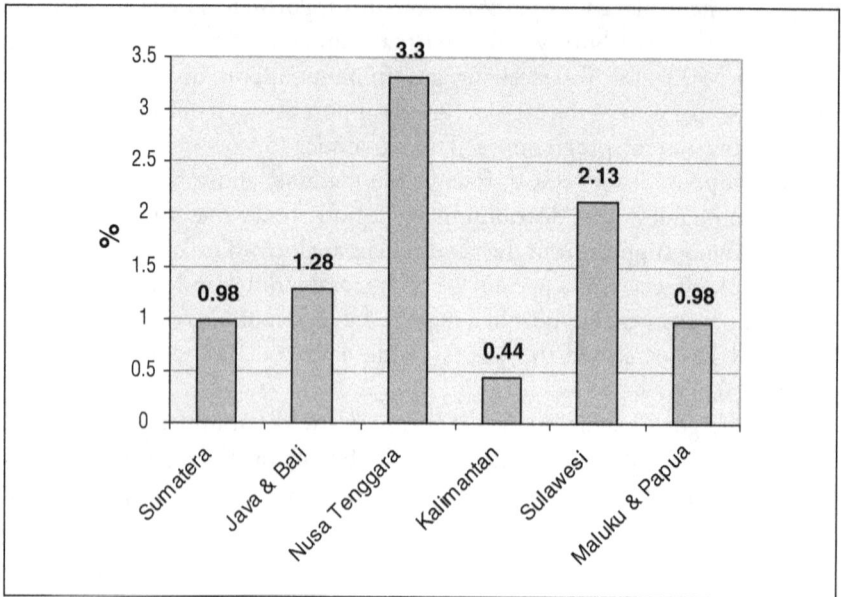

Source: BPS (SUSI 2003).

would be to measure the net benefit, not only to MIEs and SMEs receiving support. While programmes may provide significant benefits for the MIEs and SMEs, they also accrue cost. Programme benefits must thus be measured against the costs they incur.

Despite the lack of published data to measure the net benefit of a programme, the findings of some studies have indicated that most of the above SME development programmes have not been successful.[16] Whether a programme is successful or not should not only be assessed from the input side, that is the coverage of the programme, but also from its output side, that is the commercial performance of the participating MIEs and SMEs.

That looking only at the number of MIEs and SMEs participating in a programme is not enough to measure the success of a programme is, for instance, also evident with the establishment of KOPINKRA, the Co-operatives of Small-Scale Industries. The BPS SUSI data show that the majority of MIEs and SMEs were not members of KOPINKRA. The reason for this has been mentioned by Klapwijk (1997) as follows:

In view of the wide definition of small industry employed by the Ministry, much of the promotion efforts may have bypassed the smallest enterprises that are most in need of assistance. ... The extension officers generally have little technical or business experience, and training or other technical facilities have been largely provided according to the directions of central planners, rather than having been adapted to local needs. (p. 65)

Another more comprehensive technical assistance programme has been the establishment of technical service units (UPT) located in existing SME clusters of similar industries. These units provide extension and technical services and training courses. Government technical officers who have received special training staff the units. Based on his survey, van Diermen (2004) concluded that the UPT extension service programme has done poorly. It has failed to deliver efficient services, target appropriate recipients and address the important criteria of providing a net benefit to society and/or effectively addressing equity or fairness objectives. Van Diermen mentioned other problems with the implementation of the UPT, namely (i) the UPT services were supply driven rather than demand driven; (ii) although these UPT units were initially equipped with modern machinery, over the years and especially after the Asian economic crisis of 1997–98, budget constraints prevented the replacement of the existing equipment. At present, most of the machinery and other capital equipment are obsolete; (iii) the UPT services were delivered indiscriminately to clusters; (iv) the UPT staff had not had the appropriate training to respond adequately to the needs of the SMEs; and (v) because the UPT units were government units, there was not enough flexibility in the system to respond quickly to the changing needs of SMEs.

To assess the effectiveness of MIE and SE assistance programmes, SMERU (2004) conducted a field study on 172 respondents in six districts/towns (*kabupaten/kota*), including Kabupaten Sukabumi, Bantul and Kebumen, and Kota Padang, Surabaya, and Makassar, consisting of MIEs and SEs in trade, industry, and services. These were informal, non-legal entities whose turnover and number of employees fluctuated, and which operated with only simple technology. Because a large number of assistance programmes recorded in the field were capital assistance programmes, the impact on respondents was generally economic. Other effects were unknown, for example, whether there had been an increase in knowledge or technological capability as a result of the training or technical assistance received. As can be seen in Table 6.10, a large number of MIEs (58.6 per cent) and SEs (63 per cent) stated that by obtaining assistance their business had improved in terms of increased revenues. Some MIE owners stated that they had been able to develop their business satisfactorily.

Table 6.10
The Impact of Assistance Programmes on MIEs and SEs

	MIEs	*SEs*
None	18.6	15.2
Business improved	58.6	63.0
Able to send children to school	10.0	2.2
Able to build a house	2.9	4.3
Other	10.0	15.2
Total	100.0	100.0

Source: SMERU (2004).

The above data show that a majority of the MIEs and SEs did claim that their business had improved because of the assistance programmes. However, the data shed no light on how and in which way the business of these MIEs and SMEs had improved.

With regard to training programmes for the SMEs, Sandee (2000) found that the training materials or information provided did not always match the needs of the producers. As Sandee put it,

> In practice, direct assistance frequently concerns brief training sessions of one or two days for a selected group of producers. Such sessions are characterized by a great deal of theory and little attention paid to how to improve the actual running of the business of particular activities. (p. 152)

Studying the effects of the macro- and micro-policy environments on rural industries in Indonesia, van Diermen (2004) found that (i) few of the micro-policies (programmes) implemented by the government had a lasting impact in terms of improving the performance of rural SMEs; (ii) a significant number of macro- and micro-policies put additional costs and burdens on rural SMEs. Hence, many of the MIEs and SMEs preferred to operate outside of the formal economy; and (iii) macro-policies that created a favourable economic environment, as reflected by consistently high growth rates of GDP, not biased in favour of LEs, provided the best stimulus for SME growth.

Van Diermen argued that

> measured by the above criteria, namely targeting the problem effectively; setting the right duration, scale and target group; being administratively efficient for government; and not imposing excessive compliance burdens on firms, most of the above programmes would score badly. There is no

doubt that many SMEs have gained benefits under the micro-policies…
But the more relevant question is at what cost were the benefits gained? The
cost of programmes should be measured in terms of economy-wide loss in
efficiency and the specific costs to other sectors of the economy. (p. 53)

The evidence on the success or lack of success of government promotion
programmes for non-farm firms is mixed. Based on their study of a furniture
cluster in Jepara (Central Java), Sandee et al. (2000) concluded that public
intervention was likely to have contributed to the success story of this cluster.
A comprehensive development package, including technical upgrading by the
provision of a common service facility for wood drying, export training, and
support to trade fair participation, and investment in the improvement of the
regional infrastructure (container facilities, roads, telephone) helped the cluster
to gradually develop export markets. On the other hand, Sato's field study
(2000) of several clusters in the metal-working and machinery industries in
Java found that the successful development of these clusters has been achieved
without significant government support.

Sato's finding about the lack of effectiveness of government SME
programmes is also supported by Tambunan's findings (1998*b*) in the rattan
industry in Padang (West Sumatra) and Tambunan's and Keddie's findings
(1998) in their study on the leather industry in Yogyakarta, which concluded
that the government's efforts to support the clusters had not yielded effective
results. To be sure, in many clusters many local government agencies, such as
the regional offices of the Office of the State Minister for Cooperatives and
Small Enterprises and of the Department of Industry, the local universities,
and the Workers' Training Centres (*Balai Latihan Kerja*) of the Department
of Manpower, have provided some support to the SMEs. However, in
implementing the various promotion programmes, there was no effort towards
any coordination between the various agencies, and sometimes these agencies
even implemented similar schemes/programmes.

5.2. The Role of Banks and the Private Sector

Although many banks provide credit to SMEs (see Table 6.11), no credits are
given for long-term investments, because the existing credit schemes are
mainly designed for working capital (short-term financing).[17]

In Part 3.2 it was observed that there is little evidence of linkages
between rural non-farm firms and universities or research institutes,
particularly in rural areas, because the research conducted in these institutions
are largely supply-driven with little relevance to the actual needs of the non-
farm firms. Moreover, the universities and research institutes are located

Table 6.11
Banks Involved in Financing SMEs in Indonesia, 2003

Bank	Types of credit
Bank Indonesia (BI)	Programme credit – Partnership development between bank and self-development community group (PHBK) – SE development programme (PPUK) – Micro-credit project – Coordinated information system for SEs development (SI-PUK) – Development of MIEs and SEs
Bank Bukopin	*Swamitra* *Sudara* credit *Sudara* expansion credit *Pundi* credit *Kekesra Mandiri*
Bank Central Asia (BCA)	*Peduli Usaha Mikro BCA* credit programme Partnership programme with Perum Pegadaian
Bank Mandiri	SE credit (KUK) Food sustainable credit programme (KKP) Credit for members of primary cooperatives (KKPA) Empowerment of SEs and cooperatives (PUKK)
Bank Negara Indonesia (BNI)	Micro credit Credit for cooperatives (KKop) KKPA *Kekesra Mandiri*
Bank Niaga	Programme credit (KKPA, KKP) Cooperation with other financial institutions (BPR, multi-finance) Partnership programme (commercial forward and backward linkages)
Bank Rakyat Indonesia (BRI)	Rural General Credit (Kupedes) Rural saving (Simpedes) *Mitra* credit *Candak Kulak* credit Income improvement of small farmers-fisheries project (P4K) Programme credit (KKP) SE and cooperative facilitation (PUKK)

Source: SMERU (2004).[18]

mainly in urban areas with little interest in the problems of rural non-farm firms. The available literature confirms that spillovers from universities or research institutes to non-farm firms depend on geographical distance (e.g. Anselin et al. 1997).

Based on a report from the SMERU Research Institute, during 1997–2003 there were ten large private companies active in supporting SMEs (see Table 6.12). However, only a few of the companies provided training and technical assistance; while others mostly provided capital assistance for working capital. Moreover, sixteen domestic non-government organizations (NGOs) were also actively assisting SMEs; though only some of them provided technical training and assistance.[19]

Table 6.12
Private Companies Actively Supporting SMEs, 1997–2003

Company	Types of support
PT Astra International Tbk	Venture capital SME empowerment
PT Bahana Artha Ventura	Microfinance
Koperasi Bina Masyarakat Mandiri	Microfinance
PT Caltex Pacific Indonesia (CPI)	Community development programme, local business development
PT ISM Bogasari Flour Mills	Business partnership programme with SMEs
PT Pertamina	Business partnership programme with SMEs, SME, and cooperative empowerment
PT Pos Indonesia (Persero)	Business partnership programme with SMEs
PT Pupuk Kaltim Tbk	Partnership and environment assistance programme
PT Sucofindo	SME and cooperative facilitation
PT Unilever Indonesia	Sustainable SME development

Source: SMERU (2004).

6. Policy Implications

This review of literature and empirical studies in Indonesia, including the Tegal case study suggests the following recommendations for policy-makers and the private sector in efforts to support capacity-building, especially with respect to technology, in non-farm SMEs in Indonesia.

(i)   Promote commercial interaction with actors outside the local economy. One of the key lessons from the above analysis is that an outward orientation is critical to success. This is true at a national level where the government should promote an export-led technological learning strategy. According to this strategy, Indonesia's exports should gradually move up the technological ladder from labour-intensive light to heavier manufacturing products or from standardized manufacturing processes to more advanced stages of process engineering, product-process interfacing, and product design. But it is also true at the local level. Bali's garment industrial success lies in part because of its unique access to foreign tourists, but the "outside actors" that bring new ideas and techniques do not have to be foreign. Facilitating voluntary linkages with more modern firms/LEs in nearby urban centres can help to expand the domain of trade and the depth of technical capacity in rural areas.

(ii) Promote private sector driven technological learning. Perhaps, the one overriding message from the above analysis is that the knowledge diffusion is not something that government does to SMEs. It is something that happens when SMEs work together with LEs on mutually profitable activities. Both the provision and the absorption of new knowledge happen more effectively when there is a strong incentive for the supplier and the user of that knowledge. The job of the government in such learning is primarily to facilitate such private interactions by reducing the "search costs" for suitable partners both SMEs and LEs.

(iii) Creating a culture of innovation in the educational system. It has been shown elsewhere that innovative economic systems cannot function well without a highly educated workforce. Improving the quality of secondary- and tertiary-level science and technology skills to encourage creativity and enlarge the number of innovators is a critical strand of policy in supporting technology/innovation capacity-building in enterprises. For this end, the central government should improve the educational curriculum to place greater stress on science and technology and on innovation and creativity more generally. The district governments, on the other hand, have the responsibility of effectively monitoring or in creating incentives for improvements in the delivery of educational services.

(iv) Improving the capabilities of R & D institutions and universities and making them more demand driven. This should be achieved through the implementation of a national strategy for technological development and would involve increasing the government budget for science and technology, particularly to (i) improve salaries to attract high-calibre staff; (ii) to upgrade their facilities (including equipment) so they can meet best practice requirements; and (iii) to increase capacity in those agencies working in remote rural areas to engage in meaningful outreach activities for the targeted client groups. But Indonesia's research institutes and universities also need to be made more demand driven. This can be done by creating incentives for links with the private sector. The R & D institutes should implement three important steps: (i) changing their mission statements and philosophies from supply towards demand driven; (ii) adopting a more progressive approach to selling their developed technologies or innovations and to disseminate information to the private sector; and (iii) providing incentives through various measures including opening access to funding for R & D activities or providing direct subsidies for R & D institutes and universities, granting them greater managerial autonomy; enforcing greater observance of intellectual property rights; requiring universities to obtain co-funding from the private sector to obtain certain government-funded research projects; and giving awards for the most active universities or R & D institutions in conducting R & D activities and dissemination of their findings to the private sector.

(v) Make government (and other business development services) a facilitator of demand driven training rather than a provider. Government facilitated technical training can be useful. However, evidence from many empirical studies show that this training was generally of poor quality and of limited relevance to recipients. The government needs to shift from being the principal provider of such training to crowding in demand-driven private sector provision of training and other business development services. For example, government could help to bear the costs of identifying the types of training which are needed by SMEs in a local area and disseminating this information widely.

(vi) Evaluate the effectiveness of specific programmes and scrap those that do not work. Given that many of the existing government support programmes are not effective in boosting the technological capacity of the vast majority of non-farm SMEs, the government urgently needs to undertake a comprehensive evaluation of the outcomes (rather than merely the inputs) of these programmes and scrap those that create no net benefits. More importantly, it should learn the lessons from those programmes that are more successful and apply these to the redesign and implementation of the remaining programmes.

NOTES

1. Technology and knowledge will be used interchangeably in this study, because technology is a quantum of knowledge resulting from the accumulated experience in design, production, and investment activities that is retained by individual teams of specialized personnel. This knowledge is mostly tacit and often (is) not made explicit in blueprints or manuals (Rosenberg & Frischtak 1985).
2. As stated in Hill (1998), transfer of technology is between countries, while transfer from one firm to another firm within a country is technology diffusion.
3. As generally realized, there is no universally accepted definition of technology and technological progress. The most common approaches define technology as a collection of physical processes that transform inputs into outputs and the knowledge and skills that structure the activities involved in carrying out these transformations (Kim 1997, p. 4); see also note 1. As a result, all technology indicators have serious conceptual and empirical limitations. Besides TFP or partial productivity for labour or capital, other indicators are patents and the proportion of output or exports originating from "technology-intensive" activities. These indicators are empirically slippery, however (Hill 1998).
4. See also previous studies on productivity in Indonesia (particularly in manufacturing) from e.g. Hill (2001), Ito (2004), Takii (2005), Timmer (1999), Rice and Abdullah (2000), and Takii and Ramstetter (2004).
5. See e.g. Rice and Abdullah (2000), Sandee and van Hulsen (2000), Sandee et al. (2002), Sato (2000), Smyth (1990), Tambunan (1994), and Tambunan and Keddie (1998).
6. See among others Liedholm and Mead (1999), and Berry and Mazumdar (1991).
7. This issue will be discussed later on.
8. There is a growing literature on spillover effects of technology transfer; see e.g. Kokko et al. (1996) and Blomstrom and Kokko (1998) for a survey of the spillover literature.
9. See e.g. Soepardi (1996), PASMI (1996), Harianto (1993), Kitabata (1988), Sato (2000), Supratikno (2001), Goeltom (1997), and JICA (2000).
10. See e.g. Basu et al. (2002), Foster and Rosenzweig (1996), and Yusuf (2003).
11. See international literature on development of SMEs development, e.g. Richard (1996), Goodman and Bamford (1989), Piore and Sabel (1984), Rabellotti (1995), and Sengenberger et al. (1990).
12. See Agrawal (2001) for a review of this literature.

13. Unfortunately, evidence on constraints faced by LEs is very rare, and there is no data from BPS. Although some reports on competitiveness and business environment may give some idea about business constraints faced by LEs such as distorted market, labour disputes, red tape, business unfriendly tax system, lack of infrastructure, too many retributions, and many others. However, there is data on the constraints on technology acquisition.

14. See also Sandee (1994; 1996), Sandee and ter Wingel (2002), and Sandee et al. (2000; 2002).

15. For more detailed information about each programme from each institution, including the name of the programme, type of assistance, programme executor, time frame, fund used, area, beneficiaries, status, problems and potential, see SMERU at <http://smeru.or.id>.

16. For discussion explicitly or implicitly on the government programmes to support SMEs in Indonesia, see for instance Sandee and van Hulsen (2000), Tambunan (1998*a*, *b*, *c*; 2000), Tambunan and Keddie (1998), Klapwijk (1997), Sandee (1994; 1995), Sandee et al. (1994; 2000; 2002), Damanik (1994), van Dierman (1997; 2001; 2004), Godfrey (1993), Thee (1992; 1993), O'Connell (1993), Sato (2000), and Smyth (1990*a*, *b*, *c*).

17. Arief (1995), Berry and Levy (1994; 1999), JICA (2000), SMERU (2004).

18. For more details about each of these credit types by the individual banks, please visit its website: <www.smeru.or.id>.

19. See further SMERU through <www.smeru.or.id>.

REFERENCES

Agrawal Ajay. "University-to-Industry Knowledge Transfer: Literature Review and Unanswered Questions". *International Journal of Management Review* 3, no. 4, 2001.

Anselin, L., A. Varga, and Z. Acs. "Local Spillovers between University Research and High Technology Innovations". *Journal of Urban Economics* 42, no. 3, 1997.

Arief, H. "Venture Capital for Small Entrepreneurs in Indonesia: Empirical Study and Its Prospect". Paper presented at the APEC Venture Capital Workshop, Seoul, 20–22 September 1995.

Basu, K., A. Narayan, and M. Ravallion. "Is Literacy Shared Within Households?". *Labor Economics* 8 (2002): 649–65.

Bayoumi, T., David T. Coe, and Elhanan Helpman. "R&D Spillovers and Global Growth". *Journal of International Economics* 47 (1999): 399–428.

Ben-David, D. and M. Loewy. "Free Trade and Long-Run Growth". CEPR Working Paper 1183, 1995.

Berry, Albert and Brian Levy. "Indonesia's Small and Medium-Size Exporters and their Support Systems". Policy Research Working Paper 1402. Policy Research Department, Finance and Private Sector Development Division. Washington D.C.: World Bank, 1994.

————. "Technical, Financial and Marketing Support for Indonesia's Small and Medium Industrial Exporters". In *Fulfilling the Export Potential of Small and Medium Firms*, edited by B. Levy, A. Berry, and Jeffrey B. Nugent. Boston: Kluwer Academic Publishers, 1999.

Berry, Albert and D. Mazumdar. "Small-Scale Industry in the Asian-Pacific Region". *Asian-Pacific Economic Literature* 5, no. 2, 1991.

Berry, Albert, Edgard Rodriguez, and Henry Sandee. "Small and Medium Enterprise Dynamics in Indonesia". *Bulletin of Indonesian Economic Studies* 37, no. 3, 2001.

Blomstrom, Magnus. "Host Country Benefits of Foreign Investment". NBER Working Paper no. 3615. Cambridge, MA: National Bureau of Economic Research, 1991.

Blomstrom, Magnus and A. Kokko. "Multinational Corporation and Spillovers". *Journal of Economic Surveys* 12 (1998): 247–77.

Branstetter, L. "Is Foreign Direct Investment a Channel of Knowledge Spillovers? Evidence From Japan's FDI in the United States". NBER Working Paper no. 8015. Cambridge, MA: National Bureau of Economic Research, 2000.

Caselli, F. and W.J. Coleman. "Cross-Country Technology Diffusion: The Case of Computers". NBER Working Paper no. 8130. Cambridge, MA: National Bureau of Economic Research, 2001.

Cole, William. "Bali's Garment Export Industry". In *Indonesia's Technological Challenge*, edited by Hal Hill and Thee Kian Wie. Canberra: Research School of Pacific and Asian Studies, Australian National University, and Singapore: Institute of Southeast Asian Studies, 1998*a*.

————. "Bali Garment Industry: An Indonesian Case of Successful Strategic Alliance". Mimeographed. Jakarta: The Asia Foundation, 1998*b*.

Dahlman, Carl J., Bruce Ross-Larsson, and Larry L. Westphal. "Managing Technology Development: Lessons from the Newly-Industrializing Countries". *World Development* 15, no. 6 (1987): 759–75.

Damanik, K. "Promotion of Small Enterprises in Indonesia". Paper presented at seminar "Policies and Strategies for SME Development". Turin, Italy: ILO, 19 September–14 October 1994.

Djankov, S. and B. Hoekman. "Foreign Investment and Productivity Growth in Czech Enterprises". *The World Bank Economic Review* 14, no. 1 (2000): 49–64.

FIAS. *Indonesia — A Pilot Project to Promote Backward Linkages — A Private Public Partnership*. Washington D.C.: Foreign Investment Advisory Service, June 1996.

Foster, A.D. and M.R. Rosenzweig. "Technical Change and Human-Capital Returns and Investments: Evidence from the Green Revolution". *American Economic Review* 86 (1996): 931–53.

Godfrey, M. "Labour Market Monitoring and Employment Policy in a Developing Country: A Study of Indonesia". New Delhi: World Employment Programme, International Labour Organisation, 1993.

Goeltom, Miranda S. "Development and Challenges of the Machinery Industry in

Indonesia". In *Waves of Change in Indonesia's Manufacturing Industry*, edited by Mari E. Pangestu and Yuri Sato. Tokyo: Institute of Developing Economies, 1997.

Goodman, E. and J. Bamford, eds. *Small Firms and Industrial Districts in Italy*. London: Routledge, 1989.

Görg, H. and E. Strobl. "Multinational Companies and Productivity Spillovers: A Meta Analysis". *Economic Journal* 111, no. 475 (2001): F723–39.

Grossman, G.M. and E. Helpman. "Growth and Welfare in a Small Open Economy". NBER Working Paper no. 2970. Cambridge, MA: National Bureau of Economic Research, 1989.

Hall, Bronwyn H., Adam B. Jaffe, and Manuel Trajtenberg. "The NBER Patent Citations Data File: Lessons, Insights and Methodological Tools". NBER Working Paper no. 8420. Cambridge, MA: National Bureau of Economic Research, 2001.

Harianto, Farid. "Study on Subcontracting in Indonesian Domestic Firms". *Indonesian Quarterly* 21, no. 3 (1993): 331–43.

Hill, Hal. *Foreign Investment and Industrialization in Indonesia*. Singapore: Oxford University Press, 1988.

———. "Indonesia's Industrial Technology Capability: Past Experience and Policy Options for the 1990s". Report prepared for BAPPENAS/DSP II, Jakarta, 1991.

———. "Introduction". In *Indonesia's Technological Challenge*, edited by Hal Hill and Thee Kian Wie. Canberra: Research School of Pacific and Asian Studies, Australian National University, and Singapore: Institute of Southeast Asian Studies, 1998.

———. "Small and Medium Enterprises in Indonesia: Old Policy Challenges for a New Administration". *Asian Survey* 41, no. 2, 2001.

Hill, Hal and Thee Kian Wie. *Indonesia's Technological Challenge*. Singapore: Institute of Southeast Asian Studies, 1998.

Hobday, Michael. "Export-led Technology Development in the Four Dragons: The Case of Electronics". *Development and Change* 25, no. 2 (1994): 393–61.

———. *Innovation in East Asia: The Challenge to Japan*. Vermont: Edward Elgar, 1995.

Hu, Albert G.Z. and Adam B. Jaffe. "Patent Citations and International Knowledge Flow: The Cases of Korea and Taiwan". NBER Working Paper no. 8528. Cambridge, MA: National Bureau of Economic Research, 2001.

Humprey, John and Hubert Schmitz. "Principle for Promoting Clusters and Network of SMEs". Paper commissioned by Small and Medium Enterprise Branch, Institute of Development Studies, University of Sussex, Brighton, 1995.

Iqbal, Farrukh. "The Impact of Deregulation on the Manufacturing Sector". In *Deregulation and Development in Indonesia*, edited by Farrukh Iqbal and William E. James. Connecticut: Praeger, Westport, 2002.

Iqbal, Farrukh and William E. James. *Deregulation and Development in Indonesia*. Connecticut: Praeger, Westport, 2002.

Ismawan, Bambang. "The People's Economy and the Role of Microfinance". *SMERU News*, The Smeru Research Institute, 10 April–June 2004.

Ito, Keiko. "Foreign Ownership and Productivity in the Indonesian Automobile Industry: Evidence from Establishment Data for 1990–1999". In *Growth and Productivity in East Asia*, edited by Takatoshi Ito and Andrew Rose. National Bureau of Economic Research, East Asia Seminar on Economics, vol. 13, University of Chicago Press, 2004.

Jacob, Jojo and Christoph Meister. "Productivity Gains, Technology Spillovers and Trade: Indonesian Manufacturing, 1980–96". *Bulletin of Indonesian Economic Studies* 41, no. 1 (2005): 37–56.

Jaffe, Adam B. and Manuel Trajtenberg. "International Knowledge Flows: Evidence from Patent Citations". *Economics of Innovation and New Technology* 8, nos. 1–2 (1999): 105–36.

Jaffe, Adam B., Manuel Trajtenberg, and Rebecca Henderson. "Geographic Localization of Knowledge Spillovers as Evidenced by Patent Citations". *Quarterly Journal of Economics* 108, no. 3 (1993): 577–98.

Jaffe, Adam B., Manuel Trajtenberg, and Michael S. Fogarty. "Knowledge Spillovers and Patent Citations: Evidence from A Survey of Inventors". *American Economic Review, Papers and Proceedings* (May 2000): 215–18.

Jakubiak, Malgorzata. "Transmission of Knowledge and Innovation into Poland: Role of Trade and Foreign Investment". Study report (GDN). Warsaw: CASE, June 2002.

JICA. "Study on Inter-Firm Linkages and Financial Needs for the Development of Small and Medium Scale Manufacturing Industry in Indonesia". Jakarta: Japan International Cooperation Agency in cooperation with PT Kami Karya Nusantara, 2000.

Kathuria, V. "Productivity Spillovers from Technology Transfer to Indian Manufacturing Firms". *Journal of International Development* 12, no. 3 (2000): 343–69.

———. "Foreign Firms, Technology Transfer and Knowledge Spillovers to Indian Manufacturing Firms: A Stochastic Frontier Analysis". *Applied Economics* 33 (2001): 625–42.

Keller, Wolfgang. "Trade and The Transmission of Technology". NBER Working Paper no. 6113. Cambridge, MA: National Bureau of Economic Research, 1997.

———. "Are International R&D Spillovers Trade-Related? Analysing Spillovers among Randomly Matched Trade Partners". *European Economic Review* 42 (1998): 1469–81.

———. "How Trade Patterns and Technology Flows Affect Productivity Growth". NBER Working Paper no. 6990. Cambridge, MA: National Bureau of Economic Research, 1999.

———. "Geographic Localization of International Technology Diffusion". NBER Discussion Paper no. 7509. Cambridge, MA: National Bureau of Economic Research, 2000.

Kim, Linsu. *Imitation to Innovation: The Dynamics of Korea's Technological Learning.* Boston: Harvard Business School Press, 1997.

Kinoshita, T. "R&D and Technology Spillovers via FDI: Innovation and Absorptive Capacity". CERGE-EI Working Paper no. 163, November 2000.

Kitabata, T. *Report on the Subcontracting System in the Indonesian Machinery Industries.* Tokyo: Japan International Cooperation Agency, 1988.

Klapwijk, Martin. "Rural Industry Clusters in Central Java, Indonesia: An Empirical Assessment of their Role in Rural Industrialization". Unpublished Ph.D. dissertation, Tinbergen Institute Research Series no. 153, Vrije Universiteit Amsterdam, 1997.

Koch, A. *Constructing the Analytical Framework of a Competence-Based Theory of International Competitiveness.* Melbourne: Academy of Marketing Science, 1995.

Kokko, A., R. Tansini, and M.C. Zejan. "Local Technological Capability and Productivity Spillovers from FDI in the Uruguayan Manufacturing Sector". *Journal of Development Studies* 32, no. 4 (1996): 602–11.

Lall, Sanjaya and Kishore Rao. *Indonesia: Sustaining Manufactured Export Growth.* Vol. 1, Main Report, Revised draft report submitted to the National Planning Board (Bappenas), Jakarta, August 1995.

Liedholm, Carl and Donald Mead. *Small Enterprises and Economic Development: The Dynamic Role of Micro and Small Enterprises.* London: Routledge, 1999.

Mathews, John A. and Cho Dong-Sung. *Tiger Technology: The Creation of a Semiconductor Industry in East Asia.* Cambridge: Cambridge University Press, 2001.

McKendrick, David. "Obstacles to 'Catch-Up': The Case of the Indonesian Aircraft Industry". *Bulletin of Indonesian Economic Studies* 28, no. 1 (1992): 39–66.

Navaretti, Barba Giorgio and David Tarr. "International Knowledge Flows and Economic Performance: A Review of the Evidence". *World Bank Economic Review* 14 (2000): 1–15.

O'Connell, C. "Stability, Jobs and Income Generation in Indonesia". Report to the International Labour Organisation, Jakarta, 1993.

PASMI. "The Current Status of the Indonesian Motorcycle Market on the Motorcycle Industry". Paper presented at the 6th Asian Motorcycle Conference, 9–10 October 1996, Penang.

Perry, C. and R. Pyatt. *The Space of Network Relationships in a Southeast Asian Setting.* Melbourne: Academy of Marketing Science, 1995.

Piore, Michael J. and Charles F. Sabel. "Italian Small Business Development: Lessons for U.S. Industrial Policy". In *American Industry in International Competition*, edited by John Zysman and Laura Tyson. Ithaca, NY: Cornell University Press, 1983.

Piore, M.J. and C.F. Sabel. *The Second Industrial Divide: Possibilities for Prosperity.* New York: Basic Books, 1984.

PPTA and The Asia Foundation. *Provincial SME Development — Draft Final Report, Part I: Provincial SME Development in Indonesia.* ADB PPTA 4281 INO, August 2005.

Rabellotti, R. "Is there an 'Industrial District Model'? Footwear Districts in Italy and Mexico Compared". *World Development* 23, no. 1, 1995.

Revesz, J. and R. Lattimor. "Statistical Analysis of the Use and Impact of Government Business Programmes". Production Commission Staff Research Paper. Canberra: AusInfo, 2001.

Rice, R. and I. Abdullah. "A Comparison of Small and Medium/Large Indonesian Manufacturing Enterprises from 1986 and 1996 by Sector". Mimeographed. Jakarta: Partnership for Economic Growth Project, USAID, 2000.

Richard, Friedrich. "Principal for Promoting Clusters and Networking of SMEs". Paper presented at the IX International Conference on Small and Medium Enterprises, 17–19 April 1996, WASME, New Delhi.

Rodriguez-Clare, A. and L. Alfaro. "Multinationals and Linkages: An Empirical Investigation". Economia 4, no. 2, 2004.

Romer, P. "Endogenous Technological Change". *Journal of Political Economy* 98 (1990): S71-102.

Rosenberg, Nathan and Claudio Frischtak, eds. *International Technology Transfer: Concept, Measures, and Comparisons.* New York: Praeger, 1985.

Rowbotham, J. "Enterprise Networks Draw New Strength from Numbers". *Business Review Weekly*, 16 August 1991, pp. 70–74.

Sandee, Henry. "The Impact of Technological Change on Interfirm Linkages. A Case Study of Clustered Rural Small-Scale Roof Tile Enterprises in Central Java". In *Flexible Specialization: The Dynamics of Small-Scale Industries in the South*, edited by P.O. Pedersen, A. Sverrisson, and M.P. van Dijk. London: Intermediate Technology Publications, 1994.

———. "Innovation Adoption in Rural Industry: Technological Change in Roof Tile Clusters in Central Java, Indonesia". Unpublished Ph.D. dissertation, Vrije Universiteit, Amsterdam, 1995.

———. "Small-Scale and Cottage Industry Clusters in Central Java: Characteristics, Research Issues, and Policy Options". Paper presented at the International Seminar on Small Scale and Micro Enterprises in Economic Development Anticipating Globalization and Free Trade, Satya Wacana Christian University, 4–5 November 1996, Salatiga.

Sandee, Henry and H. Weijland. "Rural Cottage Industry in Transition: The Roof Tile Industry in Kabupaten Boyolali, Central Java". *Bulletin of Indonesian Economic Studies* 25, no. 2, 1989.

Sandee, Henry and J. ter Wingel. "SME Cluster Development Strategies in Indonesia: What Can We Learn from Successful Clusters?". Paper presented for JICA Workshop on Strengthening Capacity of SME Clusters in Indonesia, 5–6 March 2002, Jakarta.

Sandee, Henry and S.C. van Hulsen. "Business Development Services for Small and Cottage Industry Clusters in Indonesia: A Review of Case Studies from Central Java". Paper presented at International Conference "Business Services for Small Enterprises in Asia: Developing Markets and Measuring Performance", 3–6 April 2000, Hanoi.

Sandee, Henry, P. Rietveld, Hendrawan Supratikno, and P. Yuwono. "Promoting Small Scale and Cottage Industries: An Impact Analysis for Central Java". *Bulletin of Indonesian Economic Studies* 30, no. 3 (1994): 115–42.

Sandee, Henry, Roos Kities Andadari, and Sri Sulandjari. "Small Firm Development during Good Times and Bad: The Jepara Furniture Industry". In *Indonesia in Transition: Social Aspects of Reformasi and Crisis*, edited by C. Manning and P. van Dierman. Canberra: Indonesia Assessment Series, Research School of Pacific and Asian Studies, Australian National University, and Singapore: Institute of Southeast Asian Studies, 2000.

Sandee, Henry, B. Isdijoso, and Sri Sulandjari. *SME Clusters in Indonesia: An Analysis of Growth Dynamics and Employment Conditions*. Jakarta: International Labor Office (ILO), 2002.

Sato, Yuri. "The Transfer of Japanese Management Technology to Indonesia". In *Indonesia's Technological Challenge*, edited by Hal Hill and Thee Kian Wie. Canberra: Research School of Pacific and Asian Studies, Australian National University and Singapore: Institute of Southeast Asian Studies, 1998.

———. "Linkage Formation by Small Firms: The Case of a Rural Cluster in Indonesia". *Bulletin of Indonesian Economic Studies* 36, no. 1, 2000*a*.

———. "How did the Crisis Affect Small and Medium-Sized Enterprises? From a Field Study of the Metal-Working Industry in Java". *The Developing Economies* XXXVIII, no. 4 (2000*b*): 572–95.

Schiller, J. and B. Martin-Schiller. "Market, Culture and State in the Emergence of an Indonesian Export Furniture Industry". *Journal of Asian Business* 13, no. 1 (1997): 1–23.

Sengenberger, W., G.W. Loveman, and M.J. Piore, eds. *The Re-Emergence of Small Enterprises: Industrial Restructuring in Industrialized Countries*. Geneva: International Institute for Labour Studies, 1990.

Shepherd, W.F., A. Szirmai, and D.S. Prasada Rao. "Indonesia Manufacturing Sector Output and Productivity: An Australian Comparative Perspective, 1975–90". *Bulletin of Indonesian Economic Studies* 34, no. 2 (1998): 121–42.

Sjoholm, Fredrik. "Exports, Imports and Productivity: Results from Indonesian Establishment Data". *World Development* 27, no. 4 (1999*a*): 705–15.

———. "Productivity Growth in Indonesia: The Role of Regional Characteristics and Direct Foreign Investment". *Economic Development and Cultural Change* 47, no. 3 (1999*b*): 559–84.

SMERU. "Mapping Assistance Programmes to Strengthen Microbusinesses". *Smeru News*, no. 10, April–June 2004.

Smyth, Ines A. "Agglomeration of Small Scale Industries in Developing Countries: A Case Study of the Indonesian Rattan Industries". Paper presented at the Research Seminar on Rural Development Studies, 10 January 1990*a*, Institute of Social Studies, The Hague.

———. "The Rattan Industry of Tegalwangi (Indonesia): A Success Story for Small-Scale Enterprises?". Mimeographed. The Hague: Institute of Social Studies, 1990*b*.

————. "Collective Efficiency and Selective Benefits: The Growth of the Rattan Industry of Tegalwangi". Working Paper Series, B.11. Bandung: AKATIGA, December 1990*c*.

Snodgrass, D.R. and T. Biggs. *Industrialization and the Small Firm: Patterns and Policies.* San Francisco: International Centre for Economic Growth and the Harvard Institute for International Development, 1996.

Soepardi. "Pengalaman PT Astra International dalam Pembinaan Usaha Kecil, Menengah dan Koperasi" (The experience of PT Astra International in Assisting Small and Medium Business and Cooperative). Paper presented at the International Seminar on Small Scale and Micro Enterprises in Economic Development Anticipating Globalization and Free Trade, 4–5 November 1996, Satya Wacana Christian University, Salatiga.

Soesastro, Hadi. "Emerging Patterns of Technology Flows in the Asia-Pacific Region: The Relevance to Indonesia". In *Indonesia's Technological Challenge*, edited by Hal Hill and Thee Kian Wie. Canberra: Research School of Pacific and Asian Studies, Australian National University and Singapore: Institute of Southeast Asian Studies, 1998.

SRI International. "Technology Development Plan for Indonesia's Engineering Industries". Draft final report for the Ministry of Industry, Republic of Indonesia, Jakarta, 1992.

Supramono, H. Sandee, P. Yuwono Kuntadi, L. Suharti, and Wiratmo. "Inovasi pada Industri Anyaman Bambu" (Innovation in Bamboo Handicraft Industry), Seri UPPW no. 30. Salatiga: Christian University of Satya Wacana, 1992.

Supratikno, Hendrawan. "Partnership Between SMEs and Large Firms: Trap or Trajectory?". Working paper, Faculty of Economics, Satya Wacana University, Salatiga, 1996.

————. "Subcontracting Relationship in Indonesian Manufacturing Firms". *Gadjah Mada International Journal of Business* 3, no. 2, 2001.

————. "The Strategies of Cluster Upgrading in Central Java". A Preliminary Report to Depperindag, Salatiga, 2002.

Styles, C. *Exporting Marketing Performance: A Relational Perspective.* World Marketing Congress, 1995.

TAF. "Strategic Alliances and Development of Small and Medium-Scale Enterprises in Indonesia". Final Report, May 2000, The Asia Foundation, Jakarta.

Takii, Sadayuki. "Productivity Differentials between Local and Foreign Plants in Indonesian Manufacturing, 1995". *World Development* 32, no. 11 (2004): 1957–69.

————. "Productivity Spillovers and Characteristics of Foreign Multinational Plants in Indonesian Manufacturing 1990–1995". *Journal of Development Economics* 76, no. 2 (2005): 521–42.

Takii, Sadayuki and Eric D. Ramstetter. "Employment, Production, Labour Productivity, and Foreign Multinationals in Indonesian Manufacturing, 1975–2000". Working Paper no. 25. Kitakyushu: International Centre for the Study of East Asian Development, 2004.

————. "Multinational Presence and Labour Productivity Differentials in Indonesian Manufacturing, 1975–2001". *Bulletin of Indonesian Economic Studies* 41, no. 2 (2005): 221–42.

Tambunan, Tulus T.H. *The Role of Small-Scale Industries in Rural Economic Development: A Case Study in Ciomas Subdistrict, Bogor District, West Java, Indonesia.* Amsterdam: Thesis Publishers, 1994.

————. "Present Status and Prospect of Supporting Industries in Indonesia". In IDEA, "Present Status and Prospects of Supporting Industries in ASEAN (I), Philippines and Indonesia". Tokyo: Institute of Developing Economies, Japan External Trade Organization, March 1998*a*.

————. "Cluster Diagnosis in Kuningan Fried Onion Cluster and Proposed Action Plan". Study report. Jakarta: UNIDO, October 1998*b*.

————. "Cluster Diagnosis in Padang Rattan Industries and Proposed Action Plan". Study report. Jakarta: UNIDO, October 1998*c*.

————. "The Performance of Small Enterprises during the Economic Crisis: Evidence from Indonesia". Mimeographed. Jakarta, Indonesia: LP3E-Kadin, 1999*a*.

————. "The Needs Assessment Study of Agroprocessing Small-and Medium-Scale Industries with Special Focus on Women Entrepreneur, Environment and Gender Issues, and the Likely Impact of the Crisis". Paper prepared for Economic and Social Commission for Asia and The Pacific/United Nations Development Programme (ESCAP/UNDP). Jakarta, Indonesia: LP3E-Kadin and UNDP, 1999*b*.

————. *Development of Small-Scale Industries During the New Order Government in Indonesia.* Aldershot: Ashgate Publishing, 2000.

————. "Peluang, Potensi dan Kendala IK Logam Dalam Peta Hubungan Industrial Antara IK dan IMB. Kasus IK Komponen dan *Spare Part*" (Opportunity, Potential and Constraint of Metal SI in the Map of Industrial Relation between SI and MLI. The Case of SI of Components and Spare Parts). Paper presented at the National Policy Dialog. Jakarta: USAID and ASEMHAKI, October 2002.

————. *Development of Small and Medium Enterprises in Indonesia from the Asia-Pacific Perspective.* Jakarta: Trisakti University Press, 2006.

Tambunan, Tulus T.H. and James Keddie. "Draft Cluster Diagnosis and Action Plan. Yogyakarta Area Leather Goods Cluster". Study report. Jakarta: UNIDO, February 2005.

Thee Kian Wie. "Subcontracting in the Engineering Sub-Sector in Indonesia: A Preliminary Survey". Study report. Jakarta: PEP-LIPI, September 1984.

————. "Kaitan-kaitan vertikal antara perusahaan dan pengembangan sistim subkontraktor di Indonesia: beberapa hasil studi permulaan" (Vertical Integrations between Firms and Development of Subcontracting System in Indonesia: Some Results of Preliminary Study). *Masyarakat Indonesia* XII, no. 3, 1985.

————. "Indonesia: Technology Transfer in the Manufacturing Industry". In *Technological Challenge in the Asia Pacific Economy*, edited by Hadi Soesastro and Mari Pangestu. Sydney: Allen & Unwin, 1990*a*.

————. "Prospects for Cooperation in Technology". In *Cooperation in Small and Medium-Scale Industries in ASEAN*, edited by Kim Seung Jin and Suh Jang Won. Kuala Lumpur: Asian and Pacific Development Centre, 1990*b*.

————. "Promoting Small-Scale Industries in Indonesia". *Prisma* 52 (1992): 3–13.

————. "Industrial Structure and Small and Medium Enterprises Development in Indonesia". EDI Working Paper. Washington D.C.: World Bank, 1993.

————. "The Development of the Motor Cycle Industry in Indonesia". In *Waves of Change in Indonesia's Manufacturing Industry*, edited by Mari E. Pangestu and Yuri Sato. Tokyo: Institute of Developing Economies, 1997*a*.

————. *Pengembangan Kemampuan Teknologi Industri di Indonesia*. Jakarta: UI-Press, 1997*b*.

————. Determinants of Indonesia's Industrial Technology Development. In *Indonesia's Technological Challenge*, edited by Hal Hill and Thee Kian Wee. Canberra: Research School of Pacific and Asian Studies, Australian National University, and Singapore: Institute of Southeast Asian Studies, 1998.

————. "Competition Policy in Indonesia and the New Anti-Monopoly and Fair Competition Law". *Bulletin of Indonesian Economic Studies* 38, no. 3 (2002): 331–42.

————. "The Major Channels of International Technology Transfer to Indonesia: An Assessment". *Journal of the Asia-Pacific Economy* 10, no. 2 (May 2005): 214–36.

Thee Kian Wie and Mari Pangestu. "Technological Capabilities and Indonesia's Manufactured Exports". Revised report for UNCTAD/SAREC Project on Technological Dynamism and the Export of Manufactures from Developing Countries, January 1994.

Timmer, Marcel P. "Indonesia's Ascent on the Technology Ladder: Capital Stock and Total Factor Productivity in Indonesia Manufacturing, 1975–95". *Bulletin of Indonesian Economic Studies* 35, no. 1, 1999.

Trajtenberg, Manuel. "Innovation in Israel 1968–97: A Comparative Analysis Using Patent Data". *Research Policy* 30, no. 3 (March 2001): 363–90.

van der Kamp, Rick, Adam Szirmai, and Marcel Timmer. "Technology and Human Resources in the Indonesian Textile Industry". In *Indonesia's Technological Challenge*, edited by Hal Hill and Thee Kian Wie. Canberra: Research School of Pacific and Asian Studies, Australian National University and Singapore: Institute of Southeast Asian Studies, 1998.

van Diermen, Peter. *Small Business in Indonesia*. Aldershot: Ashgate Publishing, 1997.

————, ed. "SME Policy in Indonesia: Towards a New Agenda". Occasional Paper Series on SME Development no. 1. Manila: Asia Development Bank, 1997.

————. "The Economic Policy Environment for Small Rural Enterprises in Indonesia". In *The Indonesian Rural Economy Mobility, Work and Enterprise*, edited by Thomas R. Leinbach. Singapore: Institute of Southeast Asian Studies, 2004.

van Velzen, Anita. "Small Scale Food Processing Industries in West Java: Potentialities and Constraints", 1992.

Weaver, K. Mark and Pat H. Dickson. "Towards a Unified Model of SME-based Strategic Alliances: Transaction Costs, Resource Dependencies and Social Controls". Paper submitted to the Academy of Management Entrepreneurship Division, Department of Management and Marketing, The University of Alabama, January 1995, Tuscaloosa, Alabama, 1992.

WEF. *The Global Competitiveness Report 2004–05*. New York: Palgrave Macmillan, 2004.

Weijland, H. "The Role of Middlemen in Rural Industry: An Empirical Study of Rural Industry in 25 Indonesian Provinces". Mimeographed. Amsterdam: Faculty of Economics, Free University, 1992.

———. "Trade Networks for Flexible Rural Industry". In *Flexible Specialization: The Dynamics of Small-Scale Industries in the South*, edited by P.O. Pedersen, A. Sverrison, and M. P.van Dijk. London: Intermediate Technology Publications, 1994.

World Bank. *Indonesia — Industrial Technology Development for a Competitive Edge.* Report no. 15451-IND. Washington D.C.: World Bank, 2005.

———. *Raising Investment in Indonesia: A Second Generation of Reforms*. Report no. 31708-IND. Washington D.C.: World Bank, 24 February 1996.

Yusuf, Shahid. *Innovative East Asia: The Future of Growth*. World Bank and Oxford University Press, 2003.

7
Marketing and Competition in the New Indonesia

Hal Hill and Pantjar Simatupang

1. Introduction

Marketing and competition in Indonesia are in a state of rapid transition. The Indonesia of 2006 looks very different from that of a decade ago, and bears little resemblance to the early Soeharto era. Thirty years ago, the modern retail sector hardly existed, and marketing networks were dominated by informal, small-scale, multi-tiered trade and traders. Similarly, the modern sector of the economy was principally in the hands of a small number of state, foreign, and domestic conglomerates, alongside an extensive small-medium sector. Modern sector commerce was also slowly recovering from an ill-fated attempt to nationalize large-scale trading activities, and the removal of long-established ethnic Chinese traders from rural areas. But, over the past decade in particular, there has been a technological revolution in marketing, while ownership structures have changed substantially. The policy environment has changed significantly. There is a new set of commercial actors. And the international environment, and Indonesia's connections to it, have altered profoundly.

There are several key drivers of these changes, but they principally centre on technological and policy factors. Some of these are global and universal, while others are specific to Indonesia.

The former includes ongoing telecommunications-based technological change, which is rapidly reducing the costs of information and distribution. Accompanying this is the trend towards agglomeration and scale in retail market networks.

The major factor in Indonesia has been the transition from a centralized, authoritarian, predictable, high-growth regime to one where political and commercial power is increasingly dispersed, and policy outcomes are fluid and unpredictable. Governments have a diminished capacity to provide crucial growth-enhancing public goods, especially infrastructure. Indeed, the huge expansion in physical infrastructure investments over the three decades to 1997, which resulted in strong domestic economic integration and greatly facilitated the spread of formal market networks, has come to a halt. The road and power networks, in particular, have evidently deteriorated since the crisis (see Chapter 5).

It needs to be emphasized that, as would be expected in the world's largest archipelagic nation, there is no single "Indonesian story". Geography and the uneven distribution of physical infrastructure dictate that the evidence from Java, where most of the detailed research has been undertaken, will differ from that of much of the Outer Islands, especially in more remote regions such as Papua. There are also significant rural-urban differences, a factor reinforced by differential policy treatment, for example regarding the entry of hypermarkets. Thus there is no single paradigm in which to view these issues.

Competitive market structures and efficient marketing networks benefit consumers through lower prices and better services, thus raising their real purchasing power. They also contribute to dynamic efficiency by offering potential new entrants clear, undistorted market signals and a more level playing field. But there are also possible losers: uncompetitive firms and farmers facing intensified competition, and traditional trading networks rendered obsolete by the intrusion of direct "harvest-to-shelf" sales channels. Thus, change is inevitable and on balance desirable. As with all new technologies, it will benefit those who are best placed to connect to and take advantage of the drivers of change. The policy challenge is to facilitate adjustment for the potential losers, either upgrading within their current industry, or exiting from it.

There is some case study and anecdotal evidence on these issues, which inevitably is limited in coverage, sometimes dated, and region and/or sector-specific. There are virtually no secondary data which can usefully be marshalled for this research. We draw on the results of the RICS where possible.

With particular reference to non-farm rural enterprises (NFEs), this chapter examines marketing and competition issues in Sections 2 and 3 respectively, while in the concluding section we connect these findings to some salient policy questions. While the two issues are closely inter-related, we place more emphasis on marketing. We refer where relevant to the other modules in the RICA Project, especially infrastructure and technology diffusion.

2. Marketing

How have Indonesian marketing channels changed in recent years, in response to liberalized entry provisions governing giant MNE retail chains, continuing urbanization, and the telecommunications revolution? In the absence of comprehensive economy-wide data, we draw on a number of informative case studies, principally Simatupang (2005), in an attempt to develop a composite picture. We briefly summarize each study, and then draw some general conclusions. The following sub-section examines the even more sketchy picture for manufactures.

Simatupang (2005) provides a comprehensive analysis of agricultural marketing and competition issues. His analytical framework is shaped by four factors: missing market, high transaction costs, imperfect competition, and uncoordinated supply chains.

He first examines "traditional" marketing channels, dispelling the notion, dating back to Boeke's dual economy thesis, of backward-sloping supply curves and lack of entrepreneurial capacity. He cites a variety of empirical evidence, including the influential Hayami-Kawagoe (1993) study to show that, when markets "work" (i.e. price signals are effectively transmitted, infrastructure provision opens up a "vent for surplus", etc.), farmers and traders invariably respond. Traditional marketing channels are "long, inter-twined, uncoordinated and seller-driven", and reflect the realities of transaction costs in dealing with small, spatially dispersed producers, the timing of harvests influenced by climatic factors, and economies of scale in processing and transportation. However, these multi-tiered chains, while possessing their own economic logic, are "institutionally inefficient" in the sense of relatively high margins between producers and final consumers. Price signals as a spur to improved quality may also be suppressed, owing to the problem of "traceability", which arises because the output of many small farmers is pooled, with limited grading for quality. Information is asymmetrical, in that traders have superior knowledge of market conditions and opportunities. Marketing margins are typically high, but this reflects at least in part uncertainty and high wastage rates. Producers are generally poorly connected to retailers and consumers, and they are slow to alter their product mix. In consequence, these arrangements are prone to the problem of supply-demand mismatches.

Simatupang next assesses the role of the government in these arrangements. Especially prior to the major deregulation of 1999, intervention was pervasive, and frequently perverse. A wide range of monopolies was in place, including the state logistic bureau (Bulog), various trade monopolies (increasingly cornered by the Soeharto family in his last decade of power), crop-specific monopolies (e.g. cloves, Jeruk Pontianak, Nusa Tenggara sandalwood, rattan). A second set of barriers related to inter-regional trade, such as in livestock and sugar. While these too have largely been abolished, quasi-legal, inter-regional trade taxes, which were widespread in the 1950s and 1960s as central authority over the regions weakened, have reappeared, particularly since the 1997–98 crisis and the 2001 decentralization package. For example, he cites the case of an eight-ton consignment of oranges from Karo (North Sumatra) to Jakarta having to pay levies totalling Rp 190,000 at 45 collection points. These levies were equivalent to Rp 24 per kilo. By way of comparison, the farm price of the oranges was approximately Rp 1,850 per kilo, and trucking costs were estimated to be about Rp 692 per kilo. Thus these levies appear to be quite trivial, equivalent to less than 5 per cent of total transport costs. However, account need to be taken of the time lost and inconvenience, in addition to the general unpredictability of these levies.[1]

Inevitably, each anecdotal report differs, and thus it is difficult to draw firm conclusions regarding the incidence and intensity of these levies. Recent field research in Aceh, for example, suggests they may be a good deal higher. But perhaps this province is a special case in view of its history of conflict.[2]

In principle, most of these regional levies should have been abolished, and in early April 2006 the GOI released a draft law formally outlawing them. But since 1998 regional governments have been emboldened by a weakened central government and increased fiscal autonomy. There are no accurate statistics on the magnitude of these regional charges and levies. A monitoring team in the Ministry of Finance (MoF) recorded that, for the period 2001 to January 2006, some 13,520 "perdas" (peraturan daerah, regional regulations on levies and charges) had been issued, 12,950 by second-tier governments (*kabupaten/kota*) and 570 by provinces.[3] The MoF had received 9,573 of these perdas (71 per cent of the total). Of these, it had examined 5,794, and recommended that 611 (11 per cent) be abolished or revised as inconsistent with national laws.

This is of course an incomplete picture. The above data refer to "official" levies imposed by regional governments and reported to the central government. Unofficial levies and those which are not reported to the central government are almost certainly more numerous. This is not the place to discuss the causes of these levies and their regional incidence. But it is important to emphasize that these levies are not primarily a local governance problem. For example, organs of the central government, most notably the army and the police, are among the most active perpetrators.

At the central government level, although most of the Soeharto-linked monopolies have been dismantled, domestic monopolies continue to be an ever-present feature of Indonesia, and the current Minister for Trade has found them more difficult to deregulate than most international trade issues. This is especially the case for politically sensitive products such as rice and sugar (Marks 2004). Bulog's monopoly was abolished in 1999. But since 2002, import permits for white sugar were given to just four state-owned sugar factories, who in turn have arrangements with private sugar traders which entails an obligation to purchase all of the factories' output. The private traders and state companies in effect have complete control over the domestic sugar market. Inter-island shipping of sugar has also been curtailed. The Commission for the Supervision of Business Competition (KPPU, Komisi Pengawas Persaingan Usaha), discussed in more detail below, has warned that this sugar regulation policy may conflict with the Competition Law, but thus far no action has been taken. Moreover, in 2005, Bulog regained its monopoly right over the importation of rice. The fertilizer trade was also re-regulated over this period.

Alongside these traditional markets is the rapidly emerging modern retail industry, including department stores, hypermarkets, supermarkets, minimarkets, and specialist outlets. While the overall trends are clear, there are limited aggregate data. Pantjar cites data for the period 1997–2001 which report that modern retail sales grew by 26 per cent per annum, to about 17 per cent of the total. Both supermarkets and hypermarkets are growing quickly, by about 26 per cent and 30 per cent respectively over this period. They are both quite highly concentrated, with four-firm ratios of around 60 per cent in 2001. Supermarkets have spread to practically all provinces, whereas hypermarkets are still located mainly in the large urban centres. By contrast, over the same period traditional retail markets contracted by 3 per cent per annum. According to an AC Nielson survey, the modern market is growing by 31 per cent per annum, and the traditional sector shrinking by 8 per cent. An estimated 400 small "kiosks" are forced out of business every year.

Pantjar also draws a distinction between traditional, seller-driven markets for agricultural produce, alongside these modern buyer-driven networks. He emphasizes that the latter have introduced "harvest-to-shelf" schedules, based on efficient and highly organized logistics, which deliver produce to supermarket shelves within twenty-four hours of harvest. Such a chain is important where refrigerated transport is expensive and still quite uncommon, as it is in Indonesia.

The services offered by these two outlets differ significantly. Table 7.1 summarizes the contrasting characteristics of the two sets of markets, which we will now briefly discuss.

Table 7.1
Contrasting Characteristics between
Traditional and Modern Market Systems

Characteristics	Traditional market	Modern market
1. Retailers market place	Bazaars, wet markets, petty shops, peddler: • Inconvenient • Assisted-service	Super/hypermarkets, mini markets: • Convenient • Self-service
2. Distribution	Decentralized: • Overlapping chains • Unmanaged supply chain • No conditions	Centralized: • Unique chain • Managed supply chain • Coordinated by a chain champion
3. Quality and delivery	'Disorderly': • No standard • No quality differentiation • No delivery protocol	Assured: • Standardized • Distinct quality differentiation • Tight delivery protocol
4. Transaction arrangement	On-the-spot negotiation: • Unplanned/unorganized • Once-only • Open-actors	Predetermined contact: • Planned/organized • Recurrent • Exclusive actors
5. Traceability	Impossible: • Disorganized distribution line • Many producers and middlemen	Assured: • Organized distribution line • Unique producers and middlemen
6. Transparency and credibility	Inapplicable: • No information on quality • No supplier identity (unbranded)	Assured: • Revealed quality attributes • Revealed supplier identity (branded)
7. Key driver	Producers (sellers)	Consumers (buyers)
8. Price	Low	High

Source: Simatupang (2005).

The modern outlets are ceramic floored, air conditioned, self-service, fixed price, and offer a very wide range of goods and services. Goods are typically branded and packaged, and quality control is high. They tend to cater to urban, middle-class consumers.

The modern outlets have also revolutionized marketing channels. Producers follow these outlets' product specifications, as transmitted via consumer buying preferences. Farmers' production plans are coordinated to ensure supply is met. Supply chains are direct and speedy. Traditional trade networks are by-passed, and costs are lower. These modern outlets typically have formal, tightly specified contracts with a substantial number of suppliers.[4] As in manufacturing subcontracting arrangements, to be discussed shortly, relationships are frequently durable, and the buyers transfer a package of inputs including market information, technology,[5] and sometimes finance. They also "benchmark" their suppliers for price, quality, and reliability. Generally, suppliers need to reach some minimum size to be able to fulfill orders. Cooperative farming arrangements, including nucleus estates, are encouraged, to meet large-volume orders. Village collectors typically play a coordinating role in this process,[6] while innovative local 'pioneer suppliers' often provide an important demonstration effect. The Malang case study also draws attention to the key role played by a major seed supply company, Tanindo, which entered the supermarket supply chain in 2001.[7]

Orders are issued daily, and require quick responses, including delivery within twenty-four hours from "harvest-to-shelf". Modern logistics technologies, the telecommunications revolution, and improved transportation networks (at least compared to the 1970s) underpin the system.

The Malang case study further documents these trends, while bearing in mind the caveats associated with a single area study.[8] Farmers are quickly adopting HVC's, driven by higher profitability, good information flows, and a well-developed set of middleman/trading networks, which perform information and risk-sharing functions. The expansion of cellular telecommunication services has been particularly important in providing timely and accurate information.

Traditional markets play a buffer role in relation to these modern chains. They take residual produce, including that which fails to meet demanding quality control checks. They sometimes sell to the modern sector in times of scarcity or sudden loss of supplies. Prices in the traditional markets are also used as a reference point for the modern sector. Thus, although the latter is gradually supplanting the former, in reality the market segments are as much complementary as competitive. Direct government intervention in these modern market chains is minimal, except in cases where supermarket entry is restricted. Contrary to some popular perceptions, there is very little evidence that these modern outlets engage in anti-competitive behaviour. Whilst it is true that, as noted above, seller concentration indictors are quite high, the market is contestable as barriers to entry are modest. In any case, traditional markets also serve to place a cap on modern sector market power. Moreover, buyers generally wish to develop long-term, trustworthy, cooperative relationships with sellers, and are therefore reluctant to engage in short-term opportunistic behaviour.

Nevertheless, the potential for collusive behaviour among the modern retail outlets remains, and there is probably therefore a role for KPPU to regularly monitor price comparisons. In addition, owing to the political sensitivities associated with the displacement of small-scale traditional traders, the issuance of licences for the development of supermarkets, now in the hands of *Kabupaten* governments,[9] needs to be undertaken in a transparent manner involving public awareness and consultation.

Contrary to some common perceptions, small farmers, even those with holdings as little as 0.1 hectare, are able to profitably access these modern chains, provided they meet the more demanding market schedules. In the process, the signals from the modern outlets induce agricultural diversification towards high value crops. As small farmers shift out of these traditional low value crops (such as rice, soybean, bananas, etc.) to high value crops such as sweetcorn, lettuce, melon, etc., the returns are potentially very much higher. Table 7.2 indicates some indicative yield differentials. Moreover, there are additional potential benefits from planting the HVC's: cropping times are shorter, income flows can be balanced throughout the year, and crop diversity can be extended.[10]

Table 7.2
Cost and Profitability Indicators of Vegetable and Fruit Farming as a Ratio to Rice in Irrigated Land

Crops	Location/year	Cost ratio (1)	Profit ratio (2)	Profitability ratio (3)= (2)/(1)
Onion1	Indramayu, 2001	3.49	7.79	2.23
Curl Chili1	Agam, 2001	2.09	9.90	4.74
Red chili1	Kediri, 2001	2.48	13.38	5.40
Melon1	Ngawi, 2001	6.26	28.53	4.56
Lettuce2	Malang, 2005	1.94	4.42	2.28
Broccoli2	Malang, 2005	1.70	2.66	1.56

Source: Simatupang (2005).

The Malang case study reinforces this story of potentially very large gains to farmers. But risks also rise, owing to more expensive inputs and the demanding top-end product quality standards. In particular, there are very high returns to innovation.[11] Hence, farmers sensibly manage risk by diversifying, generally planting both conventional crops and HVC's, and catering to both the lower return traditional markets alongside the supermarkets. The Malang case study also finds a similar risk-management strategy at work. The implication is that there is a premium attached to farmer's skill, initiative, and adaptability. Those unable to compete may suffer the fate of all "innovation laggards": reduced returns, and being consigned to low yield segments of the market.[12] They are also more vulnerable to sudden large price declines in times of periodic over-supply.[13]

A key feature of the modern markets is their connections to the global economy. Their product quality and production process standards are converging to international standards. They are more likely to sell imported products, especially now that Indonesia has relatively few import barriers for these products, and they offer the prospect of connecting domestic producers to these international markets, both directly and indirectly.

Against these benefits, there are constraints and potential barriers to participation in the booming modern sector. Good quality telecommunications and a paved-road network are essential, as otherwise local farmers will struggle to compete with imports. This is especially an issue as HVC's in Indonesia are often produced in somewhat remote, high-altitude areas where these infrastructure facilities are often deficient. Moreover, public extension services are deeply rooted in traditional agricultural crops, especially rice, and have been slow to diversify their focus. Local governments may also be able to play a light-handed role in encouraging the development of agricultural clusters which are better able to service the high-volume modern sector demand. More generally, competition among regions for lucrative supermarket contracts is likely to intensify. Regional (*kabupaten*) governments have a major role to play here, in the provision of efficient marketing infrastructure,[14] together with the removal of complex licensing requirements and informal levies.

Simatupang (2005) stresses that this story relates primarily to Java-Bali, whereas markets and know-how are generally less well developed in other regions. For the latter, the "Hayami-Kawagoe framework" is useful, with the development of markets crucially shaped by the quality of the road infrastructure. For example, supermarkets in South Sulawesi and South Kalimantan are generally sourcing their fruit and vegetables from East Java, even though there are suitable local production sites.

Much more research is needed on these issues. The continuing large regional price differences for both agricultural products and manufactures (Nashihin 2007) constitute strong prima facie evidence that markets, especially off Java-Bali, are still not well integrated, and that many lucrative trading opportunities exist.[15]

To sum up, there are at least six key features of these rapidly changing agricultural marketing channels:

• They feature great diversity, from traditional local markets to well-established domestic supermarkets and the more recent entry of the global giants.

• There is an apparent coexistence of these channels, but in the context of the inexorable rise of the modern end of the spectrum.

• The new arrangements typically embed a range of technologies, including new logistical arrangements and buyer-transmitted information on prices, quality benchmarks, agro-ecological advice, and product mixes.

• Small farmers are by no means excluded from these networks. Indeed, there is strong competition among buyers for efficient, reliable suppliers. However, to be able to participate in these new chains, farmers need to quickly adapt to the buyers' tightly specified requirements.

• This is a microcosm of Indonesian marketing in transition. The farmers are competing with other regions of Java, and at the top end with international suppliers.[16] It is not yet clear whether and to what extent these global buying chains have been introducing Indonesian producers to export markets. There are some cases where this is already occurring: for example, the foreign-owned PT Java Golden Singosari in East Java has commenced exporting exotic vegetables produced by small farmers.

• There are potential losers, and there is a role for public policy in managing this inevitable structural adjustment. Some margins are squeezed, especially for producers of standardized products. There is reduced "natural protection" for some existing producers, as marketing costs decline. Those in the now by-passed trade networks may also be adversely affected, including the ubiquitous market "kiosks".

Marketing of manufactures: So much for agricultural marketing. There is even less research on the marketing of manufactures in Indonesia. In thinking about manufacturing market channels, a useful typology is the nature of the relationship between large and small firms. It may be complementary (via subcontracting networks), competitive (producing similar products) or specialized (non-competing).

We can gain partial entrée into manufacturing marketing patterns via three literatures: some general studies, research related to SME export success, and studies of subcontracting networks. In principle, one might hypothesize that the general findings from the agricultural marketing literature would also apply to manufactures. However, on a priori grounds, there are also likely to be substantial differences. One is that perishability is not such a concern for most manufactures, and thus the imperative for a rapid, highly efficient logistics supply chain is less important. (Although of course working capital tied up in stocks compels suppliers to move goods quickly.) The second difference is that manufactures are more likely to be product differentiated than agricultural produce, and therefore their bargaining power *vis-à-vis* retail chains may be stronger. Third, the size and spatial distribution of manufacturing plants differs from agricultural producers. In particular, the former are on average larger (and hence their knowledge of markets and capacity to negotiate is likely to be more developed), and they are generally in closer proximity to major urban markets.

The general literature is diverse and provides little overall guidance. One strand, for example enunciated by the Bandung-based think tank Akatiga (2004), argues that the development of SMEs is hampered by the allegedly "exploitative" behaviour of the large supply chains. This is a frequently heard criticism in Indonesia and elsewhere. For small firms producing low quality, undifferentiated products, and with limited marketing capabilities, margins are indeed likely to be low. However, as a generalized model of marketing, it lacks analytical persuasion, since the framework does not illuminate the bases for many well-known business success stories growing out of small enterprises.[17]

Tambunan (2006; see also Tambunan and Thee Chapter 6) has also examined the marketing chains of SME manufacturers, finding as would be expected of a diverse set of arrangements.[18] He reports on the 1996 BPS Survey of SMEs, which found that collectors/agents were the most important marketing channel (73 per cent of firms), followed by personal marketing efforts (38 per cent), traders/exporters (2 per cent) and cooperatives (0.1 per cent).[19] In terms of sales destination, only 0.2 per cent of firms engaged in direct export. Among micro/household enterprises (i.e. those with fewer than five employees), the shares were collectors/agents (48 per cent), own marketing (21 per cent), retailers (19 per cent), consignments (5 per cent), and cooperatives (0.2 per cent). Thus, agents or "middlemen" dominate the channels. Despite their policy significance, cooperatives appear to be almost irrelevant. The more recent 2002 Survey of SMEs concluded that, while most of these enterprises were formally involved in the government's long running *Bapak Angkat* (literally "foster parent") scheme, in practice very few (9 per cent of small enterprises, 3 per cent of household enterprises) marketed their products through or with the help of SOEs.

Major MNEs are another means by which SME suppliers better connect to the national and global economy. The case study of PT Unilever Indonesia, one of the largest and oldest established MNEs in Indonesia, is illustrative of these channels.[20] In 2003, Unilever worked with 334 suppliers in the home and personal care sector, and its procurements totalled approximately Rp 3.6 trillion, 84 per cent of which was with domestically owned firms. While it is best known for its range of personal toiletries, Unilever's supply chain includes a diverse array of agricultural raw materials, with tea, palm oil, cassava, black soybean, and coconut sugar being the most important. The report provides several case studies showing how Unilever has acquired branded products and developed a national distribution strategy which has rapidly increased production. There are also cases where it has worked with national institutions (e.g. Gadjah Mada University) to upgrade quality and introduce greater product diversity. Thus, many of the elements noted with respect to supermarket entry also apply to its operations: technology transfers, new products and processes, quality control, delivery timing; but also rigorous competitive benchmarking, which precludes some suppliers. What is crucial, and as yet undocumented, is the extent of spillovers from these commercial relationships. For example, how quickly do they diffuse to other firms, and the extent to which firms within the Unilever supply chain are able to connect to export markets over time.

Second, on SME export success, although these firms generally cater to the local market, there have been some interesting Indonesian case studies that have demonstrated how selected firms can engage in profitable employment-generating export opportunities. Two case study literatures particularly deserve brief mention.[21]

The Bali garment industry, which grew spectacularly in the 1980s and is almost exclusively based on small firms, was practically an "accidental" case of industrialization (Cole 1998). Foreign tourists, mainly surfers wishing to support a recreational lifestyle, saw commercial opportunities in Balinese garments and its indigenous design capacity. They were able to act as marketing intermediaries, connecting local producers with retail outlets abroad, in the process dispensing important information on designs and production techniques. Later, as the island's fame spread, these links developed quickly, and the industry mushroomed from its seasonal, cottage origins to larger production units and some local design capacity. It was also a magnet for creative designers and entrepreneurs from other parts of Indonesia, who sought to emulate Bali's successes in their own regions.

By contrast, export-oriented SME furniture manufacturers in Jepara, northern Central Java, had their origins further back, but here too exports began to grow quickly in the 1980s. The industry lacked the tourism connection, but it did have a good local skills base, together with access to raw materials at below international prices owing to the log export ban. Foreign buyers and traders quickly saw the opportunities for profitable export as deregulation proceeded. More recently, however, the industry's fortunes have declined, in part owing to the removal of the log export ban, resulting in firms now having to pay world market prices for their timber (see Loebis and Schmitz 2004).

These studies suggest a model of successful and innovative SME development in which the following ingredients appear to be important. First, there was some prior basic industrial competence in a particular field of activity (e.g. sewing, artistic design, and wood-working in these cases). Second, there was generally a conducive macroeconomic environment (except at the peak of the 1997–98 crisis), including especially a competitive exchange rate. Third, there was reasonably good physical infrastructure, including proximity to adequately functioning import and export facilities. Finally, of importance also have been injections of technical, design, and marketing expertise which link small producers to new ideas and major markets.[22]

With the partial exception of the first ingredient, all four elements are directly amenable to public policy. These case studies also have important implications for government policy. Neither resulted from any deliberate government promotional measures. The government did play an important role in providing a supportive macroeconomic environment and in the provision of a rapidly improving infrastructure. In Bali, the local government generally adopted a fairly open policy towards the presence of foreign entrepreneurs, and export procedures were not unduly burdensome most of the time. These of course hardly constitute "contributions" from government, except in the negative sense of avoiding a harshly restrictive regulatory regime.[23]

The third strand in the SME marketing literature relates to subcontracting networks. These networks are prominent particularly in the automotive and electronic industries, where specialist SME firms supply end-product assemblers/ producers. Successive governments have sought to develop these networks via mandatory deletion programmes and the so-called "Bapak Angkat" scheme. Such an approach accords with philosophical notions that large firms have a responsibility to "membimbing" (literally develop, protect, foster) SMEs, while Indonesian industrial policy-makers have always found the dirigiste Japanese industrial policies and experience (including subcontracting) attractive. From the late 1970s, the government's mandatory deletion programmes required that auto assemblers not only had to meet ambitious local content ratios but, in addition for finely specified product categories, this goal had to be achieved through arms' length subcontracting.

These initiatives have been largely unsuccessful, owing to the heavy-handed nature of the intervention and the highly fragmented, inefficient auto industry (see Sato 2000 and the literature cited therein). Although the auto industry and the range of products produced domestically grew rapidly until 1997, the expected dense subcontracting arrangements failed to materialize. Assembler-supplier relationships are often shallow, short-term and non-exclusive, bearing little relationship with the Japanese model.[24] The reasons for such an outcome are not difficult to explain: the market is small, and was highly protected and fragmented until 1998. In order to achieve economies of scale, suppliers necessarily sold to several assemblers. Technology transfers associated with these short-term relationships have been minimal, with the possible exception of the Astra group. Government industrial extension efforts in support of these SME producers have also been weak and sporadic. Here too we lack data which provide a picture on these marketing networks both in aggregate and over time. The most one can postulate is that these vertical linkages are common but not strongly developed, and there is no clear trend over time.

However, market-driven networks are emerging, linked in turn to MNE supply chains. Indeed, more important than the domestic subcontracting networks is the scope such arrangements provide for Indonesian firms to connect to global networks, including both buying networks and MNE global factories. In both cases, there is some cause for concern. In spite of its highly competitive exchange rate, Indonesia has been steadily losing market share in major manufacturing markets such as the U.S. and Japan. It has also been a relatively small player in the rapidly expanding global electronics industry (Yusuf and Associates 2003; Kimura 2006). Along with a range of supply-side, policy-related factors, the modest MNE presence since 1998 has contributed to this decline, especially where (as in electronics) these firms dominate an industry. Moreover, foreign ownership (both its presence and its enterprise ownership share) has been a critical determinant of firm-level recovery since the 1997–98 crisis (Narjoko 2006).

Additional insights on marketing issues for NFEs can be gleaned from the Rural Investment Climate Survey (RICS) conducted by the University of Indonesia's LPEM. In total, 2,549 NFEs were surveyed, 19 per cent in manufacturing, 44 per cent in trade, and 36 per cent in other services. These enterprises were mainly located in rural areas (62 per cent), and overwhelmingly (90 per cent) consisted of household enterprises. The enterprises were virtually all (domestic) privately owned, by individuals. The NFEs surveyed were distributed in roughly equal numbers across six *kabupaten* in as many provinces: Malang (East Java), Kutai (East Kalimantan), Labuhan Batu (North Sumatra), Sumbawa (West Nusa Tenggara), Badung (Bali) and Barru (South Sulawesi). Retrospective questions provided data for both 2002 and 2005, corresponding to periods of slow and recovering growth against the backdrop of some political uncertainty, and the return to stronger growth and a more predictable political/commercial environment.

The RICS contains two main tables of relevance to marketing issues. These relate to the procurement and marketing areas of trading enterprises, summaries of which are presented in Tables 7.3 and 7.4 respectively. In both cases, markets are defined spatially, in an ascending hierarchy: same village, same sub-district (*kecamatan*), same district (*kabupaten*), and same province, together with national and international markets. The data refer to "dominant products" in order that the results are not skewed by trade in minor goods and services.

By far the most important finding in both years is that these NFEs buy and sell predominantly in their immediate locality. In 2005, 31 per cent of the NFEs procured mainly from within their own village, and a further 24 per cent from other villages in the same sub-district. In all, 94 per cent of NFEs procured mainly from within their province. International procurements are minuscule, and occur only in one special case, Badung (Bali). Of course, there may be indirect procurement channels which are not detected in the survey, but the findings appear to be reasonably robust and consistent. In 2002, the percentages are almost identical: respectively 34 per cent, 27 per cent, and 90 per cent.

The survey identified three broad product categories, unprocessed and processed agricultural products and non-agriculture. The results generally accord with a priori expectation, in the sense that procurement areas for the first two groups are very localized, much more so than for the non-agriculture group. In fact, the latter group of NFEs, which is two-thirds of the survey, accounts for 90 per cent of the observed extra-provincial procurements. This share appears to be rising between the two survey years.

As would be expected, there are differences across the six regions, reflecting differences in infrastructure conditions, the density of local market networks, output compositions, connections to the regional and national economies, and commercial histories. Thus, for example, in Badung 10 per cent of NFEs procure from outside the province, reflecting Bali's strong, tourism-related connections to the rest of Indonesia, and abroad, and also the province's small size. The extra-provincial share is also somewhat higher for the Malang NFEs,

Table 7.3
Procurement Area of Non-Farm Trading Enterprises in RICS *Kabupaten*

	Procurement area													
	2005							2002						
Kabupaten/Dominant product	Same Village	Same Sub-District	Same District	Same Province	Different Province	Different Country	Total	Same Village	Same Sub-District	Same District	Same Province	Different Province	Different Country	Total
Labuhan Batu														
a. Unprocessed ag. product	56.4	20.5	13.3	9.8	0.0	0.0	100.0	35.3	29.6	18.6	16.5	0.0	0.0	100.0
b. Processed ag. product	50.7	44.4	2.6	2.3	0.0	0.0	100.0	46.5	48.4	4.5	0.5	0.0	0.0	100.0
c. Non ag. product	22.3	45.7	22.2	9.0	0.8	0.0	100.0	16.4	68.7	11.5	3.3	0.0	0.0	100.0
Total	38.0	37.5	16.1	8.1	0.4	0.0	100.0	26.9	53.6	12.6	6.9	0.0	0.0	100.0
Malang														
a. Unprocessed ag. product	42.0	28.3	9.1	20.6	0.0	0.0	100.0	34.8	41.1	8.7	15.4	0.0	0.0	100.0
b. Processed ag. product	53.2	24.7	13.2	1.6	7.3	0.0	100.0	55.0	25.5	12.0	0.0	7.6	0.0	100.0
c. Non ag. product	20.6	17.4	33.0	18.1	10.8	0.0	100.0	31.0	17.3	36.0	12.8	2.9	0.0	100.0
Total	27.6	20.0	26.9	16.8	8.7	0.0	100.0	35.6	23.0	27.1	11.2	3.1	0.0	100.0
Badung														
a. Unprocessed ag. product	7.0	26.5	46.0	20.5	0.0	0.0	100.0	3.3	2.9	64.1	29.7	0.0	0.0	100.0
b. Processed ag. product	31.3	25.5	25.7	14.4	3.1	0.0	100.0	27.4	25.2	31.3	12.4	3.8	0.0	100.0
c. Non ag. product	34.2	5.7	15.9	27.9	16.0	0.2	100.0	32.5	8.4	22.1	22.6	14.5	0.0	100.0
Total	30.8	14.8	22.1	22.3	9.9	0.1	100.0	27.5	15.6	30.1	18.5	8.3	0.0	100.0
Sumbawa														
a. Unprocessed ag. product	59.7	29.2	5.2	5.9	0.0	0.0	100.0	56.6	31.5	5.6	6.4	0.0	0.0	100.0
b. Processed ag. product	17.7	41.0	41.2	0.0	0.0	0.0	100.0	17.8	39.5	42.7	0.0	0.0	0.0	100.0
c. Non ag. product	27.6	40.1	25.9	3.8	2.7	0.0	100.0	31.1	41.4	21.5	2.5	3.5	0.0	100.0
Total	31.0	38.4	25.6	3.3	1.7	0.0	100.0	34.5	38.8	21.7	3.0	2.1	0.0	100.0
Kutai														
a. Unprocessed ag. product	39.1	56.6	4.3	0.0	0.0	0.0	100.0	42.9	50.3	6.8	0.0	0.0	0.0	100.0
b. Processed ag. product	61.6	18.3	3.9	13.8	2.4	0.0	100.0	73.5	0.0	4.7	18.3	3.4	0.0	100.0
c. Non ag. product	36.3	20.7	10.9	29.3	2.8	0.0	100.0	31.7	18.5	10.8	30.7	6.2	0.0	100.0
Total	41.8	23.1	8.9	23.7	2.5	0.0	100.0	44.6	16.4	8.7	24.2	4.8	0.0	100.0
Barru														
a. Unprocessed ag. product	5.1	13.0	50.6	31.3	0.0	0.0	100.0	5.9	14.9	45.3	34.0	0.0	0.0	100.0
b. Processed ag. product	21.2	27.7	27.5	13.9	9.8	0.0	100.0	31.9	19.4	13.1	20.9	14.8	0.0	100.0
c. Non ag. product	10.2	23.2	51.2	13.6	1.8	0.0	100.0	14.7	25.9	45.0	12.0	2.4	0.0	100.0
Total	10.3	22.8	50.4	14.6	1.9	0.0	100.0	14.5	25.0	44.2	13.8	2.5	0.0	100.0
Total														
a. Unprocessed ag. product	45.3	28.2	11.1	15.5	0.0	0.0	100.0	36.7	36.4	12.6	14.3	0.0	0.0	100.0
b. Processed ag. product	45.9	28.4	16.0	5.9	3.9	0.0	100.0	48.4	25.1	16.6	5.1	4.9	0.0	100.0
c. Non ag. product	24.0	21.7	27.8	18.1	8.3	0.0	100.0	29.2	24.8	28.9	13.2	3.7	0.0	100.0
Total	31.0	23.8	23.2	15.8	6.3	0.0	100.0	34.4	27.0	23.4	11.8	3.2	0.0	100.0

Source: Authors' calculations from the Indonesian Rural Investment Climate Survey (2006).

Table 7.4
Sales Area of Non-Farm Trading Enterprises in RICS *Kabupaten*

Kabupaten/Dominant product	*Sales area*													
	2005							*2002*						
	Same Village	*Same Sub-District*	*Same District*	*Same Province*	*Different Province*	*Different Country*	*Total*	*Same Village*	*Same Sub-District*	*Same District*	*Same Province*	*Different Province*	*Different Country*	*Total*
Labuhan Batu														
a. Unprocessed ag. produdct	69.5	13.6	16.5	0.4	0.0	0.0	100.0	62.5	16.5	20.4	0.7	0.0	0.0	100.0
b. Processed ag. product	75.0	25.0	0.0	0.0	0.0	0.0	100.0	59.4	40.6	0.0	0.0	0.0	0.0	100.0
c. Non ag. product	69.7	24.2	2.1	4.0	0.0	0.0	100.0	71.5	20.1	1.9	6.5	0.0	0.0	100.0
Total	70.5	21.1	6.2	2.2	0.0	0.0	100.0	66.9	22.2	7.2	3.7	0.0	0.0	100.0
Malang														
a. Unprocessed ag. produdct	48.9	30.0	14.4	6.8	0.0	0.0	100.0	62.5	18.8	8.1	10.5	0.0	0.0	100.0
b. Processed ag. product	39.1	48.9	12.0	0.0	0.0	0.0	100.0	37.1	50.5	12.4	0.0	0.0	0.0	100.0
c. Non ag. product	52.6	24.8	15.2	6.7	0.8	0.0	100.0	69.6	14.2	7.4	7.1	1.6	0.0	100.0
Total	50.5	28.2	14.7	6.0	0.6	0.0	100.0	62.7	21.4	8.4	6.5	1.0	0.0	100.0
Badung														
a. Unprocessed ag. produdct	79.0	19.1	0.0	1.9	0.0	0.0	100.0	70.3	27.0	0.0	2.7	0.0	0.0	100.0
b. Processed ag. product	73.8	25.6	0.0	0.0	0.0	0.6	100.0	69.1	30.5	0.0	0.0	0.0	0.4	100.0
c. Non ag. product	41.5	8.8	6.3	10.6	3.9	28.9	100.0	29.9	13.3	0.6	19.2	2.1	34.9	100.0
Total	57.1	16.1	3.3	5.8	2.1	15.6	100.0	52.4	22.8	0.2	8.5	0.9	15.2	100.0
Sumbawa														
a. Unprocessed ag. produdct	35.1	44.7	17.4	2.3	0.5	0.0	100.0	38.1	43.1	15.9	2.4	0.6	0.0	100.0
b. Processed ag. product	87.9	12.1	0.0	0.0	0.0	0.0	100.0	98.3	1.7	0.0	0.0	0.0	0.0	100.0
c. Non ag. product	80.2	8.7	10.1	1.1	0.0	0.0	100.0	77.2	16.9	4.3	1.6	0.0	0.0	100.0
Total	74.0	15.7	9.2	1.0	0.1	0.0	100.0	69.1	22.2	6.9	1.7	0.1	0.0	100.0
Kutai														
a. Unprocessed ag. produdct	52.5	31.3	0.0	16.1	0.0	0.0	100.0	60.0	30.8	0.0	9.2	0.0	0.0	100.0
b. Processed ag. product	70.7	26.8	2.5	0.0	0.0	0.0	100.0	88.9	7.5	3.6	0.0	0.0	0.0	100.0
c. Non ag. product	71.8	25.0	2.0	0.6	0.5	0.0	100.0	66.6	27.0	3.8	1.4	1.2	0.0	100.0
Total	69.9	25.9	2.0	1.8	0.4	0.0	100.0	72.2	21.9	3.3	1.8	0.8	0.0	100.0
Barru														
a. Unprocessed ag. produdct	65.6	13.0	21.4	0.0	0.0	0.0	100.0	21.5	5.1	3.5	0.0	69.9	0.0	100.0
b. Processed ag. product	13.2	41.4	10.5	13.7	21.2	0.0	100.0	7.9	44.4	15.9	0.0	31.9	0.0	100.0
c. Non ag. product	66.9	7.0	8.2	17.2	0.8	0.0	100.0	58.7	9.2	8.1	22.9	1.1	0.0	100.0
Total	65.2	8.4	9.0	16.0	1.4	0.0	100.0	50.7	9.3	7.4	18.2	14.3	0.0	100.0
Total														
a. Unprocessed ag. produdct	53.9	27.1	13.7	5.2	0.0	0.0	100.0	58.6	22.3	10.7	6.8	1.5	0.0	100.0
b. Processed ag. product	61.3	33.3	5.2	0.0	0.1	0.1	100.0	56.1	36.9	6.9	0.0	0.1	0.1	100.0
c. Non ag. product	58.6	22.2	11.1	5.6	0.8	1.7	100.0	67.7	16.3	5.7	7.0	1.2	2.0	100.0
Total	58.2	24.7	10.7	4.7	0.6	1.1	100.0	63.7	21.5	6.9	5.6	1.1	1.2	100.0

Source: Authors' calculations from the Indonesian Rural Investment Climate Survey (2006).

and is indicative of that region's longer history of commercial networks, principally through Surabaya. By contrast, NFEs in the four regions outside Java and Bali rarely procure beyond their province. In all cases the extra-provincial share is less than 3 per cent. Here too the results are similar for 2002, except that the inter-provincial shares for both Badung and Malang are higher in 2005, perhaps indicating a slight strengthening of inter-provincial trade networks over this period.

One might expect that the NFEs would be more widely distributed in their marketing than their procurements, on the principle that by their very nature they develop commercial activities based on locally available inputs. In fact, the distribution of marketing regions is broadly similar to that of their procurements, in the sense that the great majority of the NFEs sell in very localized markets. In 2005, 58 per cent of NFEs sold their output mainly in the local village, and a further 25 per cent just within the same sub-district. Almost 94 per cent of sales were within the same province. That is, compared to procurements, the NFEs were even more "village-oriented" in their sales. At the provincial level, the shares are identical (both 94 per cent), suggesting that procurements are more likely to come from other villages in the same province, as compared to sales. The importance of same-village sales declined somewhat, as compared to the 64 per cent recorded in 2002, but the provincial share was marginally lower (92 per cent) in 2002. Although small in both years, international sales were slightly higher than extra-provincial (but domestic) sales in both years.

The results are also broadly similar across the three product groups and the six localities. For the three product groups, unprocessed and processed agricultural products are much more likely to be sold in local regions. Perhaps surprisingly, processed goods are actually the more localized of the two. One might expect processing to reduce perishability and weight, therefore increasing their "tradability". Although the figures are small, non-agricultural products are more likely to be sold outside the province and internationally. In fact, virtually all the recorded exports come from this group. The proportions are similar in 2002.

Across the six localities, the findings for procurements and sales are also similar. The NFEs in Badung have quite well developed international connections, with 16 per cent exporting, and a further 2 per cent selling domestically but beyond the province. In fact, all the exports found in the survey originated from the Badung NFEs, no doubt reflecting the impact of tourism and related spin-offs. As with procurements, the Malang NFEs are less (same) village-oriented than the other five localities. But the figure is still high (51 per cent), and sales within the same *kabupaten* dominate. In all four localities outside Java and Bali, the same-village shares are very high: 70 per cent in Labuan Batu, 74 per cent in Sumbawa, 70 per cent in Kutai, and 65 per cent in Barru.

In sum, the clear picture which emerges is that these predominantly household NFEs buy and sell overwhelming in their local neighbourhood, most of all in the same village. For all the discussion of national market integration and globalization, the fortunes of these NFEs are linked primarily to the local village economy. The two reference points of the survey are not sufficiently wide apart to draw definitive conclusions regarding trends. But it is important to remember that these findings come after the thirty years of massive Soeharto-era infrastructure expansion, and a broadly open economy. For all the discussion of "SME export success stories" and the intrusion of MNE-linked buying chains into the village economy, most NFEs remain heavily local. Of course, this conclusion has to be qualified by emphasizing that the focus in the survey was on the "micro" end of NFEs, and very few SME "factories" were included. Account also needs to be taken of indirect procurement and marketing chains, in that the NFE respondents may be referring only to the final link in the procurement chain and the first link in marketing. Factoring in these second tiers may alter the conclusions, but they are unlikely to be fundamentally different.

3. Competition

The literature on ownership concentration typically encompasses two inter-related and complementary approaches, one which attempts to measure a range of concentration indicators, and a second which focuses on barriers to competition.

The first approach comprises two broad measures: concentration indicators such as the standard four-firm ratio (the percentage of an industry's output produced by the four (or three, five, etc.) largest establishments or firms), and various measures of corporate conglomeration. To capture the notion of market power accurately, n-firm ratios ideally need to be computed for finely disaggregated industrial groups, preferably at the five-digit ISIC level. Since practically all manufactures are tradable, they also need to be adjusted for some measure of import competition. That is, high levels of seller concentration per se constitute no grounds for concern provided producers are subject to the discipline of import competition. The latter is typically captured through some measure of import protection or import market share. Quantitative analysis of the effects of concentration typically adopt a structure-conduct-performance (SCP) framework, in which levels of concentration are positively correlated with (and co-determined by) industry profitability and other measures.

Corporate conglomeration seeks to identify a broader measure of market power, as revealed by the size of major industrial groups. These groups usually vary considerably in terms of their industrial diversification, and thus it is usually not possible to employ formal quantitative analysis. But these measures are a useful supplement to the SCP analysis, in addition to connoting the extent of corporate concentration in aggregate.

Surprisingly, in spite of Indonesia's relatively good database, there has only been one detailed analysis of industrial concentration in Indonesia at the aggregate level, by Kelly Bird (1999, based on his doctoral dissertation of the same year). He found high levels of concentration, typical of those in relatively small, late-industrializing nations. Over the period 1975–93, concentration levels were declining steadily, though in the latter year the simple average four-firm concentration ratio was still 54 per cent. Concentration ratios fell significantly once allowance is made for imports. He also confirmed the statistical relationship between concentration and industry profitability.

Indicators of corporate conglomeration in Indonesia are more difficult to obtain owing to data limitations. Few major corporations are prepared to place the majority of their assets in public hands, and no accurate records are reported to public authorities. However, various business surveys do provide at least an approximate picture. Illustrative of this sort of approach is Claessens et al. (2000). For nine East Asian economies, they found that more than two-thirds of firms are controlled by a single shareholder, that corporate wealth is concentrated among a few families, and that managers of closely held firms tend to be relatives of the controlling shareholder's family. Among the nine countries, Indonesia was found to have the most concentrated ownership patterns in 1996, with the top family owning 16.6 per cent of listed corporate assets, and the top ten families owning 57.7 per cent of the total. The shares would almost certainly be significantly lower post-crisis.

The RICS also contained some information on competition issues. Table 7.5 shows the number and frequency of trading enterprises reporting more than five competitors and buyers. In almost all cases, these NFEs clearly operate in very competitive markets. Moreover, the most frequent source of competition in aggregate comes from the same village. This applies to most of the localities. The exceptions occur in two of the locations off Java and Bali, Labuhan Batu and Kutai, but here there are competitive pressures from NFEs in other villages in the same sub-district. The patterns are generally similar across the three product groups and for both years. That is, one might have expected less competitive pressures for

Table 7.5
Number of Trading Enterprises Who Reported That There are More Than Five Competitors and Buyers

Kabupaten/Dominant	Competitor								Buyer							
	2005				2002				2005				2002			
	Village	Sub-District	District	Province	Village	Sub-District	District	Province	Village	Sub-District	District	Province	Village	Sub-District	District	Province
Labuhan Batu																
a. Unprocessed ag. product	1,325	4,031	3,846	3,294	1,072	2,635	2,611	2,058	2,536	2,392	1,100	1,627	1,607	1,660	487	992
b. Processed ag. product	996	1,355	1,252	1,206	696	671	605	559	3,000	298	140	140	1,690	168	26	26
c. Non ag. product	3,230	6,257	4,731	4,823	1,618	4,654	2,748	2,732	8,442	4,643	2,593	2,439	5,160	3,332	1,926	1,880
Total	5,551	11,644	9,828	9,322	3,386	7,960	5,964	5,349	13,978	7,334	3,833	4,206	8,456	5,160	2,439	2,898
Malang																
a. Unprocessed ag. product	5,516	4,729	2,453	2,453	5,491	3,420	1,144	1,144	7,817	4,446	2,240	2,327	6,468	3,097	892	978
b. Processed ag. product	5,294	3,755	1,847	1,847	5,000	3,462	1,700	1,700	8,658	4,567	2,348	2,278	8,365	4,421	2,202	2,132
c. Non ag. product	23,801	20,278	13,408	18,008	7,972	8,514	4,587	3,584	47,321	21,664	8,789	8,421	24,429	13,368	4,091	3,724
Total	34,610	28,762	17,707	22,307	18,463	15,396	7,431	6,427	63,796	30,678	13,377	13,026	39,262	20,887	7,184	6,833
Badung																
a. Unprocessed ag. product	872	505	346	337	622	255	96	87	885	452	292	274	629	196	36	18
b. Processed ag. product	2,479	2,631	2,479	1,276	1,917	2,227	2,103	900	3,256	2,339	435	435	2,645	2,141	387	387
c. Non ag. product	4,951	4,792	3,972	3,034	2,809	2,243	1,802	1,172	4,018	2,072	1,743	1,650	1,585	906	545	446
Total	8,302	7,927	6,797	4,646	5,348	4,724	4,001	2,158	8,158	4,864	2,470	2,360	4,859	3,243	968	851
Sumbawa																
a. Unprocessed ag. product	1,006	779	297	0	842	667	297	0	1,721	1,009	297	0	1,662	950	297	0
b. Processed ag. product	1,373	459	0	0	587	0	0	0	1,888	402	0	0	537	0	0	0
c. Non ag. product	4,324	2,746	632	98	3,137	1,628	348	98	6,275	2,184	356	0	4,291	992	237	0
Total	6,702	3,984	929	98	4,566	2,295	645	98	9,884	3,595	653	0	6,490	1,943	534	0
Kutai																
a. Unprocessed ag. product	583	746	485	485	305	469	207	207	1,076	612	109	232	581	370	109	109
b. Processed ag. product	2,208	2,688	2,470	2,368	1,328	1,722	1,903	1,801	3,193	2,772	1,897	1,804	2,227	1,807	1,704	1,611
c. Non ag. product	6,826	8,676	6,390	4,901	3,707	4,402	2,783	2,376	10,936	8,439	4,567	3,307	5,410	4,111	2,085	1,475
Total	9,617	12,110	9,345	7,753	5,340	6,593	4,893	4,383	15,205	11,823	6,573	5,344	8,219	6,288	3,899	3,195
Barru																
a. Unprocessed ag. product	79	30	12	7	300	30	12	7	81	64	0	0	300	64	0	0
b. Processed ag. product	42	46	33	21	28	30	17	15	48	35	24	8	40	25	15	8
c. Non ag. product	1,365	858	481	243	893	665	394	237	1,286	811	420	230	827	621	357	227
Total	1,486	934	526	271	1,222	726	423	259	1,414	909	444	238	1,168	710	372	235
Total																
a. Unprocessed ag. product	9,379	10,819	7,438	6,575	8,632	7,475	4,366	3,503	14,115	8,975	4,038	4,460	11,247	6,338	1,819	2,097
b. Processed ag. product	12,391	10,935	8,080	6,716	9,558	8,113	6,327	4,973	20,043	10,414	4,845	4,665	15,504	8,562	4,334	4,163
c. Non ag. product	44,496	43,606	29,614	31,107	20,135	22,107	12,662	10,199	78,278	39,814	18,469	16,048	41,703	23,330	9,242	7,751
Total	66,267	65,361	45,132	44,398	38,325	37,694	23,356	18,675	112,436	59,203	27,351	25,173	68,454	38,230	15,395	14,011

Source: Authors' calculations from the Indonesian Rural Investment Climate Survey (2006), using sampling weights.

the (presumably) more differentiated non-agricultural products, but this does not appear to be the case. Buyer networks are similarly competitive, in the sense that the locality where most firms say there are "more than five buyers", is the same village. Thus, with the caveats noted above (in particular, the heavy concentration in the survey at the micro end of NFEs), it appears that markets are competitive, and that buyers are not able to exert oligopsonistic power. At a policy level, these enterprises are outside the purview of the KPPU, but in any case there does not appear to be any grounds for the Commission to intervene.

An alternative, but complementary, approach is to attempt to identify barriers to competition, or at least some notion of contestability, and to examine the characteristics of industries which might be regarded as having a "competition problem". Here a useful framework is to first identify the barriers to competition. In principle, these barriers might arise from:

(i) Government-imposed or sanctioned barriers to entry. These may, and in the case of Indonesia, take many forms, including restraints on competition to protect the monopoly position of SOEs and other favoured investors, and complex entry procedures which inhibit the entry of new firms. Examples of the latter include the bureaucratic requirements associated with BKPM provisions for foreign firms, and those domestic firms wishing to avail of its (now very limited) fiscal incentives. Indonesia's regulatory environment is widely regarded as one of the most complex in developing Asia. This proposition receives empirical support from numerous comparative business surveys.[25]

In the case of agriculture, there has been renewed political pressure in recent years to re-regulate international and domestic trade, as noted above. In services, in spite of some significant recent deregulations, many sectors remain highly regulated and SOE-dominated.

(ii) Collusive behaviour on the part of sellers. This is difficult to document, although the KPPU reports over time will provide useful information. A working hypothesis is that it is more likely to arise in highly concentrated industries which are insulated from import competition. Therefore, the structural and regulatory characteristics of these industries need to be examined: for example, major players, extent of firm "churning" over time, and regulatory policies. High concentration can of course be a case of "Schumpeterian efficiency", and therefore it does not necessarily provide grounds for public policy intervention, as long as the industry is contestable.

The KPPU was established in 2000, following the enactment of a competition law in 1999, itself the result of one of the conditions in the IMF recovery packages.[26] Although drawing on international best practice in its design, the KPPU operates in the context of its prescribed objectives. An important factor, unusual for commissions of this type, is its implicit "affirmative action" mandate, designed to protect cooperatives, SMEs and (implicitly) *pribumi* ("native") enterprises.

It is too early to offer a definitive assessment of the KPPU's operation, and its effectiveness in any case is circumscribed by limited resources. Over the year 2003–04, for example, it received 54 reports and complaints, and was able to issue 6 decisions. Of the latter, 3 were accepted by the relevant parties, 2 were contested and 1 withdrawn. A good deal of its work relates to alleged "bid rigging" and the operation of cartels. In principle, it may investigate the anti-competitive practices of SOEs, but thus far it has focused on the private sector. It has also had little to do with M&As, which typically occupy much of the work of these agencies in OECD economies.

Thee (2006) judges that the Commission's early record provides grounds for optimism that it will foster a more competitive business environment in Indonesia. Moreover, and contrary to some earlier reservations, he finds no evidence thus far that it will have a deleterious impact on business, or pursue a political agenda (e.g. SME promotion and anti "big business") and introduce another layer of bureaucratic complexity with which firms have to contend.

The Commission has already been engaged in a case of relevance to this study. In a high-profile, political case in mid-2001, the KPPU ordered the Indomaret mini-market retail chain to cease its expansion into locations where there is a large number of small, traditional retailers. This was not a case of anti-competitive behaviour on the part of Indomaret, but the Commission was implementing its "economic democracy" charter. The outcome of the case involved an apparently acceptable compromise, in which the chain was required to reserve a certain part of its premises for these small retailers.

(iii) Infrastructure bottlenecks, which result in markets not being able to operate effectively. These are discussed in detail in Chapter 5.

The empirical work referred to above was undertaken in the late Soeharto period, and surprisingly — for all the interest the subject attracts in Indonesia — there has been no detailed analytical research on competition since the 1997–98 crisis. But it is very likely that competitive pressures have increased since then, for at least four reasons. First, this has been a period of corporate volatility and restructuring. The major Soeharto-linked business empires (Bimantara, Humpus, etc.) have collapsed, while many of the major private sector conglomerates have experienced significant changes, either related to financial workouts, or the loss of crony privileges, or both. Foreign ownership shares have increased in most major industries, and this has generally (though not always) led to increased competition. Second, levels of import protection have very likely declined, although there are no systematic studies. The principal driver of this process has been the IMF conditionality packages, resulting in increased competitive pressures (Basri and Soesastro 2005). Third, there has been some, though limited, additional deregulation in key, mainly SOE-dominated, sectors. Notable examples include domestic civil aviation and telecommunications. As noted, the establishment of the KPPU has probably also increased competition through its scrutiny of collusive arrangements. Moreover, there is less blatant "palace corruption" related to competition, of the type for example which was prevalent in the late Soeharto era; e.g. projects such as the national car ("Mobnas") and the clove monopoly (both associated with Tommy Soeharto).

In addition, the decentralization programme of 2001 has shifted power away from the centre, and with it the concentration of regulatory authority and bureaucratic rents. The effects are probably thus far quite limited, and local monopolies may have meanwhile increased. But over time, there is likely to be increased competition for business investment among regions, and this will probably on balance be conducive to increased competition. For example, the authority to issue business licences has been transferred to regional (*kabupaten*) governments. Of direct relevance to the previous section, some of these governments have been cautious in deferring to local sentiment, and decisions on the entry of large supermarket chains have become highly politicized.

To repeat, though, these are essentially empirical questions, and remain as working hypotheses until secondary data can be analysed and case studies undertaken.

Finally, and to return to the Schumpeterian theme — even though beyond the immediate scope of this chapter — it is important to emphasize the dynamic and wide-ranging impacts of a more competitive commercial environment. For example, competition is likely to have beneficial employment effects: there is considerable evidence demonstrating that managers in competitive environments are more likely to adopt labour-intensive technologies, as compared to the preferences of monopolists who prefer the "quiet life" of more capital-intensive technologies and "engineering man".[27] Competition is also a powerful spur for firms to seek out new market opportunities. This was evident in the Indonesian context in the late 1990s, where in response to the deep economic crisis and significant deregulations, firms in more competitive circumstances appeared to be able to adapt and adjust more quickly (Narjoko 2006).

4. Conclusion

By way of summary, at least ten general policy issues deserve mention:

(i)   Although Indonesia's commercial policy environment remains quite unpredictable as compared to the Soeharto era, there can be no doubt that markets are more competitive, and that this on balance is good for consumers and most producers. Prices are cheaper, and there is a more level playing field, with less arbitrary political intrusion, in the business sector.

(ii) There have been several major, high-profile deregulation measures that have been unambiguously desirable for consumers: domestic civil aviation and telecommunications. However, the former needs to be accompanied by greater supervisory controls and the latter is incomplete (see Lee and Findlay 2005), and various agricultural monopolies remain. Moreover, for all the problems related to poor financial supervision in the wake of the 1988 financial deregulation, elements of the reform were highly successful in introducing more competition and making it work for the poor. For example, the BRI small-scale credit programme continued to be effective through the crisis (Patten et al. 2001; see also Chapter 4).

(iii) But the state of physical infrastructure has deteriorated significantly since 1997, owing to the sharp contraction in the central government's development budget, in addition to its inability to establish a clear and commercially viable framework for long-term private sector infrastructure providers (see Chapter 5). Moreover, in the wake of the economic crisis, and lingering hostility towards international financial institutions in some quarters, there appears to be a reluctance to tap into concessional finance. The January 2005 Infrastructure Summit achieved little, although further initiatives are to be released shortly. As noted, high quality infrastructure, especially rural roads, is absolutely critical to marketing, competition, and the effective functioning of markets. It lowers distribution and logistics costs, and it enables more traders (and therefore competition) to enter isolated regions. This is arguably the most important policy challenge for the government in this area.[28]

(iv) Moreover, markets need to be able to operate more effectively, and much more deregulation is desirable. These reforms will be good for both efficiency and in most cases equity. For example:

- Land market rigidities and complexities, which in turn enable small firms and farmers to access formal credit markets (see Feder et al. 1988).
- The regulatory/licensing regime is unnecessarily complex, and Indonesia ranks poorly in most comparative surveys. This is a major anti-competitive factor, since it operates as a de facto barrier to entry.
- The regime also impinges disproportionately on the poor since there are pecuniary economies of scale in having to circumvent regulatory complexities and pay bribes (Thee 1994; Akatiga 2004). These costs are variously estimated to be at least 10 per cent higher for SMEs as compared to larger firms. The regulatory complexity also hurts the SMEs (especially the very small ones) disproportionately since they are more vulnerable to arbitrary bureaucratic harassment especially given the quasi-legality of their business operations, itself in part a product of regulatory complexity.
- Regional governments are continuing to tax and restrain inter-regional trade, though perhaps less than occurred at the peak period around 1998–2002.
- Many government-sanctioned monopolies remain, including most of all in the BUMN/SOE sector. Indeed, there has been limited reform of the SOE sector since the crisis, and thus far their operations appear to be beyond the purview of the KPPU. The trade in several significant agricultural products, notably rice and sugar, remains tightly controlled.

(v)   Competition at the border remains one of the most powerful commercial pressures, and it is surprising that this factor continues to be overlooked in some Indonesian policy discussions. Indonesia is now a largely open economy as indicated by its formal trade regime. However, there are major barriers to the cross-border flow of goods. Shipping services are slow and expensive by best-practice regional standards. Customs arrangements similarly under-perform, and are characterized by widespread corruption. Also, much services trade is highly regulated. For example, Indonesia has the most restrictive foreign employment regulations among the original ASEAN Five.

(vi) Especially for smaller enterprises (SMEs, small farmers), clusters may be useful for marketing purposes and to facilitate knowledge spillovers, as a means of exploiting scale economies, and achieving external efficiencies. But other than perhaps specialized infrastructure provision and some extension services, there is arguably little role for government. These are market-driven commercial arrangements. In any case, the empirical evidence on the effectiveness of clusters is mixed. As noted, the Tegal case study refers to their importance in the metalworking industry, while noting also that the cluster as yet appeared unable to have spawned a viable industry association to address collective action issues. Perhaps this is indicative of industrial infancy and lingering post-crisis firm workouts.[29] Perhaps it also indicates that market channels are not working effectively, in the sense that they do not transmit the necessary mix of price and quality information.

(vii) The intrusion of large commercial units and the demise of small-scale enterprises is always a highly sensitive issue in Indonesia, and one easily amenable to political exploitation. This is especially so if the large units are foreign or non-*pribumi* owned, as most are, and in the wake of the perceived heavy-handed treatment of Indonesia by donors, the IMF, and global capital markets in the wake of the economic crisis. Hence the entry of large new hypermarkets has to be handled in an open, transparent, consultative manner, with due recognition of, and perhaps remedial action for, the displaced traders. The KPPU appears to be playing a useful and constructive role in this context, although the micro-management of these issues is not customarily the responsibility of such an agency.

(viii) Related to this, there needs to be a systematic evaluation of the operation of the KPPU. The general impression is that it has not had a major impact on the competitive environment (it could hardly be expected to have), but that at the margin it is perhaps operating as a useful restraint on the exertion of monopolistic power. That is, firms are conscious of its existence, and its thus far constructive approach, and would not wish to become involved in a case before it.

(ix) Getting the regional policy framework right is absolutely critical for competition and marketing. That is, there needs to be "healthy competition" among the 440 or so *kabupaten/kota*, so that those which offer a sustainable, business-friendly environment are rewarded with more investment and employment (see Chapter 8).

(x) Since there is such a large non-tradable component in marketing networks, and "natural monopoly" considerations are relevant for some major infrastructure sectors, the provision of competitive market structures will need to be supplemented by a range of benchmarked indicators of best practice. This is especially the case with infrastructure provision.

NOTES

1. See Simatupang (2005, Table 3) and Montgomery et al. (2002) for further discussion of these inter-regional trade barriers.
2. For example, a development agency carefully monitored a cross-Aceh consignment. It observed twelve checkpoints, and estimated that the levies were equivalent to eleven per cent of the value of the goods. In late 2005, the BRR and the World Bank began monitoring levies imposed on trucks plying the Banda Aceh-Medan route. They found that trucks pay on average about Rp 340,000 per trip. Encouragingly, the levies appear to have declined after the military withdrew as part of the peace settlement. Conversely, other illegal payments (e.g. by over-weight trucks at weigh stations) have risen.
3. See MoF, *Monitoring Peraturan Daerah: Pajak Daerah, Retribusi Daerah*, Jakarta, March.
4. For example, in East Java the large Hero supermarket group has supply contracts with more than fifty fruit and vegetable suppliers.
5. For example, seed varieties and agro-chemicals, especially for fruits and vegetables, where public research institutes have a limited capacity to support innovation.
6. According to the RICA Malang case study, about 75 per cent of supermarket suppliers rely on these collectors (*pengepul*), who also play a role in quality control and market intelligence.
7. The study found that Tanindo carefully selected good quality, innovative farmers on the basis of its extensive local knowledge. Tanindo provides seeds for high-value crops on credit, oversees planting and harvesting, and undertakes rigorous quality control.
8. Note in particular that Malang is nearby and well connected to Indonesia's second largest urban conurbation, it is home to one of Indonesia's major universities (and with a strong concentration on agriculture), and its pleasant mountain climate attracts many wealthy residents.
9. Although a 1992 zoning law specifying that hypermarkets (defined as facilities in excess of 2,500 square metres) not be allowed outside *kabupaten* capitals still remains in place.
10. For example, one farmer in Pantjar's survey planted twenty-eight kinds of vegetables on two hectares of land.
11. For example, see the case study of Buah Indah, a large vegetable and fruit supplier in Kabupaten Batu, as reported in the Malang case study.
12. As an illustration, Herlambang (2006) worries that the mango producers of Probolinggo (East Java) appear to be unable to adapt. These are small cultivators, typically with two to five trees. Yields are low, quality is variable, post-harvest technologies are deficient, and price information is limited.
13. See for example the so-called "vegetable bombs" story in the Malang case study.
14. Such as the Sub Terminal Agribisnis Mantung referred to in the Malang case study.

15. For example, an Indonesian trader (personal discussions, Jakarta, July 2005) recently observed that there were large price differences between Surabaya and regional markets in Southeast Sulawesi for a range of simple consumer goods (clothing, footwear, bags), much larger than could be explained by transport costs. He then proceeded to develop a profitable trade in these goods out of Surabaya.

16. As trade liberalization continues and transport/logistics costs decline, such competition may be expected to intensify. It is evident, for example, in infrastructure-deficient Philippines, where Thai suppliers are able to compete against suppliers from the southern island of Mindanao in upper value niches of the Manila market.

17. In passing, it is useful to recall that the statistical observation of a declining share of small enterprises in industrial output does not necessarily indicate this sector's demise. Since size shares are typically measured on a "current year" basis, a declining share could just as easily indicate that these firms are dynamic and graduating to larger class sizes. In fact, in the only empirical study on this issue of which we are aware, this is precisely what Aswicahyono et al. (1996) found to be the case for Indonesian firms over the period 1977–91.

18. See also Rice (2004) who provides a detailed profile of these firms based on the BPS Surveys.

19. Note that firms were able to select more than one marketing channel.

20. See Oxfam-Unilever (2005), especially Chapter 4, on which this paragraph draws.

21. Important studies include Berry and Levy (1999), Berry et al. (2001), Cole (1998), Papanek (2006), Sandee and van Diermen (2004), Sandee et al. (2000), Schiller and Martin-Schiller (1997), and SMERU (2004).

22. Much is made of the injection of technical expertise embodied in market intelligence, especially in the case of the Jepara furniture manufacturers. However, recent research there suggests that many firms have yet to adopt modern technologies. See for example the IFC 2005 field report, which notes that kiln drying constitutes a serious quality control obstacle for many Jepara producers, with at best "rudimentary controls for temperature and humidity". One of the authors spent a week in this town almost thirty years ago, and the head of the furniture cooperative made a similar observation.

23. As Cole (1998) puts it, "[b]eyond these points, the role the government played seems more positive in its absence than in its actions."

24. The RICA Tegal case study of metal working enterprises comes to a broadly similar conclusion, alluding to "unhealthy competition" and "lack of trust" among producers and buyers within the cluster, including alleged espionage among competing firms and shoddy quality control.

25. For example, according to the 2005 IFC/World Bank report on *Doing Business in 2005*, it is estimated to take on average 151 days to register a business in Indonesia, one of the longest among the 145 nations surveyed. By comparison, the OECD average is reported to be 27 days, while that for East Asia is 61 days.

Note, however, that the estimates for Indonesia are regarded as an overestimate. The LPEM survey reports a (still-lengthy) start-up period of 80 days.

26. This and the following two paragraphs draw heavily on Thee (2006).
27. See Wells (1973) for an early Indonesian case study supporting this proposition.
28. In passing, the similarities with post-crisis Philippines might be noted. That country's infrastructure spending (as a percentage of GDP) is about half the East Asian average and is a major bottleneck on growth (Llanto 2007). There are three major explanations, all relevant to Indonesia: very tight fiscal constraints, resulting in the deferral of most development expenditures; an uncertain investment climate, which deters private, long-term infrastructure providers; and, in the newly decentralized policy environment, coordination difficulties between and among various tiers of government.
29. The auto industry, which many of these firms supply, was hit particularly hard during the crisis, and it has experienced deep structural change since (Aswicahyono et al. 2000).

REFERENCES

Akatiga. *Pola-Pola Eksploitasi dalam Usaha Kecil.* Bandung, 2004.

Aswicahyono, H., M.C. Basri, and H. Hill. "How Not to Industrialize? Indonesia's Automotive Industry". *Bulletin of Indonesian Economic Studies* 36, no. 1 (2000): 209–41.

Aswicahyono, H., K. Bird, and H. Hill. "What Happens to Industrial Structure When Countries Liberalize?". *Journal of Development Studies* 32, no. 3 (1996): 340–63.

Basri, M.C. and H. Soesastro. "The Political Economy of Trade Policy in Indonesia". *ASEAN Economic Bulletin* 22, no. 1 (2005): 3–18.

Berry, A. and B. Levy. "Technical, Financial and Marketing Support for Indonesia's Small and Medium Industrial Exporters". In *Fulfilling the Export Potential of Small and Medium Firms*, edited by B. Levy, A. Berry, and J.B. Nugent. Boston: Kluwer, 1999.

Berry, A. et al. "Small and Medium Enterprise Dynamics in Indonesia". *Bulletin of Indonesian Economic Studies* 37, no. 3 (2001): 363–84.

Bird, K. "Industrial Concentration in Indonesia". *Bulletin of Indonesian Economic Studies* 35, no. 1 (1999): 43–73.

Claessens, S., S. Djankov, and L.H.P. Lang. "The Separation of Ownership and Control in East Asian Corporations". *Journal of Financial Economics* 58 (2000): 81–112.

Cole, W. "Bali's Garment Export Industry". In *Indonesia's Technological Challenge*, edited by H. Hill and Thee K. W. Singapore: Institute of Southeast Asian Studies, 1998.

Feder, G. et al. *Land Policies and Farm Productivity in Thailand*. Baltimore: Johns Hopkins Press for the World Bank, 1988.

Hayami, Y. and T. Kawagoe. *The Agrarian Origins Commerce and Industry: A Study of Peasant Marketing in Indonesia.* New York: St Martin's Press, 1993.

Herlambang, T. "Modernization of the Agro-Commodity Supply Chain: Supermarkets in Indonesia". Seminar presentation, ANU, 1 February 2006.

Kimura, F. "International Production and Distribution Networks in East Asia: 18 Facts, Mechanics, and Policy Implications". *Asian Economic Policy Review* (2006): 320–45.

Lee, R.C and C. Findlay. "Telecommunications Reform in Indonesia: Achievements and Challenges". *Bulletin of Indonesian Economic Studies* 41, no. 3 (2005): 341–65.

Leinbach, T.R., ed. *The Indonesian Rural Economy: Mobility, Work and Enterprise.* Singapore: Institute of Southeast Asian Studies, 2004.

Llanto, G.M. "Infrastructure". In *The Dynamics of Regional Development: The Philippines in East Asia*, edited by A.M. Balisacan and H. Hill. UK: Edward Elgar, 2007.

Loebis, L. and H. Schmitz. "Java Furniture Makers: Globalisation Winners or Losers?". *Ekonomi dan Keuangan Indonesia* 52, no. 3 (2004): 297–308.

Marks, S.V. "Survey of Recent Developments". *Bulletin of Indonesian Economic Studies* 40, no. 2 (2004): 151–75.

Montgomery, R. et al. "Deregulation of Indonesia's Interregional Agricultural Trade". *Bulletin of Indonesian Economic Studies* 38, no. 1 (2002): 93–117.

Nashihin, M. *Poverty Incidence in Indonesia, 1987–2002: A Utility-Consistent Approach based on a Survey of Regional Prices.* Ph.D. dissertation, Australian National University, 2007.

Narjoko, D.A. *Indonesian Manufacturing and the Economic Crisis of 1997–98.* Ph.D. dissertation, Australian National University, 2006.

Oxfam-Unilever. "Exploring the Links Between International Business and Poverty Reduction: A Case Study of Unilever in Indonesia". Oxford, 2005.

Papanek, G. "The *Pribumi* Entrepreneurs of Bali and Central Java (or how *not* to help indigenous enterprise)". *Bulletin of Indonesian Economic Studies* 42, no. 1 (2006): 79–93.

Patten, R.H., J.K. Rosengard, and D.E. Johnston. "Microfinance Success Amidst Macroeconomic Failure: The Experience of Bank Rakyat Indonesia During the East Asian Crisis". *World Development* 29, no. 6 (2001): 1057–69.

Rice, R. "The Contribution of Household and Small Manufacturing Establishments to the Rural Economy". In *The Indonesian Rural Economy*, edited by T.R. Leinbach. Singapore: Institute of Southeast Asian Studies, 2004.

Sandee, H. and P. van Diermen. "Exports by Small and Medium-Sized Enterprises in Indonesia". In *Business in Indonesia: New Challenges, Old Problems*, edited by M.C. Basri and P. van der Eng. Singapore: Institute of Southeast Asian Studies, 2004.

Sandee, H. et al. "Small Firm Development during Good Times and Bad: The Jepara Furniture Industry". In *Indonesia in Transition: Social Aspects of Reformasi and*

Crisis, edited by C. Manning and P. van Diermen. Singapore: Institute of Southeast Asian Studies, 2000.

Sato, Y. "Linkage Formation by Small Firms: The Case of Rural Clusters in Indonesia". *Bulletin of Indonesian Economic Studies* 36, no. 1 (2000): 137–66.

Schiller, J. and B. Martin-Schiller. "Market, Culture and State in the Emergence of an Indonesian Export Furniture Industry". *Journal of Asian Business* 13, no. 1 (1997): 1–23.

Simatupang, P. "Agricultural Marketing and Competition". Paper submitted to the World Bank, Jakarta, October 2005.

SMERU. "Transitions to Non-Farm Employment and the Growth of the Rattan Industry: The Example of Desa Buyut, Cirebon". In *The Indonesian Rural Economy*, edited by T.R. Leinbach. Singapore: Institute of Southeast Asian Studies, 2004.

Tambunan, T. *Development of Small and Medium Enterprises in Indonesia from the Asia-Pacific Perspective*. Jakarta: LPFE University of Trisakti, 2006.

Thee K.W. "Indonesia". In *Industrial Structures and the Development of Small and Medium Enterprise Linkages: Examples from East Asia*, edited by S.D. Meyanathan. Washington D.C.: EDI Seminar Series, World Bank, 1994.

———. "Indonesia's First Competition Law: Issues and Experiences". In *Competition Policies and Deregulation in Asian Countries*, edited by C. Lee. Kuala Lumpur: University of Malaya Press, 2006.

Wells, L.T. "Economic Man and Engineering Man: Choice in a Low Wage Country". *Public Policy* 21, no. 3 (1973): 319–42.

Yusuf, S. and Associates. *Innovative East Asia: The Future of Growth*. New York: Oxford University Press for the World Bank, 2003.

⑧
Local Tax Effects on the Business Climate

Blane D. Lewis and Bambang Suharnoko Sjahrir

1. Introduction

This chapter reviews the state of our knowledge about local taxation in Indonesia and analyses the effects of local taxation on the business climate. We employ a simple cost-benefit framework to organize the discussion of such effects. Costs include the revenue burdens and compliance costs associated with local taxation that are borne by private businesses. Benefits comprise the public services delivered to businesses that are funded from local tax payments. The chapter also summarizes the state of the art regarding the effectiveness and efficiency of local tax administration, as well as corruption attendant to local taxation. We focus on the influence of local administrative ineffectiveness and inefficiency and corruption on tax burdens, compliance costs, and service delivery.

We examine local jurisdictions as a whole in this chaper; that is, we do not differentiate between *kabupaten* and *kota*. The distinction between *kabupaten* and *kota* has less meaning than one might imagine in the current context. The administrative categories of *kabupaten* and *kota* are not good proxies for rural and urban, for example. About one-third of the total *kabupaten* population is urban and the urbanization rate ranges from zero to 90 per cent across all *kabupaten*. While 95 per cent of total *kota* population is urban, the rate of urbanization varies from 55 per cent to 100 per cent across *kota*. Moreover, we cannot organize all relevant cost and benefit data according to a *kabupaten* and *kota* classification scheme.

We adopt a loose and implicit definition of the business climate. We simply assume that tax burdens and compliance costs have a negative impact on the business climate and that public service delivery has a (potentially) positive effect on the business climate.

The chapter proceeds as follows. First, we provide some rather extensive background material on local taxation. Here we examine local government own-source revenue and (central) property tax revenue, pre- and post-decentralization, as well as review certain issues related to newly created local taxes and charges during the post-decentralization period. Second, we outline our cost-benefit analytical framework in more detail. Third, we review the available evidence regarding the costs and benefits of local taxation and the impact of administrative ineffectiveness and inefficiency and corruption on such costs and benefits. Finally, in a concluding section, we summarize the main points of the chapter and draw some conclusions that might be important for the future development of sub-national tax policy.

2. Background

This section of the chapter provides some basic data on local revenues. We examine local government own-source taxes and charges as well as the property tax, pre- and post-decentralization. In addition, we describe briefly the state of our knowledge about new local revenues created in the post-decentralization period.

2.1. Pre- and Post-Decentralization Local Revenues

Law 34/00 enumerates specific allowable local government taxes. These so-called positive list taxes comprise those on hotels, restaurants, entertainment, advertisement, electricity use, Class C mineral extraction, and parking. Law 34/00 also permits local government to create supplementary new taxes, given the satisfaction of a number of "good tax" conditions.[1]

In addition, the law authorizes *kabupaten/kota* to levy three different types of user charges, including those on (pure) public services, public services that possess certain private good characteristics, and licences and fees of various kinds. The law does not enumerate particular user charges that local governments are allowed to create but instead authorizes local governments to establish charges in these three categories under certain rules.[2] Typical pure public service charges include those associated with public health clinics, public markets, and refuse collection and solid waste removal, for example. Common user fees for services with private good characteristics include those for slaughterhouses, wholesale markets, and auction houses, among others. Standard licences include construction permits, land utilization permits, and, especially, business operating licences.

The vast majority, if not all, of local government taxes and charges would appear to be levied at least to some extent on private businesses. Some of the taxes and charges are levied on both businesses and individuals, of course. Relatively few, if any, of the revenues would appear to be levied exclusively on individuals.[3] The *puskesmas* service charge is sometimes raised as the exception to the rule, although, it appears that some businesses also cover the *puskesmas* health expenses of their employees.

Table 8.1 provides a summary of local government revenues, focusing on those derived from own-sources, during the period 1994/95 to 2003. Only the most important (and identifiable) individual own-source taxes and charges are shown. The table presents three sets of data. The top-left portion of the table shows the rupiah amounts of revenue (in constant 2003 terms) generated by local taxes, local charges, and other local sources, as well as other revenues (i.e. transfers of one kind or another) over the period in question. The top-right corner of the table presents real annual growth rates of revenue, by source, both for the pre-decentralization period and for the entire period under consideration. In addition, this section of the table shows the absolute real increase in revenue from 1999/00 (the last full year before decentralization) to 2003, as well as each individual revenue source's contribution to that increase in percentage terms. Finally, the bottom portion of the table shows local own-source and other revenue in percentage terms.

There are many things that one might say about the information presented in Table 8.1. For now, we highlight four main sets of points. The first set of points concerns the structure of local taxation, pre- and post-decentralization. Note that as of 2003, taxes, charges, and other sources of revenue contribute roughly equal amounts to total own-source revenue. The structure of own-source revenues has changed significantly since 2001. In the mid-1990s, user charges were the most important source of local revenue, followed closely by local taxes; by the late 1990s the reverse was true. Before decentralization, "other" revenues made up only a relatively small share of local own-source revenues. Currently, the principal taxes are on electricity sales and hotels and restaurants. These taxes make up over 90 per cent of total tax revenue. The main user charge is *puskesmas* health service fees. The latter comprise about one-third of total user charges. Market fees contribute less than 8 per cent to the total. The most significant category of user charges is "other", which

Constant (2003) Rupiah (Blns)

	1994/95	1995/96	1996/97	1997/98	1998/99	1999/00	2001	2002	2003	Average Year Growth 1994/95–1999/00	Average Year Growth 1994/95–2003	Total Increase 1999/00–2003	Percentage
Local Taxes	1,468.8	1,742.1	1,863.6	2,004.7	1,497.5	1,633.2	2,095.5	2,489.5	2,744.1	2.1%	7.4%	1,111.0	23.6
Electricity	494.6	710.9	797.6	854.2	620.4	692.6	1,011.2	1,398.2	1,676.9	7.0%	15.0%	984.3	20.9
Hotel/Restaurant	601.7	687.4	739.9	830.4	717.2	772.7	904.5	869.7	807.2	5.1%	3.4%	34.5	0.7
Other	372.5	344.0	326.1	320.0	159.9	168.0	179.7	221.6	260.1	-14.7%	-4.0%	92.1	2.0
Local Charges	2,378.8	2,550.5	2,681.5	2,634.8	1,329.6	1,396.1	1,984.7	2,465.5	2,823.1	-10.1%	2.0%	1,427.0	30.3
Health	379.5	396.4	393.4	402.4	372.4	455.0	608.6	819.7	935.4	3.7%	10.9%	480.4	10.2
Market Fees	314.5	326.4	335.4	325.7	189.4	186.0	191.1	216.9	213.3	-10.0%	-4.3%	27.4	0.6
Other	1,684.8	1,827.7	1,952.7	1,906.7	767.8	755.2	1,185.0	1,428.9	1,674.4	-14.8%	-0.1%	919.2	19.5
Other OSR	522.1	643.8	632.1	622.3	577.2	522.7	1,385.8	2,487.1	2,695.1	0.0%	20.6%	2,172.4	46.1
Total OSR	4,369.7	4,936.5	5,177.2	5,261.7	3,404.2	3,552.0	5,465.9	7,442.1	8,262.3	-4.1%	7.6%	4,710.4	100.0
Other Revenue	30,830.1	33,082.8	35,301.7	38,343.6	29,335.3	35,555.2	85,843.0	101,872.1	106,528.5	2.9%	15.2%		
Total Revenue	35,199.7	38,019.3	40,478.9	43,605.3	32,739.5	39,107.1	91,308.9	109,314.3	114,790.8	2.1%	14.5%		

Percentage Terms

	1994/95	1995/96	1996/97	1997/98	1998/99	1999/00	2001	2002	2003
Local Taxes	100.0	100.0	100.0	100.0	100.0	100.0	100.0	100.0	100.0
Electricity	33.7	40.8	42.8	42.6	41.4	42.4	48.3	56.2	61.1
Hotel/Restaurant	41.0	39.5	39.7	41.4	47.9	47.3	43.2	34.9	29.4
Other	25.4	19.7	17.5	16.0	10.7	10.3	8.6	8.9	9.5
Local Charges	100.0	100.0	100.0	100.0	100.0	100.0	100.0	100.0	100.0
Health	16.0	15.5	14.7	15.3	28.0	32.6	30.7	33.2	33.1
Market Fees	13.2	12.8	12.5	12.4	14.2	13.3	9.6	8.8	7.6
Other	70.8	71.7	72.8	72.4	57.7	54.1	59.7	58.0	59.3
Taxes/Total OSR	33.6	35.3	36.0	38.1	44.0	46.0	38.3	33.5	33.2
Charges/Total OSR	54.4	51.7	51.8	50.1	39.1	39.3	36.3	33.1	34.2
Other OSR/Total OSR	11.9	13.0	12.2	11.8	17.0	14.7	25.4	33.4	32.6
Total OSR/Total Revenue	12.4	13.0	12.8	12.1	10.4	9.1	6.0	6.8	7.2
Other Revenue/Total Revenue	87.6	87.0	87.2	87.9	89.6	90.9	94.0	93.2	92.8

Source: World Bank Database.

notably, business licences and fees of various kinds. The third category of own-source revenues is a catch-all group of "other revenues". A close look at the primary data suggests that the most important type of revenue in this category is interest earnings on bank balances. It is well known that local governments have built up large surpluses since decentralization and these funds have led to considerable interest earnings.

Second, own-source revenues have grown quite rapidly since decentralization. Real own-source revenues declined an average 4.1 per cent per year from 1994/95 to 1999/00;[4] but the average annual real growth rate of own-source revenues was 7.6 per cent over the entire period 1994/95 to 2003. This clearly indicates the importance of own-source revenue growth in the post-decentralization period.

The third set of points concerns the contribution of various types of own-source revenue to post-decentralization growth. As Table 8.1 shows, the absolute increase in the level of own-source revenues between 1999/00 and 2003 was about Rp 4.7 trillion (in real terms). Nearly half (46 per cent) of the absolute increase was accounted for by "other own-source revenues". These revenues are, as already noted, local government interest earnings on bank balances, for the most part. About 20 per cent of the post-decentralization increase in own-source revenues was from the tax on electricity sales. Another 20 per cent of the absolute increase was derived from "other user charges". As mentioned, much, although not all, of this revenue is likely to come from business licences of various kinds, many of which were newly created by local governments under decentralization. Finally, about 10 per cent of the absolute increase in own-source revenues is from *puskesmas* user charges.

Fourth, while the growth of own-source revenues may be deemed impressive in the post-decentralization period, such revenues still make up only a very small portion of local resources. As of 2003, own-source revenues accounted for just over 7 per cent of total local government revenues. Moreover, the relative importance of own-source revenues has actually declined since decentralization, down from 12.4 per cent in 1994/95. This indicates the strong and growing importance of transfers to local government budgets in the decentralization period. The dominance of transfers has not led to reduced local own-source revenue effort, however, as has been found elsewhere (Zhuravskaya 2000). Lewis (2005) finds that, in post-decentralization Indonesia, increasing per capita transfers stimulate increases in per capita own-source revenues, across local governments as a whole.[5]

The property tax is a central tax in Indonesia. The central government defines the tax base, sets the effective tax rates, manages the tax cadastre, assesses tax liability, collects the tax, and enforces tax payment. Local governments do, however, play a supporting role in tax collection. Property tax receipts are shared among the provinces and *kabupaten/kota*. Provinces and local governments receive 16.2 per cent and 74.8 per cent of total property tax receipts, respectively. According to law, allocations to provinces and *kabupaten/kota* are done by derivation, except in the mining sector.[6] The centre keeps 9 per cent of the property tax to cover the cost of administration (Lewis 2003*a*).

The government has considered decentralization of the property tax periodically over the course of many years, most recently in 2005, in the run-up to revising Law 34/00. It may or may not eventually devolve some control over some aspects of the tax to local governments. In any case, the tax is local in character and all private businesses are liable to pay property tax. As such, the tax is included in our discussion here.

Table 8.2 presents some data on property tax receipts, by sector, for the period 1994/95 to 2003. The information shown is similar to that presented in Table 8.1 and is organized in the same manner. The data suggest four points worthy of mention.

First, property taxes from the mining sector (98 per cent of which is from oil and gas) predominate.[7] Receipts from this sector accounted for 56 per cent of the total property tax in 2003.[8] Urban sector property taxes are the next most important category, making up just over one third of the total. Property taxes from the other sectors are comparatively insignificant. Receipts from the rural, estates, and forestry sectors make up less than 10 per cent of the total property tax.

Second, like local government own-source revenues, property taxes have shown reasonably strong growth in the post-decentralization period. From 1994/95 through 1990/00, property tax receipts actually declined in real terms, at an average rate of 6.3 per cent. (Again the downturn was largely the result of the economic crisis.) But real annual growth over the entire period shown in the table, i.e. after accounting for the post-decentralization years, was 5.6 per cent.

Third, not surprisingly, most of the post-decentralization growth is accounted for by property taxes in the mining sector. Property tax receipts in mining make up almost two-thirds of the total real increase between 1999/00 and 2003 (Rp 5.5 trillion). Urban property taxes contribute slightly more than one-third of the total real increase during the post-decentralization period. Property taxes in the other sectors have not added much to the post-decentralization growth.

Fourth, note the overall level of property taxes. As of 2003, total property taxes were approximately Rp 10 trillion. This figure is about 20 per cent

Table 8.2
Property Tax, by Sector, 1994/95 to 2003

Constant (2003) Rupiah (Blns)

	1994/95	1995/96	1996/97	1997/98	1998/99	1999/00	2001	2002	2003	Average Year Growth 1994/95–1999/00	Average Year Growth 1994/95–2003	Total Increase 1999/00–2003	Percentage 2003
Urban	1,785.91	2,398.59	2,397.40	2,329.44	1,514.52	1,431.65	1,930.81	3,179.59	3,462.80	−4.3%	7.9%	2,031.1	36.7
Rural	641.32	721.63	710.38	659.67	400.34	370.05	363.40	425.71	445.71	−10.4%	−4.1%	75.7	1.4
Estates	234.28	310.77	272.19	265.67	295.37	279.00	276.06	284.60	311.76	3.6%	3.3%	32.8	0.6
Forestry	614.72	808.00	641.81	566.60	441.82	242.27	191.50	184.86	159.36	−17.0%	−14.3%	−82.9	−1.5
Mining	2,984.37	3,964.55	3,557.71	3,471.24	2,518.11	2,196.54	3,201.01	3,865.31	5,680.06	−5.9%	7.6%	3,483.5	62.9
Total	6,260.59	8,203.55	7,579.50	7,292.62	5,170.16	4,519.52	5,962.78	7,940.06	10,059.69	−6.3%	5.6%	5,540.2	100.0

Percentage Terms

	1994/95	1995/96	1996/97	1997/98	1998/99	1999/00	2001	2002	2003
Urban	28.5	29.2	31.6	31.9	29.3	31.7	32.4	40.0	34.4
Rural	10.2	8.8	9.4	9.0	7.7	8.2	6.1	5.4	4.4
Estates	3.7	3.8	3.6	3.6	5.7	6.2	4.6	3.6	3.1
Forestry	9.8	9.8	8.5	7.8	8.5	5.4	3.2	2.3	1.6
Mining	47.7	48.3	46.9	47.6	48.7	48.6	53.7	48.7	56.5
Total	100.0	100.0	100.0	100.0	100.0	100.0	100.0	100.0	100.0

Source: World Bank Database.

higher than total own-source revenues (which were just over Rp 8 trillion rupiah in 2003). But property taxes in the urban and rural sectors, which are more relevant for most businesses, constitute just less than Rp 4 trillion, or about half of total local government own-source revenue (and about 60 per cent of local own-source taxes and charges).

2.2. Newly Created Taxes and Charges Post-Decentralization

Perhaps the most frequently mentioned phenomenon regarding post-decentralization taxation at the local level concerns the creation of new taxes and charges. The following paragraphs review what we know about new revenue instruments established since decentralization. We consider issues related to the number and kind of new taxes and charges created, sectors and locations in which they were established, and certain specific procedural issues and outcomes concerning their formation and cancellation.

Local governments have apparently established new revenue instruments in a rather aggressive manner since decentralization. An early study estimated that just fewer than 1,000 new taxes and charges were created by *kabupaten/ kota* in the run-up to and during the first year of decentralization (Lewis 2003*b*). More recent work indicates that local governments may have established as many as 6,000 new taxes and charges during the period 2000 to mid-2005 (LPEM-FEUI 2005*a*). A caveat is in order with regard to the figure of 6,000 "new taxes and charges". The latter number actually represents the number of new tax and charge by-laws (*peraturan daerah* — perda) issued from 2000 to mid-2005. Some of these new perda undoubtedly were written in order to change the tariffs and/or bases of existing taxes and charges, as allowed by Law 34/2000. That is, the new perda did not, in all cases, authorize new tax and charge instruments. As such, the quoted figure might best be thought of as an upper bound on the number of newly established revenues.[9]

The vast majority of new revenue instruments authorized by local governments would seem to be user charges. Lewis (2003*b*) reports that about 90 per cent of a large (but non-random) sample of the total number of new revenue instruments created during the run-up to and the first year of decentralization were charges. Care should be taken in interpreting this figure. Experience shows that sometimes revenues that have been identified as charges by local governments are really just disguised taxes. In other words, many of the newly created user charges do not appear to be associated with the delivery of particular public services (i.e. either pure public services or those with private good characteristics) or the granting of permissions, as they should be by law.

The primary sector appears to have been the principal focus of new taxes and charges established by local governments since decentralization. Lewis (2003*b*) provides some evidence to suggest that about 40 per cent of the newly created taxes and charges during the period 2000–01 were on primary sector commodities. No particular product was singled out as the main target of new taxes and charges. Indeed, the list of primary sector goods taxed in those early years is remarkable for its variety and seems mostly to depend on location: fish in Sumatra, tea and tobacco in Java, rubber and timber in Kalimantan, cloves and cashew nuts in Sulawesi, and livestock in Eastern Indonesia, for example. Services constitute the second most important sector for new charges (21 per cent of the total), followed by distribution (12 per cent), the secondary sector and government administration (both at 11 per cent), and "other" (5 per cent).

Local governments on Sumatra and Java-Bali seem to have been most assertive in establishing new taxes and charges, at least during the initial years of decentralization. Lewis (2003*b*) reports that *kabupaten/kota* in those locations created about 38 per cent and 30 per cent of the total number of newly created revenue instruments during 2000–01, respectively. Local governments in Sulawesi, Kalimantan, and Eastern Indonesia created 16 per cent, 9 per cent, and 8 per cent, respectively, of the total number during that period. Unfortunately, there is no more recent evidence on this question.

It might be useful to note that local governments have apparently created many of their official new revenue instruments in an extra-legal manner. Lewis (2003*b*) estimated that only about 40 per cent of the newly established taxes and charges in 2000–01 were submitted to the central government for review and evaluation, as required by law. The remainder were presumably implemented directly via perda without central government appraisal and therefore contrary to applicable legislation. More generally, LPEM-FEUI (2005*a*) reports that the central government has only managed to review 47 per cent of 13,520 (tax and non-tax) perda sent in for evaluation from 2000 to mid-2005.

A related and final issue concerns the result of perda appraisals conducted by central government. Lewis (2003*b*) estimates that central government cancelled just less than 30 per cent of all new tax and charge perda it reviewed by the end of 2001. The cancellations were made because the submitted tax and charge perda contradicted in some way central guidelines for the establishment of new revenue instruments. A review of the cancelled perda suggests that the bulk were rejected on the grounds that the authorized tax or charge would somehow harm the regional economy. A second important reason for cancellation was that the good or factor in question was already considered to be sufficiently covered by another tax or charge; this is what Indonesian officials typically refer to as "double taxation". More recently, researchers at LPEM-FEUI (2005*a*) calculated that the central government cancelled about 448 of 6,456 tax and charge perda it evaluated between 2000 and mid-2005 (about 6.9 per cent). Again, it is important to keep in mind that the latter estimate refers both to new local taxes and charges as well as to perda that revised in some manner already existing revenue instruments.

Ministry of Finance has recently drafted revisions to Law 34/00 on regional taxation, which have been forwarded to DPR for review. Pending amendments to the law do not devolve additional authority over any significant local tax bases (e.g. property tax) to local governments. Further reform of central-local tax assignments would appear to be a longer term goal. The draft revisions do, however, restrict sub-national governments' authority to levy taxes and charges to those enumerated on positive lists. Thus local governments will no longer be allowed to create their own new revenue instruments as they have in the recent past. The government expects that the new policy will reduce the proliferation of nuisance and harmful sub-national taxes.

3. Analytical Framework

This section of the chapter outlines some specific matters regarding the analytical cost-benefit framework that is used later in the examination. We define terms and discuss basic issues concerning revenue burdens, compliance costs, service delivery, administrative ineffectiveness and inefficiency, and corruption. The first two items are firms' costs related to local taxation, the third is a benefit to firms, and the fourth and fifth influence firms' benefits and costs as defined here.

3.1. Revenue Burden

The revenue burden of a tax is equal to the amount of tax paid. A tax may be applied to a good or service (commodity) or to a factor of production. The tax burden of a commodity tax is shared between consumers and producers of the commodity. The relative amount of the tax burden borne by consumers and producers depends on the elasticities of demand for and supply of the taxed commodity. In general, the more elastic the demand and the less elastic the supply, the more the tax burden is borne by producers; and the more elastic the supply and the less elastic the demand, the more the burden is borne by consumers. The burden of a tax on a production factor (land, labour, capital, entrepreneurship) is shared between the users (firms) and suppliers (or owners) of the factor. Again, the relative amount of the burden borne by factor users and providers depends on the elasticities of demand for and supply of the taxed factor, in the same way as previously described. In the end, the entire burden of any tax is borne by individuals not businesses. Thus, the producer's share of a commodity tax and the user's or supplier's share of a factor tax are ultimately allocated across owners of factors of production. The share of the burden assumed by various factors of production depends, in the first instance, on the relative intensity of factor use. In general, the more intensively a factor is used, the greater the decline in its relative price (given a tax) and the more the tax burden is borne by owners of that factor.[10]

Taxes also typically create a burden in excess of revenue generated. The excess burden derives from economic distortions created by the tax. For example, individuals may consume less of a taxed commodity and more of some other (less desired) good or service and businesses may use their factors of production to make other less heavily taxed goods (less cost-effectively). The excess burden (deadweight loss) associated with a tax represents an efficiency cost and a loss of private welfare. The size of the excess burden is a function of the elasticities of demand for and supply of the commodity (or factor), the total pre-tax spending on the commodity (or factor), and the tax (squared).[11] Excess burdens are difficult to estimate in practice. We do not consider the costs imposed by excess burdens in this chapter in any depth.

3.2. Compliance Costs

Compliance costs are those costs borne by businesses (and individuals) in the context of abiding by local tax regulations. Such costs may include both money and time spent in paying taxes, user charges, and other fees. Compliance costs are typically not trivial and generally exceed the cost of administering taxes by a significant amount, although such costs are usually considerably less than the tax revenue generated, of course (at least in more modern economies).

3.3. Public Service Delivery

Benefits received by businesses in return for local tax payments are in the form of services delivered by local governments. In theory, publicly provided infrastructure services may serve as a direct input to private production, as a factor that augments the productivity of private capital and labour, and, as amenities that encourage firm creation and development (and, perhaps, relocation). Each of these uses might be expected to benefit private enterprises and stimulate local economic growth.

3.4. Administrative Ineffectiveness and Inefficiency

Tax administration is concerned with the identification of taxpayers, assessment of tax liability, tax collection, and enforcement of tax payment. The main objective of tax administration is to produce the requisite public revenue at a minimum cost, all other things remaining the same. The analysis of the tax administrative performance of governments typically focuses on realizations and/or costs. The former concentrates on the extent to which generated tax revenues approach potential levels (administrative effectiveness) and the latter on the degree to which the costs of tax administration have been minimized (administrative efficiency). Ineffective tax administration results in fewer tax revenues than could potentially be collected. And inefficient tax administration reduces the availability of collected tax revenues for service delivery.

3.5. Corruption

Finally, the effects of corruption related to local taxation must be considered. Our framework integrates three kinds of corruption. The first is corruption that is linked to the payment of official taxes. Such bribery might be expected to decrease the actual level of taxes paid (relative to statutory liabilities) but increase compliance costs associated with taxation (e.g. because of the time required in negotiation). Bribery is assumed to have no direct impact on the level of public services delivered. The second kind of corruption taken into account in the framework is that associated with the spending of fiscal resources attendant to the delivery of public infrastructure services. This kind of corruption includes input price mark-ups, contractor kickbacks, and the like. Such corruption would be expected to reduce the level of public services delivered, for any given level of available tax resources. The third type of corruption relates to the payment of strictly illegal levies. The payment of illegal taxes increases a firm's overall tax burden (and perhaps its compliance costs) but offers no public service benefits in return.

4. Review of the Evidence on Costs and Benefits of Local Taxation

This section of the chapter examines the available evidence on local taxation in Indonesia with a view to establishing some initial ideas about costs and benefits, as outlined above.

4.1. Revenue Burden

We take the total local revenue burden to be that associated with local government own-source taxes and charges and the central property tax.[12] The sum of these revenue sources in 2003 was Rp 15.6 trillion. This figure represents just 0.75 per cent of GDP. An alternative and perhaps more plausible assumption would be that the local tax burden comprises local government own-source taxes and charges and central property tax from the urban and rural sectors only (i.e. excluding, most importantly, gas and oil "property taxes"). The total amount of revenue generated from these sources was equal to Rp 9.5 trillion in 2003 or about 0.5 per cent of GDP.

RICS data provide a picture of the revenue burden associated with central, provincial, and local taxation for firms in the sample. As Table 8.3 shows, the total tax burden amounts to 0.97 and 1.84 per cent of total firms' sales and costs, respectively. Apparently provincial taxes are the most burdensome, followed by local and central taxes.

Table 8.3
Official Tax Burden

	% of Total Sales	% of Total Costs
Central Taxes	0.11	0.18
Provincial Taxes	0.57	1.12
Kabupaten Taxes	0.19	0.47
Total Official Taxes	0.86	1.73
Total Official Charges	0.11	0.18
Total Official Taxes & Charges	0.97	1.84

Of course only some portion of the local revenue burden as defined above would be borne by firms (in the first instance). And ultimately, the entire amount would be borne by individuals.[13] What would seem to be of special interest in the current context would be the portion of the firms' tax burden that is borne by owners of the firms. However, without more information about tax (burden) shifting and secondary market effects we cannot be more precise about actual burden sharing.

In any case, the main point here is that, overall, the local revenue burden would not appear to be particularly significant. This conclusion would seem to be corroborated by the views of firms themselves. A recent survey carried out by LPEM-UI (2004) found that only about 10 per cent of firms in urban centres considered the amount of taxes that they paid to be burdensome. RICS data show that just over 20 per cent of firms in the sample consider official taxes to be a problem at all and only 6 per cent found taxes to be a "big problem". Table 8.4 provides the details.

Table 8.4
Problems Related to Official Taxes

Severity of Problem	% of Respondents
Not a Problem	78.3
Small Problem	7.5
Medium Problem	8.0
Big Problem	6.1
Total	100.0

4.2. Compliance Costs

Compliance costs associated with the major local taxes do not appear to be very substantial. A firm's tax liability attendant to electricity use is indicated on its monthly electricity bill; payments can be made to PLN via most local banks. Hotels and restaurants are notified in writing of their tax liability on a monthly basis (in theory) and taxes are collected by local officials on the premises. Businesses (and individuals) are made aware of their property tax liabilities by mailed or hand-delivered notifications from deconcentrated offices of the Ministry of Finance (Directorate General of Tax) or from local governments; the tax can easily be paid at a variety of locations, including local branches of designated state banks.

Ease of compliance may not be the case for many local user charges, however. The most onerous compliance costs are those associated with business licensing. Such compliance costs tend to be measured in days spent in compliance and not in monetary amounts. LPEM-UI (2005*b*) has estimated that it takes 80 days to register a new business in Indonesia.[14] Most of the time to register a new business is taken up with satisfying central government requirements, especially those of the Ministry of Law. About 24 days (out of the total), however, are needed in order to comply with the attendant requirements of various local government offices according to the LPEM-UI survey.

Having obtained the required start-up permits, it is necessary for a business to secure a variety of other licences. LPEM-UI (2005*b*) lists six different local licences and permits that most businesses need to secure before they can legally operate: environmental permit, building licence, location permit, principle permit, nuisance permit, and work safety permit. The time required to obtain these permits and licences is estimated to range between 43 and 180 days.[15] Other authorizations may also be required, depending on the exact nature of the business. The LPEM-UI study lists an additional 20 permits that many firms may need to secure; a single business would require 24 days to obtain each of these permits, on average. In addition, to save time spent obtaining various business licences, some firms pay top-offs to local officials in order to speed up the process (LPEM-UI 2005*b*; von Luebke 2005).

Firms sampled in the RICS offer a significantly different picture of compliance costs. The average waiting time to obtain necessary permits for those businesses amounted to just 1.1 days, on average. Again only about 20 per cent of firms in the sample found compliance costs to be any kind of a problem; and just less than 4 per cent of firms found such costs to be a "big problem". See Table 8.5 for the specifics. The noteworthy difference in views must be related at least in part to the informal nature of business covered by the RICS. That is, it is likely that firms operating in the informal sector are able to avoid capture by local regulators.

4.3. Service Delivery

Given the scale of decentralization in Indonesia and the rapid manner in which it was implemented, it is perhaps noteworthy that public service delivery did not totally break down during the transition (World Bank 2003). Moreover, the public perception seems to be that the quality of many local

Table 8.5
Problems Related to Compliance Costs

Severity of Problem	% of Respondents
Not a Problem	80.8
Small Problem	10.5
Medium Problem	5.1
Big Problem	3.7
Total	100.0

public services has actually improved slightly since decentralization. A recent survey (World Bank 2004*a*) indicates that about 60 per cent of households (in eight provinces) perceive that local government, health, education, and administrative services have improved under decentralization.[16]

On the other hand, many private firms complain that they get little service benefit in return for the taxes that they pay (von Luebke 2005). Among the most important public services according to businesses are electricity, water, and (local) roads (KPPOD 2004; LPEM-UI 2005*b*).[17] Electricity is centrally provided, although local governments tax its use (and ostensibly employ the revenues to provide street and public park lighting, among other things). Water and roads are local government services. The LPEM-UI (2005*b*) study suggests that both electricity and water services have deteriorated in quality over the past two years. And while issues related to local roads were not formally included in the survey, researchers found that the majority of businesses interviewed declared the quality of roads to be problematic.

4.4. Administrative Ineffectiveness and Inefficiency

Lewis (2003*a*) estimates that recently only around 40 per cent of urban and rural property tax potential has been realized under central administration. Property valuations are the most problematic aspect of administration; the evidence suggests that government appraisals of taxable property make up only 60 per cent of real market values, on average. Tax coverage and collection are apparently less worrisome but still weaker than one might expect; moreover, improvements here would appear to have stalled in recent years.[18] The relevant coverage and collection ratios are currently around 80 per cent for both, as they have been since at least the mid-1990s.[19] No empirical evidence exists regarding local government own-source revenue administrative effectiveness.

A simple measure of a government's tax administrative cost efficiency is the cost of tax administration divided by tax revenue generated (cost-to-yield ratio). All other things being equal, as the cost-to-yield ratio rises, governments are seen as increasingly cost inefficient, as regards to tax administration. Lewis (2006) provides some evidence to suggest that the average *kabupaten/kota* cost-to-yield ratio was 53 per cent in 2003. The ratio ranged from a low of 15 per cent to a high of 264 per cent across all local governments. Interestingly, about 10 per cent of local governments had cost-to-yield ratios that exceeded 100 per cent, indicating that the cost of administering taxes was greater than the revenue collected.[20] There are no comparable data for central government costs of administering the property tax. The central government keeps

9 per cent of total property tax revenue as an administrative fee but the extent to which this covers actual costs is unclear.

4.5. Corruption

Kuncoro (2004) examines bribery linked to official local taxation in a survey covering more than 1,800 firms in 64 local government jurisdictions. He provides evidence to suggest that the level of bribes paid by firms is just less than 40 per cent of taxes the firms pay (at the margin). He finds that bribe payment is also positively related to the number of business licences that a particular firm must obtain in order to operate legally. Finally the author notes that service sector firms, businesses operating in natural resource-rich locations, and firms situated in urban areas pay higher bribes; while more established and larger businesses pay lower bribes, all other things being equal. Another study (KPPOD 2003) estimated that, on average, firms pay about 60 per cent of their total taxes and charges in bribes to local officials. Kuncoro (2004) notes that bribery also creates additional and significant compliance costs, largely in the form of time spent in negotiating bribe payments, but offers no precise estimates of costs in this regard.

Corruption associated with the spending of local fiscal resources has been a topic of a number of recent studies. The World Bank in an internal memo (that was widely distributed) famously estimated that about 30 per cent of the finance associated with its development projects was stolen in one manner or another. A more recent case study of Kabupaten Lebak (in the province of Banten) by a team of World Bank researchers (World Bank 2004*b*) estimated that leakages related to the implementation of all development projects ranged between 30 and 40 per cent of total amounts available for spending. Compliance costs associated with this type of corruption would appear to be zero for most firms.[21]

The payment of strictly illegal fees has also been considered by a number of researchers (KPPOD 2003; Ray 2003; von Luebke 2004, 2005). Such fees seem for the most part to be paid to institutions other than local governments, including, most importantly, the judiciary, police, and community groups. These illegal fees can be quite significant for firms operating in some sectors, especially transportation (Ray 2003; von Luebke 2004). Unfortunately, there are no estimates of the precise magnitude of this kind of corruption.

RICS data provide an overall view of unofficial tax payments. The revenue burden associated with unofficial payments of all kinds would appear to be rather small for firms in the sample. As Table 8.6 shows, on average firms pay just 0.21 per cent and 0.35 per cent of total sales and costs in illegal taxes and fees of various kinds.

Table 8.6
Unofficial Tax Burden

	% of Total Sales	% of Total Costs
Central Unofficial Taxes	0.00	0.00
Provincial Unofficial Taxes	0.00	0.00
Kabupaten Unofficial Taxes	0.02	0.03
Others Unofficial Payment	0.19	0.32
Total Unofficial Taxes	0.21	0.34
Total Unofficial Charges	0.01	0.01
Total Unofficial Taxes & Charges	0.21	0.35

Table 8.7
Problems Related to Unofficial Taxes

Severity of Problem	% of Respondents
Not a Problem	81.4
Small Problem	8.0
Medium Problem	6.7
Big Problem	3.9
Total	100.0

In general, firms surveyed by RICS do not appear to find corruption associated with unofficial taxes and fees to be overly problematic. Again only about 20 per cent of firms find unofficial payments to be any kind of a problem at all. And less than 4 per cent of firms surveyed find unofficial charges to represent a "big problem". Table 8.7 supplies the full details.

5. Conclusion

The evidence regarding the impact of local taxation on the business climate is mixed. Certainly, tax burdens would not appear to be especially problematic. The aggregate revenue burden associated with local taxes is low relative to GDP; individual firms surveyed by RICS report limited tax liabilities in relation to business revenues and costs. The amount of local taxes that a typical business pays is significantly lower than its statutory tax liability. The shortfall is a function of ineffective local government tax administration and bribery of local officials (which buys down tax payments).

On the other hand, the effect of compliance costs is less clear. Mandated compliance costs associated with local taxation may be significant for some larger firms, especially as related to business licensing. Compliance costs may be even higher than those officially authorized because of the need to pay top-offs in order to expedite procedures. On the other hand, (smaller, informal sector) firms surveyed by RICS do not appear to find compliance with tax and licence regulations to be particularly onerous.

Whatever the level of official and unofficial tax payments and compliance costs, associated public service delivery is very limited. Official tax revenues that might be used to deliver services are diminished by inefficient local government tax administration and by corruption attendant to the spending of funds. Bribes made in order to reduce a firm's tax payments result in no public service delivery, of course. And strictly illegal fees paid by some firms to local administration officials offer no services in return.

Forthcoming regional tax legislation will most likely claw back local governments' authority to create their own taxes, charges, and fees. Local revenues will be confined to those that appear on a positive list of allowable instruments. The Ministry of Finance hopes that the new restrictions will help reduce some of the nuisance and economically harmful effects of local taxation; the central government's ability to monitor compliance with forthcoming legislation will be a key determinant in the success or failure of the intended reforms. But new tax legislation will not address problems related to ineffective and inefficient local tax administration, inadequate local public service delivery, and corruption. Progress in these areas is part of a much longer-term and more difficult reform agenda.

NOTES

1. The good tax criteria assert that (1) tax objects should be located in the particular district and possess relatively low mobility across district boundaries; (2) the tax should not contradict the public interest; (3) the tax should not constitute a national or provincial tax; (4) tax revenues should be elastic with regard to regional income; (5) implementation of the tax should not have a negative impact on the local economy; (6) development of the tax should take into consideration issues of fairness to and capacity of local residents; and (7) the tax should safeguard the environment.

2. The conditions under which user charges may be established are similar to those under which taxes can be created, as reported just above.

3. The law defines a regional tax to be an obligatory levy, non-excessive and balanced, paid to regional government by private persons or bodies, that is used to finance regional government and regional development. A regional user

charge is defined as a fee for a service or permission provided by regional government for the benefit of private individuals and institutions.

4. The downturn was largely a function of the financial and economic crisis, the effects of which were most strongly felt in fiscal year 1998–99, as can be seen in the table.

5. Two explanations have been put forward for this finding. The first is straightforward: as transfers increase, savings grow, and interest earnings rise. As noted, interest income is categorized as own-source revenue in local budgets. The second reason is more behavioural in nature: local governments and parliaments insist that their overhead budgets keep pace with increases in total revenue and these expectations drive increases in local taxation (the funding source for overhead expenditure) in response to growing transfers from the centre.

6. The allocation of property tax revenues in the gas and oil sub-sector depends on whether it derives from on or offshore production. Onshore amounts are distributed by derivation. Offshore amounts are distributed in ad hoc ways which vary from year to year. Often, offshore gas and oil allocations are based, at least in part, on the distribution of urban and rural sector receipts. In this case, a local government's allocation from the oil and gas sector (offshore) depends directly on its relative contribution to overall urban and rural sector receipts. As such, the distribution of tax revenues in this sub-sector across sub-national governments is even more than one would expect, given the spatial concentration of gas and oil production in the country.

7. The oil and gas property tax actually operates a bit more like a sales tax than it does a property tax. The capital value (i.e. the usual basis for property appraisals in Indonesia) of productive land in the gas and oil sector is estimated to be 9.5 times the annual gas and oil sales of Pertamina under its production sharing arrangements with various contractors and partners.

8. Estimates for 2004 suggest that mining sector property taxes make up nearly 65 per cent of the total.

9. In the earlier study cited (Lewis 2003*b*), about one-third of total tax perda submitted to the centre for review concerned changes to existing revenue instruments and two thirds (i.e. about 1,000) were for new taxes and charges.

10. This is just the naive single market, comparative static version of the standard model for analysing the insidence of taxes. The model may be extended to incorporate multi-market and dynamic features but the simple model is sufficient for our practical purposes.

11. The formula for calculating the excess burden is: $0.5 \overline{\left(\dfrac{1}{\eta} + \dfrac{1}{\varepsilon} \right)} Pq \, t^2$ where P is the pre-tax price, q is the pre-tax quantity, $\dfrac{1}{\eta}$ is (compensated price) elasticity of demand, $\dfrac{1}{\varepsilon}$ is the elasticity of supply, and t is the tax.

12. We assume that all "other" local government own-source revenue derives from interest earnings and, as such, does not constitute a tax burden.

13. Lewis (2005) estimates the marginal tax rate (for total local own-source revenues) to be 1.5 per cent of personal income in the pre-decentralization period and 2.5 per cent during post-decentralization times.

14. The estimate is derived from a survey of local notaries in five cities. The World Bank (2005), based on interviews with lawyers in Jakarta, calculates that it takes up to 151 days to register a new business.

15. It takes on average 43 days to secure the environmental permit, the longest amount of time for any of the permits listed. The sum of days required to obtain all six licences is 180; this is the upper bound on time spent.

16. About two-thirds of survey respondents believe that the quality of police services (a national function) has deteriorated since decentralization.

17. The importance of telephone services (land lines) was also highlighted by businesses in both the KPPOD (2004) and LPEM-UI (2005*b*) surveys. This service is centrally provided and financed. As such we do not consider it here.

18. Property tax enforcement is rather lax; it was assumed to be costless in the cited study (Lewis 2003*a*).

19. The shortfall from potential amounts is a function of pure administrative ineffectiveness and also purposeful ineffectiveness — i.e. corruption. In practice it is not possible to distinguish between the two.

20. By comparison, cost-to-yield estimates from the United States range from less than 1 per cent for most local taxes to around 1.5 per cent for the property tax (Mikesell 1982). The U.S. cost-to-yield ratios are calculated on a net revenue basis. That is, the cost-to-yield ratio is administrative cost divided by revenue net of cost. Using this method, the average cost-to-yield ratio for local governments in Indonesia would be 110.5 per cent.

21. However, firms contracted by local governments to implement development projects would be expected to face some compliance costs; such costs have not been estimated by any study.

REFERENCES

KPPOD. *Daya Tarik Investasi Kabupaten/Kota di Indonesia, 2003.* Jakarta: The Asia Foundation and USAID, 2003.

―――. *Daya Tarik Investasi Kabupaten/Kota di Indonesia, 2004.* Jakarta: The Asia Foundation and USAID, 2004.

Kuncoro, Ari. "Bribery in Indonesia: Some Evidence from Micro-Level Data". *Bulletin of Indonesian Economic Studies* 40, no. 3, 2004.

Lewis, Blane D. "Property Taxation in Indonesia: Measuring and Explaining Administrative (Under-) Performance". *Public Administration and Development* 23, no. 3, 2003*a*.

―――. "Tax and Charge Creation by Regional Governments under Fiscal

Decentralization: Estimates and Explanations". *Bulletin of Indonesian Economic Studies* 39, no. 2, 2003*b*.

———. "Indonesian Local Government Spending, Taxing, and Saving: An Explanation of Pre- and Post-Decentralization Fiscal Outcomes". *Asian Economic Journal* 19, no. 3, 2005.

———. "Local Government Taxation: An Analysis of Administrative Cost Efficiency". *Bulletin of Indonesian Economic Studies* 42, no. 2, 2006.

LPEM-FEUI. "Construction of Regional Index of Doing Business". Mimeographed. Jakarta, Indonesia, 2003.

———. "The Impact of Regional Taxes and Levies, Interregional Trade Barriers, and Cost of Doing Business on Poverty Reduction". Mimeographed. Jakarta, Indonesia, 2004.

———. "The Impediments to Doing Business in Indonesia". Mimeographed. Jakarta, Indonesia, 2005*a*.

———. "Monitoring the Investment Climate in Indonesia". Mimeographed. Jakarta, Indonesia, 2005*b*.

von Luebke, Christian. "Preliminary Findings of the First District Case: Kabupaten Klaten". Mimeographed. Canberra: Australian National University, 2004.

———. "Political Economy of Local Business Regulations: Findings on Local Taxation and Licensing Practices from Four District Cases in Central Java and West Sumatera". Mimeographed. Canberra: Australian National University, 2005.

Mikesell, John. *Fiscal Administration: Analysis and Applications for the Public Sector*. Homewood, Illinois: Dorsey Press, 1982.

Ray, David. "Decentralization, Regulatory Reform, and the Business Climate, Overview/Summary". Mimeographed. Jakarta, Indonesia, 2003.

Wasylenko, Michael. "Taxation and Economic Development: The State of the Economic Literature". *New England Economic Review*, March/April 1997.

World Bank. *Decentralizing Indonesia*. Jakarta, Indonesia: World Bank, 2003.

———. "Decentralization, Service Delivery, and Governance in Indonesia: Findings from the Governance and Decentralization (GDS) 1+/2004". Mimeographed. Jakarta, Indonesia: World Bank, 2004*a*.

———. "Budgeting Process in Lebak: Review of the Roles of Legislative and Executive in Ensuring Transparency and Accountability". Mimeographed. Jakarta, Indonesia: World Bank, 2004*b*.

———. *Doing Business in 2005: Removing Obstacles to Growth*. Washington, D.C.: World Bank, 2005.

Zhuravskaya, E.V. "Incentives to Provide Local Public Goods: Fiscal Federalism, Russian Style". *Journal of Public Economics* 76, 2000.

⑨
Leadership and Voice in Local Governance

Christian von Luebke

1. Indonesia's Rapid Transition

Decentralization has become a salient feature of governance reforms[1] around the world. More than 80 per cent of all developing and transitional countries with populations of more than 5 million have started to reshape their governance structures by transferring power to lower government levels (Dillinger 1994, p. 302). Among these countries, Indonesia's case represents a remarkable example of substantial reform in terms of scope and speed. After decades of authoritarian rule, the Indonesian government implemented administrative, political and fiscal decentralization reforms in 2001 after a brief preparation period of eighteen months. Formerly concentrated in Jakarta, Indonesia has been devolving a wide range of authorities to more than 440 districts, making it — at least in administrative terms — one of the most decentralized countries of the world.

Indonesia's rapid transition was set in motion by the onset of crisis. The breakdown of Southeast Asia's financial markets and Soeharto's resignation in 1998 opened up a policy space, a historic window of opportunity, for radical reforms (Turner and Podger 2003). A small group of key policy-makers — namely Ryaas Rasyid, Rapiuddin, and the "Group of Seven" — crafted the new Regional Government Law 22/99 behind closed doors in the Ministry of Home Affairs. As a consequence, many senior officials in

Jakarta, including ministers of former cabinets, were taken aback by the rapid decision-making when Indonesia' new decentralization laws were presented to the public in 1999.[2]

Undoubtedly, the high momentum of Indonesia's decentralization reforms has its tradeoffs. Extensive administrative and democratic changes[3] — tightly scheduled between May 1999 and January 2001 — represented an endeavour of "building [a] ship while sailing" (Buente 2004). District governments became responsible to autonomously manage local economies in terms of infrastructure, agriculture, education, industry and trade, investment, development planning, and manpower affairs. More than two million public servants were transferred from Jakarta to the regions to facilitate this ambitious administrative task (World Bank 2003). Today, five years after implementing decentralization, it appears that districts are still struggling to establish functional accountability checks and service capacities (Brodjonegoro 2004; Sumarto et al. 2004).

Indonesia's decentralization to date indicates that costs may — at least in the short term — outweigh benefits for district economies. This is prominently displayed in the declining tendency of district business conditions since the enactment of decentralization. Empirical work shows a rise in policy uncertainties, trade-distorting taxes, and administrative bribe practices — inevitably leading to a decline in business attractiveness. In most districts private sector respondents report that business environments have, if anything, deteriorated since decentralization (KPPOD 2004, 2005; Lewis 2003*b*; LPEM-FEUI 2002; REDI 2003; Rusiani 2003; Suhirman 2002).

One economic indication for the critical state of district business climates is the stagnant flow of domestic and foreign investment. Indonesia was once referred to as an "Asian Tiger" and recognized as a part of the "East Asian Miracle" (World Bank 1993), side-by-side with Thailand and Malaysia. Now it has fallen behind in terms of investment and economic growth. Although the Indonesian government has successfully improved macroeconomic stability since the crisis, including sound inflation and interest rates (Hill and Aswicahyono 2004), investments remain stagnant (Castle 2004). The fact that foreign and domestic entrepreneurs are reluctant to invest, despite sound macroeconomic conditions and high resource endowments, points to governance-related problems. Given the decentralized setting, these are no longer solely concentrated in Jakarta but dispersed to district bureaucracies throughout the country.

Corruption is one of these impediments. According to annual surveys of Transparency International (TI), corruption practices in Indonesia are among the highest in the world (see Figure 9.1). Between 1998 and 2001 corruption perceptions aggravated further, pushing Indonesia's young

Figure 9.1
Corruption Rankings of Indonesia and its Neighbouring Countries over time

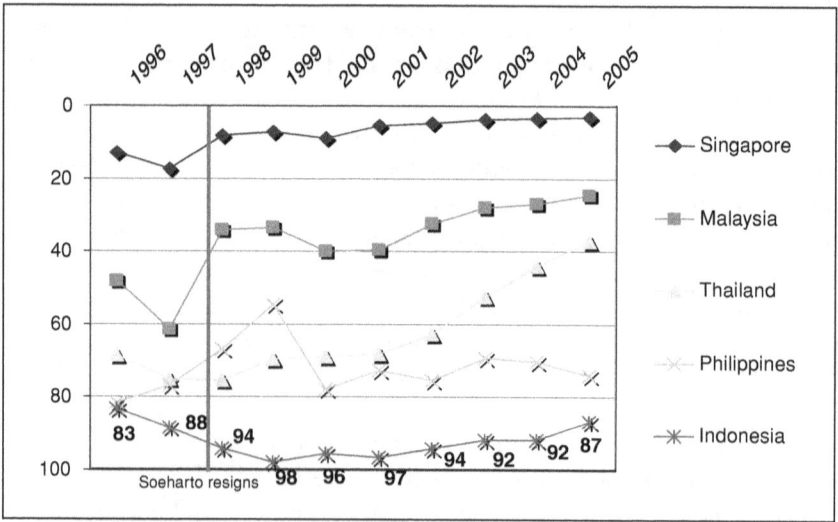

Note: This figure uses a standardized scale, where rank '100' denotes the lowest position of each year.
Source: Transparency International — Corruption Perception Index, 1996–2005.

democracy to the very bottom of the TI scale. Since 2002 the indicators have been improving, but still remain higher than prior to Indonesia's transition; and higher than in other Southeast Asian countries such as Malaysia, Thailand, and the Philippines. Anti-corruption measures have taken centre stage in Indonesia's policy debate on domestic and foreign investment. Donor agencies identify corruption — both in national and local governments — as a major obstacle to business development.[4]

Yet, it is important to note that business obstructions are *not* uniform across Indonesian districts. Local governance studies and rankings of business attractiveness clearly indicate that some districts have done better than others. Existing empirical work (KPPOD 2003, 2004, 2005; LPEM-FEUI 2002; REDI 2003; Timmer 2004) suggests that the degree to which local governments release distortionary regulations and extract rents through predatory licence procedures varies significantly throughout the country. Two key questions arise in this context, which will be addressed consecutively in this chapter:

(1) To what extent does the empirical evidence from West Sumatra, Central Java, Bali, and NTB affirm a rise of predatory licensing practices and distortionary taxation?

(2) What explains the variance among districts? Does government leadership, given by the will and power of a district head (*Bupati*), or private sector pressure, given by "voice" and "exit" options of local businesses, have a significant effect on district business conditions?

While addressing the first question helps to expand basic empirical knowledge on Indonesia's decentralization and its impact on local businesses, the latter question sheds new light on what actually drives local governance outcomes.

2. Case Evidence on District Business Climates

The Indonesian experience to date hardly confirms theoretical propositions that more favourable business environments arise with increasing decentralization. On the contrary,[5] empirical accounts point to stagnant or deteriorating government practices and services. According to the Regional Autonomy Watch (KPPOD 2004, 2005), many of Indonesia's 440 district governments have produced unsatisfactory business regulations and continue to obstruct the private sector with predatory licence practices. Lewis affirms that "many of the new regional taxes and charges have been judged as inappropriate by one standard or another" (2003, p. 16) and reports that the central government cancelled 28 per cent of assessed district regulations in the first decentralization year. In its Public Expenditure Review of 2003, the World Bank concludes that many new local taxes "are seen to be damaging the business environment" (2003, p. 30); and that "business undoubtedly felt the pinch of decentralization" in terms of the "plethora of taxes, levies and fees that were issued by the regions under the new law on regional taxes" (2003, p. 21).

Our field research[6] in eight district cases in Central Java (Klaten and Kebumen), West Sumatra (Solok and Pesisir Selatan), Bali (Gianyar and Karang Asem), and NTB (Lombok Timur and Bima) provides a similarly critical account but also displays the strong variation among districts. Asked on how local government policies have affected their business activities since decentralization, 61 per cent of the 1,014 respondents perceive no change, 21 per cent perceive deteriorating conditions, and 19 per cent feel that business conditions have improved. The district-level breakdown of these figures, however, indicates considerable variation. While respondents in Klaten, Pesisir and Lombok indicate a deterioration, respondents in Solok, Kebumen, Gianyar, Karang, and Bima report an improvement of local business climate conditions since the implementation of decentralized governance in 2001.

Moreover, the average business perception[7] suggests that policies tend to be slightly more conducive for local economic development before rather

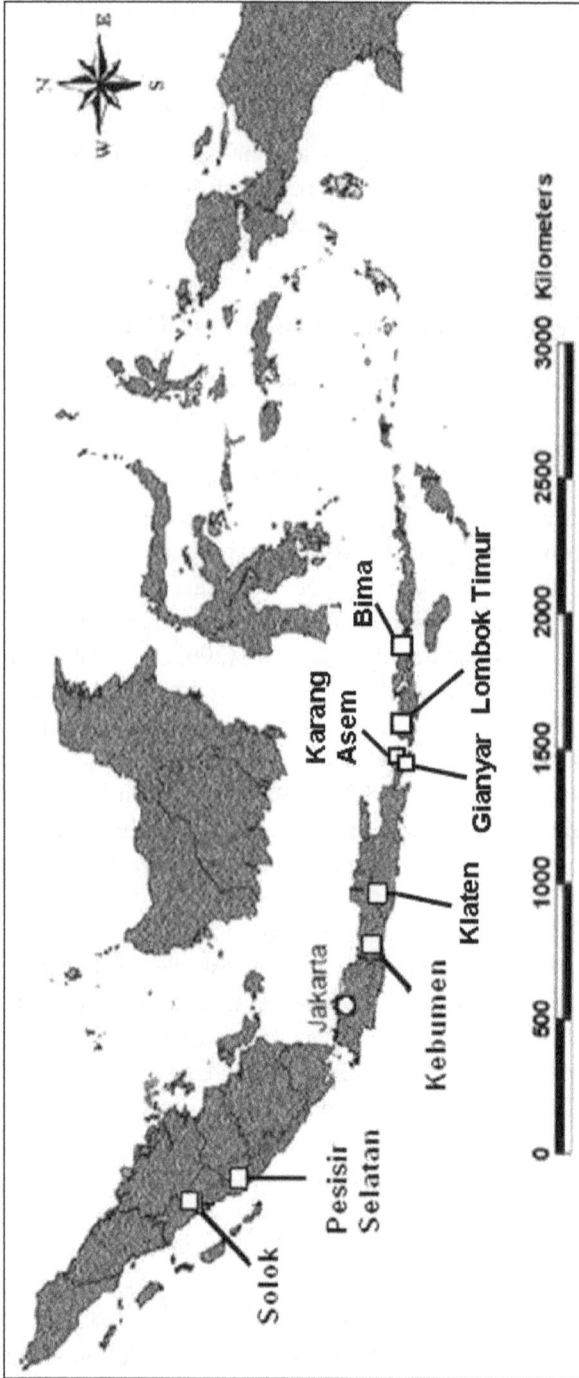

Figure 9.2
Location of the Eight District Cases

Source: Author's map, adapted from Eckardt (2006).

Table 9.1
Influence of District Policies on Business Activities since 2001

	Obstructive	No change	Supportive
1) Klaten	35.5%	58.7%	5.8%
2) Kebumen	9.1%	77.7%	13.2%
3) Solok	20.8%	46.2%	33.1%
4) Pesisir Selatan	35.5%	48.9%	15.6%
5) Gianyar	9.0%	75.7%	15.3%
6) Karang Asem	14.4%	65.6%	20.0%
7) Lombok Timur	25.6%	55.8%	18.6%
8) Bima	14.3%	55.6%	30.2%
Average	20.5%	60.5%	19.0%

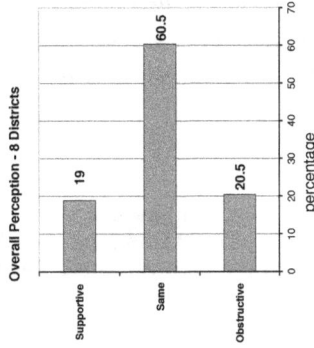

Source: Survey data based on 1,014 randomly selected business respondents in eight districts.

Overall Perception - 8 Districts

Supportive: 19
Same: 60.5
Obstructive: 20.5

percentage

than after decentralization (see Figure 9.3). According to our survey, 46 per cent of local businesses perceive district policies as "very conducive" or "conducive" for their local economy *before* decentralization; while 28 per cent and 29 per cent feel the same regarding *early* and *current* decentralization, respectively.

Figure 9.3
Perceptions of Local Business Policies During
Subsequent Governance Periods

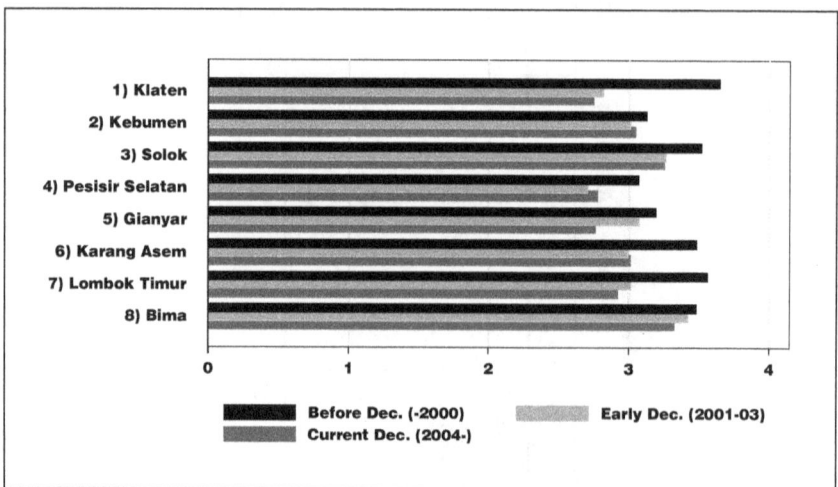

Note: 1 = very unconducive, 2 = unconducive, 3 = fair, 4 = conducive, 5 = very conducive.
Source: Survey data based on 1,014 randomly selected business respondents in eight districts.

Asked to what extent different policy aspects represent an obstruction to their businesses, respondents declared "policy uncertainty" (58 per cent), "unofficial licence payments" (47 per cent), and "licence administration time" (45 per cent) as the three major obstacles, followed by problems of "unofficial payments during tax collection" (40 per cent), "official tax expenses" (40 per cent), "official licence costs" (35 per cent), and "security payments" (19 per cent).

The following section discusses business climate problems in further detail by taking a closer look at (1) predatory business licensing and (2) distortionary taxation.

Table 9.2
Ranking of Perceived Business Problems

Rank	Problem	Obstacle (%)	Likert Mean	Std. Dev.	Resp.
1	Uncertainty of District Policies	58.17	2.29	1.35	1,016
2	Unofficial Payments for Licenses	46.80	1.93	1.20	1,015
3	Time Spent for License Administration	45.37	1.82	1.09	1,016
4	Unofficial Payments during Tax Collection	39.73	1.78	1.14	1,012
5	Official Tax Costs	39.69	1.69	0.99	1,018
6	Official License Costs	34.68	1.63	1.01	1,018
7	Security Payments	18.88	1.31	0.75	985

Note: Likert Scale ranges from 1 (no obstacle) to 5 (very strong obstacle).
Source: Author's estimates based on 1,041 randomly selected business respondents in eight districts.

2.1. Predatory Business Licensing

Predatory[8] licensing practices are not a new phenomenon for Indonesian business people. In fact, most interview respondents admit to having repeatedly experienced administrative transgressions during the Soeharto era. But existing studies also suggest that decentralization has brought little to no improvements.[9] Local bureaucracies continue to require a high number of licences and a large amount of administrative paperwork. The "chain of desks" remains long and cumbersome and technical departments are reluctant to let go of monopolistic licence authorities. In most cases, government officials consider licences as a revenue instrument — priced well above cost recovery — and rarely understand its steering function for the local economy (Ray 2003; Suhirman 2002). Overall, the complexity of licensing procedures in most districts not only includes unnecessary transaction costs but also gives way to rent seeking opportunities for local bureaucrats.

Indeed, our district surveys show that *capture practices* during the administration of business licences have increased in a majority of cases. According to current business perceptions (see Table 9.3), five out of eight district governments have an increasing demand for "unofficial payments". On average, local firms report a slight increase in administrative capture (1.81 to 1.90) and indicate that most business people currently pay around 10 per cent corruption premiums on top of their official licence cost. The data suggests that the highest rise in corruption payments occurred in Gianyar, whereas Solok's licensing practices mark a positive exception.

Table 9.3
District Evidence on Licence Procedures — Administration Time and Capture

District	Administration Capture*				Administrative Time**			
	−2000	2001–03	2004–05	Change	−2000	2001–03	2004–05	Change
1) Klaten	1.96	2.01	2.18	11.0%	3.19	2.67	2.64	−17.4%
2) Kebumen	2.24	2.27	2.33	4.1%	2.86	2.72	2.71	−5.3%
3) Solok	1.72	1.48	1.41	−18.1%	1.89	1.50	1.45	−23.3%
4) Pesisir S.	2.04	2.17	2.16	6.3%	2.30	1.82	1.82	−20.7%
5) Gianyar	1.87	2.08	2.49	33.5%	3.55	3.97	4.27	20.4%
6) Karang A.	1.43	1.46	1.42	−1.3%	2.40	2.46	2.46	2.6%
7) Lombok T.	1.63	1.57	1.58	−2.8%	1.94	1.80	1.78	−8.3%
8) Bima	1.58	1.62	1.62	2.2%	1.83	1.62	1.52	−16.8%
Average	1.81	1.83	1.90	4.4%	2.49	2.32	2.33	−8.6%

Note: * Capture Scale: 1 = none, 2 ≤ 10%, 3 = 11–20%, 4 = 21–30%, 5 = 31–50%, 6 = 51–70%, 7 = 71–100%, 8 ≥ 100%
** Time Scale: 1 = 1–7 days, 2 = 8–14 days, 3 = 15–21 days, 4 = 22–30 days, 5 = more than one month; "Change" describes the difference of capture/time between the periods "before 2000" and "2004–05"; the presented figures reflect business perceptions in 2005 as well as "recall perceptions" of early and pre-decentralization years.

Source: Author's estimates based on 1,041 randomly selected business respondents in eight districts.

The required *administration time* for business licences, on the other hand, has been improving in most districts. In six districts, current administrative procedures require less time than before decentralization. However, district cases in Central Java and Bali continue to exhibit high administration times, suggesting that many businesses spend two weeks and more for obtaining their licences. Once again, Solok receives the best evaluation within the group, as indicated in Table 9.3, the majority of respondents receive their paperwork within one week.

An example on how licensing practices can differ among districts is illustrated in Table 9.4. The comparison of administrative procedures of the two West Sumatran districts Solok and Pesisir Selatan demonstrates that time and cost requirements for five basic business licences can vary considerably.[10]

One-Stop Licensing Services (OSS) represent another illustrative example of differences in local business conditions. Our observations indicate varying OSS qualities ranging from very good to very poor. Based on the interviews with six to eight business people in each district and direct observations during unannounced visits, we evaluated the performance levels of OSS in terms of (1) transparency and access of licence information, (2) authority to decide on licence applications, (3) human capacity, (4) physical facilities, (5) data management, (6) anti-corruption measures. Table 9.5 summarizes these perceptions in a simple scoring board. Karang Asem and Bima have not established OSS units and hence do not appear in the scoring exercise.

The low score of Klaten's OSS, for example, is a result of its overall low standards. During a spontaneous visit (see Figure 9.4), licence information was unavailable and duty officers were not able to provide any technical

Table 9.4
Administration Time and Official Prices for Basic Business Licences

Licence	Admin. Time (days)		Official Price ('000 Rps)	
	Solok	Pesisir	Solok	Pesisir
Trade Licence (SIUP)	5	7–14	35–200	35–150
Industry Licence (TDI)	5	7–14	30–250	35–150
Disturbance Permit (HO)	5	5	100–250	700
Principal Business Agreement				
(*Ijin Prinsip*)	7	7	No costs	1,000
Building Permit (IMB)	9	7	50–200	> 350

Source: District documents and interviews with officials at technical departments (Perindag, Bag. Ekonomi).

Table 9.5
Scoring Board on One-Stop Licensing Services

Indicator	Kla	Keb	Sol	Pes	Gia	Lom
Transparency of Information — Brochures, Boards, Web	1	3	4	2	4	3.5
Authority Level — Discretion to decide on applications	1	1	3	1	1	1
Human Capacity — Impression of Service and Qualification	1	3	4	2	4	3
Physical Facilities — Room, Counter, Signs, Waiting Area	1	2.5	4	2	4.5	3
Data Management — Computer Equipment, Filing System	1	3	4	2	4	3
Anti-Corruption Measures — Curbing "Bribe Payments"	—	1	4	—	1	1
Average Score	0.8 Very Poor	2.3 Poor/ Fair	3.8 Good	1.5 V. Poor/ Poor	3.1 Fair	2.4 Poor/ Fair

Note: Scores range from 1 to 5: 1= very poor, 2 = poor, 3 = fair, 4 = strong, 5 = very strong.
Source: Author's evaluations based on interviews with business people and personal observations.

licence information. The dark and dusty room and the old typewriters in the corners did not create an impression of a professional service unit. Indeed, most interviewed businesses in Klaten report that they avoid the OSS altogether and prefer to approach technical departments for their licensing requirements.

In contrast, Solok's OSS ("Satu Pintu Plus") represents a positive benchmark of service provision. Since 1996, services have been continuously improved and extended for the business community. Now the portfolio includes twenty-five different types of business licenses and civil certifications. The service unit is recognized for its high level of professionalism and transparency by business people and civil society alike. Each applicant receives a well-designed information brochure[11] precisely determining required documents, costs, and administration times for each licence. For remote business people Solok's government has extended the access to licensing services by the so-called "Plus" option, which allows licence application through local post offices. During an unannounced visit to Solok's OSS, the four service counters were attended to by friendly and well-informed staff. The atmosphere of the clean bright room was welcoming. Offices were

Figure 9.4
Impressions of Local One-Stop Licensing Services

(1) Solok
Good (3.8)

(2) Gianyar
Fair (3.1)

(3) Lombok
Poor/Fair (2.4)

(4) Kebumen
Poor/Fair (2.3)

(5) Pesisir
Very Poor/Poor (1.5)

(6) Klaten
Very Poor (0.8)

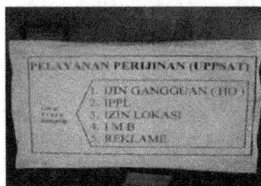

Source: Author's pictures (taken during visits to local OSS in 2005 and 2006).

equipped with modern computer technology and colourful information boards. Anti-corruption stickers ("No Grease Money") appeared on each counter window — an indication of Solok's enlarged efforts to curb administrative transgressions.

2.2. Distortionary Taxes

Distortionary[12] taxes and user charges have been reported in various empirical studies. KPPOD, an independent think tank assessing the impact of decentralization on regional investment climates, declares that local governments have enacted an alarming amount of distortionary regulations. Based on their assessment of 896 business-related tax regulations in 200 sample districts, KPPOD demonstrates that 64 districts (32 per cent) have released distortionary regulations, while only in 29 districts (14 per cent) regulations can be considered business-friendly (KPPOD 2004, p. 71). Besides general conflicts with national laws and tax duplications with national or provincial charges, district authorities are imposing imprudent charges on intra-regional trade, which distorts rather than supports local economic development.

In our study we find distortionary tax regulations in three districts. Moreover, our findings indicate a considerable loss of local revenues due to administrative inaccuracy and negotiation practices during tax collection. Regarding the first point, the following examples from Pesisir Selatan, Bima, and Lombok illustrates how district bills can obstruct local economies.

Pesisir's introduction of road *maintenance levies* (district regulation 13/ 2001 —*Retribusi Pemiliharaan Jalan*) raises the concern of local and external observers alike. In fact, before their official enactment in 2001, road levies had already caused public uproar among farmers and fishermen. In 1999, two collection posts, one at the border to Padang and one at the local bus terminal in Sago, were burned down by locals and had to be rebuilt (interview with a businessman in Pesisir). KPPOD recommends abolishing the road levy as it obstructs regional trade flows. According to an internal evaluation of KPPOD, Pesisir's bill to charge commercial vehicles for road usage overlaps with existing provincial vehicle charges and petrol taxes. It burdens local entrepreneurs and fails to stimulate inter-district trade. This point is affirmed — from a different angle — by research of SMERU (2001). This study demonstrates the negative impact of road and border levies on local businesses by assessing cumulative road fees of an average orange transporter from North Sumatra to Jakarta. According to SMERU, fees can accumulate up to Rp 1 million and reduce trade profits up to 7 per cent.[13]

Bima's export tax on local commodities provides another example of how local tax regulations can distort inter-district trade and impede economic development. Based on the district regulation 16/2000 (*Pajak Hasil Bumi*), agricultural and manufactured goods from Bima are taxed at 5 per cent; forestry goods at 10 per cent. The tax payments are levied at border posts and based on "basic commodity prices" (*harga dasar*) that are fixed quarterly by the government. According to interviews with business people in Bima, these fixed prices do not reflect actual market prices and are rarely published. Several respondents confirm that these government interventions stimulate preferentialism and inequity, in a sense that firms with close government ties can negotiate tax cuts and exemptions. However, in many cases, tax burdens are transferred downwards and borne by the least powerful in the chain: the rural poor. Eventually, due to its trade-obstructing character, Bima's tax regulation was officially cancelled by the Ministry of Home Affairs (Kepmen 42/2002). Three years after the national annulment, however, the tax is still active and contributes a major share to Bima's local revenues (PAD). Similar export taxes apply in Lombok Timur. Here, the district regulation 16/2001 (*Pajak Atas Pengiriman Barang Antar Pulau*) taxes outgoing trade with 5 per cent at port and border posts.

Even more alarming than the enactment of distortionary taxes is the way district governments collect and administer local revenues (PAD). The evidence from all eight district cases indicates that revenue collection is based on a "target system": a combination of rough estimations and personal negations.[14] Modern accountability systems are missing in both private and public sectors. Tax subjects — restaurants, hotels, shops, or home industries — are directly approached by tax officers and inspected regarding their tax potential. Both parties engage in a bargaining process and agree on a tax target based on estimated turnover figures, firm size, and financial liquidity. The agreed tax target is then collected at the end of each month.

Arguably, this target-based tax collection induces local revenue loss in two ways. First, in most districts there is little credible documentation for tax estimates — neither formal bookkeeping nor standardized receipts. This lack of accountability mechanisms creates room for misconduct. Tax subjects may understate their actual turnover, while the tax collectors may abuse administrative powers to scale up tax targets and bargain for informal rents. Moreover, field observations and interviews affirm that districts have so far been unable to install credible monitoring mechanisms for a more transparent tax collection. As illustrated in Table 9.6, local taxpayers report higher capture since decentralization in all districts but Solok and Karang Asem.[15] Interestingly, the reported capture fees rarely exceed 10 per cent of official tax fees. These

Table 9.6
Capture during Tax Collection (Percentage of Official Tax Fee)

District	District Tax Offices*			National Tax Offices**		
	−2000	2001−	Change	−2000	2001−	Change
1) Klaten	1.83	1.96	6.8%	1.42	1.50	6.0%
2) Kebumen	1.69	1.73	2.3%	1.70	1.80	6.0%
3) Solok	1.42	1.29	−9.0%	1.44	1.33	−7.4%
4) Pesisir	1.50	1.72	14.2%	1.54	1.62	5.5%
5) Gianyar	1.95	2.22	14.0%	1.60	1.89	17.7%
6) Karang	1.36	1.25	−8.3%	1.36	1.26	−6.9%
7) Lombok	1.26	1.32	4.9%	1.23	1.31	6.2%
8) Bima	1.32	1.33	0.8%	1.23	1.21	−1.6%
Average	1.54	1.60	3.21%	1.44	1.49	3.19%

Note: Capture Scale: 1 = none, 2 ≤ 10%, 3 = 11–20% , 4 = 21–30%, 5 = 31–50%, 6 = 51–70%, 7 = 71–100%, 8 ≥ 100%.
* District tax offices collect smaller charges — hotel, restaurant, advertising, small-scale mining taxes etc.
** District branches of national tax offices collect income, value-added and property taxes (PPH,PPN,PBB).
Source: Author's estimates based on 1,041 randomly selected business respondents in eight districts.

figures, however, tend to underestimate actual corruption levels, as both parties — tax collectors and payers — benefit from reducing tax payments and sharing the benefits.

Second, bargaining conventions and limited outreach induce a loss of potential revenue and an uneven division of tax burdens. Many tax subjects are not approached by tax officials — either because of staff shortage or because of remote business locations. A selection of specific examples in Box 9.1 illustrates this notion.

Administrative inaccuracy is not only a problem in terms of revenue collection but also in terms of how revenues are administered among government units. Senior officials of local tax offices in all eight districts acknowledged that they face vast challenges in their internal revenue administration. On the one hand, government units *Dinas, Kantor, Bagian* lack well-trained staff and IT facilities. On the other hand, the prevailing standard of revenue *targets* rather than clear *accounting* increases this imprecision even further. Akin to conventions with local firms, technical government units pledge to collect and transfer revenues based on predetermined target levels. One senior official in Klaten explained that — given the low level of

---

Box 9.1
Examples of Low District Tax Effort

(1) In the tile production sector, for instance, "only around 25 out of 1000 producers are paying taxes". The tax officials are not approaching 97.5 per cent of tile businesses as they are either "far from a major road, too small, or they are scared of the fierce attitude of the owners". (Interview with businessman in Kebumen.)

(2) "Local officials only approach our hotel with their tax request while other hotels in the region are not requested to pay. [...] Such treatment is not fair." (Interview with hotel owner in Pesisir Selatan.)

(3) "For example, if a restaurant tax of Rp 100.000 is due, the owner pays 50.000 of which 25.000 are captured by the tax official and 25.000 appear on the official receipt. [...] that is common". (Interview with a businessman in Klaten.)

(4) The owner of a small seaside restaurant in Pesisir Selatan, very popular with local public officials, reports that she was not asked to pay taxes for years. Now, despite a monthly turnover of approximately Rp 10,000,000 (conservative estimation of the owner), and therefore a legal tax obligation of Rp 1,000,000, the owner negotiated a fixed monthly charge of Rp 25,000 with tax officials. Other restaurants in their proximity are not taxed at all.

(5) According to Solok's budget report (ABBD 2004), the revenue officers collected Rp 41 million from 87 tax subjects (restaurants) in the fiscal year 2003. This is equal to an average tax collection of Rp 39,000 per restaurant each month. Thus, given a tax rate of 10 per cent this implies an average turnover of Rp 390,000 monthly, or Rp 13,000 daily. If we assume that an average meal in Solok ('Nasi Padang') costs around Rp 10,000, this would lead us to the conclusion that an average restaurant sells approximately one meal a day. If this would be true, most of Solok's restaurants would be bankrupt. More likely, an average restaurant sells more than fifty meals a day, suggesting that actual collected taxes cover only a fraction of the actual tax potential.

(6) The owner of a large restaurant in Solok revealed that the restaurant's daily turnover ranges between Rp 2 and 5 million. A monthly turnover between Rp 60–150 million would imply tax payments of Rp 6–15 million. The restaurant, however, has negotiated a monthly payment of Rp 250,000 with the local revenue office. In other words, payments range only between 2 and 4 per cent of the legal tax obligation.

(7) "The building of my shop was initially subject to a 'Pajak Pembangunan Sendiri' [self-construction tax] of Rp 64,000,000. Yet, I initially declined to pay this amount as the estimates were wrong. [...] Then the tax collectors came again. They said 'we can help you — we can reduce the amount to 40 million'. I rejected the offer again. They kept on disturbing me — over and over again. Finally, I paid 20,000,000 in four installments — I did not want to be bothered any longer." (Large business owner in Bima.)

(8) A large business owner in Karang Asem pointed out that the majority of business people use some sort of accountancy. But there is still much room for negotiation between tax collectors and payers. He estimated that the overall tax effort is unlikely to exceed 50 per cent of the tax potential.

accountancy and transparency standards in many administrations — these target conventions may well provide counterproductive incentives for senior officials to capture revenue surpluses. For example, if the industry department *Perindag* pledges to collect Rp 150 million for the fiscal year 2004 (e.g. through the collection of trade and industry licence fees), but happens to collect Rp 200 million, it is by no means certain that excess revenues will be delivered to the district revenue account entirely. In fact, the department may account for 170 million, receive credit for exceeding its target, and capture the remaining surplus.

2.3. Summary

To recap, our research indicates — akin to other empirical work to date — that licensing practices remain in a critical state but also vary significantly across local governments. In five out of eight district cases decentralization has seen rising rather than decreasing capture practices. Time requirements for administrative procedures have decreased during the last years but remain extensive in Central Java and Bali. One-stop licensing services in six out of eight districts are either non-existent or continue to operate on unsatisfactory service levels.

In some cases, local taxes and user charges, such as Pesisir's road levies and Bima's and Lombok's export taxes, distort local economies and inter-district trade flows. The low standard of revenue collection and administration is also alarming. The convention to strongly rely on vaguely estimated revenue targets for tax payers and government units, rather than pursing higher accountancy standards, is likely to stimulate capture practices and induce high revenue losses for district budgets.

Comparing the performance of each district (see Table 9.7), Solok's government demonstrates the best business climate in terms of its licence and tax administration. Low capture practices and efficient one-stop licensing services bear witness of these improvements. Pesisir, in contrast, receives low scores in administrative capture, distortionary taxes, and OSS quality. The comparison of the two districts in Central Java is less clear-cut than the one in West Sumatra. Business conditions in Klaten appear less conducive than in Kebumen — especially in terms of administrative capture and one-stop licensing services. In Bali, Karang Asem's licensing procedures are perceived faster and less captive than in Gianyar, even though Gianyar set up a modern one-stop licensing service. In NTB, both Lombok and Bima receive "poor to fair" grades due to the enactment of distortionary export taxes.

Table 9.7
Local Business Climates — An Overview

Business Climate Indicators (2005)	Central Java		West Sumatra		Bali		NTB	
	Kla	Keb	Sol	Pes	Gia	Kar	Lom	Bim
(a) Licensing — Capture	Poor (2,2)	Poor (2,3)	Good (1,4)	Poor (2.2)	Poor (2.5)	Good (1,4)	Fair (1,6)	Fair (1,6)
(b) Licensing — Adm. Time	Poor (2.6)	Poor (2.7)	Good (1,4)	Fair (1.8)	V. Poor (4,3)	Poor (2,5)	Fair (1,8)	Good (1,5)
(c) Distortionary Taxes	None (+)	None (+)	None (+)	Road Levies (−)	None (+)	None (+)	Export Tax (−)	Export Tax (−)
(d) Quality of OSS	V. Poor (0.8)	Poor/ Fair (2,3)	Good (3,8)	V. Poor/ Poor (1,4)	Fair (3,1)	None (0)	Poor/ Fair (2,4)	None (0)
Overall Tendency	V. Poor/ Poor	Poor/ Fair	Good	Poor	Poor	Poor/ Fair	Poor/ Fair	Poor/ Fair

Source: Summary of analyses above.

Overall, in seven out of eight districts, governance-related business conditions are either "very poor" (Klaten), "poor" (Pesisir and Gianyar), or "poor to fair" (Kebumen, Bima, Lombok, and Karang). These survey results clearly indicate that a large number of local firms are dissatisfied with government tax and licensing practices.

Some of the explanations for the varying degrees of unsatisfactory business conditions are found in the local dynamics of district decision-making. Following the argument of Bardhan (1997), in order to attain a better understanding of local policy outcomes, we must comprehend the features of their political economy. The following section sets out to do this by assessing the eight districts cases in terms of institutional frameworks, prevailing bureaucratic conventions, democratic oversight, governmental leadership, and civic pressures.

3. Political Economy of Local Business Regulations

Indonesia's rapid transition to decentralized governance, after more than thirty years of Soeharto's centralized regime has created long-term opportunities as well as short-term threats.[16] While district governments are empowered to respond better to local needs, they also have ample space to misuse enhanced discretions and pursue private rather than common interests. The degree to which governments establish favourable business conditions depends on the constellation of their political economies. More specifically, it relates to the interplay between existing institutions (both national and local; formal and informal) with prevailing interest structures.

According to a large body of literature, institutions are paramount for governance and development.[17] Following North (1990, p. 3), they are the "[rules] that structure political, economic, and social interactions". Institutions are the result of a natural process of selection, in which the most durable rules, norms, and values are integrated within a society (Hayek 1967). Applied to the context of this study, these rules appear both as *formal institutions*, such as Indonesia's national laws or district regulations, and as *informal institutions*, such as prevailing conventions and behavioural norms (Furubotn and Richter 1991) — determining the interaction of public and private actors in a district. The following paragraphs discuss examples of formal and informal institutions that produce adverse incentive structures. According to our district findings, poor oversight by local parliaments and endemic bribe conventions in the civil service are likely to induce government misconduct. Finally, in the latter part of this section, governmental leadership and civic pressures are assessed on their potential to counterbalance administrative misconduct and improve local business conditions.

3.1. Deficient Institutions — The National Level

The assessment of national institutions — most notably, Indonesia's decentralization laws and regulations — reveals two problematic aspects for local business climates: (1) the vague wording of the regional tax law 34/2000, (2) and the insufficient capacity of national ministries to monitor new district tax regulations.

The enhanced authority of local revenue generation is a core element of the Indonesian decentralisation concept. It is embodied in the "law on fiscal decentralisation" (25/1999 and 33/2004) and specified in the "law on regional revenue generation" (34/2000). While major taxes, such as income, value-added and property taxes remain with the centre, Law 34 authorizes districts to administer smaller taxes — such as hotel, restaurant, advertising, parking, and small-scale mining taxes. Moreover, it allows local governments to introduce new revenue instruments, as long as they do not oppose the law. The introduction of new taxes and user charges, however, has given rise to many problems. The legal wording, that new taxes are not to "obstruct economic development" or the "common good" and are not to target "goods with a high mobility",[18] is vague and provides insufficient guidance for local policy-makers. Moreover, with Law 34, the burden of proof lies with the central government. National ministries have to prove legal shortcomings of the districts *ex post* ("innocent until proven guilty"), as opposed to the common practice that districts have to defend regulations *ex ante* ("guilty until proven innocent") (Ray 2003, p. 23). As a consequence, the Ministry of Finance (MOF) is struggling to evaluate an ever-increasing number of local tax regulations (World Bank 2003, p. 29) based on a vaguely specified law.

This evaluation task is hardly achievable, given the capacity constraints and missing enforcement structures. In fact, Lewis (2003*a*; 2003*b*) reports that the MOF was only able to review around 40 per cent of the tax regulations of the fiscal year 2001. Moreover, national officials have no credible penalty instruments in case districts fail to comply and revise rejected tax regulations. This deficiency is further accelerated by bureaucratic complexities at the national level. While the MOF can only recommend rejections, final decisions to annul district regulations are made by the Ministry of Home Affairs. This inter-ministerial separation of technical recommendations and decision-making bears institutional uncertainty and further undermines the credibility of national oversight.

Overall, the imprecise legal wording of the district revenue law combined with the limited supervisory capacity and authority of the Ministry of Finance creates adverse incentives for district governments. Given these deficiencies, districts may disregard the principles of Law 34 when enacting new business regulations. As illustrated in the district cases of Pesisir, Bima, and Lombok, distortionary taxes that obstruct regional trade flows tend to have increased under this vaguely-specific tax law.

3.2. Deficient Institutions — The District Level

At the district level, two institutional features have a significant effect on the political economy of local business regulations: one arising in the legislative and one in the executive sphere of government. First, due to prevailing election and budget rules, district parliamentarians (DPRD) seem detached from the interests and needs of local constituencies. And second, case findings indicate that public recruitment procedures are prone to considerable corruption. The combination of these two features raises the risk of administrative misconduct and increases the likelihood of business distortions.

Between 1999 and 2004, DPRD councillors were elected on the basis of closed party lists. District residents were able to vote for parties but not yet entitled to directly vote for their representatives.[19] Interview respondents argue that party lists lacked transparency and party programmes were insufficiently publicized. In this early stage of democratization, where political parties are in search of distinct programmatic profiles and people's awareness of democratic rights just unfolds, a general detachment between parliaments and constituencies is a likely result. The survey confirms this detachment from a different angle. It indicates a strong dissatisfaction in the local business community towards DPRD representatives (see Figure 9.5). According to survey results, 60 per cent of the 1,041 respondents are "dissatisfied" or "very dissatisfied" with their local council, compared to only 7 per cent who are "satisfied" or "very satisfied".[20]

Another problem arises in the context of local parliament budgets. Budget lines are linked to the amount of local revenues (PAD) of a district, rather than its economic growth. Pursuant to Article 14 of the Presidential Decree PP 110/2000, the budget for local parliament expenses, including salary payments and travel expenses, can account up to 5 per cent of a district's PAD. Considering that parliamentarians also enact local regulations on taxes and user charges, this decree may encourage parliamentarians to raise tax and licensing revenues without considering economic consequences. Raising parliamentary budgets on the basis of local economic growth (PDRB) rather than local revenues may be a way of delimiting the risk of distortionary taxation and providing incentives for long-term economic development. Yet, to date, this has not been considered.

The second institutional deficiency arises within public administration. Our case findings reveal a bureaucracy-specific convention that has negative bearing on district business climates: the "indebtedness" of government officals (PNS) due to bribe payments during public recruitment. Estimating bribe payments in terms of their values or frequencies is difficult and raises a note of caution. Undoubtedly, given the limited scope of our study we are not in the position to generalize. The high frequency of reported PNS bribing in our districts, however, should be noted in the ongoing local governance debate.

Our interview data displays varying but widespread conventions of bribe payments by PNS candidates.[21] The empirical data in Table 9.8 may seem dense but is nonetheless important. Respondents in seven out of eight districts, affirm that PNS applicants pay high premiums in order to be accepted in the public service. The strongest evidence of bribe payments is displayed in Klaten. Here, ten interviewees report average payments of Rp 64 million — ranging from Rp 5 to 100 million. Correspondingly, bribing incidences in Bima, Lombok, Pesisir, Gianyar, and Karang are estimated at 36 million,

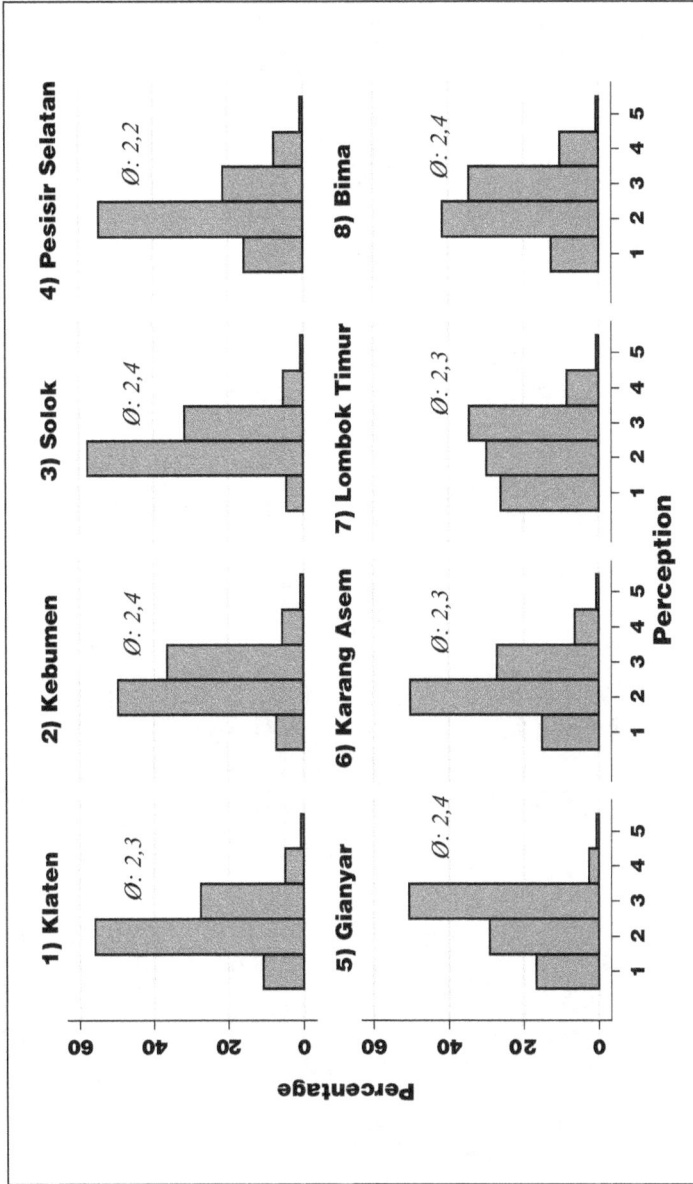

Figure 9.5
Satisfaction of Businesses towards their Representation by Local Parliaments

Note: 1 = "very dissatisfied", 2 = "dissatisfied", 3 = "undecided", 4 = "satisfied", 5 = "very satisfied".
Source: Survey data based on 1,041 randomly selected business respondents in eight districts.

Table 9.8
PNS Bribe Payments since Decentralization — Estimates from 8 Districts (million Rps)

Respondent	1) Klaten		2) Kebumen		3) Solok		4) Pesisir Selatan	
1	70 (Academic)	←	0 (Business) →		0 (Business) →		20 (Business)	←
2	50–60 (Official)	←	5–10 (Business)		0 (Business) →		Exist (Business)	
3	75 (NGO)	←	0 (Official) →→		0 (NGO)		30 (Media)	←→
4	75 (NGO)	←	5–10 (Media)		0 (Business) →→		10–20 (NGO)	
5	90 (Media)	←	Exist (Academic)		0 (Media) →		20–25 (Business)	
6	50 (Business)	←	Exist (Business)		0 (Official) →		25–30 (Business)	
7	5–90 (Media)	←	10–20 (NGO)		0 (Academic) →		Exist (Official)	
8	50–100 (Business)	—	—		0 (NGO) →		20–25 (Official)	
9	50–70 (Business)	—	—		0 (Business)		—	
10	50 (Business)	—	—		—		—	
Tendency	*Range: 5–100; Ø : 64;* ↑		*Range: 5–20; Ø : 6;* →		*Range: 0; Ø : 0;* →		*Range: 10–30; Ø : 23;* ↑	

Respondent	5) Gianyar		6) Karang Asem		7) Lombok Timur		8) Bima	
1	Exist (Business) →		5–10 (Business) →→		20–50 (NGO) ←→		Exist (Business)	←
2	30–40 (Business)		– 20 (Business)		30–40 (Media) →		40 (Official)	
3	Exist (Parliament) →		10–20 (Business) →		30 (Business)		30–40 (Business)	
4	0 (Business)		Exist (Business)		25 (Business)		40–50 (NGO)	
5	Exist (NGO)		12 (Media)		50 (Business)		20–30 (Business)	←→
6	Exist (Media)		5–24 (Academic)		30 (Business)		30 (Parliament)	
7	—		30 (Parliament) ←		50 (Academic) ←		20–40 (Media)	←←
8	—		Exist (Business)		20–50 (Parliament)		40–50 (Academic)	
9	—		30–50 (NGO)		—		30–45 (NGO)	
10	—		—		—		35–50 (Business)	
Tendency	*Range: 0–40; Ø : 18;* →		*Range: 5–50; Ø : 17;* ↓		*Range: 25–50; Ø : 36;* ↑		*Range: 20–50; Ø : 36;* ↑	

Note: Arrows (↑ / ↓) indicate perceptions that recruitment bribes increased/ decreased since decentralization; "Exist" indicates that a respondent affirms the existence of bribe payments but does not provide clear estimates.

Source: In-depth interviews with 15 respondents in each district, including: Businesses (6), Officials (3), Parliament (1), Academia (1), NGO (2), Media (2).

36 million, 23 million, 18 million, and 17 million respectively. In Klaten, Pesisir, Bima, and Lombok payments tend to rise since the enactment of decentralization, whereas the opposite applies in Kebumen, Solok, Gianyar, and Karang. The majority of respondents underlined that these bribe incidences are not uniform but nevertheless significant. The number of accepted candidates that fall into this category ranges — according to interviewees — between 10 and 50 per cent. The remaining part of PNS can be divided into two groups: *those* who are chosen on the grounds of good entrance exams and *those* who are chosen on grounds of personal connections and family ties. Solok, once again, is a clear exception in this group. All interviewed respondents assert that bribe payments do not occur. While some report incidents in the past, there is wide agreement that Solok's PNS selections are transparent and fair. An overview of selected statements on bribe payments during public recruitment is presented in Box 9.2.

Why are some citizens willing to pay enormous upfront investments in order to enter the public service? Isn't it counter-intuitive that some applicants pay, for example Rp 50 million, in order to become a public servant — especially if this forces them to take a bank loan or sell their land? Given that initial official salaries in district governments rarely account to more than Rp 1 million, such an investment is equivalent to four years of income. The reasons why some applicants willingly enter this "debt trap" seem manifold. In general, demand for PNS positions highly exceeds its supply. According to interviews in all eight districts, an opening of 50–100 government positions is generally answered by thousands of applications. This excessive demand is based on economic as well as sociocultural factors. Regarding high unemployment and a general risk aversion since Indonesia's economic crisis, many people prefer working in the public rather than the private sector. A PNS position promises secure lifelong employment, health insurance, and pension schemes. Moreover, short office hours allow for additional work on the side, thus compensating for relatively low wages. Interview data suggests that, akin to Wertheim's (1963; 1964) findings in the 1960s, the interaction between local bureaucracies and citizens remains "feudal". Interviewees report that bureaucratic positions imply high respect not necessarily high service responsibility. Rural communities consider government positions as the socially most prestigious employment option. As a businessman in Pesisir put it: "[…] The high social esteem of PNS positions are deeply rooted in the heads of our society since the Dutch colonization days.[…] Fathers want to entrust their daughters to securely employed public servants rather than successful businessmen." Thus, the pursuit of economic security and social recognition accelerates the interest in PNS positions; in some cases to such an extent that

---

Box 9.2
Perceptions on PNS Bribe Payments from Stakeholder Interviews

"In order to become a PNS, some people pay between Rp 40 and 60 million […]. Automatically — against this backdrop of putting in money upfront — one has to coordinate means in order to get a profit out of this [investment] cost. That's the law of economics. […] So what happens in the end? Incoming public servants try to get their money back. This becomes a burden to the local economy." (Interview with Senior Official in Klaten.)

"People in this district think that becoming a PNS is a 'gift of god' ('*rejeki dari tuhan*'). They assume that public servant positions can be used for family and personal interests. […] However, given our weak law enforcement and surveillance, what else can we expect?" (Interview with Businessman in Kebumen.)

"Some PNS candidates pay between Rp 25 to 30 million depending on their degree. […] Some teachers are asked for Rp 15 million […] police officers around Rp 35 million. […] I was asked myself to pay Rp 10 million in 1997 in order to get a public service position. But I declined. […] It is sad that people rarely choose to become an entrepreneur. (Interview with Businessman in Pesisir Selatan.)

"During the Order Baru times some people paid approximately Rp 2.5–10 million to become public officials. Now there are no payments any longer. Police candidates are still asked to pay Rp 30–40 million to their vertical superiors. […] I believe public servants in other districts in West Sumatra pay Rp 20–40 million to be accepted." (Interview with Academic in Solok.)

"I know of no extra fees for incoming PNS candidates in Solok. There used to be some — but under the leadership of Bupati Gawawan Fauzi they appear no longer. […] The best proof is that even a member of his own family has not been accepted as PNS last year. […] The clean PNS recruitment is directly linked to Solok's transparency reforms." (Interview with NGO Representative in Solok.)

"Before [in the early stage of decentralization] there were rumors that a high-school head had to pay Rp 19 million. […] Also, it is likely that some people had to pay a certain amount to become PNS before. […] It seems that brokers 'selling' PNS positions do not have to be in Kebumen — they can be situated in Yogjakarta. […] An interesting feature that was reported from another districts, is that the district head provided local parliament fractions or other senior officials with 'open' PNS positions. These open positions could be then sold to PNS applicants who were willing to pay." (Interview with Senior Official in Kebumen.)

"[Bribing for PNS positions] happens all over Indonesia. The strong orientation towards entering the government leads people to invest. […] If, to give an example, applicants pay 50 million, it will take many months or years to reach a break-even point. Imagine, what this investment could achieve in the private sector. [...] In Bima employment in and development of the private sector is stagnant. [...] In our culture people — even if they are poor — struggle to provide their children with the highest possible education so that they can become a public servant. [...] Business people usually have [just] a high-school degree." (Interview with Academic in Bima.)

"It is the culture of our society. People search for employment that requires low effort but provides high security. In fact, public servants should be paid for performance not position. [...] Payments [for entering the public service] with a high-school degree can be 30 to 40 million. [...] Some pay money, some promise specific services. [...] In the villages parents want their children to become PNS because [government officials] are highly respected. Actually, they should honour entrepreneurs as it is them who provide new jobs." (Interview with Businessman in Gianyar.)

applicants pursue a fast-track option and pay bribes to agents that can guarantee the desired position.

Unfortunately, these bribe payments are bound to have a negative effect on administrative conduct within a district. Assuming rational behaviour, indebted officials will pursue a "return on investment" throughout their daily routines. The administration of licences and collection of taxes has many interfaces with cash-based transactions — and is hence an easy target for absorbing rents. In other words, the more public officials are in debt, the more illegitimate rent-seeking can be expected. This economic rationale combined with low parliamentarian and legal checks and balances may explain rising predatory licensing practices, which emerged in five out of eight district cases above.

To summarize, during Indonesia's rapid transition to decentralization, some national and local institutional settings have aggravated rather than improved local governance. The vague wording of revenue law 34/2000 and the limited ministerial supervision provides districts with virtually unrestricted authority to release and administer local business regulations. The lack of checks and balances continues at the local level, where the performances of parliaments are perceived as largely unsatisfactory. Moreover, linking parliament budgets to revenue levels does little to secure critical oversight of long-term economic impacts but raises short-term interest in instant revenue generation.

Simultaneously, seven out of eight districts display an alarming trend of bribe payments for public recruitment. Given high unemployment and sociocultural conditions, it appears that a certain amount of citizens make high upfront investments in order to secure a prestigious PNS position. As a result, a number of public servants are in debt and likely to pursue illegitimate compensation during administrative tax and licensing procedures. Seen as a whole, these institutional deficiencies may well provoke the "grabbing hand" (Shleifer and Vishny 1998) — a state in which officials misuse discretion to seek private rents. The argument is summarized in Figure 9.6. Overall, adverse institutional factors — both national and local — appear to be one part of the story of unsatisfactory business conditions; another one will be offered in the next section.

Figure 9.6
Institutional Deficiencies at National and District Levels

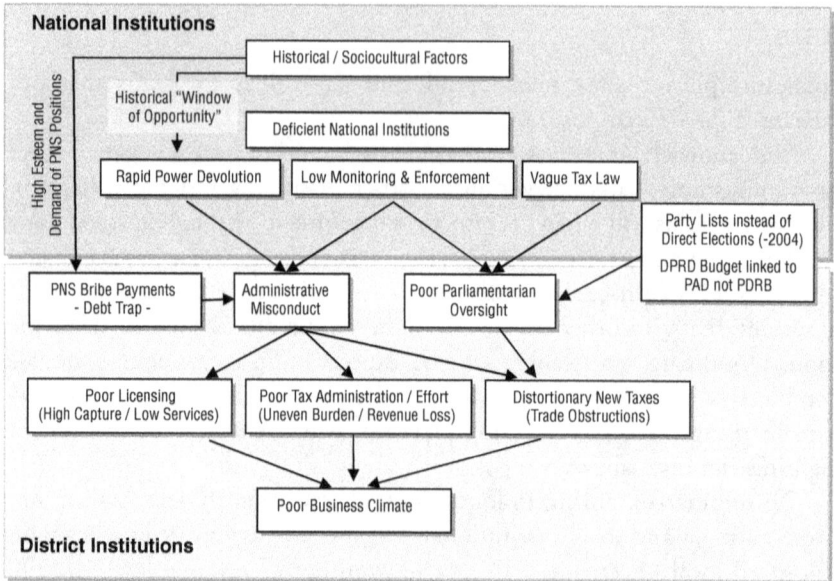

Source: Author's illustration.

3.3. Political Economy of Change

Considering that all eight district cases face similar institutional deficiencies — a vague law on regional revenues, a poor national supervision, and a poor parliamentarian oversight — an interesting question remains: why do some districts in our case study perform better than others? Why does Solok, for

Figure 9.7
Counterbalancing Factors — Governmental Leadership and Civic Pressure

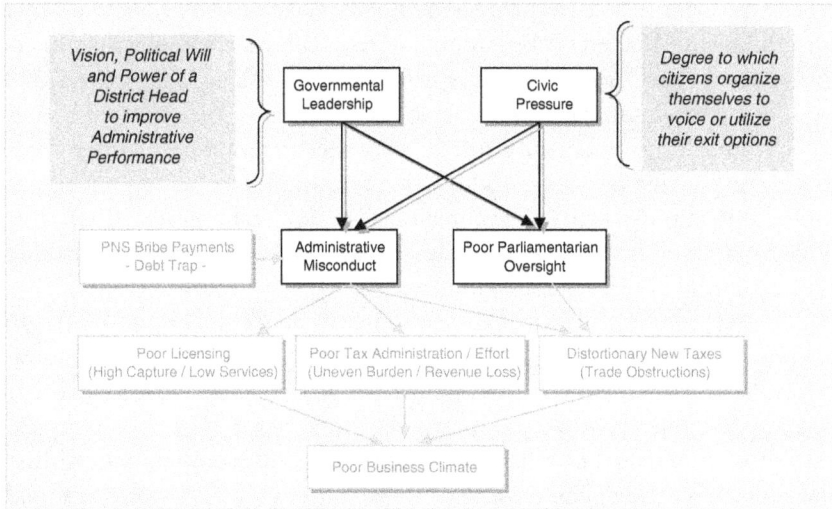

Source: Author's illustration.

instance, perform better than Pesisir in West Sumatra and Kebumen better than Klaten in Central Java? Two possible explanations come to mind (see Figure 9.7).

First, following theoretical propositions of the Fiscal Federalism and Anti-Corruption literatures, civic pressures in terms of people's exit and voice options may play an important role of counterbalancing adverse administrative conduct. And second, arising from Indonesia's specific historical and sociocultural context, governmental leadership may have a significant bearing on the performance of district bureaucracies. The impact of both of these factors is explored in the following.

(i) *Civic accountability and business pressures*
The argument that decentralizing governance will improve licensing and taxation practices by providing business people with increased means to "voice" against or "exit" from governmental misconduct, originates from theoretical discourse. Yet, regarding the first five years of decentralization, our empirical evidence hardly verifies this proposition. In this early stage, sociocultural circumstances and prevailing interest structures constrain the ability of local businesses to voice and exit.

Theoretically, decentralization creates a closer proximity between decision-makers and citizens enhancing responsiveness to local preferences and allocative efficiency (Oates 1972, 1999). This argument is often stipulated in two ways. First, following Tiebout's propositions,[22] decentralization stimulates an inter-district competition for mobile taxpayers ultimately pushing local governments to offer citizens more favourable tax-service packages (Tiebout 1956). And second, applying Hirschman's propositions,[23] decentralization may put citizens in a better position not only to "exit" a less favourable jurisdiction but also to "voice" for improvements (Hirschman 1970; Kaufmann et al. 2002; Shah 2006). Yet, both theoretic frameworks are based on a set of assumptions that are not satisfied in the Indonesian case.

In the eight Indonesian case districts, Tiebout's assumption of *high mobility* is not confirmed. In the short and medium term, sociocultural factors restrict local firms in their ability to permanently move to another district. For one, landownership is a limiting factor. Above economical reasoning as collateral or safety net, land tenure is of essential sociocultural importance to rural communities. It provides a basis for matrimonial (Sumatra) or patrimonial (Java) inheritance and a basis for annual family gatherings. Families are bound to their land. They may temporarily leave or lend it for income-generation but refrain from moving away or selling it ultimately (Bottema 1995). The notion of moving into a new district in search of lower taxes and higher services is thus an unlikely option for firms in rural Indonesia. For another, Chinese business people — who constitute a large economic force in Central Java, Bali, and NTB — are reluctant to move out of familiar district environments in fear of ethnic discrimination and bureaucratic complexities.[24]

The assumption of *high information* — a precondition for exit and voice strategies — is also rarely met in our district cases. Information on business-relevant district regulations (taxes, licences, business services) are hardly accessible by local businesses; transparency and dissemination of district policies are limited. According to our study, 50 per cent of the 1,041 respondents report to be "dissatisfied" or "strongly dissatisfied" with their information access to business-relevant government policy, while only 14 per cent declare to be "satisfied" or "very satisfied" (see Figure 9.8). Overall, it seems unrealistic to assume perfectly informed and mobile citizens while holding government conditions constant (Faguet 1997, p. 9). In fact, empirical findings indicate the contrary. Businesses continue to be constrained in terms of mobility and information access, while district governments have been changing significantly in terms of administrative structures and local elections.

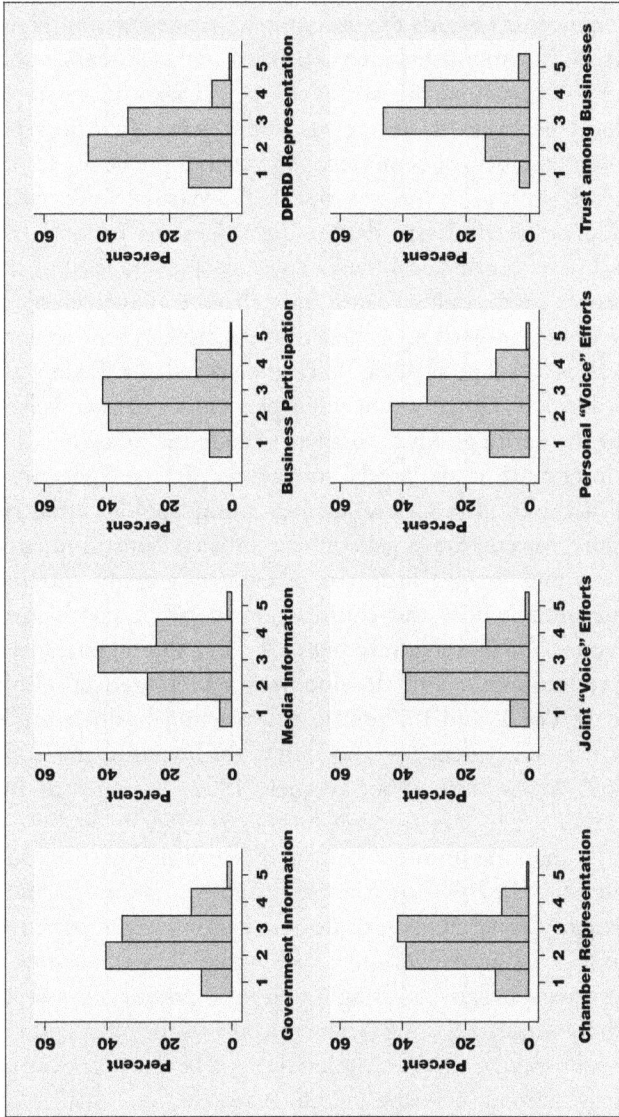

Figure 9.8
Overall Business Perceptions on Aspects of Civic Pressure

Note: Scores range from 1 to 5: 1 = "very dissatisfied", 2 = "dissatisfied", 3 = "undecided", 4 = "satisfied", 5 = "very satisfied". *Source:* Survey data based on 1,041 randomly selected business respondents in eight districts.

Hirschman and Putnam's proposition of "civic voice" or "civicness" — direct societal pressures that hold local governments to account (see note 23) — are yet to unfold. The empirical data of our eight district cases suggests that business respondents are neither fully enabled nor fully committed to voice their concerns towards the government. As depicted in Figure 9.8, the data shows local respondents are dissatisfied with (a) their involvement in new business regulations (52 versus 12 per cent), (b) the representation through local parliaments (64 versus 7 per cent), (c) the representation through local chambers of commerce (55 versus 8 per cent), (d) their efforts to voice jointly with other business people (52 versus 15 per cent), as well as (e) their individual efforts to deliver their opinions to local governments (62 versus 11 per cent). Local media coverage and the level of trust among business people are the only two indicators that are not perceived insufficient. Interestingly, the comparison of these districts displays little to no variance in the business perception of civic voice indicators (see Table 9.9). Possible reasons for low and rather homogenous perceptions of civic voice indicators throughout the entire group of districts include the following:

First, local markets are largely uncontested. In the eight case districts, a large part of the local economy revolves around public infrastructure and procurement projects. Since government projects constitute large business opportunities and involve little risk, they attract many entrepreneurs. In general, the procurement and construction of public goods involves three groups of actors: (1) senior government officials and project leaders (*Pimpro*), (2) assigned economic and development representatives of the district parliament (*DPRD*), and (3) private construction businesses (*Pemborong*). Based on anecdotal evidence — and akin to the literature on "Iron Triangles" (Lowi 1969; McConnell 1966; Michels 1962) — selected bureaucrats, parliamentarians, and construction businesses tend to establish "collusion triangles". By marking up input costs and providing lower output qualities, the members of these collusion triangles are able to capture illegitimate rents. Concrete examples of public-private rent-seeking are reported in all case districts. Box 3.3 summarizes some of the interview statements. Collusion agreements have a negative bearing on business pressures in two ways. First, they absorb the voice of existing business people — the more entrepreneurs are involved in rent-seeking activities, the less they will be able to criticize government shortcomings. Second, collusive agreements undermine market competition and, therefore, create entry-barriers for the voices of incoming firms.

Second, local chambers of commerce (KADINDA) appear dysfunctional. The interviews with KADINDA heads in all eight districts reveal alarming conditions. For decades KADINDA has been an umbrella organization for

Table 9.9
District-Specific Business Perceptions on Aspects of Civic Accountability

District	C. Java		W. Sumatra		Bali		NTB		Ø
	Kla	Keb	Sol	Pes	Gia	Kar	Lom	Bim	
(a) Information by the government	2.12	2.67	2.76	2.47	2.51	2.74	2.52	2.69	2.6
(b) Information by local media	2.73	2.98	3.02	2.79	3.07	3.10	2.92	2.77	2.9
(c) Involvement of business sector	2.39	2.59	2.61	2.55	2.83	2.55	2.45	2.67	2.6
(d) Representation through parliament	2.28	2.43	2.39	2.23	2.42	2.26	2.27	2.44	2.3
(e) Representation through chamber	2.52	2.46	2.48	2.30	2.70	2.55	2.40	2.57	2.5
(f) Joint "voice" efforts of business people	2.31	2.61	2.66	2.65	2.81	2.76	2.62	2.73	2.6
(g) Personal "voice" efforts	2.08	2.59	2.50	2.23	2.33	2.65	2.61	2.54	2.4
(h) Trust among business people	3.09	3.20	3.16	2.99	3.13	3.52	3.52	2.99	3.2
Average Score	2.4	2.7	2.7	2.5	2.7	2.8	2.7	2.7	2.7

Note: Scores range from 1 to 5: 1 = "very dissatisfied", 2 = "dissatisfied", 3 = "undecided", 4 = "satisfied", 5 = "very satisfied".
Source: Survey data based on 1,041 randomly selected business respondents in eight districts.

Box 9.3
Statements on Corruption in the Public Tender Business

(1) I am currently involved in a public infrastructure project myself. According to my calculations 30 per cent of the total value of Rp 204 million [approx. US$20,000] is captured: 15 per cent by the department of public works; and another 15 per cent by the local parliament. Initially I wanted to decline this project — but after all — what can you do? (Interview with Entrepreneur in District 1.)

(2) Endemic corruption in the public tender business has significant effects on the quality of streets in this district. In fact, only 50–40 per cent of the infrastructure budgets are used for their earmarked purposes. The rest is divided amongst actors involved in a public-private collusion system. The construction business winning the tender usually keeps between 10 and 20 per cent of the tender budget; political parties and parliamentarians capture approximately 10 per cent for their electoral campaigns; senior government officials receive around 15 per cent; construction associations asks for another 5 per cent; and security payments to police and local hoodlums amount to approximately 10 per cent. (Interview with Entrepreneur in District 2.)

(3) The government has made some efforts to make public tendering more transparent. In theory these steps are good, but their implementation will take time. We need a penalty system — a blacklist of corrupt construction companies. Moreover, as long as the rural economy is weak and people are struggling to provide basic needs and schooling for their children, the fight for greater transparency is only limitedly successful. Overall, tender practices are better than before. Yet, there is still room for corruption. Either people know each other and make up a fictive "competitive tender"; or the tender itself is legitimate but the winning applicant colludes with others during the actual implementation phase to cover up lower qualities and personal gains. Quality cuts and illegitimate rent-seeking prevails — they make up to 30 per cent of budget values. (Interview with NGO Representatives in District 3.)

(4) This year [2005] the purchase of school tables for Rp 1.5 billion [US$150,000] was openly tendered. Twenty companies joined the tender. However, all tender applications but one were fictive. It was a setup where 19 applicants were paid off for quietly withdrawing their application. These fictive tender setups are quite common. Eventually, since the winning application is based on up-scaled prices, the gain can be shared amongst the ones involved. In this case the real costs were around Rp 900 million, thus Rp 600 million [US$60,000] could be divided. The involved entrepreneur received around 70–100 million; 200 million went to government departments; the rest was shared amongst local parliamentarians and other powerful players. (Interview with Entrepreneur in District 4.)

Note: Districts are not specified to secure the confidentiality of respondents.

construction and procurement firms. Yet, with the revision of procurement legislation (Kepres 18/80/2003) these firms no longer requires KADINDA's membership nor its authorization. Unfortunately, the eight KADINDA offices in our districts have not yet succeeded to change their strategy and attract other business sectors. In fact, membership has been continuously declining over the last years — often ranging below 100 registered businesses. One reason for this low membership is the lack of attractive services, such as the provision of market information, technical training or product fairs. As a consequence, operational budgets are constantly low and most offices are situated in small run-down buildings. In light of these problems, KADINDA cannot represent the voice of district businesses in a satisfactory manner — a point that is well reflected in the business survey (see Table 9.9).

Third, the ability of local firms to freely criticize the government also depends on social and economic status. The interview data suggests that those who have higher social recognition — be it through communal achievements, family lineage, or success in their profession — are more likely to be heard; and those who hold higher economic assets are more courageous to risk public exposure and retaliation. As a consequence, the remaining group of vocal citizens is small; and it becomes even smaller once we subtract those who are reluctant to voice: Chinese minorities and government-oriented businesses.

Fourth, Indonesia's long history of authoritarian rule provides a rocky soil for the young seeds of democratization. Throughout the reigns of ancient kingdoms, Dutch colonialism, Japanese invasion, Sukarno's "Guidance Democracy", and Soeharto's "New Order", Indonesian people have continuously experienced regimes of control (Anderson 1990; Dick et al. 2002; Doorn 1983). Hence, people's awareness of democratic rights is limited and will require time to unfold. This is also reflected in the business survey. The low perceptions in personal and joint voice efforts (see Table 9.9) indicate that respondents are not accustomed to demand better business conditions.

And finally, another restrictive factor is the "mobilizing" of public voice for narrow elite interests. Anecdotal evidence suggests that many public complaints and demonstrations are not based on free personal decisions but externally induced by well-paying local elites. In Kebumen, for instance, demonstrations of small shopkeepers against the building of a new shopping mall are reported to be "stimulated" by the owner of an existing shopping mall in fear of competition. In Solok, a large drinking water producer (Aqua) withdrew investment plans after local Minang Kerbau leaders mobilized their communities to demonstrate for higher land and water prices. Ultimately, this led to the withdrawal of investment plans. In other words, not only is the voice of small businesses limited, it can also be bought or stimulated by powerful elites in certain cases.[25]

In sum, the current state of Indonesia's districts diverges from the predictions of established models. Assumptions of high mobility, high information access, and high civic engagement are not confirmed by the case evidence. Seven years of decentralized democratic governance — in a country that experienced centuries of authoritarian rule — do not suffice to produce highly informed, mobile, and vocal citizens. Civic pressures continue to be constrained by prevailing sociocultural structures and vested interests. Since voice indicators remain similarly low in all eight district cases (see Table 9.9), the variance of more or less conducive business conditions can hardly be explained by different levels of civic pressures.

(ii) *Governmental leadership*
Despite the long lineage of classic social science scholarship (Plato, Aristotle, Sun Tse, Macchiavelli),[26] the notion of leadership … has been largely neglected in economics (Hermalin 1998, p. 1,188). The focus on governmental leadership as an explanatory variable in this study arose inductively during three years of work experience in Eastern Indonesia. The observations of strong influence of district heads (*Bupati*) in policy-making and the high respect of citizen's towards leading government officials were revealing. Similar to former studies in Java by Wertheim (1964) and Doorn (1983), government bureaucracies in the Eastern districts appear strongly hierarchical.

The findings of our study suggest that governmental leadership — which constitutes the supply side rather than the demand side of governance — has a considerable bearing on district business conditions. The analysis of the survey data illustrates that better or worse licensing and taxation practices correlate to good and bad leadership qualities. We find that the ability to influence "activities of … a group in efforts toward goal achievement" (Hersey and Blanchard 1988, p. 86), or put more specifically, the skills of a *Bupati* to lead public servants towards better administrative conduct, matters.

The leadership indicators in the business survey are calculated based on the perceptions of approximately 125 businesses in each district. Survey respondents were asked to evaluate district heads in terms of (a) efforts to curb corruption, collusion, and nepotism, (b) vision and political will, (c) communication skills, (d) popularity and public support, (e) and power to bring about change.[27] As an additional feature, a score on the educational background of a district head is added.[28] Figure 9.9 and Table 9.10 summarize the results.

In contrast to civic voice indicators, leadership varies significantly across district cases. Solok's *Bupati* achieves an average score of 4.3 (strong to very strong) due to strong marks in all regards, followed closely by Kebumen's *Bupati* who achieves a score of 3.9 (strong). The leadership in Pesisir is perceived as fair (3.0), while Klaten's district head comes last (1.9) with poor evaluations in each aspect.

The case of Solok provides a good example for the leadership argument. Respondents agree unanimously that Solok's *Bupati*, Fauzi Gamawan, has played a crucial role in improving government conduct. His governance reforms — including pioneering an "anti-corruption pact" with Transparency International, abolishing unjust project allowances, and increasing government transparency (see Box 9.4) have had a substantial impact. The highly rated One-Stop Licensing Service (Satu Pintu Plus) was — according to interviewees — the result of Gamawan's own vision and effort.

The case of Kebumen is slightly less clear-cut. Although survey results indicate high leadership values, most business respondents declare that Kebumen's *Bupati* Rustriningsih — during her incumbency from 2000 to 2005 — paid less attention to the business community and more attention to rural development. While there is much praise for Rustriningsih's achievements in rural service provision,[29] her disregard of business impediments is frequently criticized. In other words, Kebumen's *Bupati* directed her efforts towards basic service provision rather than licensing and taxation aspects. Yet, in comparison to its provincial counterpart Klaten, Rustriningsih is perceived the better leader both in business surveys and interviews. Klaten's *Bupati* Haryanto was widely criticized by non-government stakeholders for his arbitrary policies and authoritarian management style.

In fact, the 2005 elections (*Pilkada*) in Central Java clearly confirm these leadership differences (see Figure 9.10): while Rustriningsih was reaffirmed with 77 per cent of Kebumen's votes — one of the best results to date — Haryanto was rejected by his party and replaced by another candidate in the run-up to elections.

If we now assess leadership, civic voice, and other institutional indicators from the political economy discussion in relation to business climate results from above (see Table 9.11), we can identify the following tendencies:

(1) Leadership "correlates" positively with better tax and licensing conditions. This holds especially true in the first two district pairs that were chosen

Figure 9.9
Governmental Leadership Indicators in Case Districts

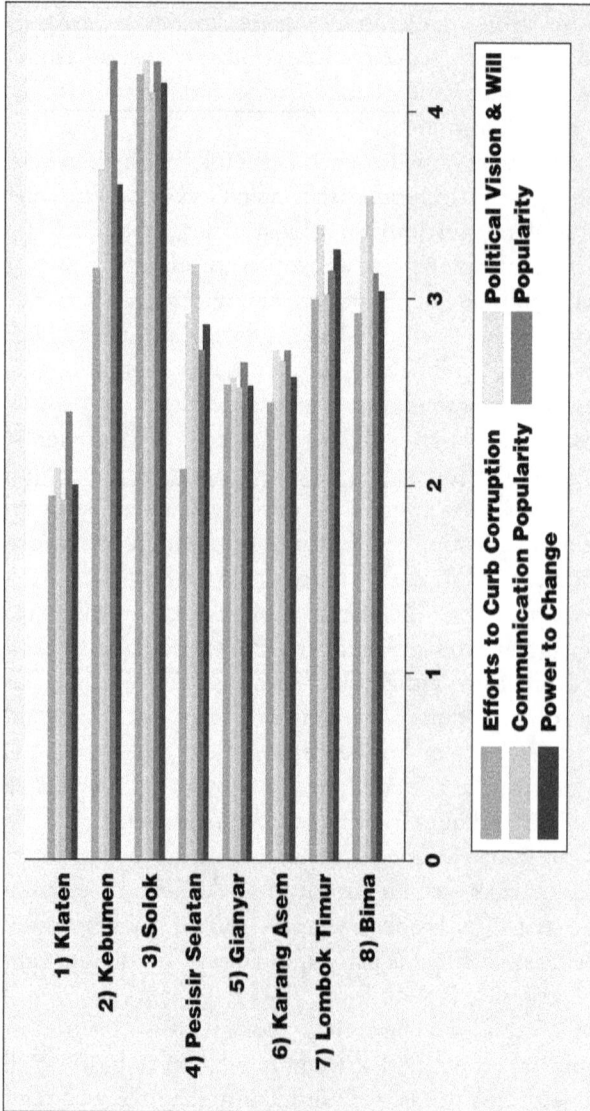

Legend:
- Efforts to Curb Corruption
- Communication Popularity
- Power to Change
- Political Vision & Will
- Popularity

Districts:
1) Klaten
2) Kebumen
3) Solok
4) Pesisir Selatan
5) Gianyar
6) Karang Asem
7) Lombok Timur
8) Bima

Note: Scores are means of a Likert Scale: 1 = "very poor", 2 = "poor", 3 = "fair", 4 = "strong", 5 = "very strong".
Source: Survey data based on 1,041 randomly selected business respondents in eight districts.

Table 9.10
Governmental Leadership Indicators in Comparison

District	C. Java		W. Sumatra		Bali		NTB		Ø
	Kla	Keb	Sol	Pes	Gia	Kar	Lom	Bim	
(a) Integrity/Efforts against Corruption	1.94	3.16	4.19	2.09	2.54	2.44	2.99	2.92	2.8
(b) Vision and Political Will	2.09	3.68	4.27	2.91	2.57	2.72	3.39	3.33	3.1
(c) Communication Skills	1.92	3.98	4.10	3.18	2.52	2.67	3.02	3.55	3.1
(d) Popularity and Public Support	2.39	4.26	4.26	2.72	2.66	2.72	3.15	3.13	3.2
(e) Power to Bring About Change	2.00	3.60	4.15	2.86	2.53	2.58	3.26	3.04	3.0
(f) Educational Background	1.00	5.00	5.00	4.00	3.00	3.00	3.00	3.00	3.4
Average Score	1.9	3.9	4.3	3.0	2.6	2.7	3.1	3.2	

Note: Scores are means of a Likert Scale: 1 = "very poor", 2 = "poor", 3 = "fair", 4 = "strong", 5 = "very strong".
Source: Survey data based on 1,041 randomly selected business respondents in eight districts.

Box 9.4
Government Reforms in Solok during the
Office of *Bupati* Fauzi Gamawan

(1) *Integrity Pact*
Solok is the first Indonesian district to have successfully implemented an "Integrity Pact" under the supervision of Transparency International (TI). The agreement was signed officially in 2003 by senior public officials, parliamentarians, and construction businesses. It represents a promising first step to eradicate corruption practices in public government projects. The monitoring of public tender procedures, often seen to be the core of Indonesian's corruption problems, is authorized to independent "watch dogs", including the local TI office and other civil society institutions. According to the interviews, *Bupati* Gawawan was determined to implement the Integrity Pact in cooperation with TI and the German Development Agency GTZ after coming back from a government transparency conference in South Korea.

(2) *Regulation on Government Transparency*
The district regulation on governmental transparency (Perda 5/2004) emphasizes the obligations of local government officials to serve its citizens. It represents a first step to set a minimum service standard by informing Solok's people of government programmes and performance. Government publications are publicly accessible (APBD, PDRB) and public servants are reported to have a "open door" policy. These policies were further enhanced by *Bupati* Gamawan through weekly "coffee mornings" in his residence — where he invited government and civil society representatives to exchange thoughts and discuss problems.

(3) *One-Stop Licensing Services (Satu Pintu Plus)*
As described in more detail above, Solok's government has continuously improved licensing services to its citizens. Customer-oriented service units provide a wide range of 25 different licenses. Based on interview and questionnaire results, processing times and capture practices are decreasing since decentralization. The concept was envisioned by Solok's *Bupati* in the late 1990s.

(4) *Abolishment of "Project Allowances"*
Bupati Gamawan took an exemplary step to abolish common "project allowances" (*Tunjangan Daerah*), an Indonesia-wide convention that secures high-level officials (*Bupati*, Deputy *Bupati*, District Secretary, and Project Leaders) high benefits from public projects. Instead, he decided to redistribute project allowances evenly amongst all public servants based on their work experience and bureaucratic rank (*Peraturan Bupati* 2/2005). Inevitably, this initiative leads to income losses for higher officials and income gains for lower-ranked officials. Moreover, it balances incomes amongst technical departments. While some departments used to be endowed with high project allowances (e.g. public works), the current bill treats all departments equally.

Comparison of Leadership Values in Kebumen and Klaten

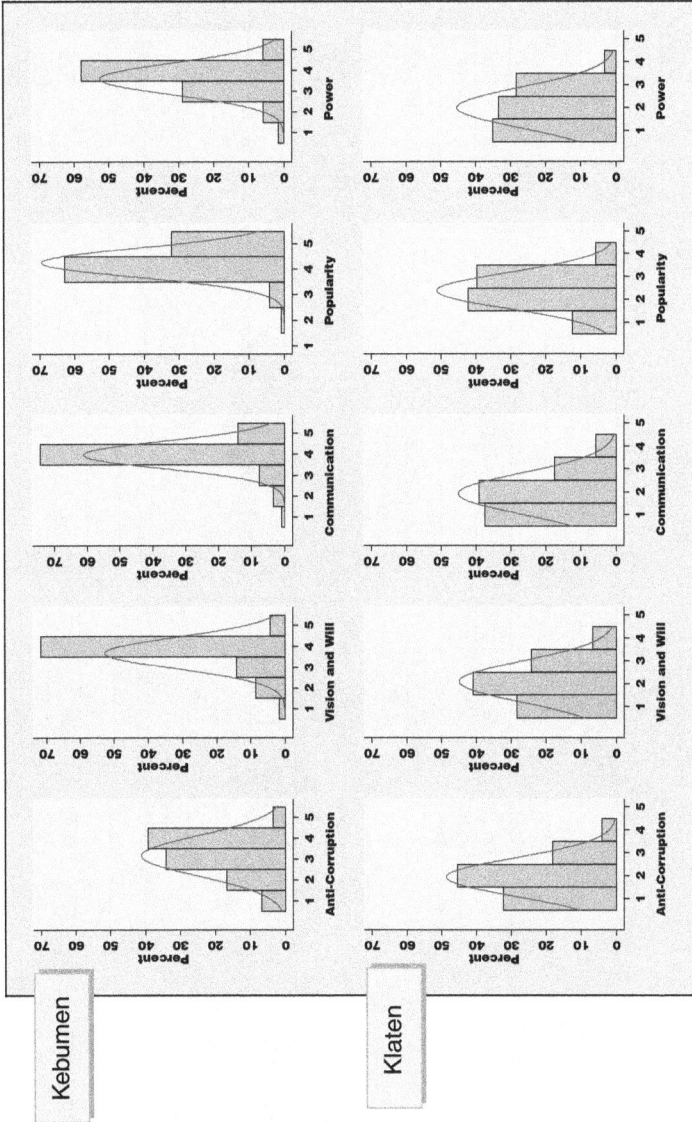

Note: Scores are means of a Likert Scale: 1 = "very poor", 2 = "poor", 3 = "fair", 4 = "strong", 5 = "very strong". Normal Distribution Curves signal means and variance of the survey responses.
Source: Business survey data from Solok and Klaten.

Table 9.11

Overview of Business Conditions in Relation to Political Economy Indicators

Aspect	Central Java		West Sumatra		Bali		NTB	
	Kla	Keb	Sol	Pes	Gia	Kar	Lom	Bim
(1) Business Conditions								
(a) Licensing — Capture	Poor (2,2)	Poor (2,3)	Good (1,4)	Poor (2,2)	Poor (2,5)	Good (1,4)	Fair (1,6)	Fair (1,6)
(b) Licensing — Admin. Time	Poor (2,6)	Poor (2,7)	Good (1,4)	Fair (1,8)	V. Poor (4,3)	Poor (2,5)	Fair (1,8)	Good (1,5)
(c) Distortionary Taxes	None	None	None	Road Levies	None	None	Export Tax	Export Tax
(d) Quality of OSS	(+) V. Poor (0.8)	(+) Poor/Fair (2,3)	(+) Good (3,8)	(–) V. Poor/Poor (1,4)	(+) Fair (3,1)	(+) None (0)	(–) Poor/Fair (2,4)	(–) None (0)
Overall Tendency	V. Poor/ Poor	Poor/ Fair	Good	Poor	Poor	Poor/ Fair	Poor/ Fair	Poor/ Fair
(2) Political Economy								
(a) National Law, Supervision, and DPRD Oversight	——————— deficiencies apply to all districts ———————							
(b) Tendency of PNS Bribing ("Debt Trap")	Very High (64 mill)	Fair (6 mill)	None (0 mill)	High (23 mill)	Fair (18 mill)	Fair (17 mill)	High (36 mill)	High (36 mill)
(c) Civic Voice	Dissatisfied/ Undecided (2,4)	Dissatisfied/ Undecided (2,7)	Dissatisfied/ Undecided (2,7)	Dissatisfied/ Undecided (2,5)	Dissatisfied/ Undecided (2,7)	Dissatisfied/ Undecided (2,8)	Dissatisfied/ Undecided (2,7)	Dissatisfied/ Undecided (2,7)
(d) Governmental Leadership	Weak (1.9)	Strong (3.9)	Strong (4.3)	Fair (3.0)	Fair (2.6)	Fair (2.7)	Fair (3.1)	Fair (3.2)

Source: Summary of analyses above — based on survey data, interviews, and personal observations.

for their distinctiveness in leadership. The positive relationship is most prominent in West Sumatra. Compared to its counterpart Pesisir, Solok's stronger leadership values clearly correspond to better business conditions. The same pattern applies in Central Java. In comparison to Klaten, Kebumen exhibits higher leadership qualities and a more favourable business climate. However, differences are not as pronounced, due to Kebumen's emphasis on rural education and village development (rather than tax and licensing improvements).

(2) Bribing conventions during public recruitment are perceived higher in cases of low leadership. Indeed, the ability of district heads to successfully monitor recruitment procedures in their district is likely to reduce the indebtedness of incoming officials and, thereby, the extent of illegitimate fees during tax and licence administration.

(3) Civic voice does not "correlate" significantly with different levels of business climates. Although the two district pairs in Bali and NTB were chosen for their differences in education levels and business participation, the results indicate no alignment between better voice indicators and better business conditions.

4. Conclusion

The empirical evidence of this study leads to three conclusions: first, district business conditions remain critical but vary substantially among the eight district cases. In tune with existing empirical work, our business surveys and personal observations confirm — in the majority of cases — rising capture practices, extensive administrative time requirements, unsatisfactory one-stop licensing services, and inadequate tax administration. Most districts administrations continue to operate on a level that is still unsatisfactory to business needs. One reason for this lies in institutional deficiencies. They manifest in vague (tax) law enforcement and insufficient legislative oversight. Equally noteworthy is the large variation in governance outcomes across district cases. While Solok represents a positive yardstick, with low rates of administrative capture and exemplary licence services, Klaten exhibits the lowest performance with high levels of public rent-seeking and low service provision.

Second, varying business conditions cannot be sufficiently explained by demand-side factors as advocated in fiscal federalism and governance literatures. Survey results show that business pressures — in terms of information access, participation in regulatory policy-making, their representation through parliaments and chambers, and individual/joint efforts to voice concerns to district authorities — are largely perceived as unsatisfactory. Interviews indicate that sociocultural features, such as strong ties to family and land (*pulang kampung*) and high integration costs of Chinese minorities (*tionghoa*), reduce the options to permanently exit a district. Assumptions of high information access and high civic engagement appear unrealistic at this stage. Businesses tend to be rarely informed of and involved in policy decisions. Individual voice efforts continue to be restricted by socioeconomic status (*tingkat sosial*), communal consensus-based decision-making patterns (*musyawarah*), and high respect towards government officials (*rasa hormat terhadap pemerintah*). Overall, the district cases hardly fit into models of inter-district competition à la Tiebout, of exit and voice à la Hirschman, or of civicness à la Putnam. Democratic transitions occurred less than ten years ago. Civic checks and awareness require time to evolve. This finding may be unsurprising to Indonesianists but relevant to Jakarta-based policy circles that debate the significance of current societal pressures.

And third, local leaders play an important role in explaining local governance outcomes. Five years into decentralization, our empirical snapshots from eight districts across Indonesia indicate that the variation of local business climates is positively related to governmental leadership indicators. It is noteworthy that high levels of leadership correspond with low levels of public recruitment bribes. This suggests that a district head can improve business conditions not only by policy initiatives (e.g. one-stop licensing services, abolition of distortionary taxes), but also by closely monitoring recruitment procedures.

In fact, decentralization has considerably altered the notion of leadership. While Indonesia has experienced strong national leaders during pre-decentralization times, the post-decentralization era has provided a platform for more than 400 sub-national leaders. Leadership has become contestable. District leaders are exposed to an increasing "yard-stick competition" (Besley and Case 1995) for donor funding and — since 2005 — for direct votes of local citizens. This mechanism of contestable leadership that has been largely missing in the decentralization debate to date and may compensate for weak civic pressures in an early stage of democratic transition.

NOTES

The author is grateful for the valuable suggestions and support of Andrew MacIntyre, Peter Timmer, Yusaku Horiuchi, Peter Larmour, Runako Samata, Taco Bottema, Sebastian Eckardt, Neil McCulloch, Hadi Susastro, Agung Prambudi, Raemond Atje, Syarif Hidayat, Koko, Thee Kian Wie, Iwan Azis, Raksaka Mahi, Sukamdi,

Blane Lewis, Hal Hill, Chris Manning, and Ross Mcleod; and greatly indebted to local students in Java, Sumatra, Bali, and NTB for their assistance in administrating business surveys.

1. Following Kaufman et al. (1999), *governance* is defined as "the traditions and institutions by which authority in a country is exercised — including the process by which governments are selected, monitored, and replaced, the capacity of the government to effectively formulate and implement sound policies, and the respect of citizens and the state for the institutions that govern economic and social interactions among them." Accordingly, *local* or *district governance* refers to the same definitional understanding but is limited to actors and their interaction within a district's boundaries.

2. Based on personal interviews with Ryaas Rasyid (key policy-maker/Minister for Regional Autonomy, 1999–2001), Berhard May (GTZ advisor to the Ministry of Home Affairs), and Sjarifuddin Baharsjah (Minister for Agriculture 1993–98). The fiscal decentralization law 25/99 was drafted by a team in the Ministry of Finance, which received additional consultancy by IMF and USAID (Turner and Podger 2003, p. 15).

3. During the last two years, for the first time in history, government heads and parliaments at various government levels have been elected directly by Indonesian people. Although many challenges lie ahead, national presidential elections and district-level elections have set an important democratic landmark — especially because they took place without major conflicts and violence (Aspinall 2005).

4. "Corruption is often at the very root of why governments do not work. Today one of the biggest threats to development [...] is corruption. It weakens fundamental systems, it distorts markets, and it encourages people to apply their skills and energies in non-productive ways. In the end, governments and citizens will pay a price, a price in lower incomes, in lower investment, and in more volatile economic fluctuations. That is a lesson Indonesia learned the hard way. ... [Corruption] now looms as a major obstacle to achieving the development successes that I believe this country is capable of, and which the Indonesian people deserve." Speech of World Bank President Paul Wolfowitz in Jakarta on 11 April 2006.

5. Undoubtedly, this theory-empirics gap arises partly because it is early days and theoretically proposed mechanisms may take more time to unfold. Yet, it may also arise because theoretical assumptions diverge too far from Indonesian reality, and cannot be approximated within a policy-relevant time frame. As Keynes once emphasized, "in the *long run* we are all dead" (1923, p. 65). In other words, policy-makers will require additional analysis on the current political economy in their districts. Some of the main theoretical arguments are presented in further detail in the latter part of this chapter.

6. In the field research from April 2005 to March 2006, we employed four methods in each district: (1) a survey of 125+ randomly selected small/medium business respondents, evenly stratified across three business sectors — trade,

manufacturing, and service; (2) 15 in-depth interviews (6 small/medium businesses, 4 public officials, 2 NGOs, 1 academic, and 2 media representatives); (3) direct observations of district licensing services and government units; and (4) the assessment of available secondary information sources — government reports, statistics, and news clippings. The eight districts were selected purposely. The four district pairs, located in four provinces that spread evenly from Western to Eastern Indonesia, come close to what Yin (2003) calls a "natural experiment". We controlled for external factors as much as possible, in order to have better explanatory traction with independent variables. Within a district pair cultural differences are minimal due to their regional proximity. In addition, the selected districts exhibit similar characteristics in terms of government transfers (APBD), regional gross domestic products (PRDB), and natural resource incomes (no oil or gas income). Most importantly, all district pairs display distinct differences in the independent variables to be explored. Hence, the pairs in West Sumatra and Central Java are chosen for their variations in "Leadership" (based on World Bank GDS data and Indonesian news coverage, Solok and Kebumen district heads exhibit high leadership qualities compared to their provincial counterparts in Pesisir and Klaten). The pairs in Bali and NTB differ in their potential for "Civic Accountability" (data sets from UNDP HDI and World Bank GDS suggest that Gianyar and Bima exhibit stronger education and participation levels than Lombok Timur and Bima). This methodological setup allows for relatively robust analysis of how government leadership and civic accountability affect district business conditions. For further details on scientific case study design, see King, Keohane, and Verba (1994, pp. 132–38), Yin (2003, p. 38), Ragin and Becker (1992, p. 222), and Geddes (1990).

7. It is important to stress that the presented values are means of ordinal (not nominal) scaled data. The common Likert-scaled variables in our business survey can be seen as a "continuous variable[s] denoting individuals' degrees of agreement [...] mapped into categories that are ordered but are separated by unknown distances" (Winship and Mare 1984, p. 514). It is therefore possible to calculate means of these perception values, but one should keep in mind that these are relative not absolute indications. For more detailed discussion on statistical inference with ordinal data, see Kerlinger and Lee (2000) and Winship and Mare (1984).

8. Predatory licensing is understood in terms of welfare reductions from a political economy perspective. It is the arbitrary act of public officials charging extensive illegal fees, which arise in the context of personal motives, interests, and local power structures. In case officials hold unrestricted monopoly positions of a required service, e.g. the issuing of licences, predatory behaviour and welfare distortions become more likely (Shleifer and Vishny 1998; Tullock 1965; Weber 1930). Overall, corrupt practices of public agents appears to be positively correlated to discretion and unrestrained power and negatively to accountability requirements (Klitgaard 1998).

9. The list of critical accounts on district licence procedures is long:
   (1) According to a study by LPEM-FEUI (2004), a leading economic research institute associated to the University of Indonesia, business licensing procedures on the district level continue to be a burden for the private sector. The study illustrates that licence requirements and the number of involved technical agencies (Dinas Teknis) are excessive. It concludes that such complex procedures weaken the position of licence applicants and make illegal charges more likely.
   (2) An earlier study of LPEM-FEUI published in 2002 and covering 1,736 businesses in 60 districts/municipalities — illustrates that the majority of businesses (79 per cent) pay additional costs when dealing with the local bureaucracy. (LPEM-FEUI 2002, p. 5). These additional costs amount to 9.7 per cent of overall business expenses in Java and up to 11.2 per cent outside Java (2002, p. 7).
   (3) The Regional Autonomy Watch, in its "Regional Business Attractiveness" report of 2004 (KPPOD 2004, p. 70), estimates the incidence of administrative corruption even higher. Based on a sample of 5,140 survey respondents, KPPOD declares that 85 per cent of the interviewed entrepreneurs pay illegal charges to public officials, while 15 per cent declined to answer. On average these illegal fees are seen to increase the costs of licences and user charges by 60 per cent.
   (4) The study on "Private Sector Perceptions on Local Business Climates in the Era of Decentralisation", affirms that "illegal extractions" are the highest ranking factor obstructing local businesses (Ray 2003, p. 13; REDI 2003).
   (5) Suhirman (2002, pp. 79–81), after studying bureaucratic practices of two districts in West Java, identifies the following tendencies: (a) In many cases licensing still involves unofficial charges ("pungutan tidak resmi"), which raise uncertainty and create high-cost economies; (b) government departments (Dinas) are in a monopolistic position to issue sector-specific licences and hardly cooperate with each other; (c) and the drafting process of licence regulations does not involve entrepreneurs and other affected citizens.
10. Rustiani (2003, p. 80) confirms the notion that licence procedures vary strongly among local governments. She supports her argument by assessing costs and time to receive a basic industry permit (*TDI*) in four local governments. Observable differences are considerable with costs ranging from Rp 5,000 (Yogyakarta) to Rp 477,000 (Bandung) and process durations ranging from 2 days (Yogyakarta) to 20 days (Medan).
11. A PDF file of the brochure can be downloaded from Solok's government website <www.solok.go.id>.
12. *Distortionary taxation* is understood in this chapter as economic welfare reductions. Undoubtedly, most taxes distort the behaviour of economic actors by changing relative prices (*substitution effect*) and by reducing available income and consumption (*income effect*) (James and Nobes 1998; Stiglitz 2000). Yet, some taxes cause more severe welfare reductions and are often referred to as "deadweight

loss" or "excess burden" (Auerbach 1985). Economic theory has shown that government tax practices are highly distortionary when obstructing trade flows (Caves et al. 1993; Ohlin 1933; Ricardo 1817; Samuelson 1962). Especially the taxation of mobile trade goods with high price-elasticity results in high welfare losses (Ramsey 1927).

13. This illustration of trade obstructions is found in SMERU (2001, p. 26). The study estimates that "the total amount of levies (official and non-official) paid to transport oranges from Kabanjahe to Jakarta ranges from Rp 268,500 to Rp 1,008,500. Paying the lowest amount would only be possible if the truck complies with its permitted capacity. Nevertheless, even when trucks comply with the regulations frequently drivers still have to pay levies." According to SMERU's calculations, the levies of sixteen truck weighing stations reduce total profits between 2 and 7 per cent.

14. "*Ya, dengan melihat, kan jadi kira-kira [...]. Misalnya warung A, omzet kira-kira setiap hari berapa, minimal, jadi kita bikin yang paling sepi lah. [... Sistem akuntansi] saya pikir masih jauh, kita tawar-menawar aja masih seperti itu.*" "We are looking at estimated values [...]. What is the daily turnover of a small restaurant A, for instance. We look at a minimal turnover — on a day that it is least frequented. [...] we are still far away from [accountancy systems]. We just negotiate — that's the way things are." (Interview at Kebumen's local revenue department.) Similar statements were made in revenue departments in all four provinces.

15. The tax office in Gianyar claims to have made strong efforts to improve tax collections by rotating tax officers during different tax collection stages (estimation, collection, and monitoring). Yet, the empirical data in Table 9.6 does not reflect such improvements.

16. McLeod (2000, 2003) argues that the transition from Soeharto's authoritarian regime to decentralisation creates more uncertainty for the business community, by putting an end to a well-established vertical system of benefit-sharing. Key administrators under Soeharto devoted their loyalty and resources to an all-informed president and — similar to a "franchise concept" — received rewards and authority in return. A decentralized form of administrative corruption, which is no longer fine-tuned by a powerful oligarch who seeks to maximize rents over time by ensuring a stable level of investment and growth (MacIntyre 2001; Olson 1993; Shleifer and Vishny 1993), may initially be more harmful to the business environment.

17. The *New Institutional Economics* literature demonstrates that efficient allocation of scarce resources can only take place if the rule of law and individual property rights are well developed within a society, and reinforced by its general value system (Furubotn and Richter 1991; Olson 1996; Weingast 1995; Williamson 1985, 1996). Moreover, due to their effect on trust and certainty, institutions determine the degree of entrepreneurial risk-taking and hence the impulses for economic growth (North 1990). Ill-defined institutions, on the other hand, give

way to short-term and self-centered individual objectives rather than long-term goals, thus endangering sustainable development.

18. Pursuant to Article 2.4, district authorities can enact any new tax or user charge that fulfils the following criteria: (a) it does not represent a national or provincial tax; (b) it does not contradict the common good; (c) it has sufficient revenue potential; (d) it does not obstruct local economic development; (e) and it does not address goods essential for basic needs; or (f) goods with high mobility.

19. This has changed in 2004 with Indonesia's first direct election of DPRD representatives. Now citizens can vote directly for DPRD members. Yet, "money politics", payments for party list nominations and mobilizing of voters through tangible incentives, remain a problem. Notwithstanding the move towards more electoral accountability, parliamentarians continue to be highly dependent on powerful party leaders (Choi 2004).

20. This dissatisfaction can be connected to the high incidents of corruption of DPRD representatives throughout the country. Based on news coverage, the Indonesian Corruption Watch (ICW) has identified a list of more than 80 DPRD corruption cases in 25 provinces since the enactment of decentralization (for more details refer to <www.icw.or.id>).

21. Bribe incidences have also been reported by Indonesian media. The Indonesian newspaper *Kompas* (2004), for instance, reports of a PNS candidate complaining to President S.B. Yudhoyono for being asked for Rp 40 million to enter the public service in Bekasi, West Java.

22. The Tiebout model argues in favour of decentralized tax administrations based on a neoclassical framework with the assumption of perfect information and mobility. It argues that citizens will make use of their rational choice and "vote with their feet" for the best available service-tax combination within their reach. Put differently, in a decentralized setting, in which local jurisdictions offer different policy packages of services and taxes, it is up to civic customers to compare and move to the location which meets their preferences best. Following this free-market logic, Tiebout envisions a scenario in which sub-national governments are forced to compete for critical tax-paying residents. The "invisible feet" of citizens pressure local governments to utilize local tax revenues efficiently and provide adequate public services.

23. *Hirschman*'s argument (1970) complements Tiebout's economic propositions by adding a political dimension. According to Hirschman, citizens have two powerful options to hold governments to account. First, akin to Tiebout's logic, citizens can decide to "exit" from public service provision, either by migrating to more attractive jurisdictions or by choosing private service providers within their jurisdiction. And second, in case exit options are limited by low mobility or bureaucratic monopoly, citizens have the option to "voice" their concerns. This assumes a certain degree of "civicness" (Putnam 1993, p. 87) — an awareness and social capacity to actively engage in the public sphere and directly express one's dissatisfaction (Hirschman 1970, p. 4). By engaging themselves in public

debates — be it through local elections, public hearings or participatory development planning — citizens improve policy environments rather than simply escaping from it (1970, p. 30). Some of these propositions are prominent in the discourse of the governance literature (Kaufmann et al. 2002; Picciotto 1995; Rietbergen-McCracken 1995; Shah 2006; World Bank 2001).

24. All in-depth interviews with Chinese business people confirmed that moving into a new district implies high costs for adapting to a new social environment and government bureaucracy. Chinese respondents clearly stated that they invested many years to establish a stable social balance with their surrounding community. They are generally anxious about moving into a new environment, as this implies high efforts and uncertainty with new government and societal pressures. Some still remember their businesses being burned down in 1965 and 1998.

25. The phenomenon of 'purchasable demonstrations' is confirmed in interviews with local parliamentarians, journalists, and senior officials in Kebumen and Solok.

26. See McGregor et al. (1966) for a more detailed discussion of classical works.

27. While the first indicator arises from the specific Indonesian context, the latter four indicators derive from business and public administration literatures. According to Bennis (1989, p. 139), "Leadership revolves around vision, ideas, direction, and has more to do with inspiring people .... A leader must be able to leverage more than his own capabilities." Leaders attempt to influence "the activities of followers through the communication process" (Donelly et al. 1985, p. 362). The Australian Public Service Commission (1998) declares that leaders in senior government positions (1) show personal drive and integrity; (2) shape strategic thinking; (3) communicate with influence; (4) cultivates productive working relationships; and (5) achieve results. For a detailed literature review on leadership see Van Wart (2003); for an analysis on the impact of leadership on economic growth refer to Jones and Olken (2005); for a discourse on Indonesian leadership see Liddle (1996) and MacIntyre (1999).

28. Education scores are based on available curriculum vitae and interview statements. Kebumen's and Solok's *Bupati* receive the highest education score due to their master degrees in Political Science (UGM) and Public Policy (Padang) respectively. Pesisir's *Bupati* finished a degree on Public Administration (LAN) during his military career. Gianyar's and Bima's *Bupati* served as national bureaucrats, whereas Karang's and Lombok's *Bupati* worked in the private sector; all of them have moderately good educational degrees. Klaten's *Bupati* receives the lowest score, since he holds a high-school degree that — according to several interviewees — is likely to be invalid.

29. Examples of rural development achievements during Rustriningsih's incumbercy (2000–04) are: (1) the rehabilitation of 2,648 classrooms in village schools; (2) the provision of more funds and fiscal authority to village bodies (APBDs); (3) and the reallocation of infrastructure budgets from construction associations to village authorities.

REFERENCES

Anderson, B.R.O.G. *Language and Power: Exploring Political Cultures in Indonesia.* Ithaca, NY: Cornell University Press, 1990.

Aspinall, E. "Political Update 2004: Indonesia's Year of Elections and the Normalisation of Politics". In *The Politics and Economics of Indonesia's Natural Resources,* edited by B. Resosudarmo. Singapore: Institute of Southeast Asian Studies and Canberra: Australia National University, 2005.

Auerbach, A.J. "The Theory of Excess Burden and Optimal Taxation". In *Handbook of Public Economics,* edited by A.J. Auerbach and M. Feldstein. Amsterdam: Elsevier Science, 1985.

Australian Government. *Senior Executive Leadership Capability Framework.* Canberra: Australian Public Service Commission, <http://www.apsc.gov.au/selc/index.html>, 1998.

Bennis, W. *On Becoming a Leader.* Reading, MA: Addison-Wesley Publishing, 1989.

Besley, T. and A. Case. "Incumbent Behavior: Vote Seeking, Tax Setting and Yardstick Competition". *American Economic Review* 85, no. 1 (1995): 25–45.

Bottema, T. *Market Formation and Agriculture in Indonesia from the Mid 19th Century to 1990.* Jakarta: Desa Putra, 1995.

Brodjonegoro, B. *Three Years of Fiscal Decentralization in Indonesia: Its Impacts on Regional Economic Development and Fiscal Sustainability.* Mimeographed. Jakarta: Department of Economics, University of Indonesia, 2004.

Buente, M. "Indonesia's Decentralization: The Big Bang Revisited". In *Thai Politics: Global and Local Perspectives,* edited by M. Nelson. Bangkok: King Prajadhipok Institute, 2004.

Castle, J. "Investment Prospects: A View from the Private Sector". In *Business in Indonesia: New Challenges, Old Problems,* edited by C. Basri and P. van der Eng. Singapore: Institute of Southeast Asian Studies, 2004.

Caves, R.E., J.A. Frankel, and R.W. Jones. *World Trade and Payments: An Introduction.* 6th ed. New York: Harper Collis, 1993.

Choi, N. "Local Elections and Party Politics in Post-Reformasi Indonesia: A View from Yogyakarta". *Contemporary Southeast Asia* 26, no. 2 (2004): 280–301.

Dick, H., V.J.H. Houben, J.T. Lindblad, and T.K. Wie. "The Emergence of a National Economy: An Economic History of Indonesia 1800–2000". Honolulu: University of Hawaii Press, 2002.

Dillinger, W.R. "Decentralization and its Implications for Urban Service Delivery". Washington D.C.: Urban Management Programme, World Bank, 1994.

Donelly, J., J. Ivancevich, and J. Gibson. *Organizations: Behaviour, Structure, Processes.* 5th ed. Plano, T.X.: Business Publications Inc., 1985.

Doorn, J.A.A.v. *A Divided Society: Segmentation and Mediation in Late-Colonial Indonesia.* Rotterdam: Comparative Asian Studies Program, 1983.

Eckardt, S. *Political Accountability, Incentives and Public Service Delivery: Theory with Evidence from Local Governments in Indonesia.* Berlin: Freie Universitaet Berlin, 2006.

Furubotn, E.G. and R. Richter. *The New Institutional Economics: A Collection of Articles from the Journal of Institutional and Theoretical Economics.* College Station: Texas A & M Press, 1991.

Geddes, B. "How the Cases You Choose Affect the Answers You Get: Selection Bias in Comparative Politics". In *Political Analysis*, edited by American Political Science Association. Ann Arbor: University of Michigan Press, 1990.

Hayek, F. *Studies in Philosophy, Politics and Economics.* Chicago: University of Chicago Press, 1967.

Hermalin, B.H. "Toward an Economic Theory of Leadership: Leading by Example". *American Economic Review* 88 (1998): 1188–206.

Hersey, P. and K.H. Blanchard. *Management of Organizational Behavior.* Englewood Cliffs, N.J.: Prentice Hall, 1988.

Hill, H. and H. Aswicahyono. "Survey of Recent Developments". *Bulletin of Indonesian Economic Studies* 40, no. 3 (2004): 277–305.

Hirschman, A.O. *Exit, Voice, and Loyalty: Responses to Decline in Firms, Organizations, and States.* Cambridge, Mass.: Harvard University Press, 1970.

James, S.R. and C. Nobes. *The Economics of Taxation: Principles, Policy, and Practice.* New York; London: Prentice Hall Europe, 1998.

Jones, F. and B. Olken. "Do Leaders Matter? National Leadership and Growth Since World War II". *Quarterly Journal of Economics* 120, no. 3 (2005): 835–64.

Kaufman, D., A. Kraay, and P. Zoido-Lobatón. *Governance Matters.* Policy Research Working Paper 2196. Washington D.C.: World Bank, 1999.

Kaufmann, D., G. Mehrez, and T. Gurgur. *Voice or Public Sector Management? An Empirical Investigation of Determinants of Public Sector Performance.* Washington D.C.: World Bank, 2002.

Kerlinger, F.N. and H.B. Lee. *Foundations of Behavioural Research.* 4th ed. C.A., USA: Wadsworth Thomson Learning, 2000.

Keynes, J.M. *Tract on Monetary Reform.* New York: Hartcourt Brace, 1923.

King, G., R.O. Keohane, and S. Verba. *Designing Social Inquiry: Scientific Inference in Qualitative Research.* Princeton, N.J.: Princeton University Press, 1994.

Klitgaard, R. *Controlling Corruption.* Berkeley: University of California Press, 1998.

KPPOD. *Daya Tarik Investasi Kabupaten/Kota Di Indonesia 2002 (Regional Investment Attractiveness 2002 — A Survey of 134 Districts/Municipalities in Indonesia).* Jakarta: Komite Pemantauan Pelaksanaan Otonomi Daerah (Regional Autonomy Watch), 2003.

————. *Daya Tarik Investasi Kabupaten/Kota Di Indonesia 2003 (Regional Investment Attractiveness 2003 — A Survey of 200 Districts/Municipalities in Indonesia).* Jakarta: Komite Pemantauan Pelaksanaan Otonomi Daerah (Regional Autonomy Watch), 2004.

————. *Daya Tarik Investasi Kabupaten/Kota Di Indonesia 2004 (Regional Investment Attractiveness 2004 — A Survey of 214 Districts/Municipalities in Indonesia).* Jakarta: Komite Pemantauan Pelaksanaan Otonomi Daerah (Regional Autonomy Watch), 2005.

Lewis, B.D. *How Many New Taxes and Charges Have Regional Government Created Under Fiscal Decentralization?* North Carolina: Research Triangle Institute, 2003*a*.

⸻. "Indonesian Regional Government Tax and Charge Creation under Fiscal Decentralization". *Bulletin of Indonesian Economic Studies* 72, 2003*b*.

Liddle, W. *Leadership and Culture in Indonesian Politics*. Sydney: Allen and Unwin, 1996.

Lowi, T. *The End of Liberalism: Ideology, Policy, and the Crisis of Public Authority*. New York: Norton, 1969.

LPEM-FEUI. *Ketidakpastian Usaha di Indonesiah: Dampak dari Otonomi Daerah dan Suap (Cost of Doing Business Survey)*. Jakarta: Institute for Economic and Social Research, Economic Faculty of the University of Indonesia, 2002.

MacIntyre, A. "Political Parties, Accountability, and Economic Governance in Indonesia". In *Democracy, Governance, and Economic Performance: East and Southeast Asia in the 1990s*, edited by J. Blondel, T. Inoguchi, and I. Marsh. Tokyo: United Nations University Press, 1999.

⸻. "Investment, Property Rights, and Corruption in Indonesia". In *Corruption: The Boom and Bust of East Asia*, edited by J.E. Campos. Manila: Ateno University Press, 2001.

McConnell, G. *Private Power and American Democracy*. New York: Knopf, 1966.

McGregor, D., W.G. Bennis, and E.H. Schein. *Leadership and Motivation*. Cambridge: MIT Press, 1966.

McLeod, R.H. "Suharto's Indonesia: A Better Class of Corruption". *Agenda* 7, no. 2 (2000): 99–112.

⸻. *After Suharto: Prospects for Reform and Recovery in Indonesia*. Canberra: RSPAS, Australian National University, 2003.

Michels, R. *Political Parties: A Sociological Study of the Oligarchical Tendencies of Modern Democracy*. New York: Free Press, 1962.

North, D.C. *Institutions, Institutional Change, and Economic Performance*. Cambridge; New York: Cambridge University Press, 1990.

Oates, W.E. *Fiscal Federalism*. New York: Harcourt Brace Javanovich Inc., 1972.

⸻. "An Essay on Fiscal Federalism". *Journal of Economic Literature* 37, no. 3 (1999): 1120–49.

Ohlin, B. *Inter-Regional and Inter-National Trade*. Cambridge: Harvard University Press, 1933.

Olson, M. "Dictatorship, Democracy and Development". *American Political Science Review* 87 (1993): 567–76.

⸻. "Big Bills left on the Sidewalk: Why Some Nations are Rich and Others Poor". *Journal of Economic Perspectives* 10, no. 2 (1996): 2–24.

Picciotto, R. *Putting Institutional Economics to Work: From Participation to Governance*. World Bank Discussion Paper no. 304, Washington D.C., 1995.

Putnam, R. *Making Democracy Work*. Princeton: Princeton University Press, 1993.

Ragin, C. and H. Becker. *What is a Case? Exploring the Foundations of Social Inquiry*. Cambridge: Cambridge University Press, 1992.

Ramsey, F.P. "A Contribution to the Theory of Taxation". *Economic Journal* 37 (1927): 47–61.

Ray, D., ed. "Decentralization, Regulatory Reform and the Business Climate". In *Proceedings of the Conference on Decentralization, Regulatory Reform and the Business Climate*. Jakarta, 2003.

REDI. *Persepsi Pelaku Usaha Terhadap Iklim Usaha di Era Otonomi Daerah (Private Sector Perceptions on Business Climates in the Era of Decentralisation)*. Jakarta: Regional Economic Development Institute, 2003.

Ricardo, D. *The Principles of Political Economy and Taxation*. London: John Murray, 1817.

Rietbergen-McCracken, J. *Participation in Practice: The Experience of the World Bank and Other Stakeholders*. World Bank Discussion Paper no. 333, Washington D.C., 1995.

Rusiani, F. "Izin: Mampukah Melindungi Masyarakat dan Seharusnya Beban Siapa? (Licenses: Are They Able to Secure Society — and Whose Burden Are They?)". In *Proceedings of the Conference on Decentralization, Regulatory Reform and the Business Climate*, edited by D. Ray. Jakarta, 2003.

Samuelson, P.A. "The Gains from International Trade Once Again". *Economic Journal*, December 1962.

Shah, A. "Corruption and Decentralized Public Governance". World Bank Policy Research Working Paper 3824, Washington D.C., 2006.

Shleifer, A. and R.W. Vishny. "Corruption". *The Quarterly Journal of Economics* 108, no. 3 (1993): 599–618.

———. *The Grabbing Hand: Government Pathologies and their Cures*. Cambridge, Mass: Harvard University Press, 1998.

SMERU. *Regional Autonomy and the Business Climate: Three Kabupaten Case Studies from North Sumatra*. Jakarta, 2001.

Stiglitz, J.E. *Economics of the Public Sector*. 3rd ed. New York: W. W. Norton, 2000.

Suhirman. *Merancang Kebijakan Perijinan yang Pro Pasar dan Sensitif Kepentingan Publik (Design of Licensing Policies: Conforming with Markets and Public Interest)*. Bandung: Bandung Institute of Governance Studies, 2002.

Sumarto, S., A. Suryahadi, and A. Arifianto. *Governance and Poverty Reduction: Evidence from Newly Decentralized Indonesia*. SMERU Working Paper 3/04, Jakarta, 2004.

Tiebout, C. "A Pure Theory of Local Expenditures". *The Journal of Political Economy* 64, no. 5 (1956): 416–24.

Timmer, P. "The Road to Pro-Poor Growth: The Indonesian Experience in Regional Perspective". *Bulletin of Indonesian Economic Studies* 40, no. 2 (2004): 173–203.

Tullock, G. *The Politics of Bureaucracy*. Washington D.C.: Public Affairs Press, 1965.

Turner, M. and O. Podger. *Decentralisation in Indonesia: Redesigning the State*. Canberra: Asia Pacific Press, 2003.

Van Wart, M. "Public-Sector Leadership Theory: An Assessment". *Public Administration Review* 63, no. 2 (2003): 214–28.

Weber, M. *The Protestant Ethic and the Spirit of Capitalism*. London: Allen & Unwin, 1930.

Weingast, B. "The Economic Role of Political Institutions: Market-Preserving Federalism and Economic Development". *Journal of Law, Economics, and Organization* 11, no. 1 (1995): 1–31.

Wertheim, W.F. "Sociological-Aspects of Corruption in Southeast-Asia". *Sociologia Neerlandica* 1, no. 2 (1963): 129–54.

————. *East-West Parallels: Sociological Approaches to Modern Asia*. The Hague: van Hoeve Ltd., 1964.

Williamson, O. *The Economic Institutions of Capitalism*. New York: Free Press, 1985.

————. *The Mechanisms of Governance*. Oxford: Oxford University Press, 1996.

Winship, C. and R.D. Mare. "Regression Models with Ordinal Variables". *American Sociological Review* 49, no. 4 (1984): 512–25.

World Bank. *The East Asian Miracle: Economic Growth and Public Policy*. New York: Oxford University Press, 1993.

————. *Decentralization and Governance: Does Decentralization Improve Public Service Delivery?* PREM Notes no. 51. Washington D.C.: Poverty Reduction and Economic Management Network, 2001.

————. *Decentralizing Indonesia: A Regional Public Expenditure Review*. Jakarta: East Asia Poverty Reduction and Economic Management Unit, 2003.

Yin, R.K. *Case Study Research: Design and Methods*. 3rd ed. Thousand Oaks, California: Sage Publications, 2003.

10
Insecurity and Business Development in Rural Indonesia

Jonathan Haughton and John M. MacDougall

1. Introduction

Anecdotes abound about day-to-day insecurity in Indonesia, and the negative effects of this insecurity on businesses. John MacDougall (2003) writes, "contemporary Jakarta is home to hundreds of localized ethnic gangs", but "organized crime ventures are not new to Jakarta". In a highly-publicised case, the world's largest retailer, Wal-Mart, pulled out of Indonesia in 1998, in large part because one of its two stores was looted and torched. And a study of truck drivers plying the road between Medan and Banda Aceh found that as recently as early 2006 they were forced to pay bribes averaging Rp 687,000 (US$74) per round trip (BRR 2006).

Suggestive as they may be, it is not obvious that the anecdotes reflect widespread insecurity. So the first task of this chapter is to sift through the available evidence in order to answer a simple question: how widespread is insecurity in Indonesia, and specifically in rural Indonesia, which has traditionally been viewed as more peaceful and safer than the urban areas.

Evidence of widespread insecurity is not, per se, sufficient to make the case that business development has been stunted as a result. By international standards the murder and incarceration rates in the United States are high, but they have not prevented the United States from achieving affluence and sustained economic growth. Thus the second task of this chapter is to determine the extent to which violence, or the threat of violence, limits business development.

Based on the empirical findings, we are then in a position to discuss the nature of insecurity in Indonesia — who are the actors, what lies at the root of the violence insofar as it affects business, and who is (or should be) in a position to do something about it.

2. How Widespread is Insecurity in Indonesia?

Internationally-published statistics on crime rates show Indonesia to be an exceptionally safe country, as Table 10.1 illustrates. If they are to be believed, the numbers show that over the period 1998–2000, the murder rate in the United States (at 57 per million population) was almost six times as high as in Indonesia, and the rate of assaults was 72 times higher.

Table 10.1
Crime Rates, 1998–2000

	Indonesia	*United States*
Homicides per million population	10	57
Assaults per million population	45	3,240
Robberies per million population	310	

Source: United Nations Office on Drugs and Crime (2006).

These numbers are not credible. They are based on incidents reported by the police, and seriously under-report actual events, as the evidence marshalled below shows.

To solve the problem of under-reporting, the United Nations in 2001 assembled a data set tracking every incident of collective violence between 1990 and 2001 as reported in two major Jakarta news sources (*Antara* and *Kompas*). This gave a total of 4,662 deaths over the 11-year period covered by the UNSFIR numbers. These numbers also understated the problem, in part because national-level publications were censored during much of this period, and also because not every local conflict was considered newsworthy at the national level. A second data set was then assembled (UNSFIR-2) using provincial-level newspaper sources and found more than twice as many deaths, i.e. a total of 10,402 deaths over the same period.

These numbers appear to be too low. In 2003 the Government of Indonesia included a module on conflict in its PODES (*Potensi Desa*) survey, which is based mainly on reports by the elected officials in the country's more than 69,000 villages and urban wards. The key findings were that in 2002, conflict had been experienced in 7.2 per cent of localities, resulting in property damage of Rp 771 billion (US$91 million) and 4,869 deaths — a rate of 22 deaths per million of population (Barron and Sharpe 2005, p. 7). Unlike the UNSFIR data, the PODES numbers showed that conflict is widespread throughout the country, and is not concentrated in a handful of provinces or regencies.

Even these numbers are too small. Barron and Sharpe (2005) gathered data from local newspapers in a total of fourteen districts in the provinces of East Java and East Nusa Tenggara (NTT). They were able to compare the number of deaths in these districts (277 deaths in 2001–03) with those reported by PODES (105 deaths) and UNSFIR-2 (45 deaths). They found 2.6 times as many deaths as reported by PODES; if this proportion applies to the whole country, then there may have been as many as 12,659 deaths in 2002 (p. 15), or 58 deaths per million population.

Barron and Sharpe include deaths that are the result of individual versus individual conflicts (43 per cent of their total), while the UNSFIR data cover "group" conflicts only. Even so they make a compelling case that "the more local the news source used, the more accurate the picture of conflict given" (p. 13). They also find that very few of the cases, even where someone is killed, go to court.

In East Java most of the violent incidents were related to vigilantism or retribution, with about 10 per cent of the cases involving issues related to resources or "administration", while in NTT conflicts over land (particularly communal land) were relatively frequent (26 per cent of the total), as were disputes related to "administration". About four-fifths of the cases of violent conflict were handled by the police, rather than by local groups or individual citizens.

In sum, Indonesia, including rural Indonesia, is far less internally peaceful than the international statistics would lead one to believe. The homicide rate, at least, appears to be comparable to that of the United States.

3. Is Insecurity Rising?

There is some evidence that the level of insecurity rose rapidly in the last years of the New Order regime, peaked in 2000, and has fallen sharply since then. Figure 10.1 illustrates this, showing the number of incidents of social violence

Figure 10.1
Incidents of Social Violence in Indonesia, 1990–2003

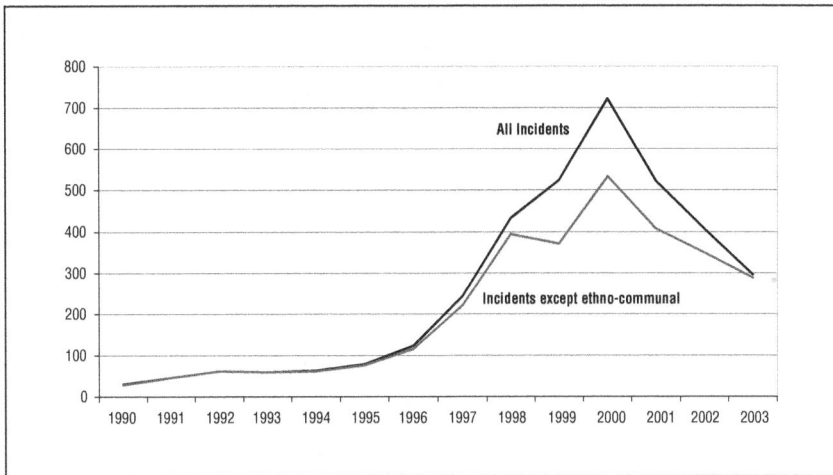

Source: UNSFIR-2.

that were recorded for 1990–2003 (using UNSFIR-2). If the degree of under-reporting did not change over time, then this graph may be used to show the trend, if not the absolute level, of violent incidents in Indonesia.

Some additional evidence on this issue comes from the National Economic and Social Survey (SUSENAS) of 2000, which asked respondents whether, over the previous three years, their level of security from peace and order (*Rasa aman dari gangguan kamtibmas*) had improved or worsened. Of the 59,203 responses, 19.6 per cent said that the security situation was "better" or "much better" while 4.2 per cent said it was "worse" or "much worse".[1]

The SUSENAS data show that the perception of change in the security situation varied somewhat from area to area, but was unrelated to the level of household expenditure. There were minor differences in the perception of the extent to which the security situation had changed, depending on the employment status of the household: households that ran informal businesses were slightly less upbeat, while those with at least one employee were slightly more likely to report an improvement in the security situation, but as Table 10.2 shows, the differences were very slight. The table also shows that rural households were somewhat more likely than urban households to report an improvement in the security situation.

Table 10.2

Perceived Change in Security Situation over the Three Years up to 2000

	Self-employed	Self-employed with part-time employees	Self-employed with full-time employees	Employees	Unpaid employees	Urban	Rural
Score	4.054	4.047	4.054	4.064	4.049	4.052	4.054
p-value	0.64	0.00	0.02	0.00	0.00		0.00

Note: Score varies from 1 (security situation is much worse) to 6 (security situation is much better). The p-value refers to the comparison between the given category (e.g. households where at least one person is an employee) and the rest of the sample (e.g. no household member is an employee) based on a chi-square test. There are 59,142 valid observations. The results are not weighted.

Source: SUSENAS (2000).

A separate part of the SUSENAS questionnaire asked whether respondents faced a problem with teenagers congregating (6.3 per cent said yes), teenage drunkenness (6.7 per cent said yes), and drugs (2.3 per cent said yes). These are relatively modest levels of exposure to social problems of this nature.

4. The Emergence of a New Security Regime

The apparent rise, and subsequent fall, in the crime rate requires an explanation. Soeharto's New Order (1965–98) was characterized by the centralization of all security, economic, and political/bureaucratic decisions. Internal security was the preserve of the military, which had an elaborate territorial command structure; prior to 1999, the police had the same basic training as the army, and its officers graduated from the national military academy. To maintain control over the internal movement of goods and people, eighty ports were closed in the late 1970s, concentrating commerce through just a handful of main harbours.[2] District-based authorities were appointed rather than elected, and many of the local leaders were recruited from the army. Youth militias, which supported GOLKAR's political campaigns and helped enforce "land clearance", were provided with funds and some turf, under the umbrella of the military.

The economic crisis of 1997–98 severely damaged this system of "policed capitalism". The crisis created sudden high unemployment, inter-regional migration, social unrest and conflict, and was followed by several years of political and institutional transition under four administrations. As the security situation deteriorated, provincial elites demanded greater decentralization, and by late 1998 a multi-party electoral system had been put in place. Local militias, freed from army coordination, were increasingly employed by local elected officials to enforce local regulations; they also filled part of the security vacuum that was left when, in 1999, the role of the armed forces (TNI) was reduced to defence and the police force (POLRI) found itself overwhelmed.

From 1999 to 2003, political parties (as opposed to politicians) were ascendant, under an electoral system where the public voted for a political party, and the party subsequently chose who would fill the seats. This favoured local leaders who could mobilize local militias and their supporting populations. In some parts of the country the development of community-security militias, ostensibly geared towards countering crime, but with strong links with a political party, was extraordinary. John MacDougall (2007) writes that in reaction to widespread theft (especially of motorbikes) in Lombok, "starting in 1998", local security groups (*pam swarkarsa*) "absorbed roughly 25 per cent of Lombok's men for the sole purpose of hunting down the island's thieves". In other areas this period saw an increase in gangsterism (*premanism*), which is often viewed with some ambivalence (as with Robin Hood).

A key institutional change occurred in 2004, when the rules were altered so that voters would elect individuals rather than vote for parties. This allowed Soesilo Bambang Yudhoyono to be elected president despite coming from a totally new and undefined party (Partai Demokrat), and despite the fact that the GOLKAR Party won a majority in most provincial legislatures. One of the unexpected effects, both of the institutional change and of the election of President Yudhoyono, is that gangs and paramilitaries are now on the wane. Local leaders appeal directly to the people who might elect them, and do not have to bargain with (or bully) local legislatures. General Sutanto, the president's choice to head the police, is no friend of civilian militias or the back door politics they espouse.

Thus a new security order is emerging, even if it is still a work in progress (International Crisis Group 2004). At the top of the hierarchy are the police, who are now independent of (and less lethal than) the military. Many police augment their modest salaries with bribes and kickbacks, but this does at least ensure that motorcyclists wear helmets. There are still occasional turf battles with the military.

At the next rung are the registered security guards (*satpam*), believed to number about 250,000.[3] They receive four weeks of formal training by the police, and although their job is typically to protect businesses, they constitute a security presence of some importance. They are not a unified group, and so do not represent a threat to the security order.

The office of every *bupati* (district), mayor, and governor has guards (Tramtib and Satpolpp) who are paid by the day, but are nonetheless civil servants. Their job is to enforce regional regulations and ordinances passed by local legislatures, and directives issued by *bupati*, mayors, and governors. In Jakarta, the Tramtib are widely hated by the city's poor because of the coarse and sometimes brutal methods they employ to clear squatters from properties, arrest sex workers, and destroy unlicensed businesses around market areas. They are rarely used, however, to terrorize citizens with rightful claims to business or property.

Although their role is declining, the tradition of people's militias remains alive. The *pam swakarsa* often start out as crime fighters, but all too easily turn to protection rackets and extortion. Most recently they have tried to skim the rent on migrant labour contracts; and to control who gets hired by businesses (in order to extract payments from potential employees).

At one side the military remains a diminished, if still substantial, presence. It continues to operate numerous companies, but its officers may take temporary leave in order to engage in politics, which provides a productive outlet for the more ambitious among them.

After the massacres of 1965, the Soeharto New Order brought order and security for three decades. But its centralized nature also made it vulnerable once the political and economic sands shifted in 1997, after which point is ceased to be viable. The transitional period that followed, with rising conflict and strife, is now over, and a new security order has emerged that, while far from perfect, does appear to be sustainable. This is widely understood, which helps explain why, when they were surveyed in late 2005, most rural businesses were not particularly concerned about security issues, as the evidence marshalled in the next section shows.

5. Business Perceptions of Insecurity

In late 2005, the Rural Investment Climate (RICS) project undertook a survey of 2,520 household enterprises in six selected *kabupaten* (districts) in rural Indonesia. The survey collected a wide array of information about enterprise activities, including turnover, profit, costs, and employment. It also asked the operators to indicate for each of fifty-seven items — such as the cost of electricity, the quality of local roads, corruption, and so on — whether the item was not a problem (0), a minor problem (1), somewhat of a problem (2) or a major problem (3). The answers for existing firms are summarized in column 1 of Table 10.3, and are based on weighted averages.[4]

By this measure, the major obstacle to an enterprise's operations and growth is "financial services", which essentially measures access to finance and received a score of 0.96. The next most serious obstacles were access to markets (0.76), transportation (0.70), and "government" (0.67). This latter may be broken down into the parts shown near the bottom of Table 10.3, and this exercise shows that uncertain economic policy (0.78), corruption (0.65) and restrictive laws and regulations (0.59) are all seen as relatively serious obstacles to business growth and development.

The survey results also show that safety concerns rank near the bottom. Most business people do not view "criminality, theft and lawlessness" as a major concern (score of 0.21), while "conflict and social friction" (0.14) is seen as one of the least important obstacles faced by firms.

5.1. Security and Existing Enterprises

The main difficulty with these numbers is that they do not give a good sense of whether the obstacle is important or not. Thus land use regulations

Table 10.3
Weighted Measures of the Four Main Obstacles to the Enterprise's Operations and/or Growth: Existing Firms

	Existing enterprise		Firm Never Created	Firm No Longer in Operation
	Obstacle? Scale: 0 (not a problem) – 3 (major problem) (1)	Main obstacle % (2)	Main obstacle % (3)	Main obstacle % (4)
A Electricity	0.48	9.8	3.4	1.8
B Telecommunications	0.28	2.8	2.0	0.0
C Water	0.37	3.1	1.0	0.0
D Postal Service	0.21	0.1	0.1	0.0
E Transportation	0.70	14.6	8.5	6.7
F Financial Services	0.96	31.3	52.3	45.5
G Marketing	0.76	19.3	16.2	25.9
H Government	0.67	10.1	1.8	7.1
I Security	0.18	1.5	2.1	3.6
J Technology	0.22	0.8	1.0	7.6
K Registration & Permits	0.32	1.2	1.4	0.9
L Taxation	0.36	2.7	0.8	0.0
M Labour Issues	0.26	1.0	1.6	0.9
N Land	0.19	0.9	4.2	0.0
O Non-Agricultural Product Trade Policy	0.26	0.3	1.8	0.0
P Environmental Policy	0.26	0.5	1.8	0.1
Total	0.44	100.0	100.0	100.1
Memo				
H1 Corruption	0.65	3.8		3.6
H2 Uncertain Economic Policy	0.78	5.2		0.0
H3 Restrictive Laws and Regulations	0.59	1.1		3.6
I1 Criminality, Theft and Lawlessness	0.21	1.3		3.6
I2 Conflict and Social Friction	0.14	0.3		0.0
Sample size	2,002	2,002	88	17

Note: For the method used to construct the measures see the accompanying text. The results in column (1) use enterprise weights.

might be restrictive, for instance, but if most firms do not have to worry about land, then this restriction is unlikely to be very damaging. This difficulty may be avoided by using the answers to another question in the RICS (question 13.A), which asked respondents to list up to four main obstacles and then to attach weights to each. In about half of the cases the weights add up to 100 per cent; in most other cases they add up to less than this — presumably there are obstacles other than the four listed, or those listed have just modest effects.

Our procedure is straightforward. First, for households whose weights summed to more than 100 (!) we recomputed the weights so they summed to 100. Then we measured the proportion of all weights that were assigned to concerns about electricity, government, land, and the like. The results for the 2,002 enterprises for which there were usable responses are shown in the second column in Table 10.3, and they are striking; fuller details are shown in Appendix Table 10.A. Almost a third of the concerns about the obstacles faced by firms are directed at financial services (i.e. access to credit), with significant concerns about access to markets (19 per cent), transportation (15 per cent), government policies and corruption (10 per cent), and the price and reliability of electricity (10 per cent). Security issues take a back seat, accounting for just 1.5 per cent of the weighted total of all concerns about obstacles to firm development.

It thus appears that security concerns are near the bottom of the list for most enterprises. However, these numbers refer to surviving firms only, and so do not represent the whole story, because it is quite possible that the households most affected by a lack of security either did not create enterprises in the first place, or created firms that have now gone out of business. We now consider these cases.

5.2. Security and Enterprises Never Created

There were just eighty-eight responses to a question (12.B in Module A) that collected information from households that had wanted to set up an enterprise but were deterred from doing so for one reason or another. It is of interest to ask what the key obstacles to creating a business are, as perceived by these households.

The results are shown in Table 10.3, column 3, and again are based on the weighted averages of the four main obstacles that were cited as standing in the way of starting a business. In this case, financial services and marketing accounted for over half of the (weighted) responses.

Although security is mentioned as a top-four concern in just 2.1 per cent of cases, this is substantially higher than the proportion (1.5 per cent) found for existing firms. There is thus a very slight suggestion that some firms may have been frightened out of coming into existence.

The governance variable (1.8 per cent) was far less important for firms that were not created than for firms that are currently operating (10.1 per cent), although the results may be somewhat influenced by the design of the question, which was not broken down in as much detail for the case of firms that were never created. One might speculate, however, that would-be entrepreneurs underestimate the problems of corruption and uncertain government regulation, while those who run actual enterprises are keenly aware of these issues.

5.3. Security and Failed Enterprises

With only seventeen households responding to the questions about the four main obstacles faced by their now-defunct businesses, it would be unwise to put much weight on the results. However, for what they are worth, they are shown in the last column in Table 10.3. Problems related to government were mentioned 7.1 per cent of the time, which is comparable to the value of 10.1 per cent found for those running existing firms. Insecurity, in the form of criminality, theft, and lawlessness, was also a factor of negligible importance (3.6 per cent).

Yet the most striking feature of Table 10.3 is its consistency. Whether a firm is currently operating, or whether a firm has failed or not been willed into existence, the dominant obstacles to growth are seen as access to finance and access to markets. By comparison, concerns about security, and even about government (including corruption, and uncertain or restrictive rules) are of relatively minor importance.

5.4. Disaggregating the Responses

It is possible that the aggregate responses, presented in the previous section, hide important differences in the perception of safety and corruption by location or type of firm. Are security problems mainly urban? Do they affect partnerships more than single proprietors? Are there regional differences?

The results set out in Table 10.4 capture the flavour of this analysis, while the remaining results are to be found in Appendix Tables 10.B1, 10.B2, and 10.B3. For each category (e.g. urban, rural) and for each of the five listed obstacles of interest (government corruption, uncertain economic policy, restrictive laws and regulations, security/criminality, and security/social

Table 10.4
Breakdown of Government and Security Obstacles to Enterprise Development by Urban/Rural and Ownership

	Urban	Rural	Total	Proprietor	Partnership	Other	Total
Government: corruption							
A problem? (0=no, 3=major)	0.58	0.69	0.65	0.65	0.47	0.85	0.64
% saying it is a major problem	16%	16%	16%	16%	11%	27%	16%
Number of observations	892	1,478	2,370	2,232	76	31	2,341
p value, Chi-square test			0.004				0.000
Government: Uncertain economic policy							
A problem? (0=no, 3=major)	0.66	0.85	0.78	0.78	0.75	0.78	0.78
% saying it is a major problem	15%	22%	19%	20%	12%	24%	19%
Number of observations	898	1,462	2,360	2,221	76	31	2,331
p value, Chi-square test			0.317				0.000
Government: restrictive laws & regulations							
A problem? (0=no, 3=major)	0.46	0.66	0.59	0.59	0.48	0.77	0.59
% saying it is a major problem	9%	14%	12%	12%	10%	24%	12%
Number of observations	889	1,461	2,350	2,212	76	31	2,321
p value, Chi-square test			0.026				0.000
Safety: criminality, theft & lawlessness							
A problem? (0=no, 3=major)	0.21	0.21	0.21	0.2	0.22	1.31	0.21
% saying it is a major problem	4%	3%	3%	3%	4%	37%	3%
Number of observations	904	1,482	2,386	2,245	78	32	2,357
p value, Chi-square test			0.002				0.004
Safety: conflicts and social friction							
A problem? (0=no, 3=major)	0.09	0.18	0.14	0.13	0.2	0.92	0.15
% saying it is a major problem	1%	1%	1%	1%	5%	6%	1%
Number of observations	896	1,462	2,358	2,219	76	31	2,329
p value, Chi-square test	0.023	0.000					

Note: The p-values are derived from a Chi-square test of whether there is a difference in the value of the "A problem?" variable between the groups shown (e.g. urban vs. rural); a p-value below 0.1 means that there is at least a 90 per cent probability that there is indeed a difference between the two groups.
Source: RICS (2005).

conflicts), we present an index that measures whether the obstacle is a problem (0 = no, 3 = major problem), the percentage of respondents saying that it is a major problem, the number of observations, and the p-value from a Chi-square test. A low value of the p-value — less than 0.1 is conventionally taken to be "low" — indicates that there is a statistically significant difference in the index across the groups in question.

Approximately five-eighths of the respondents to the RICS lived in rural areas. The first three data columns of Table 10.4 show that for existing firms, rural areas are more likely than urban areas to perceive corruption, uncertain economic policy, and restrictive rules as obstacles to firm growth, but the differences are not very large. The right-hand side of Table 10.4 shows that partnerships are less concerned about government and more concerned about security than are single proprietors.

Although corruption is found in all districts surveyed (see Appendix Table 10.B1), there are marked differences across the *kabupaten* surveyed, with high levels of perceived corruption and uncertainty in Labuhan Batu and Badung, and low levels in Malang and Kutai. The districts with high government obstacles were generally also those with higher levels of concern about security; this is consistent with the idea that areas with a poorly-led or venal police force (high corruption) might also be areas with more lawlessness.

It is widely believed that the mining sector is particularly vulnerable to corruption, and the numbers confirm this (see Appendix Table 10.B2), with 37 per cent of respondents in that sector saying that corruption is a major problem and 48 per cent indicating that uncertain economic policy represents an obstacle. On the other hand, mining firms are not particularly worried about security, in contrast to the transportation sector, where 10 per cent of firms reported that criminality, theft, and lawlessness are a major problem. This too is in line with the widely-held view that transportation firms are vulnerable to protection rackets and concerned about theft and the safety of the goods and passengers they carry.

Corruption and uncertain economic policy are less serious for local firms than for branches of firms headquartered outside the district (see Appendix Table 10.B3). This is not unexpected: "outside" firms are often seen as ripe for plucking, while firms that are local to an area may have social and other links that help protect them from predators.

6. Does Insecurity Affect Business?

The results of the RICS are in line with those found by a number of other researchers, which provides some useful validation for our results.

The Regional Autonomy Watch (*Komite Pemantauan Pelaksanaan Otonomi Daerah*, or KPPOD) has, since 2002, undertaken a series of studies that rate towns (*kota*) and regencies (*kabupaten*) based on the perception of their attractiveness to business. The most recent report refers to 2004, and rates 214 of the country's 440 *kota* and *kabupaten* based on data on 42 variables. Fifteen of the variables use data from secondary sources — for instance, wage rates from BPS — while the remainder are largely based on a field survey of business people. The overall ratings are based on an index that uses a complex weighting mechanism.

For our purposes, the most interesting feature of the KPPOD surveys is that they consistently collected data on the perceptions of a number of variables related to security, as detailed in Table 10.5.

The actual scores for each of these variables for 2002 and 2004 are shown in Table 10.6, along with the maximum possible values for each score; higher scores are "good" (i.e. they represent less social conflict or fewer strikes, etc.). A very clear pattern emerges: over that two-year period there was a marked improvement in political stability and a reduction in social conflict, including strikes. However, businesses appear to have perceived a worsening in their own security, including the safety in the neighbourhoods where they operated. The 2003 KPPOD report on the business environment comments:

> Most business people in Indonesia maintain that the socio-political conditions in their operating regions — security conditions, social conflicts (inter-village conflicts, ethnic wars, etc.), the political environment and strikes — are conducive to investment. ... Large companies tend to be more exposed than their smaller counterparts to the effects of the socio-political conditions in their operating areas. (p. 85)

Table 10.5
Security Variables Used in KPPOD Surveys

Variable	Variable	Weight in overall index (%)
Extortion/Criminal activity	Pungli di Luar Birokrasi	1.86
Political stability	Stabilitas Politik	2.86
Social conflict	Konflik Masyarakat	1.82
Strikes	Unjuk Rasa	1.04
Security in area near business	Gangguan Masyarakat	3.12
Business security	Gangguan Usaha	5.20
Speed of response of security officer	Kecapatan Aparat	7.28

Table 10.6
Scores for KPPOD Variables, 2002 and 2004

Variable	Score, 2002	Score, 2004	% improvement in score	Maximum possible score
Extortion/Criminal activity	0.0030	0.0036	+20	0.0099
Political stability	0.0059	0.0112	+90	0.0116
Social conflict	0.0040	0.0089	+123	0.0095
Strikes	0.0022	0.0044	+100	0.0049
Security in area near business	0.0071	0.0043	−39	0.008
Business security	0.0116	0.0084	−28	0.0254
Speed of response of security officer	0.0130	0.0112	−14	0.0214

Note: A higher value of the score represents an improvement. The numbers are unweighted averages of the 134 *kota* and *kabupaten* for which comparable data were available both for 2002 and 2004.
Source: KPPOD (2005).

7. Security, Extortion and Corruption

When insecurity is widespread, firms will be reluctant to expand, because their investments are vulnerable and their profits are squeezed. There are several ways in which violence, actual or latent, can deter investment.

The simplest is theft. If thieves are not caught, or not even pursued, then firms will either have to sustain losses from theft or pay more for their own security. However, the RICS data from 2005 find that the cost of replacing stolen goods comes to less than 0.1 per cent of business costs.

A second source of vulnerability, for businesses, is from gangsters (*preman*), who frequently operate protection rackets and extort payments from transportation companies, retailers, and others. They may also pressure newly-hired workers to pay a fee. There is some evidence that *premanism* weighs most heavily on medium-sized enterprises; small firms are not worth troubling, and large firms have more ability to resist pressure from thugs.

Most businesses in Indonesia pay bribes and make other "unofficial" payments. However, it is difficult to identify which payments are the result of actual, or implicit, violence, and which are paid to speed the way for permits or other favours from officials (such as low tax bills) that might actually reduce the cost of doing business. With this in mind, it is helpful to summarize the main points in the literature.

Ari Kuncoro (2004) reports on the results of a survey of businesses in Indonesia that was undertaken between September 2001 and July 2002. Out of 1,808 firms interviewed, 1,333 (74 per cent) reported paying bribes in 2001. For those firms that paid bribes, the (unweighted) average was 10.8 per cent of production costs, which can be broken down into 8.2 per cent for large firms, 10.4 per cent for small firms, and 11.6 per cent for small-medium firms. Among firms that reported paying them, bribes were higher in urban areas (11.8 per cent of costs) than rural areas (10.3 per cent). In some areas the reported "bribe rates" were remarkably high, exceeding 15 per cent in Jakarta, in contrast to just 4 per cent in Yogyakarta.

These results are in line with the findings of the KPPOD surveys. The 2003 KPPOD report found that 85 per cent of firms acknowledge that they pay illegal charges on top of official fees in order to obtain services from local government staff, and that these charges amounted to 61 per cent of the official fees paid. The report also notes that, "typically, 2 per cent of a company's total operating expenditure consists of illegal levies that have to be paid to local government officials, security officers, community groups, youth groups, mass organizations, gangsters and others. 7.3 per cent of respondents say that illegal levies account for as much as 8 per cent to 10 per cent of their operating costs" (p. 86).

It is clear that for many firms, these charges are not voluntary. As the 2003 KPPOD report put it, "illegal fees in the judicial process are seen as the most onerous (13.1 per cent of respondents), followed by illegal fees imposed by security officers (11.5 per cent), extortion by community groups (8.5 per cent), and extortion by gangsters (6.1 per cent)" (p. 86). Such levies are most prevalent among companies operating in the forestry, agri-industry, and mining sectors (p. 86).

Additional evidence comes from a report of businesses operating in five provinces (North Sumatra, West Java, East Java, Bali, and South Sulawesi) in the years up to 2002. The report notes (see Chapter 6) that in some areas, most notably North Sumatra, *premanism* is a serious constraint on the further development of medium-scale businesses. According to the report, the amounts paid directly in protection money are typically modest, representing less than a quarter of all "informal" payments among firms studied (which in turn came to 9 per cent of production costs). However, this understates the damage; forced payments also include "environmental" contributions, which represent nearly 30 per cent of informal collections; the payments are often loosely related to a firm's ability to pay, and so are very burdensome for some firms; and the "collections become disruptive in the matter of comfort in doing business" (see Chapter 6).

Thugs are not the only ones collecting from firms. A recent remarkable book published by the Partnership for Governance Reform in Indonesia

Table 10.7
Tax Payments and "Unofficial Payments" by
Firms, Indonesia 2005

	All firms		Firms reporting making unofficial payments	
	Total payments	*of which "unofficial" payments*	*Total payments*	*of which "unofficial" payments*
	(thousands of Rupiah)			
Tax payments				
Central government	198.0	0.001	817.5	0.007
Provincial government	128.7	0.004	338.3	0.040
District government	108.9	10.1	228.8	90.8
Other	71.8	59.7	562.1	535.6
of which:				
Security		9.7		86.7
Gangsters (preman)		21.1		189.8
Village officials		28.9		259.1
Licence payments		0.9		8.2
Total	507.4	70.7	1,946.7	634.6
Sales	187,799		164,045	
Estimated profit	25,977		34,738	
	(percentages)			
Unofficial payments as % of				
Sales	0.04		0.39	
Estimated profits	0.27		1.83	
Legitimate tax payments	16.20		48.37	
	(numbers)			
Observations (unweighted)	2,520		532	

Source: RICS (2005).

entitled *POLRI and Corruption Issues* (c. 2005) explains the ways in which the police extract payments from businesses and citizens, based on the findings of 132 theses written by students at the Police College. Most of the scams involve collusion between the police and the business or citizen to reduce tax payments, or avoid going to court on a criminal or drug matter. It is entirely possible that the net effect is to reduce the cost of doing business, relative to a benchmark of an honest police force and judiciary, although this is an issue that calls for further investigation.

In light of these other reports, it is surprising that the RICS found such a low level of bribery. Just 21 per cent of firms (or 11 per cent if sample weights are used) reported paying "unofficial" fees to tax or other officials or payoffs to *preman*. And the amounts were, on average, small, equivalent to

0.27 per cent of profits for all firms (or 1.83 per cent of profits for those firms that reported paying bribes), as Table 10.7 shows. On the other hand these "unofficial" payments were substantial when compared to legitimate tax payments, equivalent to 16 per cent of the tax bill for all firms, or 48 per cent for bribe-paying firms.

8. Security and Business Performance

Our fundamental interest is in the effect of various "obstacles", including insecurity, on business performance. The RICS data do not have an objective measure of insecurity, but there are a number of subjective measures that will serve adequately.

Two issues then arise. First, how is one to measure business performance? And second, how might one test for the presence of a link between insecurity and performance?

Most economists' preferred measure of a firm's success is its (economic) profit relative to sales or assets; or the growth of this measure over time. The biggest problem with profit-based measures is that it is difficult to measure profit accurately, as it is a residual obtained by subtracting cost from revenue. Moreover, profit is rarely measured in the way that an economist would prefer, using a definition of costs that includes the opportunity cost of assets and inputs that is broader than the definition typically used by accountants.

A simpler measure of success is the current size of a firm, as measured by sales or employment or costs. This is not theoretically as satisfactory — a firm with a huge turnover might have no profit, which hardly qualifies as success — but it does moderate the measurement problems. Alternatively one might measure success as the growth in the real value of a firm's sales or costs or assets.

The standard technique for testing for links between variables is regression analysis; a regression of performance on a set of variables, including a measure of the perception of insecurity, for instance, would in principle allow one to isolate the effect of insecurity, holding all other influences constant. This is the approach we take here, but it does have a serious limitation: where does causality begin? If insecurity and corruption vary in intensity across the country in a random manner, then it is indeed legitimate to use regression analysis to identify their effects, and we would expect higher levels of (say) corruption to be associated with slower firm growth and lower output. But suppose, not implausibly, that fast-growing or rich firms attract the attention of the corrupt, who want to appropriate some of the "rent" inherent in the enterprise, then higher levels of corruption might be correlated with faster firm growth and higher output! In principle this problem could be solved using instrumental variable techniques, but only in the (unlikely) event that one could find variables that influence the level of corruption while not affecting firm performance.

The key results from estimates of six different regression equations are presented in Table 10.8. The only differences between the regressions are the measures of firm performance that are used as the dependent variables. There are 32 regressors, including 6 sectoral dummy variables, 8 measures of obstacles (electricity, post and telecommunications, and so on), and 5 district dummy variables, but only the coefficients on the years of education of the manager, the mining sector dummy variable, and the government obstacles variable are reported in the table (although the full estimates for the sales equation are given in Appendix Table 10.C). The "government obstacles" variable averages the reported level of concern about the government variables (corruption, changes in laws and regulations, restrictions) and the security variables (lawlessness, social conflicts); a higher value of this variable implies a bigger problem. If the simple regression model holds, then we would expect to see a negative sign on the government obstacles coefficient.

Table 10.8
Basic Regression Results

Dependent variable:	Ln(sales)	Ln(costs)	Ln(profit/ sales)	Sales growth		Profit growth
				Full sample	Firms with positive growth	
Adjusted R²	0.204	0.250	0.133	0.011	0.028	0.007
Observations	1,770	1,754	1,701	1,312	670	1,341
Govt. obstacles						
coefficient	0.114	0.115	0.029	−777	−1,075	−3.167
p-value	0.086	0.120	0.661	0.451	0.594	0.660
Years education						
coefficient	0.097	0.120	−0.037	140.0	268.7	1.693
p-value	0.000	0.000	0.002	0.350	0.373	0.107
Mining sector						
coefficient	0.525	1.011	−1.147	−5,322	−8,074	−18.77
p-value	0.158	0.017	0.002	0.329	0.635	0.626

Notes: Ln(sales): log of the value of sales.
Ln(costs): log of the firm's costs.
Ln(profit/sales): log of profit rate.
Sales growth: Percentage, based on full sample, or on sample with positive growth rate.
Profit growth: Percentage.

The results are mixed. None of the estimated equations fits very well, as reflected in the relatively modest values for R^2, so there are other important influences on firm performance, possibly unobservable, that have not been included here. The "government obstacles" variable is statistically significant only in the equation where the dependent variable is the log of sales, and here it has the "wrong" sign. Managers with more education typically perform better. And the mining sector has higher sales and costs than the "other" sector of the economy, but slower growth and profits. In sum, when we control for the effects of other potentially important influences using regression, there is no evidence that insecurity has a measurable negative effect on firm performance, however measured.

9. Conclusion

Insecurity in Indonesia, as measured by murder rates, is comparable to that of the United States, and far higher than portrayed in standard international statistical comparisons. Furthermore, this insecurity is found throughout the country, and not just in large urban centres.

Insecurity rose sharply after 1997 as the New Order regime collapsed and was followed by a period of political uncertainty and economic decline. From 2000 onwards the economy began to recover and the political chaos receded, and Indonesia has now emerged with a more robust and sustainable political system and solid economic growth.

The Rural Investment Climate Survey was undertaken in late 2005, covering 2,520 household enterprises in six rural districts (*kabupaten*). This dataset allows one to address the question of the extent to which insecurity acts as a brake on business opportunities and expansion.

The answer is clear: concerns about safety — whether criminality, theft and lawlessness, or conflict and social friction — rank near the bottom of the list of perceived challenges faced by current (or potential, or former) business people. This by no means implies that security issues are irrelevant or that they never intrude, but for most small rural enterprises — or at least those surveyed — there are other more pressing concerns.

One of the most important of those concerns is "government", including corruption, uncertainty in economic policies, and restrictive laws and regulations. This represents insecurity of a different sort, and appears to be particularly important in the mining sector (where corruption and uncertain economic policy are seen as major problems) and in transportation. This latter is the one sector where "criminality, theft and lawlessness" are reported to be serious, as trucks and buses are especially vulnerable to extortion.

To what extent does insecurity, whether physical or under cover of government staff and policies, affect enterprise performance? Although hard to answer definitively on the basis of a survey of just six districts, the tentative answer seems to be: "not much". Regressions of a variety of measures of firm performance — sales, profit, growth, employment — on a range of variables, including measures of insecurity, found essentially no effects.

Is this plausible? After all, several other studies, not necessarily confined to rural Indonesia, have documented widespread corruption and policy uncertainty (e.g. KPPOD 2003 and 2004, Kuncora 2004), or set out the mechanisms by which the police extract payments from the public (*POLRI and Corruption Issues*, c. 2005).

It is entirely possible that, from the perspective of a firm, corruption might sometimes be helpful if, for instance, it amounts to a cheap way to evade taxes or evict squatters or get access to land or subsidies or permits. The RICS data do not allow one to distinguish between cost-lowering and cost-raising insecurity.

Apart from the unimportance of insecurity, the other real surprise in the RICS data is how small reported "unofficial" payments (including those made to *preman*) are, and what a small fraction of rural households report paying them (just 11 per cent of enterprises, on a weighted basis). One can only speculate that most such firms are too small and insignificant to be targets, or are well-enough integrated into their communities to be protected.

One aspect of the RICS results is worth noting: the level of concern about corruption and "uncertain" government policy varies sharply from one *kabupaten* to the next.

This may be the most productive direction for efforts to reduce insecurity and corruption: identify those areas where it is particularly strong, and make a concerted effort to bring it under control. This would require resources — perhaps a set of anti-corruption investigative teams that would focus on a limited number of districts, or the strengthening of local investigative capacity, along with support and training for a vigorous local press.

As the security situation has improved, investor confidence has returned; in 1999, just 12 per cent of GDP was spent on investment, but by 2004 this had risen to 21 per cent, and as the new security order takes firmer root, the investment rate is likely to rise further.

APPENDIX 1
Detailed Breakdown of the Reported Main Obstacles to Enterprise Operations and Growth

Table 10.A
Weighted Measures of the Four Main Obstacles to the Enterprise's Operations and/or Growth (Full Breakdown)

Code	Obstacle to Enterprise Operation and/or Growth	Size of obstacle: 0 (not) – 3 (serious)	% reporting item as "main obstacle"
A1	Electricity: access	0.29	1.0
A2	Electricity: quality	0.52	5.1
A3	Electricity: cost	0.65	3.7
B1	Fixed line access (household phone)	0.28	1.4
B2	Fixed line quality (household phone)	0.25	0.2
B3	Fixed line cost (household phone)	0.28	0.4
B4	Cellular access	0.25	0.2
B5	Cellular quality	0.25	0.1
B6	Cellular cost	0.35	0.5
C1	Water: access	0.37	1.5
C2	Water: quality	0.39	1.1
C3	Water: cost	0.36	0.4
D1	Postal services: access	0.20	0.1
D2	Postal services: quality	0.21	0.0
D3	Postal services: cost	0.23	0.0
E1	Road access	0.63	3.5
E2	Road quality	0.81	4.6

continued on next page

Table 10.A — cont'd

Code	Obstacle to Enterprise Operation and/or Growth	Size of obstacle: 0 (not) – 3 (serious)	% reporting item as "main obstacle"
E3	Transportation cost	0.90	4.5
E4	Traffic	0.55	0.9
E5	Facilities to transport goods	0.60	1.1
F1	Possibility to borrow from family, friends or others	0.62	3.0
F2	Possibility to borrow from formal financial institutions	1.08	10.9
F3	Interest rates	1.09	7.2
F4	Complicated bank loan procedures (too many forms)	1.01	5.7
F5	Fear of not being able to pay loan installments	1.01	4.4
G1	Access to markets (distance and cost)	0.62	4.2
G2	Difficult to obtain information on your product's market	0.60	2.8
G3	Demand for goods and services produced	1.05	12.3
H1	Corruption	0.65	3.8
H2	Uncertain economic policy	0.78	5.2
H3	Restrictive laws and regulations	0.59	1.1
I1	Criminality, theft and lawlessness	0.21	1.3
I2	Conflict and social friction	0.14	0.3
J1	Technology: lack of training	0.24	0.5
J2	Technology: research costs	0.23	0.0
J3	Access to computers	0.22	0.1
J4	Access to information technology	0.21	0.1
J5	Quality of information and technology	0.24	0.0
K1	Time and cost of registering enterprises	0.31	0.3
K2	Time and cost of obtaining enterprise permits	0.32	0.5

K3	Complicated regulations to register enterprise and obtain permits	0.32	0.4
L1	High taxes	0.40	1.9
L2	Complicated regulations to calculate and pay taxes	0.36	0.3
L3	Unofficial levies	0.33	0.5
M1	Inflexible labour regulations in hiring and firing employees	0.17	0.1
M2	High labour costs as a result of government regulations	0.18	0.3
M3	Obtaining work permits for foreigners	0.17	0.0
M4	Lack of skilled labour		0.5
M5	Difficulties in hiring labour from outside region		0.1
N1	Land use regulations	0.26	0.3
N2	Obtaining construction permits	0.27	0.4
N3	Land ownership uncertainties	0.26	0.2
O1	Export and import regulations	0.19	0.2
O2	Customs and duties regulations	0.18	0.1
P1	Food safety regulations	0.26	0.1
P2	Environmental regulations	0.26	0.4
	Total		100.0

Note: Obstacles are rated from 0 (not an obstacle) to 3 (serious obstacle).
Source: RICS (2005).

APPENDIX 2

Disaggregation of Reported Government and Security Obstacles to Enterprise Operation and Growth

Table 10.B1
Government and Security Obstacles by *Kabupaten*

	Lab. Batu	Malang	Badung	Sumbawa	Kutai	Barru	Total
Government: Corruption							
A problem? (0=no, 3=major)	1.21	0.51	1.01	0.8	0.48	0.7	0.65
% saying it is a major problem	31%	13%	26%	22%	9%	17%	16%
Number of observations	279	1,428	164	194	272	33	2,370
p value, Chi-square test							0.000
Government: Uncertain economic policy							
A problem? (0=no, 3=major)	1.25	0.61	1.29	0.89	0.86	0.4	0.78
% saying it is a major problem	32%	14%	32%	24%	22%	8%	19%
Number of observations	279	1,424	163	189	273	32	2,360
p value, Chi-square test							0.000
Government: Restrictive laws & regulations							
A problem? (0=no, 3=major)	1	0.47	0.83	0.72	0.6	0.37	0.59
% saying it is a major problem	20%	9%	20%	19%	11%	7%	12%
Number of observations	278	1,422	163	183	272	32	2,350
p value, Chi-square test							0.000
Safety: Criminality, theft & lawlessness							
A problem? (0=no, 3=major)	0.24	0.15	0.59	0.35	0.19	0.23	0.21
% saying it is a major problem	3%	2%	15%	8%	3%	4%	3%
Number of observations	284	1,420	166	206	279	32	2,386
p value, Chi-square test							0.000
Safety: Conflicts and social friction							
A problem? (0=no, 3=major)	0.19	0.09	0.28	0.36	0.13	0.16	0.14
% saying it is a major problem	1%	0%	3%	8%	1%	1%	1%
Number of observations	282	1,410	165	195	274	31	2,358
p value, Chi-square test							0.000

Source: RICS (2005).

Table 10.B2
Government and Security Obstacles by Sector

	Mining	Manufacturing	Trade	Hotels/food	Transport	Public service	Other	Total
Government: Corruption								
A problem? (0=no, 3=major)	1.42	0.38	0.56	0.33	0.66	0.84	1.03	0.65
% saying it is a major problem	37%	7%	15%	7%	17%	19%	28%	16%
Number of observations	177	305	1,019	210	301	195	162	2,370
p value, Chi-square test								0.073
Government: Uncertain economic policy								
A problem? (0=no, 3=major)	1.58	0.57	0.68	0.46	0.76	1.02	1.13	0.78
% saying it is a major problem	48%	10%	16%	12%	19%	23%	31%	19%
Number of observations	177	304	1,009	210	304	195	162	2,360
p value, Chi-square test								0.041
Government: Restrictive laws & regulations								
A problem? (0=no, 3=major)	1.47	0.36	0.46	0.36	0.61	0.8	0.89	0.59
% saying it is a major problem	37%	6%	8%	8%	17%	13%	19%	12%
Number of observations	177	303	1,005	210	300	195	161	2,350
p value, Chi-square test								0.023
Safety: Criminality, theft & lawlessness								
A problem? (0=no, 3=major)	0.27	0.14	0.17	0.09	0.39	0.23	0.33	0.21
% saying it is a major problem	0%	2%	2%	1%	10%	4%	8%	3%
Number of observations	179	302	1,031	213	304	198	158	2,386
p value, Chi-square test								0.032
Safety: Conflicts and social friction								
A problem? (0=no, 3=major)	0.27	0.09	0.12	0.07	0.23	0.13	0.27	0.14
% saying it is a major problem	0%	2%	1%	1%	3%	1%	3%	1%
Number of observations	178	300	1,014	211	302	196	156	2,358
p value, Chi-square test								0.047

Source: RICS (2005).

Table 10.B3
Government and Security Obstacles by Location of Owner of Enterprise

	Same village	Same sub-district	Same district	Same province	Different province	Different country	Total
Government: Corruption							
A problem? (0=no, 3=major)	0.68	0.27	0.61	0.98	1.49	0	0.68
% saying it is a major problem	17%	3%	19%	27%	48%	0%	17%
Number of observations	1,938	67	44	51	11	0	2,111
p value, Chi-square test							0.007
Government: Uncertain economic policy							
A problem? (0=no, 3=major)	0.81	0.44	0.58	1.06	1.85	0	0.81
% saying it is a major problem	20%	10%	17%	28%	49%	0%	20%
Number of observations	1,932	67	44	50	11	0	2,104
p value, Chi-square test							0.102
Government: Restrictive laws & regulations							
A problem? (0=no, 3=major)	0.62	0.21	0.55	0.92	1.2	0.68	0.62
% saying it is a major problem	13%	3%	7%	24%	21%	0%	13%
Number of observations	1,922	66	44	50	11	0	2,094
p value, Chi-square test							0.257
Safety: Criminality, theft & lawlessness							
A problem? (0=no, 3=major)	0.21	0.13	0.51	0.76	0.06	0	0.22
% saying it is a major problem	3%	2%	12%	17%	1%	0%	4%
Number of observations	1,962	68	38	51	11	0	2,130
p value, Chi-square test							0.052
Safety: Conflicts and social friction							
A problem? (0=no, 3=major)	0.15	0.07	0.41	0.42	0.03	0	0.16
% saying it is a major problem	1%	1%	6%	5%	0%	0%	1%
Number of observations	1,939	67	37	51	11	0	2,105
p value, Chi-square test							0.426

Source: RICS (2005).

APPENDIX 3
Estimation Results for Firm Performance Equation (Sales)

Table 10.C
Estimation Results for Model of Enterprise Sales

	Coefficient	p-value	Mean value
Dependent variable			
Log of value of enterprise sales in 2005			9.716
Independent variables			
Age of enterprise (years × 10⁵)	0.490	0.990	11.2
Age of manager (years × 10²)	0.792	0.017	41.9
Is manager male? (yes=1)	0.487	0.000	0.701
Years of education of manager	0.097	0.000	6.4
Sector of firm (dummy variables):			
Mining	0.525	0.158	0.056
Manufacturing, utilities	0.332	0.051	0.196
Wholesale, retail	0.537	0.000	0.444
Hotels, food, catering	0.402	0.029	0.087
Transportation	−0.532	0.001	0.129
Public service	−0.442	0.004	0.088
Other (construction, repair, finance, real estate, health): reference			
District (dummy variables):			
Labuhan Batu	0.612	0.000	0.110
Malang	0.441	0.002	0.619
Badung	0.640	0.000	0.065

continued on next page

Table 10.C — *cont'd*

	Coefficient	p-value	Mean value
Sumbawa	-0.055	0.707	0.083
Kutai	0.682	0.000	0.111
Barru: reference			0.013
Population of village ($\times 10^5$)	-0.652	0.120	6,274
Transportation costs ($\times 10^5$)	-0.421	0.027	19,636
Village is served by a main road (yes=1)	-0.113	0.244	0.735
Village is reachable by car (yes=1)	0.560	0.171	0.993
Village is subject to electricity blackouts (yes=1)	0.019	0.001	5.26
Household has piped water? (yes=1)	-1.630	0.026	0.05
Household has fixed line telephone? (yes=1)	1.083	0.000	0.12
Household has mobile phone? (yes=1)	-0.296	0.000	0.25
Is there a bank nearby? (yes=1; $\times 10^3$)	0.797	0.865	0.21
Index indicating whether item is an obstacle to a company's operations and growth (0=no, 3=definitely)			
Electricity	-0.169	0.731	0.484
Telecommunications and postal service	-0.039	0.685	0.242
Transportation	0.027	0.628	0.692
Financing	0.032	0.425	0.946
Governance and security	0.114	0.086	0.426
Marketing and demand	-0.076	0.091	0.745
Registration, regulation, taxation, trade restrictions	0.114	0.202	0.287
Labour, environmental policy	-0.203	0.052	0.565
Intercept	7.653	0.000	

Notes: Adjusted R^2=0.204. Number of observations: 1,770. Mean values of variables use weights.

NOTES

1. These are unweighted totals; the weighted totals are very similar.
2. The major remaining ports were Medan (North Sumatra), Tanjung Priok/ Jakarta, Surabaya (East Java), and Makassar (Southwest Sulawesi). For further information on shipping see Dick (1987).
3. Communication from then police chief Awaloeddin Djamin, October 2002.
4. The weights on enterprises are designed to correct for over- and under-sampling of certain strata of enterprises. Thus, for instance, mining enterprises were undersampled (and so have larger sampling weights) while retail enterprises were oversampled (and so have smaller sampling weights). For details, see Molyneaux (2006).

REFERENCES

Barron, Patrick, Rachael Diprose, Claire Smith, Katherine Whiteside, and Michael Woolcock. "Applying Mixed Methods Research to Community Driven Development Projects and Local Conflict Mediation: A Case Study from Indonesia". Prepared for submission to Masyarakat, Jurnal Sosiologi, Universitas Indonesia, 2004.

Barron, Patrick, Kai Kaiser, and Menno Pradhan. *Local Conflict in Indonesia: Measuring Incidence and Identifying Patterns*. World Bank Policy Research Working Paper 3384, Washington D.C., 2004.

Barron, Patrick and Joanne Sharpe. "Counting Conflicts: Using Newspaper Reports to Understand Violence in Indonesia". *Social Development Papers: Conflict Prevention and Reconstruction* 25. Washington D.C.: World Bank, 2005.

BRR/World Bank. *Trucking and Illegal Payments in Aceh*, 2006.

Crouch, Harold. "No, the Military isn't Running Indonesia". *International Herald Tribune*, 2 August 2001.

Dick, H.W. "The Indonesian Inter-Island Shipping Industry: An Analysis of Competition and Regulation". Singapore: Institute of Southeast Asian Studies, 1987.

Emmerson, Donald K., ed. *Indonesia Beyond Suharto: Polity, Economy, Society, Transition*. Armonk, NY: M.E. Sharpe, 1999.

Fielding, David. "How Does Violent Conflict Affect Investment Location Decisions? Evidence from Israel During the *Intifada*". Unpublished manuscript, University of Leicester, 2004.

International Crisis Group. *Indonesia: Rethinking Internal Security Strategy.* 20 December 2004.

Komite Pemantauan Pelaksanaan Otonomi Daerah (Regional Autonomy Watch; KPPOD). *Daya Tarik Investasi Kabupaten/Kota di Indonesia, 2004: Persepsi Dunia Usaha (Regional Investment Attractiveness Business Perception)*. Jakarta, 2005.

———. *Daya Tarik Investasi Kabupaten/Kota 2002*. Jakarta, 2003.

Kuncoro, Ari. "Bribery in Indonesia: Some Evidence from Micro-Level Data". *Bulletin of Indonesian Economic Studies* 40, no. 3 (2004): 329–54.

MacDougall, John. "Criminality and the Political Economy of Security in Lombok". In *Renegotiating Boundaries: Local Politics in Post-Suharto Indonesia*, edited by Henk Schulte Nordholt and Gerry van Klinke. The Netherlands, Leyden: KITLV Press, 2007.

———. Jakarta's Civilian Security Matrix. Unpublished manuscript, 2003.

Molyneaux, Jack. "Sample Weights". Unpublished, 9 May 2006 <http://www.jack-molyneaux.com/rics/Data/beta06/Sample_Weights.htm> (accessed 18 May 2006).

Partnership for Governance Reform in Indonesia. *POLRI and Corruption Issues*. Jakarta, 2005.

Resosudarmo, Budy. *The Politics and Economics of Indonesia's Natural Resources*. Singapore: Institute of Southeast Asian Studies, 2005.

Skaperdas, Stergios. "The Political Economy of Organized Crime: Providing Protection when the State does not". *Economics of Governance* 2 (2001): 173–202.

Suprananto, Agung. *POLRI: Financial Management Reform*. Partnership/kemitraan, Jakarta, 2005.

United Nations Office on Drugs and Crime. Compiling and comparing International Crime Statistics. <http://www.unodc.org/unodc/crime_cicp_surveys_3.html> (accessed 5 February 2006).

United States Embassy, Jakarta. Indonesia: Investment Climate Statement, 2000. <http://jakarta.usembassy.gov/econ/invest/2000/investment2000-1.html> (accessed 25 October 2007).

Index

"Bapak Angkat" scheme, 204
"bribe rates", 315
"domain of trade", 15
"Foster Father" scheme, 162, 170
2004 Decree on Temporary Working
Agreement or *Pekerjaan kerja
Waktu Tertentu* (PKWT), 70

A
absorptive capacity, 148, 151
access to credit, 86–87, 90, 99
access to electricity, 122–23, 125, 129
access to finance, 165
access to information, 148
access to infrastructure, 111, 113–14,
117, 128, 130, 135
access to irrigation, 127
access to technology, 167–68
access to telecommunications, 126
administration time, 255
administrative ineffectiveness and
inefficiency, 235, 239–40
age, 10, 54, 56–57, 60–64, 66
Agency for Assessment and
Application of Technology
(BPPT), 161–62
Agency for Industrial Research and
Development (BPPI), 161
agricultural growth multiplier, 26
agricultural linkages, 34

agricultural sector, 44–45, 51
agricultural sector growth, 42–43
arisan, 61, 65
assistance programmes, 174

B
backward and forward linkages, 26,
28, 35
backward linkages, 167
Bank Rakyat Indonesia (BRI), 165
banks provide credit to SMEs, 175
Bapak Angkat scheme, 202
BKPM, 213
BPD, 105–06
BPN, 102
BPRs, 105
BPS, 53, 97, 145, 147, 162–63, 166,
171–72, 202, 313
BRI, 101–02, 105–07
bribery, 240–41
building licence (IMB), 10
bupati, 67, 249, 280–81, 284, 306
business development services (BDS), 167
business perceptions, 307–12
Business Registration Certificate
(TDP), 10

C
capital assistance, 169, 173
capital goods, 20, 140, 149, 154–55

capital market, 148, 218
capture practices, 253, 257, 262
certificates for the land, 101
clustering, 20, 160
clusters, 160–61, 175, 217
collateral, 19, 94, 97–98, 101–04
community facility, 60, 62–65
competition, 20, 192–223
compliance costs, 21, 234, 237, 240
computable general equilibrium
    (CGE), 32, 37
constrains to credit access, 86–109
constraints faced by households and
    firms, 93
consumption linkages, 26–27, 32, 34, 43
contract workers, 70–71
corporate conglomeration, 210–11
corruption, 21, 235, 240–42, 247,
    265, 278, 280, 308–12, 314–20
credit constraints, 19, 87, 90–97
credit problems, 103
credit, 16–18, 86–87, 95, 97–101,
    103–04
cumbersome and onorous business
    regulations and restrictions, 164–
    65

D
Debtor Information System (DIS), 101
decentralization reforms, 246–47
decentralization, 246–47, 249, 252–
    53, 255, 258–59, 262, 264, 270–
    71, 274, 284, 288
deficient institutions, 264–72
deletion programmes, 157–58, 204–05
demand, 15–17
demand-pull motivation, 55
demand linkages, 17, 24–49
diffusion, 17, 19–20, 61, 140–91
distortionary taxes, 258
distress-push motivation, 55
distribution linkages, 26
DPRD, 265–66

E
education, 41, 55–57, 60–64, 66, 77,
    80
electricity, 10, 15, 112–13, 122, 124–
    25, 129–33, 135, 239, 308–09,
    318
electrification, 130
empirical estimation, 40–44
employment, 6, 27, 29–30, 36, 50–
    51, 54–56, 58–61, 70–73, 75–
    78, 81–82
employment by sector, 3, 52
extortion, 314–17

F
facilitation, 169
farm employment, 60–65
farm sector, 53, 57, 61, 65, *see also*
    non-farm sector
female employment, 54
female literacy rate, 36
financing, 90
foreign direct investment (FDI), 19,
    141, 149–54
Foreign Investment Advisory Service
    (FIAS), 167–68
formal employment, 54, *see also*
    informal employment
formal financial institutions, 94, 96,
    99–100, 104
formal institutions, 264
formal sector, 52–54, 58–59, 65, 67,
    71–72, 117, *see also* informal
    sector
formal sector employment, 53, 71–73

G
gender, 57, 60, 77
government promotion programmes,
    170–75
growth linkages, 25
growth multipliers, 24–49

H
health, 57
household characteristics, 62–65
household enterprises, 2, 4, 10, 73, 205
household expenditures, 40, 319
household income, 19, 30, 34, 121,
133
household participation, 129
household size, 58, 60, 64, 66
households, 7, 9, 18, 26, 32, 34, 53,
55–56, 58–61, 64–66, 78, 87,
98, 106
human capital, 55–59, 155
High Valued Commodities (HVC),
198, 200
hypermarkets, 218

I
income source, 29
incomes, 5, 15, 26, 45, 62–63, 65–66,
115
Indonesia Family Life Survey (IFLS),
18–19, 51, 60, 111, 118–30,
133, 135
Indonesian Central Statistical Agency
(*Badan Pusat Statistik* or BPS), 2,
27, 53, 97, 145, 147, 162–63,
166, 171–72, 202, 313
Indonesian Institute of Sciences
(LIPI), 161–62
Indonesian Rural Economy, 27–32, 44
industrial technological capabilities
(ITCs), 153
inefficiency, 21, 139, 235
infant mortality rate, 36
informal employment, 54, *see also*
formal employment
informal institutions, 264
informal labour practices, 75–76
informal non-farm enterprises, 95
informal sector, 52, 54, 58–59, 72–73,
77–78, *see also* formal sector
information transfer, 155–56

infrastructure, 8, 13–17, 19–20, 24,
36–37, 44, 66, 81, 110–39, 148,
152, 175, 193–94, 200, 204,
206, 214, 216–18, 234–35, 247,
276, 278
innovative capacity, 148
input-output table (IOT), 32, 37
insecurity, 21, 300–30
institutional deficiencies, 272, 287
institutional problems, 103
Instrumental Variable (IV) procedure,
39, 41, 43–44
inter-regional trade, 195
intersectoral linkages, 35
investment climate reforms, 21
investment linkages, 27
irrigation, 8, 36, 125–27

J
judicial system, 103

K
kabupaten, 1–2, 4–5, 8–11, 13, 16,
73, 90, 94, 100, 110–39, 152,
173, 195, 199–200, 206–09,
215, 218, 224–25, 227, 229,
231–32, 236, 239, 241, 307,
312–14, 319–20
KADINDA, 276, 279
kabupaten leaders (*bupati*), 3
kecamatan, 10–11, 206
KHM (*Kebutuhan Hidup Minimum*
— Minimum Basic Subsistence
Needs), 67 knowledge diffusion,
161–63, 178
knowledge transfer, 140–91
koperasi, 65
KOPINKRA (*Koperasi Industri
Kerajinan Rakyat* — Small-Scale
Handicraft Industry
Cooperatives), 172
kota, 2, 90, 173, 195, 218, 224–25,
227, 229, 231–32, 239, 313–14

KPPOD (*Komite Pemantauan Pelaksanaan Otonomi Daerah* — Committee Monitoring the Implementation of Regional Autonomy), 313–15
KPPU (*Komisi Pengawas Persaingan Usaha* — the Supervisory Commission on Business Competition), 20, 199, 213–15, 217–18

L
labour, 58, 77
labour-intensive industries, 67
labour market, 18, 50, 66, 71–72, 78
labour migration, 79
labour policies, 67, 81
labour practices, 73–76
labour productivity, 11, 141–47, 149
labour protection, 73
labour regulations, 50, 58–60, 66–76
lack of finance, 165–66
lack of knowledge, 99–100
lack of quick and accurate information, 101
land certification, 102
landholding, 31, 60, 65
large enterprises (LEs), 145, 157–60, 162–63, 165, 178
leadership, 21
lending, 94
letters of credit (LCs), 168
licences, 10, 199, 215, 225–26, 228
licensee, 141, 149, 153
licensing, 17, 19, 21, 73, 200, 217
licensors, 141, 149, 154
linkages, 7–8, 19–20, 25, 32–37, 45
local governance, 246–99
local revenue, 226
local tax effects, 224–45
local taxation, 235–42
local taxes, 226, 262
location, 65–66
low technological capabilities, 166–67

M
macro-economic approach, 32, 35–38
Malang case study, 198, 200
marketing, 20, 90, 192–223
medium enterprises (MEs), 159
micro or cottage enterprises (MIEs), 145–48, 156
micro-credit, 93
micro-economic approach, 32–35
microfinance, 88, 92–93, 105–07, 165–66, 177
migration, 6, 14, 18, 50, 56, 58, 60, 76–79
minimum wages, 66–67, 71–73
modern sector, 81
Multi National Enterprise (MNE), 194, 203, 205, 210
multinational companies (MNCs), 140–42, 145, 148, 151–53, 156, 168
multinomial logit estimation, 62–63, 65
multinomial logit regression model, 60–61

N
National Council of Applied Economic Research (NCAER), 33
Newly Industrialized Economies (NIE)s, 155
non-agricultural employment, 51–55, 72
non-agricultural sector, 44, 56
non-agricultural sector growth, 41
non-farm activity, 120–21, 126–27, 130, 133
non-farm business, 124
non-farm employment, 1, 5–6, 50–80, 112
non-farm enterprises (NFEs), 2, 4, 9, 13–14, 17–21, 50–191, 194, 205–06, 209–11, 213
non-farm family worker, 60
non-farm firms, 140–48, 152, 161–66, 168, 170, 175, 177

non-farm formal activities, 64–65
non-farm formal sector employment, 64
non-farm formal worker, 60
non-farm growth, 34
non-farm income, 55
non-farm linkages, 34
non-farm rural economy, 119
non-farm rural employment, 116–18
non-farm rural enterprises, 111, 116
non-farm sector, 33–34, 51, 53–54, 56–58, 65–66, *see also* farm sector
non-farm self-employment, 60–62, 66
Non-Government Organizations (NGOs), 168–69, 171, 177, 270, 278
non-household rural enterprises, 119
NPWP (*Nomor Pokok Wajib Pajak* — Taxpayer Registration Number), 98–99

O

Organization for Economic Cooperation and Development (OECD) economies, 214
official taxes, 237
omitted heterogeneity, 128
One-Stop Service (OSS), 21, 255–57, 262, 281, 284, 287–88
Ordinary Least Squares (OLS) procedure, 39, 41, 43
outsourcing, 18, 60, 70
Overseas Contract Workers (OCW), 79
own-source revenue, 21, 226, 228, 231, 239
own-source taxes, 231, 236

P

PAD (*Pendapatan Asli Daerah* — Locally Raised Revenue), 73, 266
pam swarkarsa, 305–06
perceived challenges, 319
perception of change, 303

PKK (*Pendidikan Kesejahteraan Keluarga* — Women Welfare Activities), 61
PLN (*Perusahaan Listrik Negara* — State-owned Electricity Company), 123, 135
PNS (*Pegawai Negeri Sipil* — Civil Servant), 266, 269–72
PODES (*Potensi Desa* — Village Potential Statistics), 302
population growth, 41
population mobility, 76–77
postal services, 135, 308
poverty, 5, 7–8, 25, 30, 34–37, 41, 115, 118
predatory business licensing, 253–58
preman or *jawara*, 76, 314, 316, 320
premanism (boss boys), 75, 306, 314–15
pribumi enterprises, 214
procurement, 20, 206
production and consumption linkages, 27–28
production and distribution linkages, 25, 28
production linkages, 25–26, 32, 34, 43, 157
productivity, 33–34, 37, 45, 56–57, 86, 166
productivity growth, 16, 33, 36
programmes to support SMEs, 181
promotion programmes, 20, 168–77
property tax, 21, 228–30, 233, 239, 264
property tax revenue, 240
purchasing power parities (PPPs), 145
puskesmas, 226, 228

Q

quality control (QC), 153, 203

R

reason why firms do not borrow, 94
reasons for not applying, 95
regional charges, 195

Regional Gross Domestic Product (RGDP), 40
registration, 19, 98–99
research and development (R & D), 36–37, 161–63, 179
revenue burden, 21, 233–34, 236, 240
reverse causation, 114–15, 119
road access, 16, 115, 120–22, 125, 130
road infrastructure, 120–21, 132
road levies, 258, 262
road quality, 125, 130, 133
road transport, 16, 135
roads, 15–16, 19, 36, 131–32, 200, 239
rural agricultural sector, 38–40
rural agricultural sector growth, 41, 45
rural areas, 44–45, 50–55, 58, 72, 78, 100–01, 112–13, 140, 148, 152, 156, 175, 178–79, 192, 312, 315, *see also* urban areas
rural electrification, 122–25
rural household income, 123, 134
rural households, 119, 128, 130, 133, 135
rural investment climate, 1–6, 13, 17
Rural Investment Climate Survey (RICS), 1, 4, 8–10, 15, 18–20, 22, 73, 90, 96, 100, 111, 130–36, 193, 205–08, 211–12, 236–38, 240–42, 307, 312, 314, 316, 319–20
rural non-agricultural sector, 38–40, 45
rural non-agricultural sector growth, 43
Rural Non-Farm Enterprises (RNFEs), 1–3, 5, 7–8, 10–20, 87–89, 91, 113, 165–66
rural roads, 112, 115–17, 125, 216
rural sector, 44, 231

S
Sakernas, 53, 55
sales, 20, 209
science and technology (S & T), 161, 178–79

sectoral growth multiplier, 26
sectoral linkages, 25–27, 32
security, 309, 312–18
service delivery, 234, 238
severnance pay, 67–72
SIUP (*Surat Ijin Usaha Perdagangan* — Trade Business Permit), 98–99
small and medium enterprises (SMEs), 3, 93, 101, 105–06, 145, 148, 152–53, 155–68, 170–79, 202–05, 210, 214, 217
small enterprise development, 170
small enterprises (SEs), 146–47, 156, 166–74
SMERU, 67, 71, 168–70, 173–74, 176–77, 258
social accounting matrix (SAM), 32, 37
social capital, 57–58
social network, 58, 60–66, 77
sources of capital, 87
sources of credit, 88–89
standard four-firm ratio, 210–11
state-owned enterprises (SOEs), 161–64, 203, 213–14
strategic alliances, 158–60
structural transformation, 30
structure-conduct-performance (SCP) framework, 210
subcontracting, 20, 157–59, 198, 201–02, 204–05
supermarkets, 196, 199–201
SUSENAS (*Survei Sosial Ekonomi Nasional* — National Socio-Economic Survey), 303–05
Susenas Consumption Module, 40
SUSI (*Survei Usaha Terintegrasi* — Integrated Business Survey), 94

T
tax, 21, 68, 71, 73, 82
tax administration, 235, 239, 241–42, 262, 287
tax burden, 236, 241, 259–60
tax effort, 261

tax liabilities, 237, 241
tax payments, 234, 240, 242
tax regulations, 234, 258–59, 264–65
tax revenue, 239
taxation, 16–17, 21, 224–25, 308
technical licensing agreements (TLAs),
    153–54
technical service units (UPT), 173
technological capabilities (TCs), 19,
    141, 147–48, 152, 154, 166–68,
    173
technology exclusively from licensing,
    148
technology growth, 36
technology transfer, 140–91, 203, 205
technology upgrading, 166–67
telecommunications, 19, 113, 125,
    130–32, 135, 194, 198, 200,
    215–16, 308, 318
TFPs (Total Factor Productivities), 150
time requirements, 287
TNI (Tentara Nasional Indonesia), 305
Tobit model, 133–34
total factor productivity (TFP), 141
total quality control (TQC), 153
trade, 155–56
trading licence (SIUP), 10
traditional and modern market
    systems, 197
traditional marketing, 194
training and skills, 56–57
transfer, 5, 158, 140
transfer linkages, 27
transnational corporations (TNCs),
    150–51

transparency international (TI), 247–
    48, 281, 284
transport, 115–16, 132
transportation, 16, 22, 90, 100, 130,
    164, 166, 194, 198, 240, 307–
    09, 312, 314, 319

U
unavailability of the information, 103
Unilever, 203
unofficial taxes, 241
UNSFIR (United Nations Support
    Facility for Indonesian Recovery),
    301–02
urban areas, 44, 50–54, 72, 100, 148,
    177, 240, 312, 315, *see also* rural
    areas
urban development, 43
urban employment growth, 51
urban sector, 38–39, 231
urban sector growth, 41–43, 45
urbanization, 29, 194, 224–25
user charges, 225–26, 228, 231, 234,
    258, 262, 264, 266

V
violence, 21, 301, 314
violent incidents, 302
voice, 21, 83

W
wage employment, 65
wage inequality, 34
wage regulations, 66
water, 135, 239, 308

www.ingramcontent.com/pod-product-compliance
Lightning Source LLC
Chambersburg PA
CBHW021847020426
42334CB00013B/220